ADVENTURES IN ART

ADVENTURES IN ART

ARTS & CRAFTS EXPERIENCES FOR 8- TO 13-YEAR-OLDS

SUSAN MILORD

A WILLIAMSON *KIDS CAN!* BOOK
WILLIAMSON PUBLISHING CHARLOTTE, VERMONT

Library of Congress Cataloging-in-Publication Data

Milord, Susan.
Adventures in art: art and craft experiences for 8- to 13-year-olds/Susan Milord.—Rev. ed.
p. cm.
Includes index.
Summary: Explores styles of art through the ages with over 200 artistic adventures including paints, pastels, ethnic and recycled art, sculpture, still life, batik, silkscreen, and more.
ISBN 1-885593-13-9
1. Handicraft—Juvenile literature. [1. Handicraft.] I. Title.
TT160.M494 1997
745.5—dc21 97-19327
CIP
AC

Cover design: Trezzo-Braren Studio
Book design: Susan Milord
Illustrations: Susan Milord, with selected works from the Dover Pictorial Archival Series
Typography: Superior Type
Printing: Capital City Press

Williamson Publishing Co.
Charlotte, Vermont 05445
1-800-234-8791

Manufactured in the United States of America

10 9 8 7 6 5 4

Susan Milord is also the author of *The Kids' Nature Book: 365 Indoor/Outdoor Activities and Experiences, Hands Around the World, Tales Alive!, Tales of the Shimmering Sky, Bird Tales from Near & Far, and Mexico! 50 Activities to Experience Mexico Past & Present.*

The Library of Congress previously cataloged earlier edition as follows. see page 162 in the center of the book.
ISBN 1-885593-78-3

Selected illustrations taken from the following books:

Authentic Chinese Cut-Paper Designs
Edited and arranged by Carol Belanger Grafton (Dover Publications, Inc., 1988)

The Book of Signs
Rudolf Koch (Dover, 1955)

The Cornucopia of Design and Illustration for Decoupage and Other Arts and Crafts
Edited by Eleanor Hasbrouck Rawlings (Dover, 1984)

1800 Woodcuts by Thomas Bewick and His School
Edited by Blanche Cirker (Dover, 1962)

North American Indian Designs for Artists and Craftspeople
Eva Wilson (Dover, 1984)

Ready-to-Use Old-Fashioned Animal Cuts
Edited by Carol Belanger Grafton (Dover, 1987)

Ready-to-Use Old-Fashioned Illustrations of Children
Edited by Carol Belanger Grafton (Dover, 1989)

The Styles of Ornament
Alexander Speltz (Dover, 1959)

Symbols, Signs & Signets
Ernst Lehner (Dover, 1950)

2001 Decorative Cuts and Ornaments
Edited by Carol Belanger Grafton (Dover, 1988)

For Angus

Once again I find myself fortunate to be able to offer a revised and updated edition of a favorite book. Many thanks to both Jack and Susan Williamson for making this possible. Copious thanks go to Jennifer Ingersoll, whose diligent research and insistence that we offer a glimpse into the lives of some unusual artists, have made this revised edition of *Adventures in Art* one of which I am proud.

Much research undertaken for the original edition was made easier thanks to the help of several librarians. Once again, I wish to acknowledge the contributions made by Joy Putnam of the Canaan Elementary School Library, Louise Cady of the Canaan Town Library, Mary Gove of the Grafton Town Library, and Connie Tobey of the Gale Memorial Library in Laconia. Many thanks also to Mary Ellen MacCoy, Sara Goodnow, Joe Gelbard, R.P. Hale, Lorraine Clough, Betsy Denzer, and Francisca Fay.

Finally, I wish to acknowledge the many kids and their parents who have thanked me over the years for compiling a book of art activities "just for them." Nothing pleases a writer more than learning how her work has touched another, and nothing pleases me more than hearing all about my readers' adventures in art.

CONTENTS

HOW TO USE THIS BOOK

Here's a book for everyone who loves to draw, paint, cut and paste paper, sculpt, construct . . . in short, create! There are 100 fabulous art adventures for rainy days, sunny days, and all those days in between.

Take a moment to read these next few pages so that you can make the most of your adventures. Then jump right in anywhere and let the fun begin!

ART FOR ALL AND ALL FOR ART

People have been making art since the beginning of time. It seems to be a very human need. Art is sometimes used as a way to express feelings and ideas; it's also one way to add a little beauty to our world. Of course, some art is made just because it's so satisfying making something with your own two hands, besides being a lot of fun! Whatever the reasons, the creation of art has a long history, and a bright future.

Adventures in Art is for everyone who would like to join in on the fun of creating art. It is bursting with 100 projects you can do by yourself or with your family and friends. There's lots of "fine art"—the kind you'd be proud to hang on your walls—and plenty of craft projects (sometimes called "popular art") to use and to wear. Many of the projects use techniques (originating in different countries throughout the world) that have been handed down over the centuries, but can be made with everyday materials available today.

Adventures in Art is divided into eleven sections, each having to do with a particular type of art.

The other sections are just as much fun. *The Portrait Gallery* invites you not only to paint a portrait of yourself, but to create an imaginary portrait in the form of a mask. *Lay of the Land* includes painting outdoors, as well as creating a landscape of sorts (you might call it a terrarium) indoors. And there's lots more!

You'll encounter many different art techniques in this book, too, which you can use to

MEASURING UP

Use this handy chart to help you convert the measurements found in this book into their equivalent metric measurement.

TO CHANGE	TO	MULTIPLY BY
Length		
inches (in.)	centimeters (cm)	2.54
feet (ft)	centimeters (cm)	30
yards (yd.)	meters (m)	0.91
miles (mi.)	kilometers (km)	1.6
Weight		
ounces (oz.)	grams (g)	28
pounds (lb.)	kilograms (kg)	0.45
Volume		
teaspoon (tsp.)	milliliters (ml)	5
tablespoon (T.)	milliliters (ml)	15
fluid ounces (fl. oz.)	millimeters (ml)	30
cups (c.)	liters (l)	0.24
pints (pt.)	liters (l)	0.47
quarts (qt.)	liters (l)	0.95
gallons (gal.)	liters (l)	3.8
Temperature		
Fahrenheit (°F)	Celsius (°C)	5/9 after subtracting 32

A painting is a poem without words.
Latin proverb

Artist's Profile
One of the best known Japanese printmakers was Hokusai, an artist who lived from 1760 to 1849. He made nearly 50,000 different prints and drawings in his lifetime. His styles and methods changed so much over the years that he signed his art with over 31 different names. The last name he chose for himself was Gwajyō Rōjin—"old man crazy about painting"!

give these projects your own special touch and to experiment with on your own. You'll have lots of fun discovering ways to use colored pencils, making three-dimensional objects from paper without scissors or glue, and dyeing wool with plants. There are hints for making your drawings more realistic (from still lifes to landscapes) and for modeling with everyday materials that can be air-dried or "fired" in an oven.

You'll also find lots of tricks artists use to make things easier (such as the best way to fold paper and a speedy method for cutting paper tiles for mosaics), as well as fascinating historical facts, artist profiles, and words of wisdom to inspire you. With all this, you're well-equipped for some real adventures in art! Enjoy!

STOCKING UP

Part of the fun of creating art is working with all the different materials available to artists. While some projects are best made with a specified type of paper or glue, there's a lot of leeway when it comes to choosing art supplies.

You probably already have many of the materials called for in *Adventures in Art.* Check at home for white glue, crayons, plain white paper, corrugated cardboard, and leftover bits of yarn and fabric. In fact, it's a good idea to save a number of everyday items that might come in handy in the future. Here are a few suggestions to get you started.

Paper—everything from newspaper to wrapping paper, scrap paper, and old greeting cards

Egg cartons

Milk cartons

Small jars

Cardboard—from corrugated boxes to oatmeal boxes and the backs of pads of paper

String and yarn

Fabric scraps—from old clothing to felt pieces

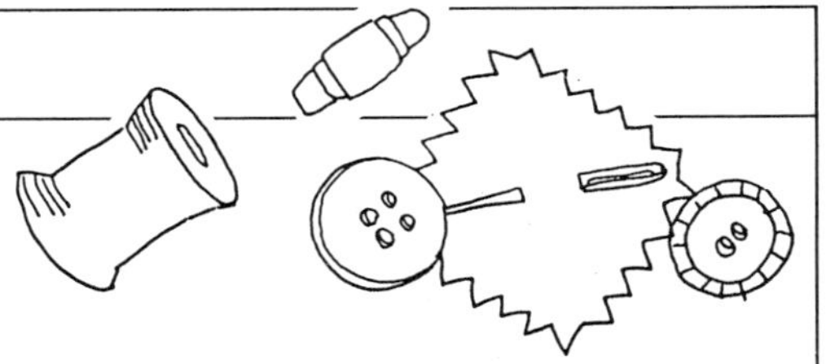

Buttons, beads, sequins, and other notions

Wood scraps

Popsicle sticks

Wooden spools

Wire, in various sizes

Pine cones, feathers, lichen, bark, and dried flower seed heads

What you don't already have at home can be bought. Basic art supplies can be found most everywhere, including many department stores and supermarkets. There you'll find tape, glue, crayons, markers, construction paper, typing paper, and poster board, as well as a limited selection of paints and inks.

For a larger selection and for better-quality materials, check out an art store in your area. You'll find printing supplies, X-acto knives, art papers (many of which sell by the single sheet), plus a full range of pencils, pens, and paints. Ask a salesperson to help you find what you need. Some things, such as brushes and paints, come in two grades—student and professional. You can save money by choosing the student-grade supplies.

Do what you can to get the most out of your art materials. Use both sides of the paper when you're sketching. Save any usable scraps of colored and printed paper—paper mosaics and collages can be made with the smaller pieces. Be sure to replace the tops on markers and tubes of paint when you're done with them. Always carefully plan any projects that call for expensive materials, so that you are sure not to waste any.

SAFETY CHECK

Most of the art materials called for in this book are perfectly safe to use. There are a few potentially dangerous materials and tools, however, that you must handle with extra care. Have an adult help you if you are unsure how to use a tool or if you're handling tricky substances.

Most of the projects that require glue recommend using white glue, but a few specify rubber cement. Rubber cement should be used with extreme care. It is flammable, which means you should store it and use it away from any heat source. Its vapors are harmful, so always use rubber cement in a well-ventilated area and cover the container tightly when you are done.

Spray paints and fixatives should also be used with caution. Spray them outdoors whenever possible. Place the object to be sprayed in a large box (this prevents your spraying the surrounding area with the paint). Avoid breathing the vapors.

Protect yourself and your clothing from those inks, paints, and dyes that stain. You'll find the instructions for a simple smock on page 142; wear it, an old shirt, or another smock or apron whenever you are working with messy materials. Wear rubber gloves to protect your hands from dyes, which readily stain skin (don't worry—dyes *do* eventually wash off!).

Handle all cutting tools with extreme care. Linoleum cutting tools are very sharp—use them properly, as described on page 38. Be very careful whenever you are using an X-acto knife. Concentrate on what you are doing, and take your time. Accidents usually happen when you're feeling rushed or frustrated. Read the pointers on page 30 for some valuable tips that will make cutting with an X-acto knife much easier.

Several projects in this book require a stove. Have an adult help you at the stove, if you aren't familiar with it or aren't allowed to use it by yourself yet. Use a potholder when you're handling hot pots and pans. Be especially careful when melting paraffin (it's flammable) and working with hot wax (a project where an adult's help is especially important).

Wood fibers were first used to make paper in the 18th century. A French naturalist studying the way wasps make "paper" from chewed wood got the idea for using small particles of wood for paper pulp.

The ideal artist's studio is lit with natural light from high, north-facing windows. The light coming from such windows doesn't create distracting shadows and doesn't have the glare of direct sunlight.

Did you know?
The word portfolio is a shortened version of *portafoglio,* an Italian word meaning "carry sheets" (as in paper).

ROOM OF ONE'S OWN

You don't really need a special room for working on art projects. Most projects can be done at the kitchen table (not right before a meal!) or at a table or desk in your room, if you have one.

It is nice, however, if you can arrange to make a little work area where you can store some of your art supplies near your table. Maybe you can set up in a corner of a family room, or in a little-used room such as a guest room or formal dining room. Getting permission to do so will probably hinge on your keeping your work area nice and neat (and possibly removing all traces of activity whenever the room is needed!).

Use a free-standing bookshelf to hold supplies, or rig your own storage system from cardboard

boxes and other containers. Small sturdy boxes with separate lids such as tomato boxes (ask for these at your market) can be stacked one on top of the other to make the most of a small space. Paint the outsides of the boxes or cover them with paper, to make the boxes nicer to look at. You can also color-code them so that you know what's where.

A bulletin board is nice to have to pin inspirational pictures and works-in-progress on. If you can't get a cork board, improvise and make your own from corrugated cardboard. Ask the manager at an art store if you can have one of the empty boxes that mat or illustration board comes in. These large, flat cardboard boxes are easily pierced with pushpins and thumb tacks. Hang the box on the wall or on the back of a door, or prop it up on the floor near your table.

These same boxes can be used to store flat artwork. Seal up the open end (usually a narrow end is opened) and slit open one of the long sides. This makes it easier to store pictures side by side, and prevents the artwork from getting lost at the far end of the box. Store the box flat. Stack several on top of one another to make your own flat file.

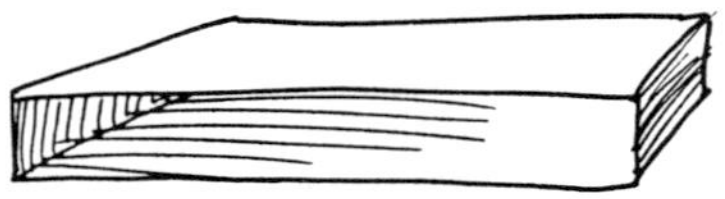

A simple portfolio is another good place to store flat artwork. Make your own from two pieces of corrugated cardboard or foam-core board. Join two pieces (the same size) on one side with strips of wide tape such as duct tape or packing tape. Poke some holes at the top of both boards, thread some strong string through the holes, and tie the string together to keep the portfolio shut. It is best to store this portfolio flat, too, but if you need to store it upright, wedge it tightly behind a piece of furniture so that the artwork inside doesn't bunch up and get wrinkled.

ON DISPLAY

With all the artwork you're making, there will be plenty to put on display. You may want to frame some pieces to hang on a wall. Three-dimensional items such as sculptures can also be given special treatment for display.

Having art framed by a professional framer is expensive. It's much less expensive, and a lot easier, to use ready-made frames. These come in lots of different styles in various standard sizes. In fact, when you want to give a framed drawing or print as a gift, for instance, you might consider buying a frame first, and limiting your artwork to its size.

Most artwork is matted before it is placed in a frame. The mat helps protect the artwork by keeping it from touching the glass of the frame. The mat also helps set off the artwork, giving it a "finished" look. To mat a picture, use an X-acto knife to cut a piece of mat board the same size as the inside dimensions of the frame. Cut a window in the center of the mat, large enough to show all but the very edges of your artwork. (Cut the window smaller if you want less of the artwork showing.) Use an uncut piece of mat board or sturdy cardboard (the same size as the first piece of mat board) to place behind the artwork.

Of course, you can simply mat artwork instead of framing it. Protect the art itself with a piece of clear acetate sandwiched between the art and the window of the top mat. Or wrap the entire mat with acetate, taping it at the back.

You can also make your own frames. Instructions for two different types of frames can be found starting on page 139.

Sculptures and other three-dimensional pieces can be displayed on table tops or shelves (or hung from the ceiling in the case of mobiles). You may want to make a base for smaller sculptures such as the Kachina figures (see page 75) or salt dough sculptures (see page 80). A scrap of wood sanded free of splinters and perhaps stained a darker shade is one possibility. Be sure to glue a piece of felt on the underside of the base to protect fine furniture from scratches.

Acetate is available at art stores. It comes in several thicknesses and finishes (clear or frosted). Frosted acetate can be painted and drawn on with water-based paints and inks, too.

VIEWING HOURS

At some point, you'll probably accumulate too many pieces of artwork to have on permanent display. This is when it's fun to set up a "gallery" or "museum" and display some of your work for a limited time.

This is even more fun when you join with other family members or some of your friends to stage a "group show." Turn a room in your house into a gallery or put on an outdoor show. Use freestanding boxes (the big appliance boxes are especially nice) to set sculptures on, or to tape or pin drawings, paintings, and prints to. Outdoors, you can hang art from a clothesline or from some rope stretched between two trees.

Advertise the art show and invite all your friends to come and see it. You can even sell your artwork, if you like. People enjoy beautiful things in their homes, and art lasts a lot longer than lemonade!

Probably the most famous painting in the Western world is the portrait known as the *Mona Lisa.* Leonardo da Vinci painted this portrait of a smiling woman in 1503. She is thought to be Lisa del Giocondo, the wife of an official of Florence. It is said that she was entertained by musicians while she posed. Do you suppose that's why she's smiling?

All great art is the work of the whole living creature, body and soul, and chiefly of the soul.
John Ruskin

PAST, PRESENT, & FUTURE

You can create art without ever seeing examples of what other artists have done. But art is something people have been making for a very long time, and there's so much to see!

Where can you find examples of art to look at? Just about everywhere! Museums are one place to go to see what has been done before. There may be a museum devoted entirely to art near you, or one with displays of art and artifacts from your town or region. You'll discover artists who worked in some of the styles and with some of the materials mentioned in this book. Up close, you can see how an artist used brushstrokes to suggest clouds in the sky or the wind rustling through trees. You'll get a chance to see how the arrangement of objects in a still life affects a painting, and how bright and pale colors can be used for different effects.

You can also view paintings, sculptures, and prints first-hand at an art gallery. Generally, you'll find contemporary (recent) work at most galleries, but many artists working today use the same centuries-old techniques.

Art reproductions offer another way of looking at paintings and prints. One place you can look for reproductions is your local library. Did you know you can borrow to take home any framed reproductions they have if you have a library card?

Libraries, of course, are also the place to go to borrow art books. The children's section should have some you'd enjoy, but check the adult shelves for an even greater selection. There are hundreds of art books, many with color pictures of every imaginable type of art, from African tribal masks to zoo art (one way of saying pictures of animals!). You'll also find lots of instructional books you can turn to, if you'd like to know more about figure drawing, for instance, or how to paint with watercolors or oil paints.

TIME FRAME

You'll find the chart on the following page helpful when you need to have some idea how long a particular project takes to complete. These are just general guidelines, of course, because not everyone works at the same rate. It's also impossible to time creativity!

These time amounts are for completing projects once you've gathered all the necessary materials together. Allow extra time if you need to construct a loom, for instance, or make a plant press or a batch of salt dough. Read through the instructions for each project from start to finish, to get a better idea of what's involved. Most, as you can see, can be completed within two hours. In fact, many of the projects that need to dry for several days can also be made in a matter of hours (papier-mâché typically needs the most drying time).

TICK TOCK

UNDER 1 HOUR

Note These times include drying time. The actual artist's time may be much less.

1-2 HOURS

2-4 HOURS

OVERNIGHT

3-7 DAYS

A WORD TO PARENTS

Every genuine work of art has as much reason for being as the earth and the sun.
Ralph Waldo Emerson

From the first scribbles made by a determined toddler, to the portraits of his family and the imaginative playthings constructed from wood scraps that come later, a child's art is an extension of himself. With the most basic materials, a child can share with others a little bit of his world, as he sees it.

Adventures in Art encourages children to continue, as they grow older, to share their vision through art. It addresses the interests of children from about 8 to 13 years of age, years when kids are looking for forms of self-expression, as well as showing an interest in "usable" art, such as kites and things to wear. Making art is nothing new, of course; this book offers a variety of media and artistic styles that have been handed down over the centuries, but are as relevant today as ever. *Adventures in Art* is more than just a collection of "things to do." It's an open invitation to discover both the "fine arts" as well as the "popular arts" or crafts that are universal avenues of artistic expression. Many countries and cultures are represented.

There are detailed instructions for 100 projects in this book plus lots of practical pointers for using a variety of materials and methods. Many of the projects suggest variations, offering choices as well as opportunities for self-expression. While some children feel more comfortable following instructions to the letter, others are more inclined to loosely interpret certain steps. There are no hard and fast rules in art, so encourage your young artists to experiment.

If you need some idea how long a project takes to complete, see the chart on page 15. There's no way to time the creative process, however, so these are loose estimates.

Please note that some of the tools and materials should be used under adult supervision; younger children will need you to actually help them. Be sure your children know to ask for help when using sharp tools (such as linoleum cutting tools and X-acto knives), when heating things on the stove, and when melting paraffin and pouring it into molds for candlemaking. Show your children how to use rubber cement properly (always in a well-ventilated area) and how to handle spray paints and fixatives.

Adventures in Art is certainly a book older children can use on their own, but don't let that keep you from lending a hand or make you shy about joining in. You may not consider yourself artistic, but you probably possess many skills you can share with your budding artists. You may have a good color sense or know something about flowers. You may be handy with a hammer and nails or be confident in your sewing. These, and many other skills, make you the perfect partner for many of the activities in this book. Making art at home is a wonderful way for families to spend time together.

Your enthusiasm, combined with the books you bring home from the library, the trips you plan to museums and art galleries, and the wall space you clear for the ever-changing gallery in your own home, will go a long way to providing your children with a lifetime love for art and a confidence in their abilities to create art of their own. After all, as Henry James once said, "It is art that *makes* life."

THE ADVENTURES BEGIN

THE ARTISTS' WAYS

In this first chapter, you'll be introduced to eight types of art—and the artists who created them. As you'll discover, the world of art encompasses everything from the folk paintings of a self-taught grandmother to hillsides draped in miles of brightly colored cloth. To make these, the artists drew on their experiences as well as on centuries-old materials and techniques.

What does it take to be an artist? Nothing more than a belief in yourself and your own visions.

JUST PLAIN FOLKS

Grandma Moses was a famous folk artist who didn't begin painting seriously until she was 78 years old! Like all folk artists, she was entirely self-taught. That didn't prevent her from painting rich, colorful scenes of the simple country living she loved. And it shouldn't prevent you from painting what you know and love either!

FOLK ART PAINTING
Paper or canvas
Colored pencils, markers or paint

1. Many folk artists use scenes from their daily lives as their inspiration. For instance, if going to the playground is something you often do, use it as the basis for your painting.

LOOK SHARP

Colored pencils are perfect for detailed drawings. Of course, they can be used anytime you're working in color.

Colored pencils can be bought individually or in sets. Art stores usually carry several brands. Some have softer leads than others, and some are even water-soluble which means they can be used like watercolor paints.

You can get different effects with colored pencils by varying how hard you press down when you draw with them. Generally they work best when you press down lightly. You can blend two colors together to make a third (add more layers to create still more colors). You can also make new colors by placing one color over another in a cross-hatching pattern.

Notice that when you press down hard, you get deep, rich colors, but you can't blend them easily. Try a technique known as burnishing, instead. Make a drawing using light pressure on the pencils. Cover the entire drawing with a white (or other light color) pencil, pressing down hard to give the drawing a glazed finish. See how the colors get brighter but are slightly lighter. This occurs because white added to any color makes it a lighter shade.

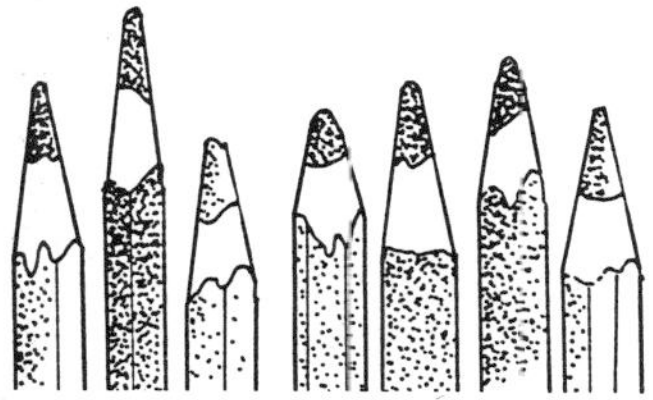

There are many kinds of American folk art in addition to paintings. Other examples of folk art include quilting, decorative paper cutting, weathervanes, ships' figureheads, cigar-store figures, and carousel animals.

2. Sketch or paint the scene as you see it in your mind. (Grandma Moses rarely painted what she was looking at; instead, she painted what she remembered or envisioned.) That means that if you think there should be girl fishing in a stream or a horse walking down a crowded city street in your picture, include them.

3. Add lots of details. In folk art, details don't have to be accurate. For instance, you don't have to create realistic faces or know exactly how that old tree in the school yard looks. Draw it how it appears in your mind when you think of it. Remember that the idea is to show your own vision.

Folk art often looks flat and two-dimensional. If you want to create a more realistic painting or drawing, try painting a landscape (see pages 107–108) or a portrait (see pages 67–69).

Folk art is enjoying a renewed popularity. You can see great examples of it on notecards, in hotels, even in fast food restaurants. Artists such as Warren Kimble are continuing the tradition of creating scenes of a bygone era. Many of these artists paint not only on canvas but on boards—sometimes on scraps of wood that happen to be around. Warren Kimble uses wood, which gives his paintings a rustic look that suits the art.

NOW YOU SEE IT...

No doubt you'll get the urge to see some of the art created by the artists named in this book. You're in luck! Your local public or college library is likely to have many art books in its collection. But for a really special treat, search for some of the originals in a location near you. Art created by the artists mentioned in this book—and hundreds of others, too—can be seen hanging on museum walls, placed in public parks, as well as in other locations all over the world.

For example, The Bennington Museum in Bennington, Vermont, has the largest public collection of Grandma Moses's art, but The Museum of American Folk Art in New York City is probably the best place to see a large collection of all kinds of folk art. (Don't forget to check out the Internet. Input a keyword or set of words and the search engine will offer up some Web sites. Popular search engines include Alta Vista, InfoSeek, and Yahoo. Grandma Moses's work can be found at www.fmhs.cnyric.org/clay/community/artlang/AL.gif/Moses.html.)

You may be surprised by the size of some art. Some paintings are much larger than you would think they'd be; others are so small you wonder how the artist was able to paint such detail (Hint: Think small brush!). When you visit an art gallery or park you can also see three dimensional sculptures as they are meant to be viewed—from all sides.

MEMORY LANE

Romare Bearden (1911–1988) was an artist who used the techniques and materials of collage to express the many moods of painting. Much of Bearden's work reflected his memories of growing up, and of life experiences of African-Americans like himself. Creating a life collage is a creative way to express something meaningful to you through art.

LIFE COLLAGE
Heavy paper or poster board
Pictures from old magazines and catalogs
Photos from your own album or collection (get grown-up permission to use them)
Paints, crayons, markers, colored pencils
Fabric scraps
Glue, rubber cement, or transparent tape

1. Cut out pictures from magazines, catalogs, and from your own photos. You don't have to use pictures as they appear. You could create a face by finding two different eyes, a nose, lips, hair, skin, and ears—all gathered from different pictures. Collages are all about using various mismatched pieces to create your own vision.

2. Use paint, markers, or crayons to color the background of the poster board. Draw designs and patterns on the background, if you like, or make it plain. If you use paint, allow it to dry completely before continuing.

3. Glue or tape on the other elements of the collage. Though collages are usually flat in appearance, Bearden sometimes used pieces of material, such as a scrap of striped shirt fabric, to create texture. You could create texture or add three-dimensional elements to your collage with fabric, cotton balls, and dried beans or seeds.

If you enjoy making collages, check out *Animal Collage* on page 55, as well as *Cut-Paper Collage* on pages 109–110, and *Pressed Flower Collage* on page 98.

Some of Bearden's most important works came out of the 1960s. That turbulent time in the lives of African-Americans, the focus of Bearden's art, is seen in his collage painting *Black Manhattan*. In this piece, Bearden celebrates the many residents of Harlem and the diversity of the city itself, creating a harmony between the two.

The Story of Art
The Chinese were the first to strain a pulp made from plant fibers through a sieve-like frame to make paper. They invented this method around 105 A.D. From China, papermaking spread to Japan and throughout Asia.

Papermaking was not introduced to the Western world until several centuries later. The first to learn of it were the Arabs who held some Chinese prisoners captive in 751. Eventually the know-how spread to other countries via the Moors. By 1276, papermaking was practiced in Italy and, soon after, in other European countries.

Tip Add vitality to your collage by manipulating your materials in different ways. Rip paper to create a jagged edge and a sense of drama. Give a girl a pleated paper skirt; tear tiny scraps of fabric to make patches on clothing. Fringe the bangs of a person's hair, or make tiny braids for corn rows.

One of Bearden's early techniques was to paint broad areas of color on various thicknesses of rice paper, glue the paper on canvas, and tear away sections of the paper until a theme emerged. Then he would add more paper and paint other elements to complete the work.

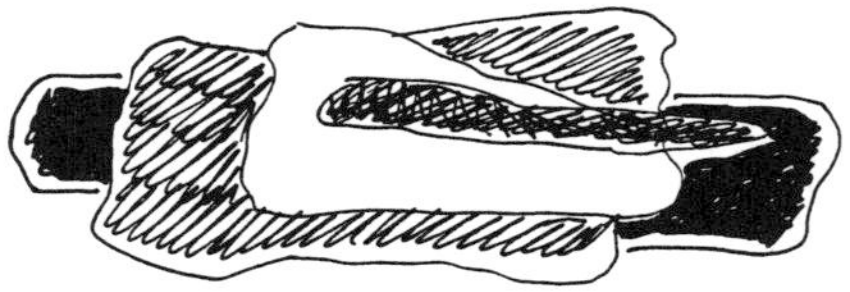

PICK A PACK OF PAPER

You're in for a surprise when you discover what kinds of paper are available to artists. The nice thing is that much of the paper sold at art stores is sold by the sheet, so you can treat yourself to lots of different kinds.

For colorful, thin paper, check out origami paper, colored craft paper, even gift wrap (you'll find the greatest selection at card and party shops). Are you looking for a heavier paper that comes in colors? There's always construction paper, but another paper that comes in every color of the rainbow, and is not as brittle as construction paper is Canson paper from France. It is sold by 19″ by 25″ sheets.

Do you need an inexpensive paper that's just right for sketching on? Ask for newsprint pads. Tracing paper is another valuable paper with a lot of uses. It's available in pads, as well as by the roll.

Watercolor papers are very heavy and can be used for constructing masks and models, as well as for painting on. Then there's poster board, which comes in colors as well as in white. Even heavier are the illustration and mat boards. Many art stores offer framing as one of their services, and you can usually buy small pieces of leftover mat board for not much money.

And then there's colored tissue paper, foil papers, Japanese rice paper . . . the list goes on and on!

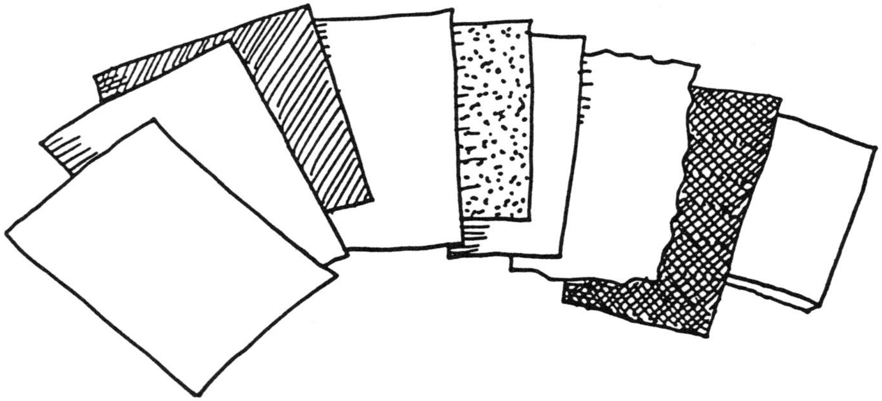

TRIMMED IN GOLD

The *Book of Kells* is a spectacularly decorated text of the four Gospels of the New Testament. Dating from the 8th or early 9th centuries, its distinctive artwork was done by Irish monks. Some of the pages feature illuminated letters, large initial letters at a section's beginning that are embellished with intricate, colorful designs. Illuminate your name in this elegant and distinctive style.

ILLUMINATED LETTER
Paper
Pencil
Paint in bright colors, including gold
Black felt-tip pen

1. Create an ornate design for the first letter of your name, sketching it first in pencil. Draw the letter as large as you like, but be sure to leave enough room on the paper for the rest of the letters of your name. (Lightly pencil the line on which they will be written.) You may want to draw animals such as a snake or bird intertwined through the letter. Or, draw the letter itself in the shape of an animal, in the traditional Celtic style of illumination.

2. Paint over the design, using bright colors, including gold. Then use the pen to write the rest of your name in a decorative style. (See *Celtic Calligraphy* on page 24 for a traditional lettering style you may wish to copy.) Carefully erase any pencil lines.

Tip To add snap to the design, go over all the lines with the black pen. This not only will give your artwork contrast, it will also cover up any uneven lines where there is color.

Variations on a Theme
The Book of Kells has 31 full-page illuminations. Choose a favorite story (or write one of your own) and decorate it the way medieval scribes did. Start with a decorated initial letter for the first word in the story; then use illumination techniques throughout for the illustrations.

The Story of Art
Illumination takes its name from the shining quality of the pictures and decorations—in part because real gold and silver were used to decorate them. The metals were pounded very, very thin into sheets known as leaf, then carefully applied to the paper wherever a little sparkle was desired.

The *Book of Kells* is written on parchment. Parchment is a specially prepared writing or painting surface made from animal skin (most usually that of a sheep or goat).

The *Book of Kells* is named for the Irish town of Kells, located near Dublin. The Book is considered by many historians to be the greatest relic of Western society.

The manuscript itself is very large, and it is no longer complete. Some of the illustrations, or illuminations, are full-page drawings of various biblical figures. Others are strange and fantastic beasts running right through the text. Some pages feature a large initial letter in an intricate design pattern that takes up one quarter of the page!

WITH PEN IN HAND

There is a wide range of pens that can be used with ink. Some nibs or points, such as the broader squared-off ones, are made especially for calligraphy, but you can use many nibs interchangeably. That's part of the fun—seeing what types of lines you can make with various pens.

Traditional pens are those that must be dipped often into the inkpot. They can be used with both waterproof and non-waterproof inks. Be sure to clean your pens after use to prevent the dried ink from clogging the nibs.

Fountain pens, on the other hand, store ink in built-in holders. They are great for taking along when you do outdoor sketching. Some cannot be used with waterproof ink, so make sure you fill those with non-waterproof inks only.

There are also pens, known as reservoir pens, that store ink. Technical pens belong in this category. These pens have points that make lines of consistent width. Draughtspeople (pronounced drafts-people) and illustrators use these quite often.

CELTIC CALLIGRAPHY
Drawing paper
Pen with slanted nib
Tracing paper (optional)

1. Irish monks had a characteristic way of writing letters. Known as half-uncials, the rounded letters were all lowercase. While most are recognizable, some of the letters were quite different from those used today.

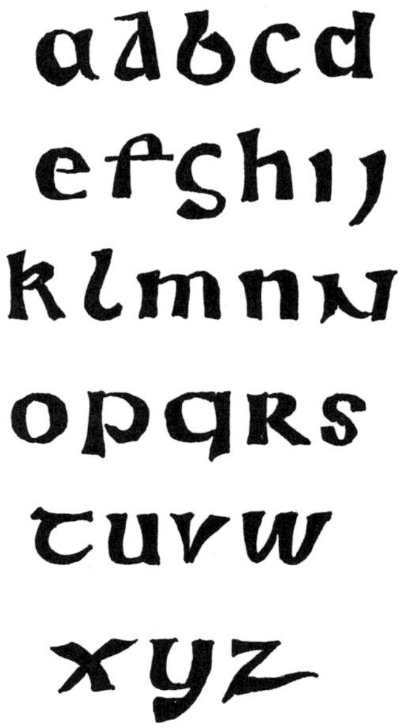

2. Rule lines on paper and practice forming the letters. (If you prefer, take this book to a copy center and have the alphabet enlarged. You can then practice forming the letters by tracing over them with tracing paper.)

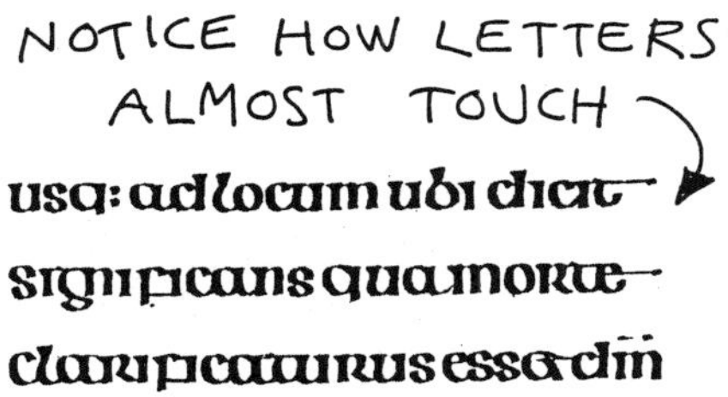

3. Use this alphabet to letter your name in the previous project, or to create your own greeting cards, labels for homemade foods, covers for school reports . . . or whatever!

The word calligraphy comes from two Greek words—*kali,* which means "beautiful," and *graphos,* which is "writing." Calligraphy is a way of turning words into art.

FROM THE EARTH

Lucy M. Lewis was an Acoma potter who lived from 1895 to 1992. Her storage jars, bowls, water jars, pitchers, and tiny seed jars were made in the centuries-old Acoma tradition. Lewis was known for her fine-line geometric designs, which were usually black on a white background. With some cornstarch clay and your imagination you can create your own Pueblo-style pot.

CORNSTARCH CLAY POT
Cornstarch clay (see page 26)
Tempera paint: white, black and red

1. Form a ball of clay and then push your thumbs into the center to create a hole.

Many Pueblo Indians make distinctive earthenware. Santo Domingo potters create stunning black pottery; San Juan potters favor two-toned pots—one part is reddish tan, the other a soft buff color.

The Story of Art
The know-how for Pueblo pottery-making originally came from Mexico. The first southwestern pottery is believed to date from 300 B.C., which is about how long people have been living in that part of the United States. Potters have been adding decorations to their wares since about 600 A.D.

Many of the decorative Pueblo motifs have remained unchanged for centuries. Animals, birds, floral designs, clouds, and the sun are the most common.

2. Build up the sides of the pot from the hole, stretching it and thinning it so the sides are evenly thick. The Acoma use a gourd to press from the inside out, but you could use a rounded tool such as a large spoon.

3. Continue shaping the pot so the top round edge overhangs slightly toward the center. The pot should have a rounded look. Be sure to flatten the bottom a little so the jar or pot can rest on its own. Once the pot is shaped, bake it in a 250°F oven (ask a grown-up to help you) until hardened.

Turn to page 75 for another Pueblo Indian project, a simple Kachina figure. Or, if you're interested in other traditions, try your hand at a Navajo sandpainting (see page 70).

4. Paint the pot white, then with a simple design using the traditional black and red colors. The Acoma use symbols and designs on their pots that have meaning to them, such as lizards, birds, and the sun.

Variations on a Theme
Work with extra clay and mold the pot in the shape of a farm animal, such as a chicken, by adding a head, a comb, and other features. This was a common style among Pueblo potters.

CORNSTARCH CLAY

Mix 1 cup baking soda, 1/2 cup cornstarch, and 2/3 cup water in a saucepan. Have a grown-up help you cook the mixture on the stove over medium heat, stirring constantly, until it resembles mashed potatoes. Remove from the stove; let cool. When it is cool enough to handle, knead the clay on your work surface, adding more cornstarch as necessary to make a soft, pliable clay.

Bake finished pieces at 250°F until hard. Flat pieces will take about 30 minutes (turning the pieces over after 15 minutes; larger, thicker pieces may take longer. You can keep any unused clay in the refrigerator in an airtight container for about a week.

For another homemade modeling material, see the recipe for salt dough on page 81.

There are many closely guarded rituals and beliefs connected with Pueblo pottery. For example, Acoma clay comes from a secret source that the Acoma will not reveal to *anyone.* It's a special clay that turns white when it is fired.

The paints used on Acoma pots are made from natural dyes, such as minerals and metals in rock form and even wild spinach juice (called *guaco*). Potters chew the tips of stiff yucca leaves to make brushes.

GOTHIC GALLERY

Gothic was the dominant structural style in Europe for about 400 years during the Middle Ages (starting around 1140 A.D.). Today we associate it with the architecture seen in the cathedrals built during that period, and with huge, looming gargoyles that jut out from old buildings. Gargoyles originally functioned as rain spouts, carrying rainwater off cathedral roofs. Here's your chance to make a new use for one.

GARGOYLE PAPERWEIGHT
Papier-mâché pulp (see page 74)
Large rock with a flat bottom
Felt
Glue

If you like creating gargoyles and other imaginary beasts, see *Mythical Monsters* on page 57 for an unusual way to paint with bleach. Or, turn a plain window into a Gothic paper "stained-glass" window (page 49).

1. Have the papier-mâché pulp ready. Press the pulp all around the rock with your hands to create an even layer that covers the rock.

2. Using the papier-mâché pulp like clay, mold the pulp into a head right onto the covered rock. Use pulp to fill in the gap between the rock and the head.

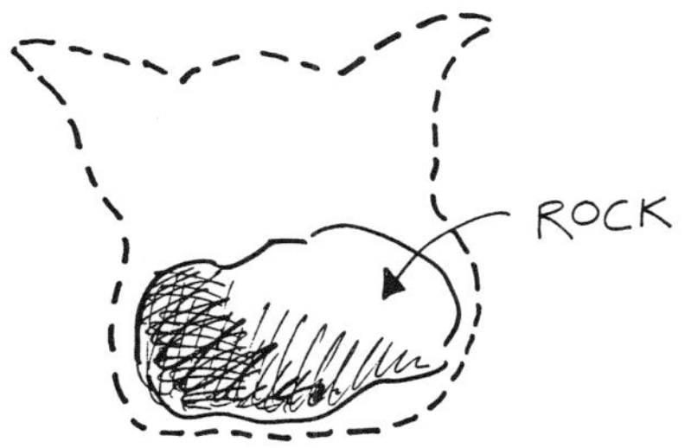

3. Press globs of pulp to the head for facial features. Gargoyles traditionally have big, bulging eyes and large, open mouths, or they are shaped like animals such as lions or eagles. There really aren't rules though, so use your imagination and create a fantastic beast!

Gargoyle comes from the old French word *gargouille,* which means "throat." Gargoyles had several original purposes. They served as rain spouts (notice their mouths are open holes) while also illustrating Bible stories or serving to scare away evil spirits. Because gargoyles were first and foremost practical, after the introduction of lead drainpipes in the 16th century their use declined.

It took many people, and many years, to construct a large cathedral. Work on Notre-Dame in Paris, for instance, was begun in 1163 and finished in 1250. Some Gothic cathedrals in Europe took up to two hundred years to complete. Unexpected events—everything from running short of money for materials and workers to natural disasters and the outbreak of War—could delay construction.

4. Let the pulp dry in a warm place for 4 to 7 days. Cut a piece of felt slightly smaller than the bottom of the paperweight; glue it to the bottom of the gargoyle.

Variations on a Theme
Gargoyles on cathedrals are the color of the stone from which they're carved. Paint your gargoyle with watercolor paints to resemble stone, if you like. Or you can add coloring to the pulp (see Mish Mash on page 130 for several ways to do this).

GOTHIC ARCHITECTURE

The style of Gothic architecture is partly practical and partly decorative. The practical aspect can be seen in the ribbed, vaulted ceilings, the pointed arches, and the flying buttresses, which are the huge supports built on the outside walls. The decorative aspect is seen in the massive stained-glass windows, exterior carving, and gargoyles. In fact, the two go together—for instance, the flying buttresses were needed to take some of the pressure off the walls so the large windows could be included.

One of the best-known examples of Gothic architecture is the Notre-Dame Cathedral of Paris, which is famous for its legendary deformed bell ringer, the hunchback. *Notre-Dame* means "our lady" (Mary, the mother of Jesus) and so is a common cathedral name in France and other French-speaking countries.

THE WILD BUNCH

Henri Matisse was a French painter and sculptor who lived from 1869 to 1954. He was the central figure in the brief art movement known as Fauvism. Its style was characterized by brilliant color, often applied right to the canvas from paint tubes, and broad paint strokes for dramatic effects. Creating a Fauve-style painting using your fingers is the perfect way to explore this art style.

FAUVE FINGER PAINTING

- Finger paints
- Paper

1. Fauve painting can be kind of messy, so be sure to cover your work space with newspaper and your clothes with a smock (see page 142 for one you can make yourself) or old T-shirt.

2. Scoop a glob of paint onto your finger and smear it on the paper. Continue adding different colors, making your paint strokes wide and thick with actual paint. Paint whatever you want using the paint however you want—the Fauves were radicals of their time and didn't mind shocking observers with their outrageous way of showing landscape scenes and people.

Tip Wait until one color dries before adding another, if you want defined areas of color.

Matisse painted a portrait of his wife in 1905 that created quite a stir. Called *Woman with the Hat (Mme. Matisse),* the painting showed a woman in the pose and dress that were popular at the time, but her face was made up of shades of green, blue, yellow, and pink. As he always did, Matisse had chosen the colors to suit himself, but Parisians of the day thought it was an insult both to Matisse's wife and to their whole idea of what it meant to be womanly. Perhaps as a result of its shocking style, the painting soon became the symbol of the Fauve movement.

The Story of Art
Fauvism was an aggressive style of painting and it surprised—sometimes greatly upset—those who observed it. The name Fauvism comes from the French word *fauve,* which means "wild beast," words a French art critic called the artists after observing the violent style Matisse and others used in their paintings during this period.

Paints used in the earliest recorded paintings, found in caves in such places as Lascaux, France, were made by mixing pigments from burned wood (black), chalk (white), and red and yellow earth with animal fat.

Many Fauves, including Henri Matisse, painted or sketched self-portraits. If you'd like to try making one, see *Me, Myself & I* on pages 67-68. To learn more about colors, including the primary colors, which were so popular with the Fauves, see *Round & Round* on page 53.

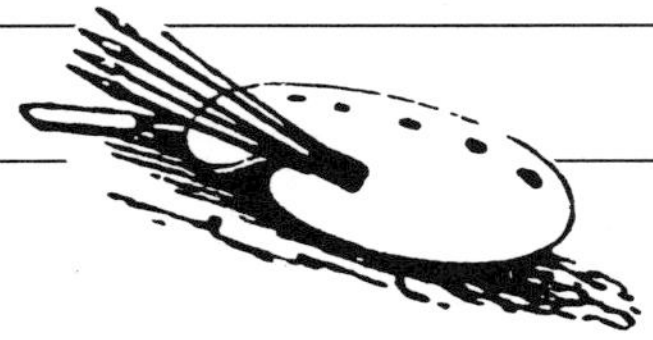

PAINT BOX

Artists use a number of different types of paint. Oils are slow-drying paints used mostly for painting on canvas. Faster drying (and water-soluble until dry) are acrylics, which are often substituted for oil paints.

Also mixed with water, and most usually used on paper, are watercolor paints and gouache (an opaque watercolor). Temperas are pigments mixed with raw egg or other binders. Poster paint is a thick, gummy paint designed for quick sign work. Because it is non-toxic and inexpensive, it's an ideal paint for children.

LARGER THAN LIFE

Diego Rivera was a Mexican mural painter who lived from 1886 to 1957. Many of his massive paintings—some of which are on the walls of public buildings—depict the history and social problems of his home country. He also painted murals inspired by important events in his own life. You can create your own mural right in your bedroom. What kind of story will your mural tell? You're limited only by the size of your wall!

Call your local newspaper office to see if they sell the ends of rolls of newsprint (the paper used for printing newspapers). It's not expensive, and it's perfect for making murals as well as all sorts of other projects.

WALL MURAL

- Large roll of paper, or several large sheets of paper taped together
- Paints, markers, or crayons

1. Get permission from a grown-up before taping or pinning the paper to one of your walls. Be sure to cover the floor, bed, or whatever else is below your workspace with newspapers or a drop cloth (an old sheet works well).

2. Sketch the scene on the paper in pencil first. (You may find it easier to draw a smaller version of the mural first, then transfer the drawing to the mural paper. See *Small, Medium, Large* below for tips on enlarging artwork.)

You might show the history of your life in different blocks of space, or create a visual story about something that frustrates you or that makes you happy. Sometimes to emphasize an object or person, muralists exaggerate their features or enlarge them.

3. Paint the mural. Some mural painters like to work on their projects in stages—maybe one section each day for a few days. That way they can look at it each time with a fresh eye. Besides, it's a lot of space to cover!

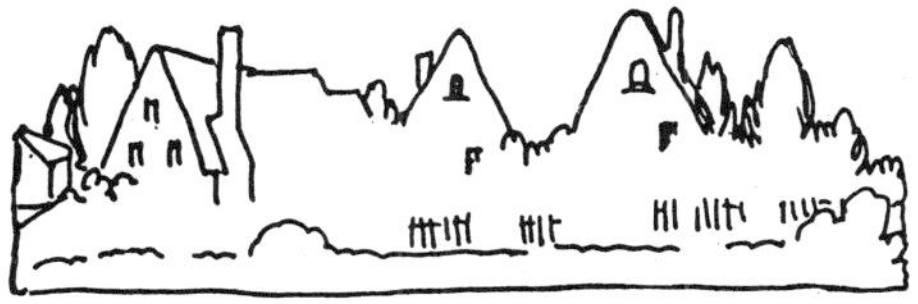

Variations on a Theme
Murals are often painted on the exteriors of buildings such as schools, stores, and even gas stations. Is there a building near your home that needs a little sprucing up? Organize a group of friends and talk to the owner or head of the building (school principal, nursing home administrator, store owner) about painting a mural on it. Find out if he or she would consider supplying the paint if you and your friends supply the artwork!

Experimenting with different styles and techniques can add pizzazz to your mural. Look on page 45 for tips on sponge-painting, or see *Distant Relations* on page 108 for techniques on adding depth. Or, create a trompe l'oeil scene as a mural (see pages 108–109).

ENLARGING ARTWORK

Here's an easy way to enlarge artwork. With a ruler, mark an even grid of squares onto the drawing you wish to make bigger. Now draw a grid of larger squares onto a larger piece of paper (or wall or other surface). Working one square at a time, transfer the lines in each of the smaller squares to the larger ones. Presto! The same drawing, only larger in size.

To reduce the size of a drawing, make the grid on your new paper smaller.

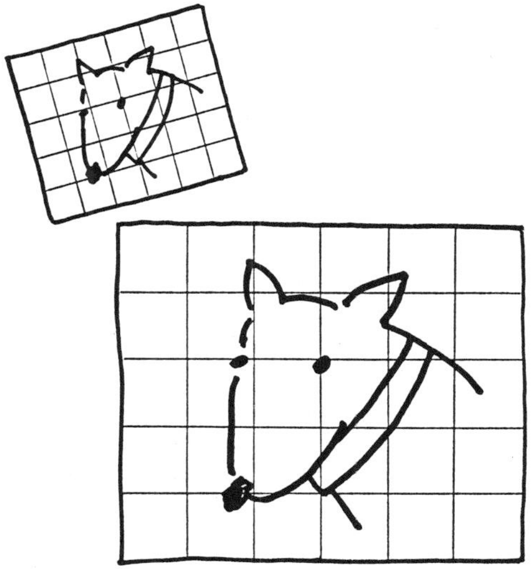

Frescoes are similar to murals. Instead of being painted on a dry wall, they are done on damp plaster. Italian frescoes are some of the most beautiful works of art in the world. One of the best-known is on the ceiling of the Sistine Chapel in Rome. During the early 1500s, artist Michelangelo spent four years flat on his back on high scaffolding creating the biblical scenes shown there.

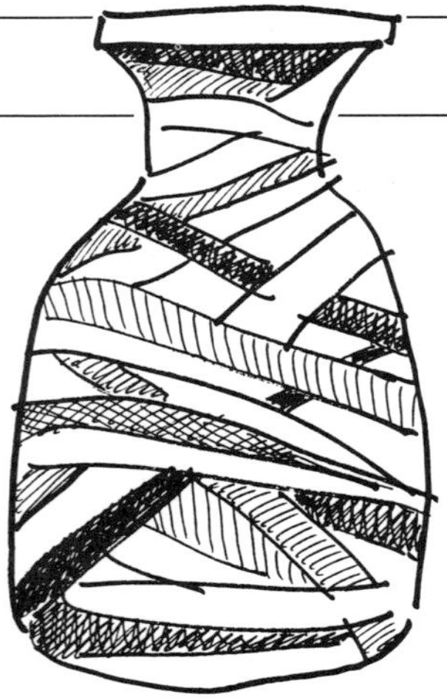

WRAP IT UP

Christo and Jeanne-Claude are married artists famous for their massive environmental art creations. Their incredible projects include wrapping entire buildings, islands, and bridges. They've even hung a curtain across a valley in Colorado! But Christo started his art career by wrapping smaller objects first. Do the same and turn a bottle or a tin can into a unique vase or a holder for pens, pencils, or kitchen utensils.

The Story of Art
Christo and Jeanne-Claude are considered two of environmental art's founders. Environmental art is intended to startle observers into reconsidering structures and spaces as more than just buildings, islands, valleys, for example.

In Burlington, Vermont, artist Jane Horner wrapped two dead trees at the public library in colorful fabric to bring attention to their deteriorating condition and to raise money for new trees. How could you use your creativity to draw attention to something important to you?

COVERED CONTAINER
Clean bottle, jar, or tin can
Crepe or tissue paper
White glue

1. Cut the paper into strips or into any decorative pattern you like. For a more three-dimensional treatment, first crumple the paper, or twist it into strands. (Braid three strands together for an even different look.)

2. With slightly watered-down glue, attach the paper strips to the container, wrapping them tightly. Overlap the strips to create different patterns. Build up extra layers along the top (or bottom or midsection) of the container, if you like as well. Both crepe paper and tissue paper bleed when wetted; take advantage of this trait when wrapping your container.

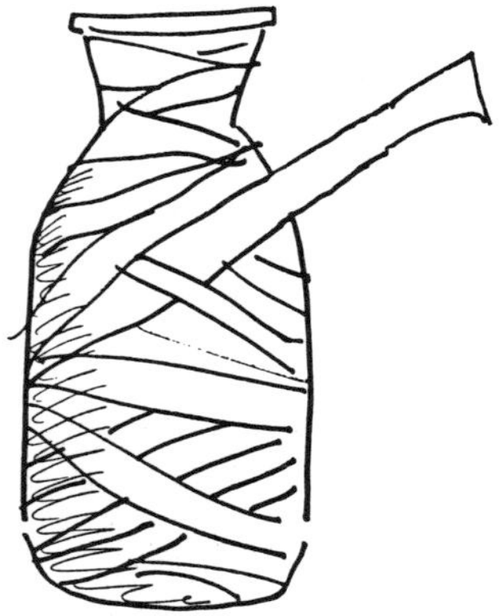

3. Allow the container to dry thoroughly. This may take several days. Then fill 'er up!

Variations on a Theme
As an alternative, decorate your container with papier-mâché. Use the recipe on page 74 to make papier-mâché pulp. The pulp can be used in the same way as the crepe paper and applied to the jar or bottle in any pattern or style you like. Or, cover the container with tissue paper first and then apply the pulp to that for a three-dimensional decorative container.

Christo and Jeanne-Claude often use brightly colored fabrics. In fact, they wrapped eleven islands outside Miami, Florida, in bright pink fabric! If you have some colorful cloth you'd like to use, consider using it to make brilliant-colored paper *molas* (see page 62). Or, bring the outdoor environment inside, and make leaf-print note cards (see page 35), pressed flower bookmarks, (see page 97), or a homegrown terrarium (see page 114).

WRAPPED TREE
Discarded Christmas tree, or dead tree branch
Used gift wrap
Tape

1. Like Christo, you may want to try working on a larger scale, even taking your art outdoors. One way to get started is with a discarded Christmas tree or dead tree branch.

2. Cut the used gift wrap into strips. (You can use other paper, or even plastic garbage bags cut into strips, instead.) Wrap these around the branches of the tree, or bind the entire tree with strips. Glue or tape the strips in place.

3. Set up the tree outdoors. Do passers-by comment on your creation? Do they wonder if you are making a statement of some sort?

Variations on a Theme
With your parents' permission, scope out a feature near your house that you could wrap with waterproof material. It might be a large rock in a rock garden, or a section of a fence. Make sure you take down the art when it begins to get tattered and torn, or when a grown-up asks you to!

Environmental art can take many years from idea to completion. And though it often makes use of our "free" natural environment, it can be very expensive. Christo and Jeanne-Claude raise money for their work by selling drawings of the plans for each project.

STARVING ARTISTS

It is popularly believed that most people who create art for a living end up as starving artists. While it's true that art is generally not a high-paying profession, artists throughout history have found ways to put both art on their walls *and* food on their tables.

Some have been helped by patrons, wealthy people who give artists money so that they can concentrate on creating their art. Others make more popular types of art, which allows them to continue making art that might not sell. Many artists work at other jobs—even teaching art—in order to pay their bills, devoting weekends or other free time to their first love, making the art that expresses their unique vision.

FIRST IMPRESSIONS

The Chinese, who invented paper, also came up with an ingenious way to use it. They were the first to use paper for printmaking. The first printing blocks were probably the same stone carvings that had been used to make designs in clay wall tiles. The Chinese artists simply dabbed some paint on the carvings and pressed them down on paper. Printmaking was born!

LEAF IT BE

You needn't go far to find something to print with. Gather some fresh leaves from outdoors or from houseplants to make some eye-catching note cards.

LEAF-PRINT NOTE CARDS
Fresh leaves
Acrylic paints, in 1 or more colors
Brush
Scrap paper
Note cards or heavy paper cut to size

Note Acrylic paints are a good choice because the paint sticks to the waxy surface of most leaves.

1. If you aren't using purchased note cards, make your own from heavy paper folded in half. Just make sure the cards fit comfortably in standard-sized envelopes.

2. Choose fresh leaves that are whole and unblemished. (Fresh leaves work best, because they are pliable and the veins are more pronounced.) On the back of a leaf, brush on an even coat of paint.

3. Place the leaf, paint-side down, on the note card. Put a scrap of clean paper over the leaf and with your fingers (or a brayer or wooden spoon) rub the paper in the general area of the leaf.

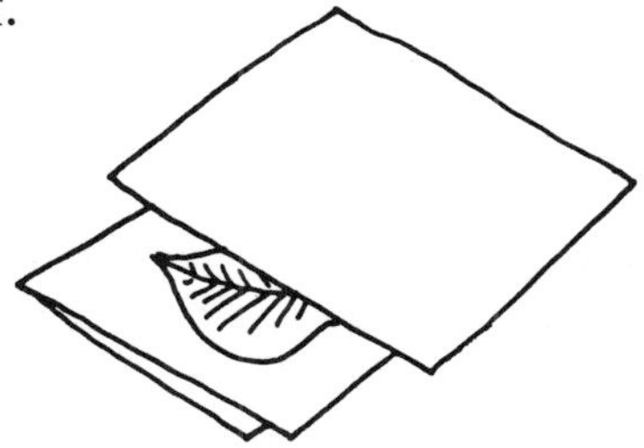

2. Remove the paper and carefully peel back the leaf. Brush more paint onto the leaf to make more prints.

Tip You can easily change colors when you're using acrylics. These paints dry so quickly that you only need to wait a minute or so before brushing on a new color. You can also get some interesting effects by adding a new color before the old one is dry.

Variations on a Theme
Use this technique to print your own gift wrap. Dress up all sorts of household items with leaf prints. Use acrylic paints (the preferred paint because it is waterproof when dry) to decorate placemats, baskets, and planters.

Add a leaf-print border to a pair of curtains or to one of your T-shirts. Printed fabrics should be heat-set as described on page 37.

Don't stop once you've mastered leaf printing! Use your leaves to make leaf rubbings (place a leaf under a sheet of lightweight paper and rub over it with the flat side of a crayon) and leaf stencils (stick a leaf to a sheet of paper with a piece of tape doubled over itself, and dab paint around its perimeter). What other ways can you think of using leaves?

Leaves come in a variety of shapes. Most leaves are *simple,* with one leaf per stalk. Others are *compound,* with at least 3 (and as many as 36) leaflets attached to each stalk.

Leaves can be as long and skinny as evergreen needles (yes—they are leaves); they can be lobed, like maples and oaks, or shaped like small fans, such as the leaves of the ginkgo are.

Mix your own paints to match the colors of the leaves when they turn in autumn.

LOST & FOUND

Ever wonder what kind of print a potato masher makes? Now's your chance to find out. Here are two methods of printing that use items found in the home.

Try this for an interesting effect: Wrap some string around your brayer and roll the inked brayer directly on your paper.

FOUND OBJECT WRAPPING PAPER

Everyday objects such as bottle caps, string, kitchen utensils, shop tools, wood, and cardboard scraps
Printing ink (see *Note*)
Piece of glass, about 8½″ × 11″
Brayer
Large sheets of thin paper

Note For the best results, use water-based printing ink which is available at art stores.

1. Apply ink to the objects you are printing with in one of two ways. You can dip the items into a shallow dish containing slightly watered-down printing ink or paint. Or you can put some ink on a sheet of glass (you can also use a cookie pan), spread it out flat with a brayer, and roll the brayer over the objects you are printing with.

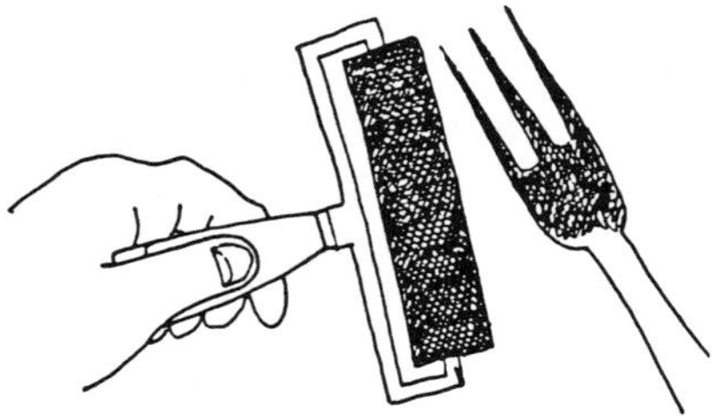

2. Press the inked objects down on the sheet of paper. Rock curved items back and forth slightly to make full contact with the paper.

3. See what kinds of designs you can make by combining various found objects.

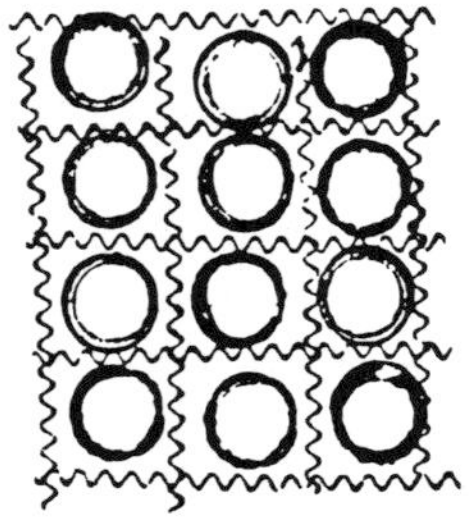

See what kinds of patterns you can create with just one object.

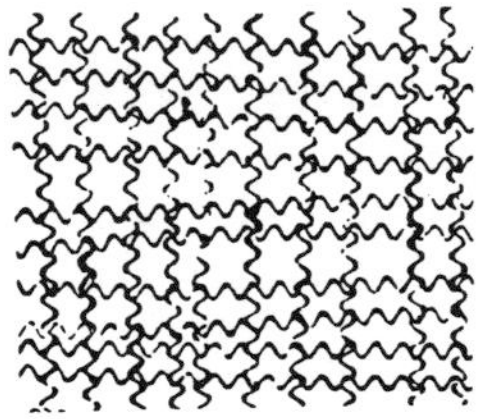

Cover the entire paper with your design. Lay flat to dry.

Variations on a Theme
One-of-a-kind prints, known as monotypes, can be made in a slightly different way. Spread some printing ink on a sheet of glass with a brayer. Draw designs directly in the ink with various tools and found objects such as Popsicle sticks, forks, and cardboard scraps. You can even make a sampler of sorts by making a checkerboard pattern of different designs. Lay a sheet of paper over the glass and roll a clean brayer over it. Peel up the paper to reveal the print. Presto!

POTATO PRINT BOOKMARK
Potato
Paring knife
Printing ink
Piece of glass, about 8½″ × 11″
Brayer
Thick paper, about 2″ × 9″

1. Slice the potato in half. Make a simple raised design on the flat face of one half. Carve away those parts you don't want to print by slicing down and then across with the knife.

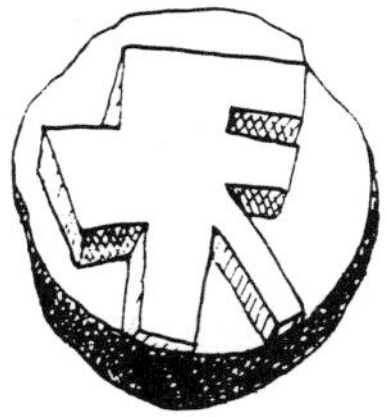

Let the potato dry for an hour or so to help the ink adhere better.

2. Spread some ink on the sheet of glass with the brayer. Dip the potato into the ink. Position the potato on the paper and press down firmly. Re-ink the potato after every one or two prints.

3. Use the potato to make a pattern that is evenly spaced, or place each print so that it is touching to create a different type of pattern.

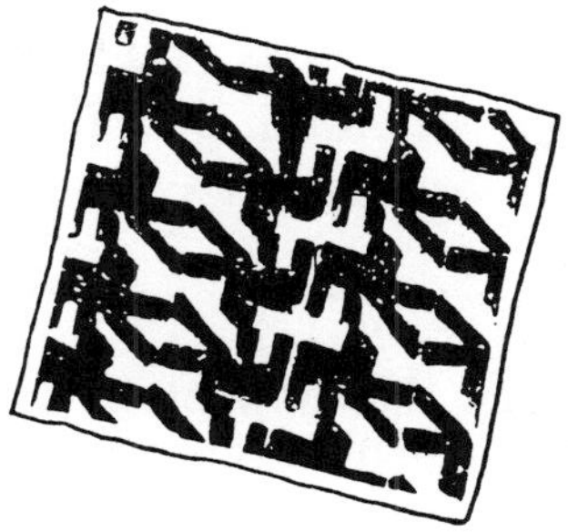

POSITIVELY NEGATIVE

A funny thing happens when you print a repeated design with a potato, especially when the designs touch one another. The printed images make a pattern (this is the *positive* design), but so do the spaces between them (the *negative* design).

You can have a lot of fun playing around with patterns. Let some patterns just "happen," but experiment with using a grid to give others form. You can lightly pencil in grid lines to help you. Erase them when the ink is dry.

Here are a few grid patterns to try:

BLOCK

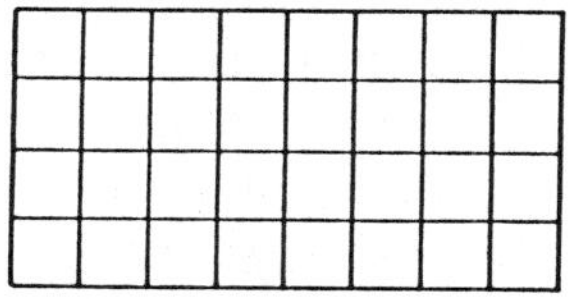

BRICK

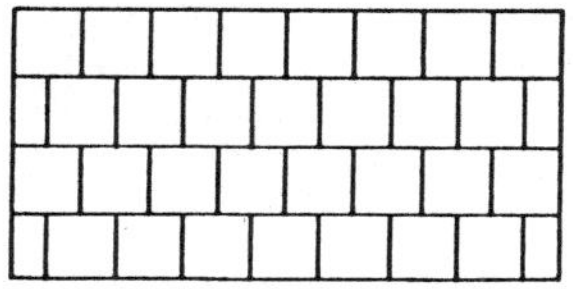

DIAMOND

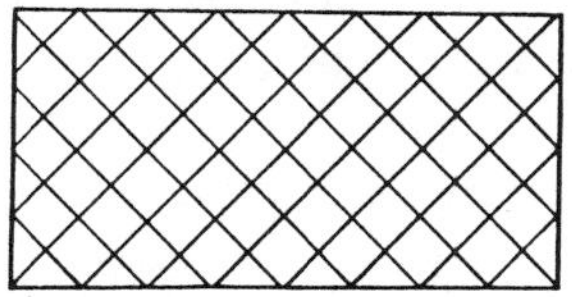

STRIPE

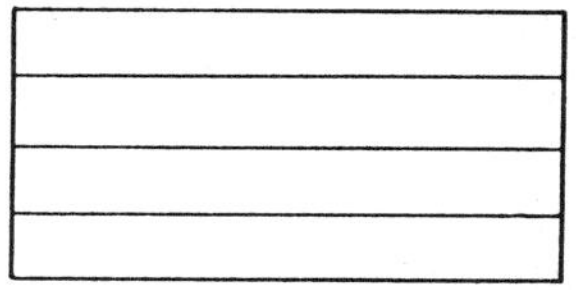

Look in your refrigerator for other vegetables and fruits to print with. Sliced green peppers, mushrooms, and broccoli and cauliflower flowerets make interesting prints. So do apples cut across the middle (see the star shape?) and citrus fruits sliced in half (let these dry for 2–5 days first).

Tricks of the Trade
Found objects and carved potatoes can also be used to print fabric. Use a water-based textile ink, and heat-set it to make it permanent and washable. Let the ink dry for 24 hours, then sandwich the fabric between clean paper towels and iron with a hot, dry iron for about 3 minutes. Keep the iron moving to avoid scorching the fabric.

RAISED CONSCIOUSNESS

Potatoes are perfect for printing small designs, but for larger images you'll want to use linoleum. Burlap-backed linoleum and the few tools used to cut it, aren't expensive. Ask for them at your local art store.

The Story of Art
Among the most beautiful woodcuts ever made are those that were made in Japan from about 1680 to the mid-1800s. At first black line prints were hand-colored with watercolors, but by 1764 full-color prints were made using inked blocks only. Ten and twelve different blocks were commonly cut for each print—one for every color.

Linoleum is harder to cut when it's cold. Warm it on a radiator (or in a 200°F oven) for a few minutes to soften it.

LINOCUT PRINTS
Linoleum, burlap-backed or mounted on wood blocks
Assorted cutting tools, plus a handle
Printing ink
Sheet of glass, about 8½″ × 11″
Brayer
Paper

Note Keep in mind that the image you make on the linoleum will print backwards. If you include any words in your design, make sure not only that they are spelled backwards, but that you form each letter in reverse. Check to see that you're doing it right by penciling the design on the linoleum (backwards) and hold it up to a mirror before cutting. It should read correctly.

1. Sketch your design on the linoleum with a pencil. Use the design shown here or make up your own. Check that any letters are facing the right direction (see *Note*). Remember that mistakes cannot be corrected. You can always cut away more from a design to make it stand out from the background, but you can't replace any of the linoleum that you've already cut!

2. Hold the linoleum steady with one hand (watch that it is never in the way of the cutting tool). Hold the cutting tool in the other hand. Cut *away* from yourself. Turn the linoleum as needed, so that you're always cutting away from your body.

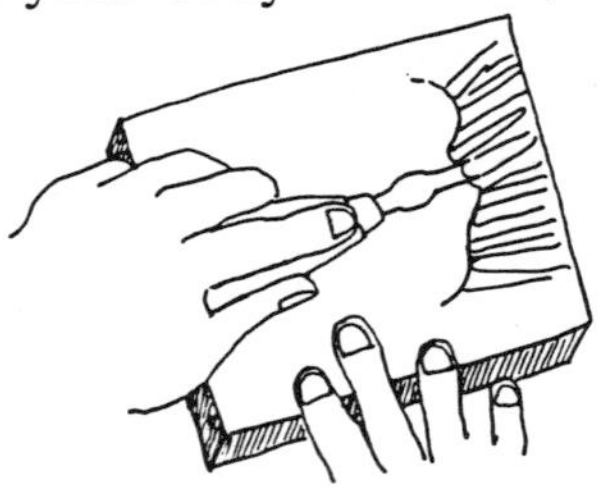

See *Gouge Gauge* on the next page for some of the effects you can get with just three blades.

3. Squeeze a little ink on the sheet of glass and spread it around with the brayer. When it is "tacky" (you can tell because it makes a smacking sound), roll the brayer over your linoleum block, covering it completely with ink.

4. Place a sheet of paper over the linoleum and apply even pressure with your hands or a clean brayer.

Or plunk the block down onto the paper. Push hard with your hands or even stand on the linoleum to make a complete impression.

Separate the linoleum and the paper, and leave the print to dry.

GOUGE GAUGE

You can achieve a variety of lines and textures with just three linoleum cutting blades. One handle can be used to hold the interchangeable blades.

The knife-blade cutter is used to cut around shapes and to make thin lines. Two cuts are made with this tool for every line—one sloping away from the shape, the other right next to it, cut at the opposite angle. This makes a thin V-shaped line.

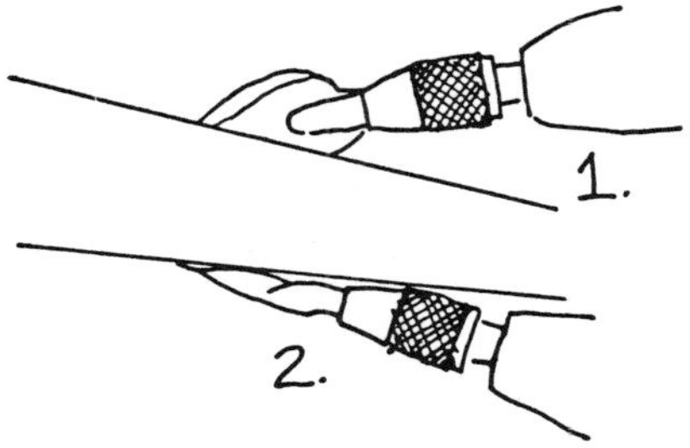

"V" tools also make V-shaped lines, but these come in a variety of widths. "V" tools are used to cut out sections of linoleum, especially where narrow but deep cuts are wanted.

Lastly, there are the U-shaped gouges, also available in several widths. These make a softer, wider line and are good for removing large areas, such as backgrounds.

For over 1,000 years, printing on paper was done solely with woodcuts. Linocuts were introduced only with the invention of linoleum in the 19th century. Linoleum is much easier to cut than wood, but it lacks some of the crisp qualities inherent in wood.

STENCIL STATEMENTS

Stenciling is sort of a combination of printmaking and painting. The same image can be made over and over (as in printmaking), but a brush is used to dab on the paint (just like painting). Stencil your own stationery, or experiment with the effects you can create on fabric.

STENCILED STATIONERY
Tracing paper (optional)
Thin cardboard, about 4″ × 6″
X-acto knife
Masking tape
Paint
Stiff-bristled brush
Typing paper, or plain stationery sheets

Note Tracing paper is handy when you are designing stencils. Use it to trace existing designs; use it also to help you position repeated designs on walls and furniture.

Use this trick to cut out stencils that are symmetrical or the same on both sides. Fold the thin cardboard in half before cutting and your time will be cut in half.

▶

The Story of Art
Stenciling probably originated in China. Some of the earliest examples we know of are paper patterns pricked with tiny holes that were used to stencil the outlines of paintings. It wasn't long before someone figured out that you could enlarge the open areas and stencil whole parts of the paintings themselves.

1. Draw the outline of your stencil on the thin cardboard. Draw it freehand, or trace an existing design and transfer it to the cardboard. (Sheets of clear acetate can also be used. Look for these wherever stenciling supplies are sold.) Use the design shown here, or make up your own.

2. Simplify your design to make it easier to "read." The outline of this apple, for instance, is made more interesting and easier to see by adding a vein to the leaf and by showing the contours of the apple with some white space.

This also allows you to stencil the apple in more than one color, if you choose. Make the apple red, the stem brown, and the leaf green, for example.

3. Carefully cut out the stencil shapes with the X-acto knife.

4. Tape the stencil in position at the top of a sheet of typing paper. With the brush, dab a little paint in the open areas, working from the edges toward the center (this keeps the paint from seeping under the stencil).

Use as little paint as possible (dab the excess off onto scrap paper first). Use a different brush for each color.

5. Let the paint dry before removing the stencil. Tape it to the next sheet of paper, and stencil it. Continue in this way until you are done.

MULTICOLORED STENCILED T-SHIRT
Tracing paper
Thin cardboard, 3 pieces about 8″ × 10″
X-acto knife
Masking tape
Water-based textile paints or acrylics, in 3 colors
Stiff-bristled brush
Newspaper
T-shirt

Note This stenciled design is meant to be made in three colors, one at a time. Separate stencils are cut for each color.

1. Draw the outline of your design on a piece of tracing paper. Use the design shown here or make up your own. Lightly pencil a box around the drawing and mark each corner of the box with a dot.

2. Transfer the outline of the earth (make a 7″ circle using a plate or compass) to one of the pieces of thin cardboard. Transfer the dots marked in the four corners, too.

Transfer the outlines of the continents to a second piece of cardboard. Transfer the dots marked in the four corners.

Lastly, transfer the word "HOME" to the last piece of cardboard. Transfer the corner dots.

3. Carefully cut out the stencil shapes on each piece of cardboard. Poke small holes in each where the dots are.

4. Lay the T-shirt on a flat surface. Fold up some newspaper and place it between the front and back of the shirt. Smooth out any wrinkles and bumps.

5. Position the first stencil on the shirt. Tape it down. Poke a sharp pencil or water-soluble fine-tipped marker through the holes in the four corners. (Make sure the dots show up on the shirt.)

6. Paint the open area of the stencil, in this case using a bright blue. Work from the edges toward the center. Use as little paint as possible, dabbing it on with an up-and-down motion. Let the paint dry; then remove the stencil.

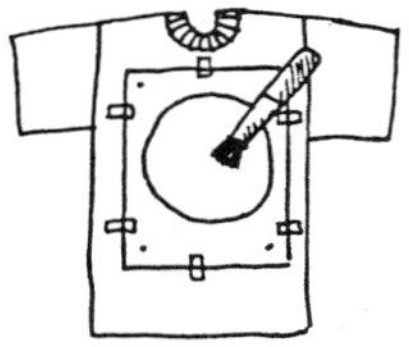

7. Position the second stencil on the shirt, matching up the marks in the four corners. Tape the stencil down. Paint the open areas, in this case, green, adding more paint in some areas to suggest shading. Let dry and remove the stencil.

Do the same with the third and last stencil, using the remaining color.

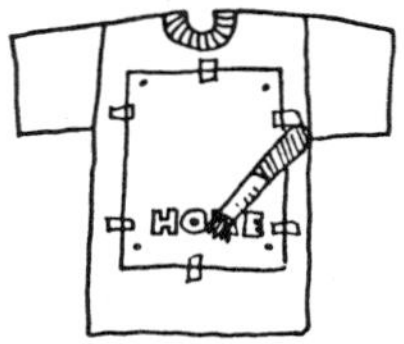

8. Let the shirt dry 24 hours. Remove the newspaper and replace it with clean paper towels. Put a few sheets of paper towels over the design. Iron the shirt for at least 3 minutes with a hot, dry iron. Keep the iron moving all the time to prevent scorching. This heat-setting makes the shirt washable.

Keep delicate parts of stencils flat by pressing them down with a pencil held in your free hand.

BRUSHING UP

Artists' brushes fall into two main categories: those made from soft hair such as squirrel hair, red sable, or synthetic hair, and those stiffer-bristled brushes made from hog hair or synthetic fibers.

The softer brushes are generally used for painting with watercolors and for very detailed work. Pointed brushes, especially, are used for precise work. Large, flat brushes known as one-stroke brushes are perfect for laying down broad expanses of color.

Bristle brushes are better suited to oil and acrylic painting. They come in a variety of shapes and sizes. Stencil brushes are stubby, round brushes made from bristles, although you can stencil with any stiff-bristled brush.

A good brush will last a very long time, if you treat it with care. Avoid getting paint on the ferrule or metal part of the brush that holds the hairs in place. The paint will gradually weaken the hair at that point and the brush will start shedding. Always clean your brushes as soon as you are done using them. Store brushes in a jar, bristle-end up, to keep the hairs nice and straight.

Stenciling was commonly used to decorate walls (and sometimes floors) in colonial America. Wallpaper was expensive and hard to come by. Traveling artists called limners went from town to town stenciling designs and painting murals on walls in homes and public buildings.

Drawing with brush and ink is highly developed in China. Brush drawing as an art form first appeared in the West in the 15th century.

SCREEN STARS

Screen printing is basically a stencil technique using a frame that has finely-woven mesh stretched over it. You can print with one, two, or more colors. Here's how to work two colors into a print.

The Story of Art
The mesh used in screen printing was originally made of silk, and the method was commonly called silkscreen printing. Silkscreen printing was used long ago to print textiles, but it wasn't until the beginning of this century that screen printing was used to make art prints.

TWO-COLOR SCREEN PRINT
Tracing paper, 2 sheets 8½″ × 11″
Medium-weight paper, 8½″ × 11″
X-acto knife
Masking tape
Screen printing ink in 2 colors
Hinged screen and squeegee (see page 43)

1. On an 8½″ × 11″ piece of paper, draw a picture or design to be printed in two colors. Use the picture shown here, or draw one of your own. Keep the shapes simple and bold.

2. Place a sheet of tracing paper directly over the drawing (have all the edges matching), and trace around those parts that are going to be printed in the lightest color. The sky and part of the water in this picture, for instance, are pale blue.

Carefully cut out these sections with the X-acto knife.

3. Do the same for the parts of your drawing that are going to be printed in the second color. In this case, the flag, the stripes on the sail, and the rest of the water are a blue-green. Make sure you place this tracing paper directly over the drawing as you did with the first piece, so that the two stencils line up properly when you put one on top of the other.

4. Place a large sheet of scrap paper on the board under the screen. Put the first stencil on top of the paper, making sure it sits exactly under the screen when it is lowered. Pour some ink at the end of the screen farthest from you. Pull the squeegee towards you, dragging the ink along. Lift the screen; the stencil is now stuck to it.

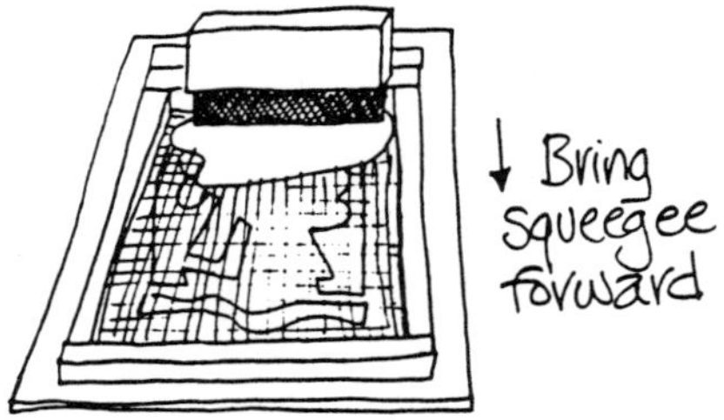

5. Place an 8½″ × 11″ piece of paper on the board under the screen. Try to position it right under the screen so that the printed image will not be crooked. Place some masking tape on the board at all four corners of the paper. Lower the screen, ink it, and make a print. Lift the screen and check to see that the print is where you want it on the paper.

Make any necessary adjustments, moving the masking tape accordingly.

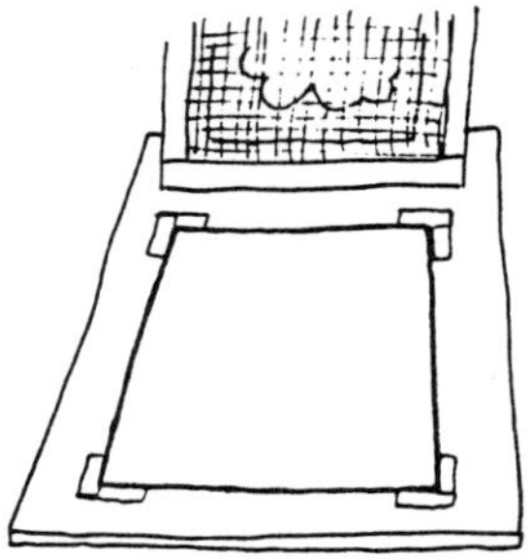

6. Make as many prints as you like, one after another, positioning the paper within the masking tape lines each time. Set the prints aside to dry.

7. Remove the stencil and wash the screen with warm, soapy water. (Wash the squeegee if you're using the plastic kind.) Let dry. Place the second stencil on the board beneath the screen; carefully position it between the masking tape. Adhere the stencil to the screen, as you did the first one.

8. Place one of the already-printed papers on the board between the masking tape lines. Lower the screen; print with the second color. Remove the paper and set aside to dry. Continue printing until you have added the second color to all the sheets. Wash the screen and squeegee.

SCREEN & SQUEEGEE

You can make your own screen printing set-up very easily with some wood, hardware, and finely-woven fabric. (You can also buy small screens and squeegees at most art stores.)

A screen with inside dimensions of 8½″ × 11″ is a good size to start out with. Have a lumberyard rip some 1″ × 3″ pine boarding down the middle. Cut four pieces and attach them at right angles with corner braces or irons.

Staple some polyester mesh to one side of the frame (ask for this at an art store, or pick up some organdy or tightly-woven curtain material at a fabric store). Cut the mesh at least 4″ larger than the frame all around, and stretch it as tightly as possible as you staple it to all four sides.

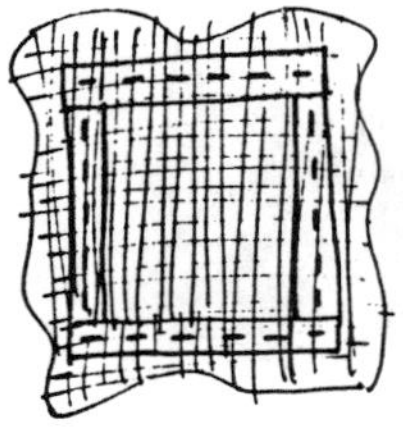

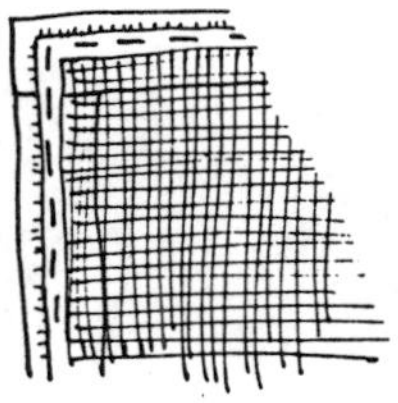

To prevent the mesh from ripping, you can place a strip of thin cardboard over it before stapling. Trim away the excess mesh.

Run masking tape along the inside of the frame to keep the ink from seeping under the screen.

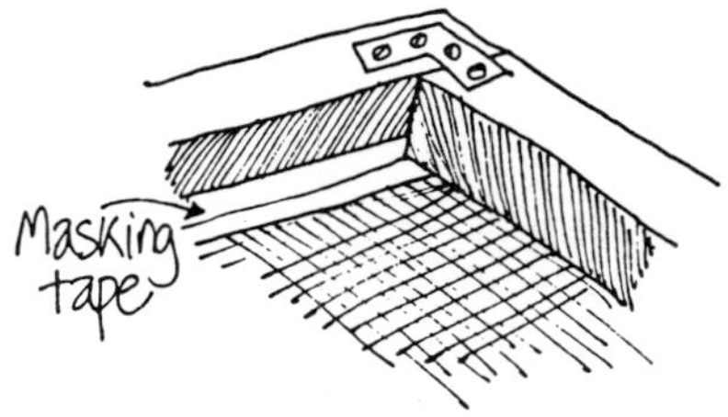

Cut a piece of masonite or ¼″ plywood 2″ larger than the frame. Bolt a piece of wood to one end of the masonite (have the nuts at the top). Place the screen (screen-side down) against the bolted wood piece. Join them together with two hinges. Screw an "arm" to one side of the screen, so you can prop the screen up.

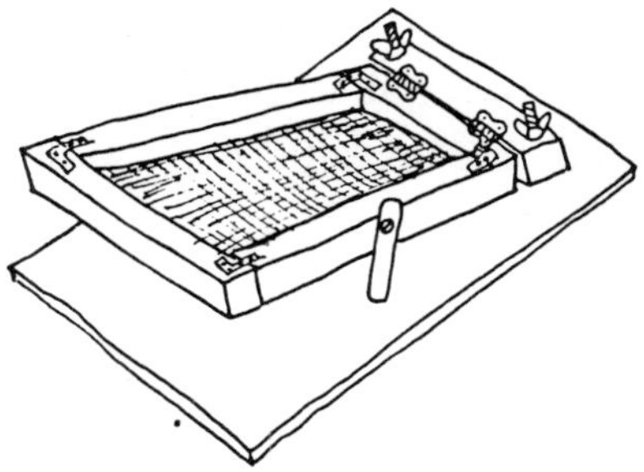

And what about a squeegee? You can easily make your own from a scrap of thick cardboard about 4″ × 8″, or you can buy the thick plastic kind at an art store.

Tricks of the Trade
There are a number of different ways of creating a stencil for screen printing. You can draw directly on the screen with lithographic tusche or crayons (just remember that what you draw on the screen will not print, but will be the color of the paper). You need to use water-based ink when you use this method (so that the ink won't dissolve the stencil), but you'll need turpentine to clean away the design.

You can also use stencil film that is coated so that it sticks to the screen when wet (some films are water-based, others shellac-based). Check to see what your art store stocks.

ANYTHING GOES

Some art tells a story; some is a record of people and places.
Abstract art is art that has no "subject."
Abstract art is appreciated for its color and form, and, in the case of collages, for its texture. There may be no recognizable objects in abstract art, but it can be very expressive.

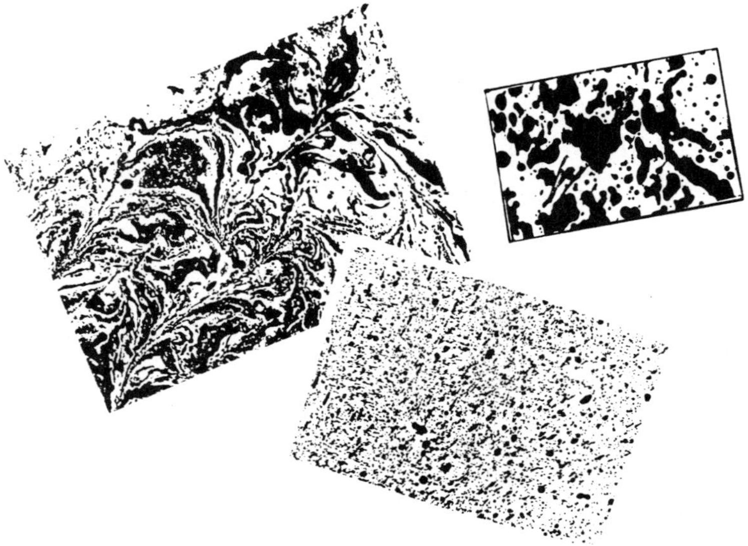

SPONGE & SPATTER

Sponge painting is a quick way to give a textured look to walls, furniture, and pottery. Use this method to make a colorful planter for yourself or as a gift for a gardening friend.

SPONGE–PAINTED PLANTER
Flower pot, terracotta or plastic
Sponge
Scissors or X-acto knife (optional)
Acrylic paint

1. Wash and dry the flower pot.

2. Tear or cut the sponge into small pieces about 2″ square. You can also cut the sponge into shapes such as circles, triangles, stars, or letters of the alphabet. Use the X-acto knife to cut out interior sections.

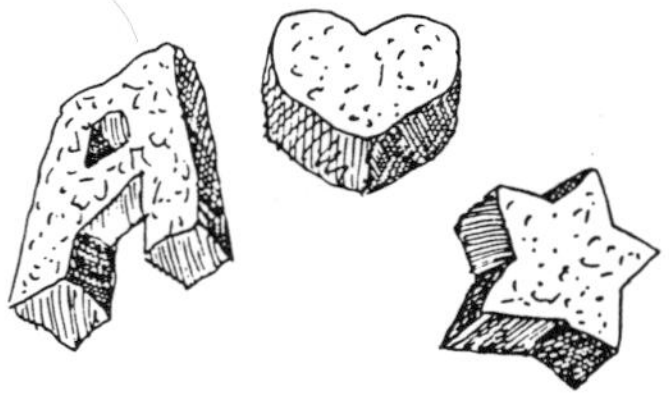

3. Squeeze acrylic paint on some newspaper and dip the sponge into it. Press the sponge on the flower pot, in a random pattern, or, in the case of letters and other shapes, with some space between each print.

Experiment with sponging a different color over the first one, or even a third color. Let the paint dry completely.

Variations on a Theme

Spatter painting is another decorating technique that's fun to do. You need an old toothbrush (or a paintbrush), a Popsicle stick, and some watery paint.

Spatter painting can be very messy! Be sure to use only water-based paints and protect both yourself and your work area from flying paint. For small pieces, do your spattering in a cardboard box. Otherwise, work outdoors if possible. Water-based paints will not harm grass or other plants.

Dip just the tip of the brush's bristles in the paint. Hold the brush over the surface you are decorating and draw the Popsicle stick across the bristles. Bring the stick *towards* you; otherwise you'll end up spattering yourself! Keep moving the brush to spread the spatters around. Repeat with different colors.

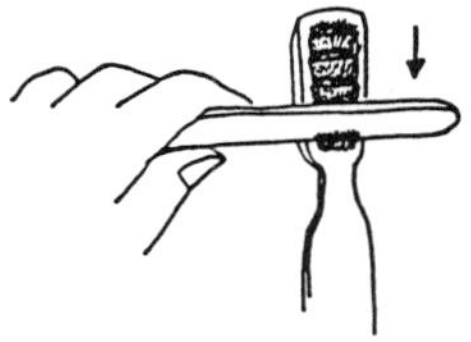

Comb painting is another decorating technique. Make a "comb" from a scrap of sturdy cardboard. (You can also buy combs made of flexible rubber or metal notched with teeth of various widths.) Cut a row of notches in the cardboard with a pair of scissors or an X-acto knife.

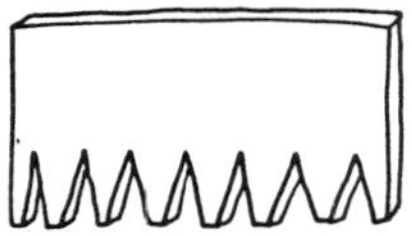

Dip the comb in some paint and pull it across the surface you are decorating. Experiment with making choppy and wavy lines, full circles and woven patterns.

Artist's Profile

One well-known painter made his mark with spattered paint. Jackson Pollack, an American painter who lived from 1912 to 1956, created many huge canvases of dripped and spattered paint. He often lay the canvas on the floor of his studio and stood over it flinging paint. Sometimes, he squeezed paint right from the tube onto the canvas or punctured holes in paint cans and swung them about. This style of painting came to be known as *action painting*.

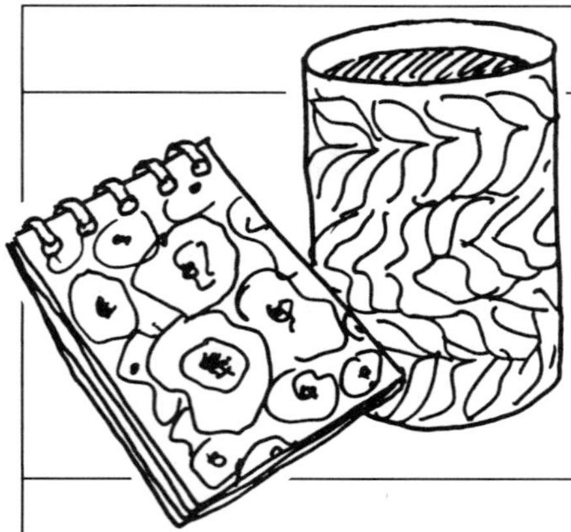

STONE CLONE

Marbling is a popular way of decorating paper used in bookbinding and desk accessories. Use your marbled paper to cover a notebook or to make a pencil holder from an empty oatmeal box.

Marbling was once a carefully controlled craft. Apprentices were taught only part of the process, so that they couldn't make marbled paper on their own.

OIL & WATER MARBLED PAPER
Medium-weight paper
Oil paints, 2 or 3 colors
Turpentine or mineral spirits
Paper cups
Plastic dishpan or deep tray
Paint brush
Small stick
Notebook
Rubber cement

Note Make sure the paper fits comfortably in the dishpan or deep tray you are using. Trim the paper if necessary.

1. Thin each oil paint color with a little turpentine in the paper cups. The paint should be thin enough to shake easily from a brush. (It shouldn't be too runny or it will spread out to nothing when it is dropped on the water.)

2. Fill the dishpan with room-temperature (65–70°F) water at least 3″ deep. With the paint brush, sprinkle small drops of each color onto the water. Use a small stick, such as a toothpick, to make swirling designs in the water. Don't overmix, or the colors will get muddy.

3. Hold the paper by opposite corners and carefully lower it onto the water. Let it lie flat, then lift it out of the water. Dry the paper flat, design-side up, on newspaper or hang to dry.

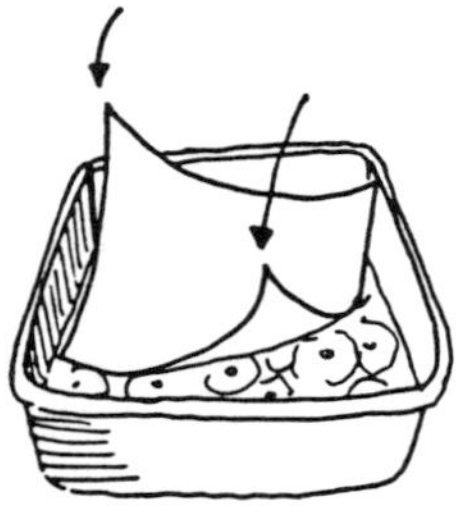

4. Glue the paper to the cover of a notebook such as a spiral-bound pad. Trim any excess off.

Tip Use the same tray of water to make more marbled designs. Simply add more drops of color to the dishpan. Or start fresh by skimming any remaining paint from the water with a strip of newspaper. Drop new paint on the water.

Marbled paper made with only one color is also effective, especially when done with colored paper.

WALLPAPER PASTE MARBLED PAPER

Medium-weight paper
Powdered wallpaper paste
Oil paints, 2 or 3 colors
Turpentine or mineral spirits
Plastic dishpan or deep tray
Paint brush
Small stick
Oatmeal box
Rubber cement
Scissors

1. In a medium-sized bowl, mix 3/4 cup of wallpaper paste with 4 cups of room-temperature (65–70°F) water. Stir until well blended. Add another cup of water to make the paste thick and sauce-like. Pour the paste into the dishpan.

2. Mix your oil paints with turpentine as described in step 1 of *Oil & Water Marbled Paper.* Drop the colors onto the paste in an all-over design. With the stick, move the colors around in swirling, zigzagging, or scalloped patterns.

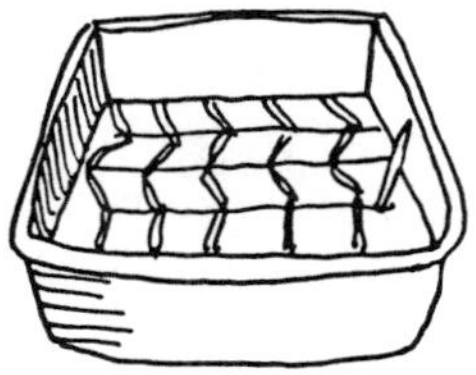

3. Hold the paper by opposite corners and lower it onto the paste. Lift the paper out of the dishpan and sponge the paste off the paper under running water. Be careful not to rub the marbled pattern off. Dry the paper flat, design-side up, on newspaper or hang to dry.

4. Cut the paper so that it is about an inch wider than the oatmeal box you are covering and 1″ to 2″ longer. Glue the paper to the box with rubber cement. Position it so there is paper overhanging at both the top and bottom of the box.

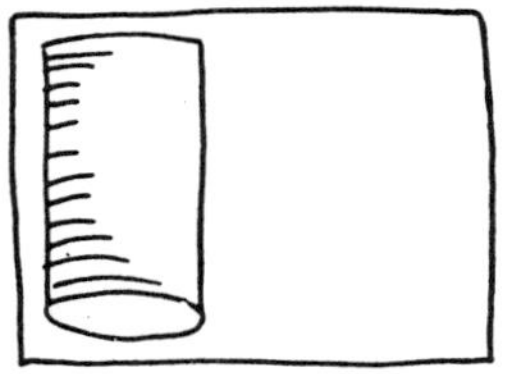

5. Turn the excess paper at the top to the inside of the box and glue it down.

6. Cut notches out of the excess paper at the bottom, and glue the paper to the bottom of the box. Cut a circle of paper slightly smaller than the bottom of the box and glue it to the bottom.

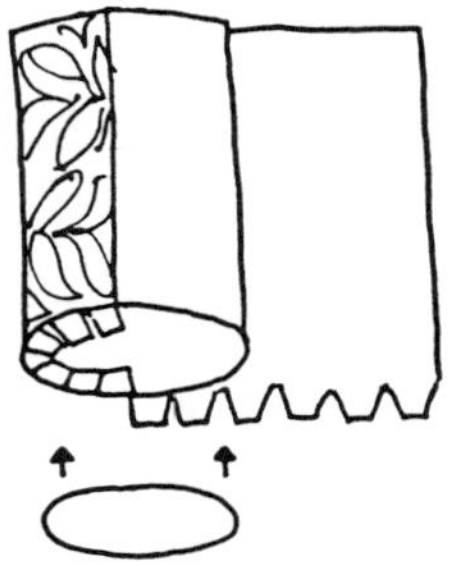

Use marbled paper to cover the books, and to make woven baskets, boxes, and rolled paper beads.

The Story of Art
The Japanese were marbling paper as early as the 8th century, but the technique was not widely used until the Persians and Turks took up the craft in the 1500s.

Examples of marbling made their way to western Europe from the Middle East. Bookbinders began using larger sheets of marbled paper as end papers. In the 17th century in England, there was a high tariff or tax on imported papers. To get around this, some merchants used marbled paper to wrap small items that were being shipped to England. As the paper was simply "packing material," it escaped being taxed. When the crates were unpacked, the sheets of marbled paper were smoothed out and sold to the bookbinders!

DIP DESIGNS

Tie-dyeing is a popular way to decorate fabric (see page 143), but you can use a similar method to color paper. This paper is pretty enough to frame, but you can also use it to wrap gifts or make covers for books.

This method of decorating paper is very popular in Japan where it is called *itajime-shibori.* Soft folded-and-dyed paper is sometimes used as napkins for special occasions.

FOLD-AND-DYE WRAPPING PAPER

- Absorbent paper, such as paper napkins and towels or rice paper
- Assorted colored inks or food colors

Note This project goes fast. Practice with inexpensive paper, such as paper towels, before using rice paper.

1. Pour the ink into small dishes. (Two or three different colors is plenty.) Thin the inks with a little water.

2. Fold a paper towel in half width-wise, and in half again.

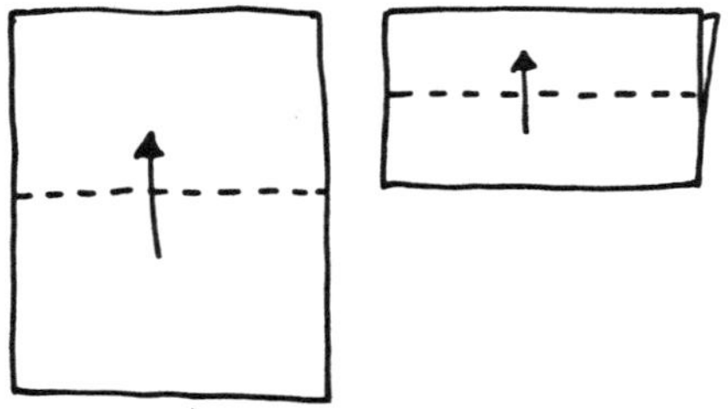

3. Fold the top left-hand corner down to the bottom edge.

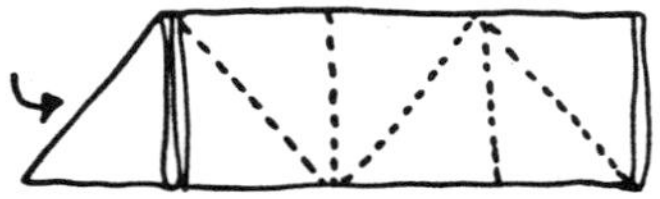

Then fold this triangular section to the back.

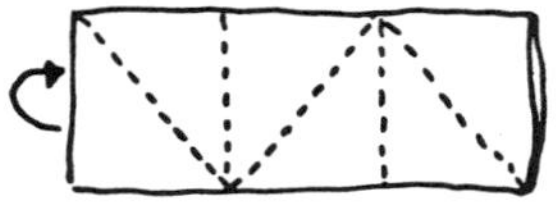

Continue folding back and forth in this way, making a series of folded triangles.

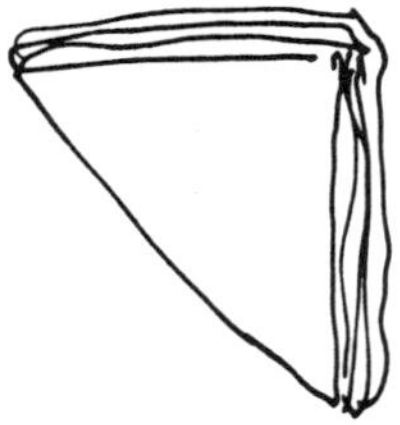

4. Compress the paper with your fingers and dip each corner of the triangle into the ink. Hold the paper in the ink for only a second or two—the paper quickly soaks up the dye.

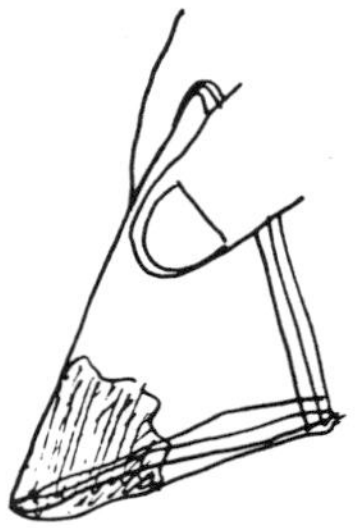

5. Carefully unfold the paper and hang to dry.

Variations on a Theme
Experiment with other ways of folding the paper before dipping it in the ink. Fold the paper into a narrow strip (as you did for the triangular folds above), but fold it into squares instead.

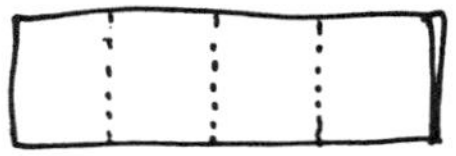

Try this variation, too. Fold the paper first one way and dye it. Let it dry and then fold it another way and over-dye it.

WINSOME WINDOWS

Colored glass windows rely on sunlight to bring them to life. The jewel-like colors can be really dazzling. Transform one of your windows into a "stained glass" window with this tissue paper technique.

PAPER "STAINED GLASS" DESIGN
Heavy-weight black paper, about 20″ × 30″
Tissue paper in assorted colors
X-acto knife
White glue

1. On a separate piece of paper, draw a geometric design. Use the design shown here or make one of your own.

Make the lines of your drawing at least 1/2″ wide. The tissue paper will be glued to the back of these lines, so they must be wide enough.

2. Transfer the design to the sheet of black paper. Carefully cut out all the open spaces with an X-acto knife.

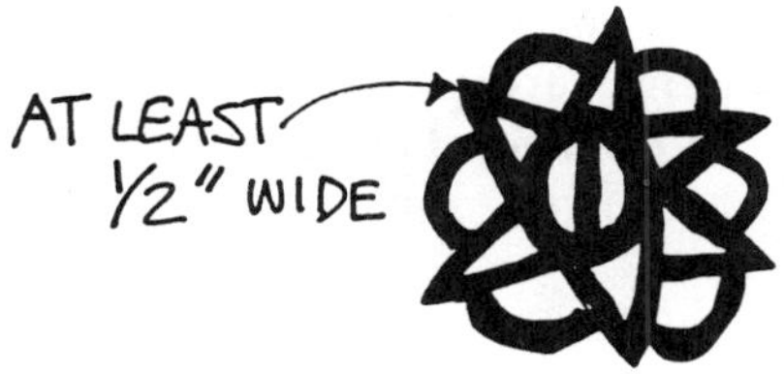

3. Choose what color tissue paper you want for each cut-out section. Do one section at a time. Cut the tissue paper roughly to size. Spread a little glue on the back of the black paper that frames that section. Place the tissue paper over the opening and press it all around. Trim off any excess tissue paper.

Continue to cover each opening with tissue paper. Let dry.

4. Hang the "stained glass" design in a sunny window, glued-side against the pane.

The art of stained glass reached its peak in the 13th century. By the 1600s, the art was nearly forgotten. It was revived in the 1800s when windows modeled on medieval examples were made once again. It wasn't long before original designs in stained glass became popular.

Tricks of the Trade
To transfer a design, rub pencil on the back of the design. Place the design pencil-side down on a second sheet of paper. Carefully trace all the lines of the design; lift the paper. The design is now on the second sheet of paper.

Originally, stained glass windows were used as instructional aids in churches and chapels. Scenes from the Bible or from the lives of the saints were illustrated for all to see in this way.

BITS & PIECES

Collages are wonderful catch-all pieces of art. You can make them with everything from sticks and stones to postage stamps and pictures cut out of magazines. Here's a collage that pays tribute to where you live.

Collages were "invented" by Pablo Picasso, a Spanish painter who created some very original art during his 92-year lifetime. Pasting items on boards is an old folk art, but Picasso is credited with turning collages into fine art.

Another name given to collages is *assemblage*—artwork made of many things assembled together.

NEIGHBORHOOD COLLAGE

Things you find in your neighborhood, from rubbings of tree bark and manhole covers to your local newspaper and candy wrappers
Sturdy cardboard (see *Note*)
X-acto knife
White glue or hot glue

Note Cardboard is fine for gluing paper and lightweight objects to. Use a heavier support, such as 1/4″ plywood or masonite, for bulkier items. Likewise, white glue works well with paper, but hot glue is a better choice for heavier items.

1. Collect items for your collage. Make rubbings of tree leaves, as well as engraved signs and building bricks. Look for things that have meaning for you—movie ticket stubs, bags from local merchants, pictures of your favorite cartoon characters.

2. Make a "frame" for your collage. (A purchased frame with glass can be used for flat collages.) Cut 1″-wide strips of cardboard and glue them around the perimeter of the cardboard you are using for the collage. This gives the collage a finished look.

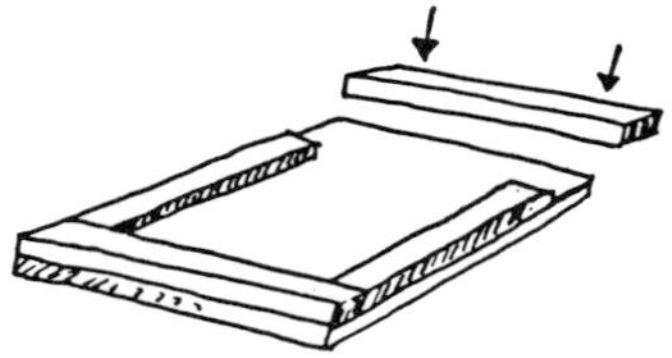

3. Play around with the arrangement of your collected items. Large flat pieces can form the background for smaller things; related items might look good grouped together. When you are happy with the way everything looks, glue the pieces down.

The word collage is from the French word *coller* which means "to glue."

Variations on a Theme
Here are some other ideas for collages.

Make a nature collage. Paste down twigs, leaves, pieces of bark, feathers, moss, rubbings of rocks . . . you name it.

Make a collage with items all the same color. If there's something you want to add to your collage, but it's the wrong shade, then paint it.

Make a collage with things you've saved from a vacation trip. This is a great way to keep those memories alive.

STICK TO IT

There are many glues available to artists, some better suited to certain materials than others. The two most often suggested in this book are white glue and rubber cement.

White glue, such as an all-purpose glue like Elmer's® glue, is perfect for porous materials such as paper, wood and fabric. Because it is a watery glue, it has a tendency to bleed through thin materials and buckle others. Use white glue very sparingly, and spread it out with your fingers to get more coverage. It can also be thinned with water and brushed on. Clean your brushes and hands with warm, soapy water.

Rubber cement is also used for gluing paper. There are two types: regular rubber cement that is brushed on both surfaces and allowed to dry before bonding, and the type known as one-coat rubber cement, which requires—you guessed it—coating just one surface. Regular rubber cement is more widely available, and is the one called for in this book.

After sticking your paper down with rubber cement, burnish (rub hard) the paper to create a good bond. Clean any excess from your artwork by rubbing it off with your fingers. Rubber cement peels away very easily. If you accidentally glue the wrong paper down, or glue it on crookedly, carefully peel the top paper off, clean the rubber cement from both surfaces and start again. Rubber cement can be thinned with rubber cement thinner if it begins to evaporate and thicken. (See *Safety Check* on page 11 for proper storage and use of rubber cement.)

Wood glue, a water-based glue used for gluing wood to wood, is useful when making collages. Wood glue (as well as such glues as epoxy and super adhesives) can be purchased at hardware and department stores.

Most glues are derived from animal substances, such as bones and skin.

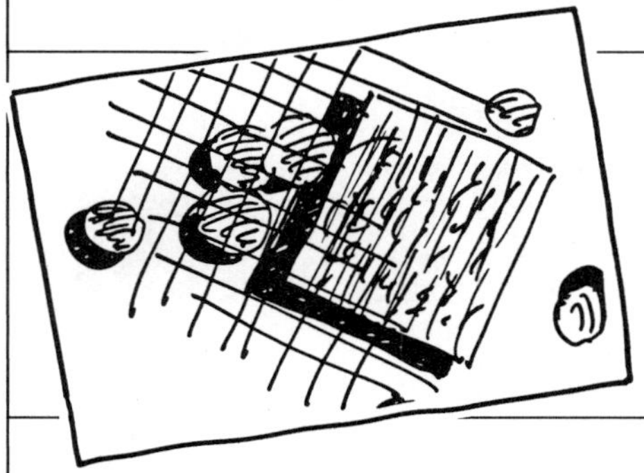

RUB DOWN

Abstract art makes the most of color and form . . . and texture. What better way to show texture than to make a rubbing? Look for rough, bumpy surfaces and those with raised patterns.

ABSTRACT RUBBING
Anything with texture, from tree bark to coins
Soft pencils or crayons
Thin paper, about 8½″ × 11″

Note Thin paper works best for making rubbings. There's a large selection to chose from. Try out such papers as tracing paper, thin typing paper, and many Asian papers.

1. Make an abstract picture of randomly placed rubbings. Place your paper over whatever you are rubbing. With your fingers, feel where the object is located. Use a soft pencil or a crayon to make back-and-forth strokes over the

Texture is all around us. Close your eyes and rub your hands along some textured items. Can you tell what they are without looking?

object. Use light pressure for the best results.

Variations on a Theme
Compose a picture made up of textures taken from various objects. A landscape can be made with different textures for fields, mountains, and clouds. Draw a portrait of a person and "clothe" him with shirt and pants made by rubbing over textured surfaces.

Many people enjoy making rubbings of old gravestones. Some of the old grave markers are decorated with quaint carvings.

COLOR CODED

Can you imagine what it would be like if everything were in black and white? Color plays an important part in everyday life. You probably respond to some colors more favorably than others. Look how some colors "respond" to one another!

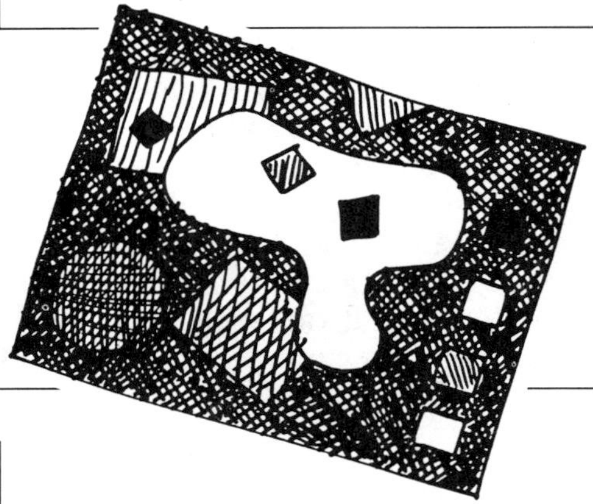

We use color names in many common expressions. When someone is sad, we say he's blue; an angry person is said "to see red." If you're green with envy, you're jealous. What other expressions can you think of?

COLOR STUDIES
Paint, markers, or crayons, in assorted colors
Brush, for paint
Masking tape (optional)
Paper or canvas

Note You can also use cut-paper for these color studies. Check your scrap box for pieces of paper in solid colors.

1. Create a series of paintings concentrating on color combinations. Start out with using just two colors. Cover the paper completely with one color; let it dry. Paint a square or other shape in the center of the paper, using the other color.

Do a series of these paintings, keeping the background color constant while changing the color of the central shape.

Notice how the background color looks different depending on the color next to it.

2. Evoke different moods with your color studies. How would you show "quiet" or "hot"? Use the brushstrokes (or marker and crayon lines) to help you express these moods.

3. Make some paintings using as many colors as you like. Which colors seem to work well together? Experiment with little paintings, and very large ones (tape together several sheets of large paper to create mural-size compositions).

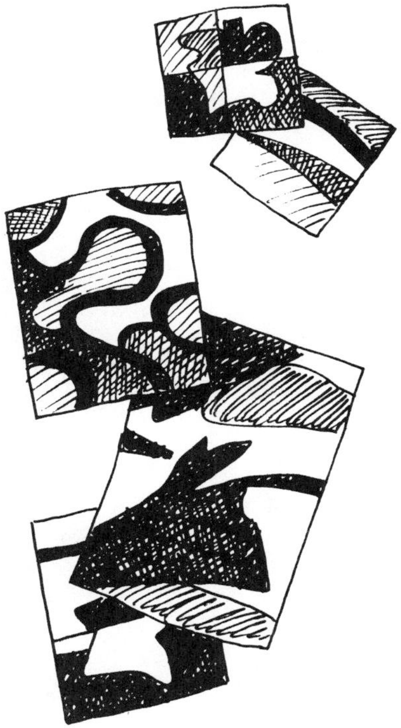

ROUND & ROUND

Color and its effects have been closely studied by artists over the centuries. You may be familiar with the basic color wheel, a tool which can help you understand the relationship between colors. You can make your own color wheel using the model shown here. Fill in the "pie slices" with colored markers or crayons.

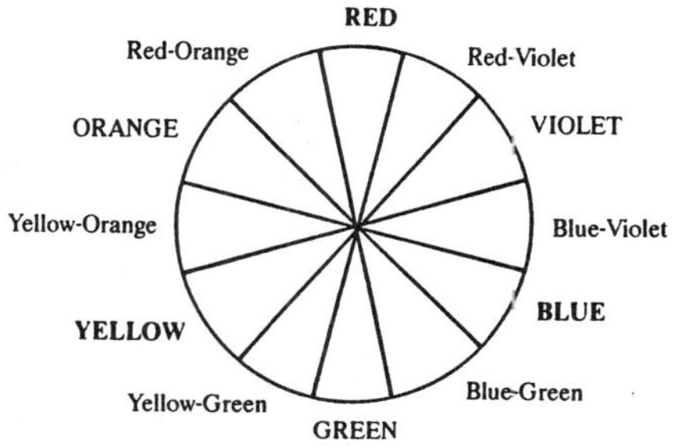

The colors in **bold type** are the *primary colors.* Mix them together to create the *secondary colors* (red + blue = violet, blue + yellow = green, yellow + red = orange). *Intermediate colors* are created whenever you mix a primary color with a secondary color (red + violet = red-violet, for instance).

The colors opposite one another on the wheel are known as *complementary colors* (red and green are complementary, for example). These are exciting colors when used together.

You can make any color lighter by adding white (the new color is called a *tint*). You can make any color darker by adding a little black (these are called *shades*).

Experiment with isolating colors with black or white strips (such as you did with the paper "stained glass" design on page 49). Placed next to black, colors seem to glow; next to white, they appear darker.

Most animals see in black and white (and shades of gray). Monkeys, apes, many birds, and some fish, however, apparently have vision similar to ours. Bees are another exception, but experiments show they are not able to distinguish the color red.

In commercial printing, full-color printing is done using three different primary colors. These are yellow, magenta (a bright purple-red) and cyan (a turquoise blue). Inks in these three colors plus black are combined to create the thousands of colors the human eye is able to distinguish.

THE ARTFUL ANIMAL

Some of the earliest art we know of was created nearly 20,000 years ago on the walls and ceilings of caves. What do you suppose those artists chose to paint? You guessed it—animals! Artists continue to try to capture the beauty, majesty, and mystery of animals in their art. But not all the animals people paint and sculpt are real. Just think of the fabulous dragons that the Chinese make or the frightening animal masks that are found in so many cultures.

PET PROJECT

There's something about animals that makes us want to touch them. Make a portrait of your pet, if you have one, or of an animal you admire, that shows how soft its fur is or how slithery its skin!

ANIMAL COLLAGE
Scraps of felt and fake fur, yarn, cotton balls, sandpaper, art papers
Dried peas and beans, spices, beads, sequins
Paint or markers
Poster board, about 8½″ × 11″
White glue

1. Draw the outline of an animal (or of several) on the piece of poster board. Place your animal in an outdoor setting, the way these sheep and cows are, or wherever you like.

2. Fill in the outlines with your chosen materials. Use white glue to hold them in place. The sheep here are made with cotton balls and black turtle beans (for the face and feet); the cows' spots are made from sandpaper cut into shapes.

Experiment with fake fur (perfect for cuddly creatures) and short pieces of yarn for manes and tails. Use overlapping sequins to create a spangled snake; crumple up some gray paper, smooth it out, and glue it down for an elephant's hide. Use shiny paper or cellophane to make a fish.

QUICK TAKES

There are other ways of making a portrait of your pet, of course. Sleeping pets, especially, are cooperative models. Spend some time making pencil sketches of the different poses your pet sleeps in.

Here's something a little different. Try "suggesting" your pet's shape with as few lines as possible. This is harder than it looks! For bolder lines, use a crayon or brush and ink. With just a few lines you can get the feeling of a solid form.

The Story of Art
The beautiful paintings of animals on cave walls and ceilings were not meant to be seen and admired. Instead, they were created for their magical powers. How do we know this? Since many primitive peoples living today use art in a similar way, we can guess that when a cave artist painted a picture of a bison, he was casting a sort of spell over a real bison. After all, our ancestors depended on animals for food and clothing, and they did what they could to make sure they had enough.

LIONS & TIGERS & BEARS

The Huichol (WEE-chole) Indians of Mexico make decorative paintings of animals using brightly-colored yarn. They press the yarn into soft beeswax spread on a board, but you can use white glue for the same effect.

Yarn and beeswax paintings are traditionally made by the Huichol men. The women make a similar type of art by pressing tiny glass beads into wax that is shaped into small animal sculptures.

YARN PAINTING
Stiff cardboard, about 6″ square
Yarn in assorted colors
White glue
Scissors

Note Yarn paintings can be any size, but because they take time to make, it's best to start small.

1. Draw the outline of an animal on the cardboard. (Most Huichol yarn paintings have a single figure, filled in with several colors of yarn.) Make the cat as shown here or draw your own animal. If there are distinct areas that you are going to fill with different colors, sketch in those lines, too.

2. Start by covering the outlines with yarn. Spread some glue in the general area, then press the yarn down, following the outline all the way around. Cut the yarn when you reach the spot where you began.

3. Fill in the figure with yarn, working from the outside in. Spread the glue in small areas and press the yarn in place, keeping the strands as close to one another as possible. The painting will have a swirling pattern. Change colors by cutting the yarn of the first color and placing the start of the second color right after it.

4. Now fill in the background. Start by making a border around the whole piece with one or more colors of yarn. Then work the background in a solid color. Again, start at the outer edge and work in. When one area gets completely filled in, cut the yarn and fill in another area.

Tip Try not to press too hard on the yarn when you are gluing it in place. It will stay nice and clean, and springy, too, if you handle it gently.

The Spanish explorers brought sheep to the New World in the early 1500s.

The art of spinning wool into yarn was developed around 4000 BC.

MYTHICAL MONSTERS

The dragon is one make-believe monster common to countries in both the West and the East. With this painting technique, you can give your fire-breathing dragon a smoky smile!

BLEACH PAINTING
Heavyweight paper, about 8½″ × 11″
Fountain pen ink (see *Note*)
Brush
Bleach
Popsicle stick

Note Some fountain pen inks work better than others for this project. Skrip® ink is recommended for the best results. Use black or a blue-black for a picture that really stands out.

1. Cover the entire sheet of paper with the ink. Swirl the ink around to make a murky background. Set aside to dry.

2. With the Popsicle stick, paint a picture of a dragon (or the beast of your choice) using the bleach. The dragon will magically appear as the liquid bleaches the ink. Make plenty of smoke coming out of the dragon's nostrils with swirling lines.

Variations on a Theme
Let the bleach completely dry. Then add color to the painting with markers, pastels, or crayons.

Be very careful handling the bleach. Do this project in a well-ventilated area and protect both your work area and yourself from splashes. A single drop of bleach will make a permanent white spot, if it falls on colored fabric.

FADE AWAY

Usually when you draw or paint, you *add* color to white paper to make an image. With bleach painting, however, you start with a colored background and bleach out those parts you want to show up. Bleach paintings are very dramatic because the reversed image (white on black or some other dark color) really stands out.

Bleach painting can also be done with dyed fabrics. Dark colors work best here, too. Use chlorine bleach (rather than the type of bleach which doesn't affect dyes) to paint a design on the fabric or to dip a tightly-wadded up ball of fabric into. (This technique is a type of tie-dyeing. For more projects using this method, see *Dip Designs* on page 48, and *To a Tee* on page 143.)

Chinese people all over the world celebrate their New Year (which falls some time in mid-February) with firecrackers and a huge dragon that dances in the streets. The dragon is actually an enormous costume that is worn by as many as 50 people!

FLYING FISH

The Japanese are famous for their kites, but they also make a wind sock in the shape of a carp, a favorite fish. It is displayed each year on May 5th during the festival called Children's Day.

The carp is a fish that swims upstream against the current. To the Japanese, the fish is a symbol of strength, courage, and determination, all qualities they want their children to have.

For a kite you can make that really flies, see page 88.

FABRIC WIND SOCK
White fabric, about 16″ × 24″
Acrylic paints
Brush
Plastic lid from a coffee can
Scissors
Needle and thread
String

Note You can also make this wind sock out of paper (in which case, glue the seams rather than sew them). It won't hold up very long if hung outdoors, but it's just as nice.

1. Fold the fabric in half lengthwise and draw the outline of a fish on it. Place the bottom of the fish on the fold of the fabric. Make sure the fish's mouth measures 4½″, so that it will fit snuggly around the coffee can lid when it's sewn. Cut along the outline.

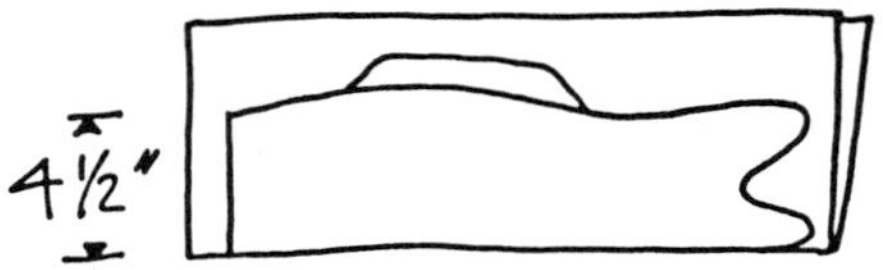

2. Open up the fabric, and place it on some newspaper. Paint the fish with acrylic paints so that both sides match. Let the paint dry.

3. Poke a hole in the center of the coffee can lid with the scissors and cut out the entire center, leaving just the rim.

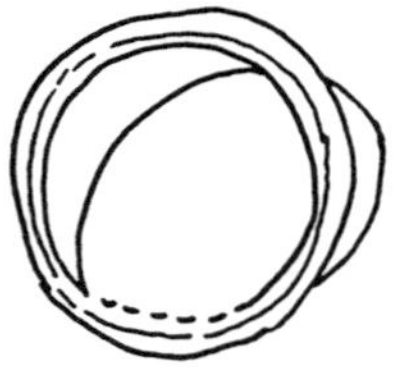

4. Fold the fish along the center fold, right sides together, and stitch the long edge with small, even stitches. Place the lid rim around the fish's mouth and fold about an inch of fabric over the rim, concealing it. Stitch the fabric in place.

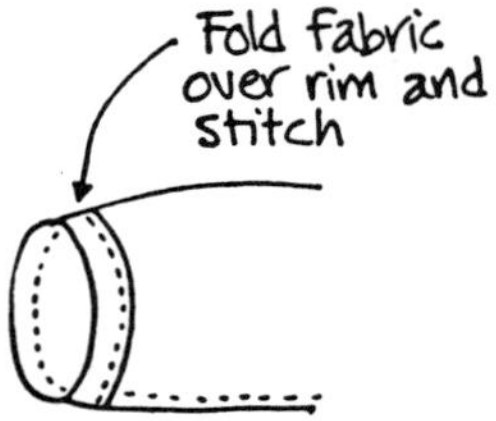

5. Turn the fish right side out. Cut a piece of string about 20″ long. Poke two small holes in the fabric on opposite sides of the mouth and tie the string to the rim. Tie another, longer string to the middle of the first one. Lash the wind sock to a pole or porch railing, so it is blown horizontally when there's a breeze.

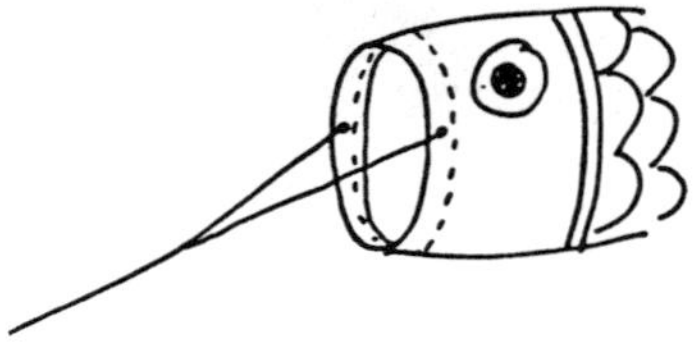

TUMBLEBUGS

Bet you've never seen an insect flip-flop quite like this one! Don't tell your friends what makes this little critter go, and see if they can guess.

TUMBLING TOY
Poster board, about 4″ × 8″
Scissors
White glue
Marble
Paint or markers
Felt or paper scraps

1. Cut a 3/4″ × 4 1/2″ strip and two ovals, 3/4″ × 1 3/4″, from the poster board.

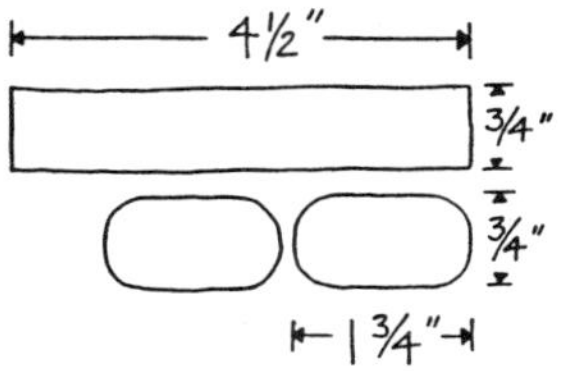

2. Glue the long strip into an oval shape, overlapping the ends about 1/4″. Hold the ends together until the glue sets. Glue one of the poster board ovals to one edge of the strip. Let dry.

3. Place the marble in the tumbler and glue the other oval in place. Let dry. Turn the tumbler into a tumblebug by adding a little paint, six felt feet, and a pair of antennae.

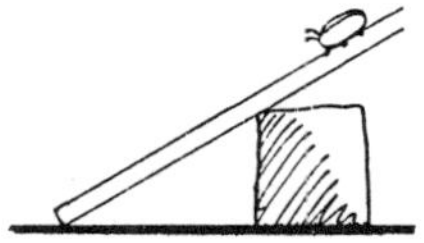

4. To get your tumblebug tumbling, place it at the top of a board propped up at a 30° angle (this is a gentle slope). Watch it fly down the runway!

Did you know?
Do you know the difference between beetles and bugs? They're both insects, but they have different body parts for eating foods. Beetles chew their food, using hard front wings and mouth parts, while bugs suck up food with soft, leathery front wings.

TWO BY TWO

You could easily make an arkful of animals using this construction method. Paint your animals as realistically as you want or invent some wild and crazy creatures all your own!

SLOTTED CARD-BOARD ANIMALS
Poster board, about 11″ × 17″
Scissors
Paint or markers

Note The instructions here are for four-legged animals, but you can easily make creatures with more legs.

This horse looks much like those the Chinese traditionally paint and sculpt. Have you ever seen any pictures of them? They have very fat bodies and delicate heads and feet. In fact, one of the most famous cave paintings is the one in Lascaux, France known as the "Chinese horse," because it looks so much like Chinese paintings of horses.

1. Draw the outlines of both the animal's body and two sets of legs on the poster board. If you want your animal to have a separate tail, draw that, too.

2. Cut all the pieces out. Now cut inch-long slits in the legs, tail, and body. Do this by cutting a narrow "V," no wider than the thickness of the poster board.

3. Paint the animal any way you like. You may find it easier to do this before you put the animal together, but since each piece is painted on both sides, you can paint the assembled animal to save time.

Variations on a Theme

To make sturdier (and larger) animals, use wood instead of cardboard. Masonite, particle board, and plywood are good choices. Use a coping saw to cut out the shapes. Just remember to make the slits as wide as the board's thickness. Sand all rough edges before painting.

TURTLE TOSS

Sturdy turtle bean bags like these can stand a lot of rough play, so have fun tossing them back and forth or through a hole cut into a piece of cardboard.

When you're not tossing your bean bag around, use it as a paperweight.

FELT BEAN BAG
Green felt, about 1/4 yard
Dried beans, peas, or rice
Needle and thread
Acrylic paints or permanent markers

Note This makes a bean bag that measures about 6″ across.

1. Sketch the outline of a turtle on a piece of paper. Make it a simple shape as shown. Make the outline about 1/2″ bigger than you want the final bean bag to be. Cut out the turtle shape.

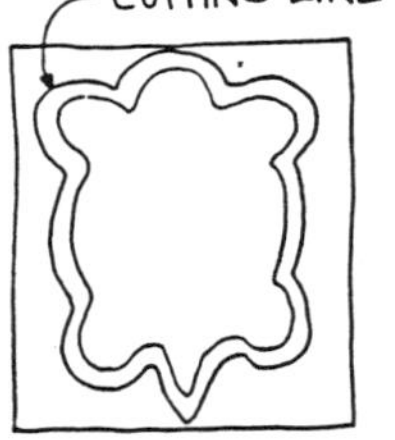

2. Fold the felt in half and pin the paper shape to it. Cut around the paper. Remove the paper pattern and stitch the two felt pieces together with small even stitches (leave a 1/2″ seam allowance). Leave a 2″ opening in the bag.

3. Turn the fabric right side out. Fill the turtle with beans, then sew the opening shut. Give the turtle some features and markings with paint or markers.

Did you know?
The turtle is the only reptile that has a shell. There are 240 species of turtles in the world, 50 of which can be found in North America.

Felt is a type of unwoven cloth. Wool, fur, and combinations of other matted fibers are "felted" by steaming them under pressure. Most craft felt is made from rayon and acrylic fibers; real fur and wool felts are used to make hats, slippers, and other items.

A STITCH IN TIME

Basic sewing is a skill anyone can acquire. Knowing how to thread a needle and make a running stitch opens up a whole world of art projects to you.

Use a medium-sized needle with a big enough eye (opening) to thread easily. Cut a length of thread about 30″ long. Thread one end through the needle's eye; bring the two ends of the thread together and knot them. An easy way to do this is to wrap the ends around your index finger once; then use your thumb to roll the thread right off your finger. As you do so, the end will tangle itself and you can pull down on the thread to make the knot.

This creates a double thread that is nice and strong, and that won't slip out of the needle by mistake.

A running stitch is a basic sewing stitch. It is used for sewing two pieces of fabric together (usually right sides facing). Make a series of "dashes" by inserting the needle into both layers of fabric from the top and bringing it back up 1/4″—1/2″ from the first hole. Pull the thread all the way through. Continue in this way until you reach the end of your sewing.

Now work your way back to the beginning, filling in the empty spaces between the first stitches.

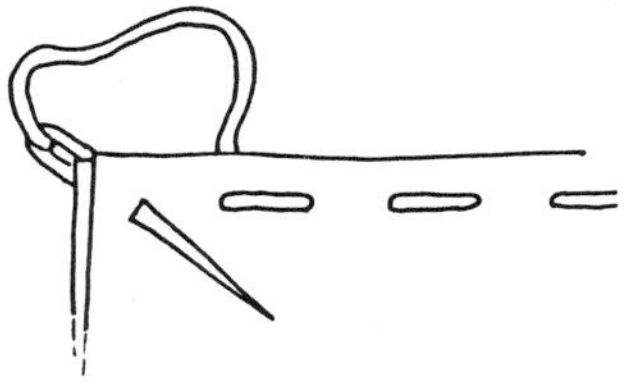

Make a knot in the thread where the sewing ends. Snip the excess thread.

Tip A 30″ thread doubled over and knotted ends up being only about 14″ long. This is an easy length to handle. While it's tempting to make your sewing thread longer (so you don't have to thread the needle as often), longer threads tend to get tangled and end up being more work.

Sewing was done by hand until the 1800s. In 1846, an American inventor named Elias Howe took out a patent for a sewing machine he invented.

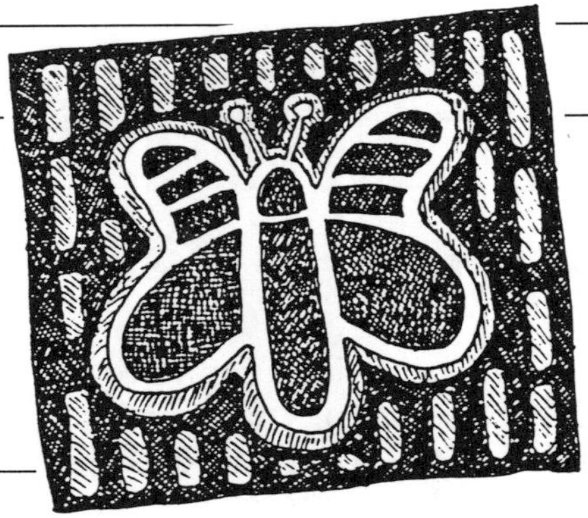

BUTTERFLUTTER

The Cuna Indians of San Blas, off the coast of Panama, create a unique art with brightly-colored fabric. You can make similar *molas,* as these panels are called, using colored paper.

Mola panels are traditionally sewn onto blouses. In fact, the word *mola* means "blouse" in the Cuna language, but it is commonly used to refer to the panels themselves.

PAPER *MOLA*
Colored paper, 4 colors about 8½″ × 11″
Scissors
X-acto knife
White glue

1. Choose which color you want to show up the most. On this sheet, draw the outline of an animal, such as this butterfly, or any one you like. Make the shape slightly oversized. Around it draw lots of short, thick, rounded lines as shown.

2. Cut out all the shapes (use the scissors for the large shape, and the X-acto knife for the smaller shapes).

3. Place this cut out paper over one of the other colored sheets. With a pencil, draw a faint outline on the second sheet about ¼″ from the cut shape of the butterfly. Cut the second sheet along this line.

4. Do the same again with the third sheet of colored paper. Add more detail to this sheet.

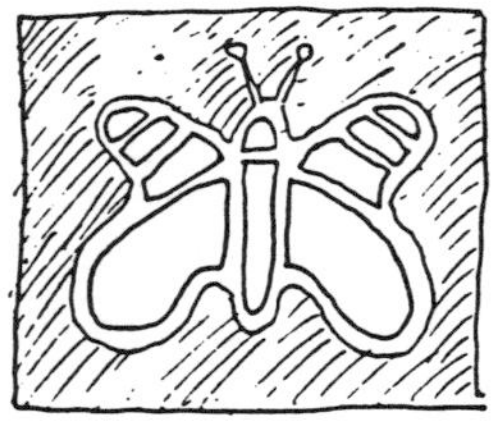

5. Sandwich all the layers together, starting with the fourth sheet that is not cut. On top of this place the third sheet you cut, then the second, and lastly, the first. Glue the four layers together in their proper order.

Tip You can add even more colors to your *mola* by slipping small scraps of paper under any of the layers that are cut out. Glue or tape them in place.

Variations on a Theme
Use colored rectangles of felt to make a *mola.* Sketch your design on a sheet of tracing paper first; then transfer it to the felt. If you find it hard to cut the felt with an X-acto knife, cut the shapes out with sharp scissors, after first slitting the felt with the knife.

Red is one of the most common colors used in *molas.* Use it and a combination of bright colors such as shocking pink, emerald green, royal blue, sunny yellow, and even black for a design in authentic colors.

IVY LEAGUE

This songbird may not awaken you with its singing, but it will certainly brighten a windowsill. In about six weeks time, ivy will completely cover the wire frame of this charming chirper.

TOPIARY BIRD
Wire, such as 14- or 16-gauge wire, about 52″ long
Wire cutters
Pliers
Twist ties
Waterproof tape
Small stones or gravel
Ivy plant, growing in a 4″ pot

1. Cut a piece of wire about 42″ long. Bend it into the bird shape shown or into your own shape. The base of this bird takes about 8″ of wire, the central "stem" another 8″, and the bird itself the remaining wire. Fasten the end of the wire to the central stem with a twist tie.

Don't worry if the wire has any kinks or bends—the ivy will eventually cover them.

2. For a fuller, more three-dimensional shape, add a 10″ circle of wire to the mid-section, as shown. Attach it with twist ties. Cover the entire frame with waterproof tape.

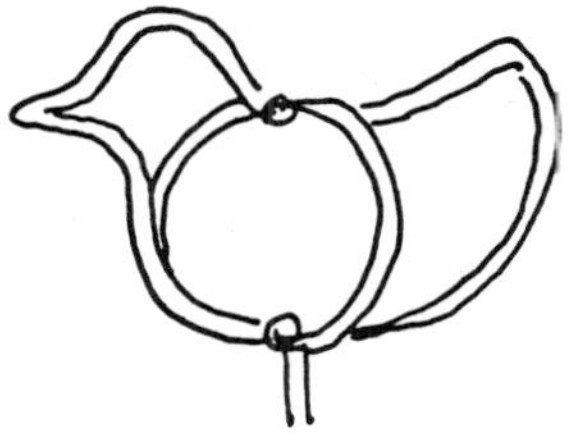

3. Remove the ivy plant from the pot by holding it upside-down and giving it a shake. The plant should drop out, soil and all.

4. Place the frame in the pot. Anchor it with some small rocks; then replace the ivy plant and its soil. Start training the plant right away by wrapping a long piece of ivy around the central stem and up to the bird shape.

5. Keep the plant in a bright spot, but away from direct sunlight (you can keep it in a windowsill but make sure it's facing north or east). Turn the plant now and again, so that it grows evenly on all sides.

Trim the plant as it grows. Wherever you cut a stem, it will branch off into two stems, which is the trick to getting the ivy to completely cover the frame.

Water the plant when the soil feels dry, but don't overwater it. Give the ivy a dose of fertilizer every month, and it should live a long, happy life.

Variations on a Theme
A topiary bird is only one of

Ask for one of these varieties of English ivy at your local garden center. They are perfect for portable topiary such as you've made.

- Itsy Bitsy
- Shamrock
- Duck Foot
- Fiesta
- Lustrous Carpet

The art of shaping plants into animals and other objects dates from about 100 B.C. Well-to-do Romans livened up the gardens of their country estates with all sorts of unusual shapes.

many fantastic forms topiary can take. Bend some wire into any animal or shape you can think of.

You can also make topiary forms outdoors. Make a frame similar to the one shown here, or clip an existing bush (ask permission first!) into a surprising shape.

People who grow herbs sometimes include in their gardens a design known as a *knot.* Low-growing plants are planted in intertwining patterns, such as the one shown here.

The different greens of the different herbs make knot gardens particularly effective. You can make a type of knot garden yourself by planting various compact flowers in interesting patterns.

SNOW SNAKE

Most snakes hibernate in winter, but not this one! This snake looks forward to a good, wet snow, when it can slither down a hill. Get your friends together to play this Iroquois Indian game.

PAINTED SNOW SNAKE
Straight branch, at least 4 feet long (see *Note*)
Short screws
Washers, to fit screws
Sandpaper
Acrylic paints

Note If you can't find a branch, you can use an old broom handle, some quarter-round molding from the lumberyard, or a length of wood, ripped to size.

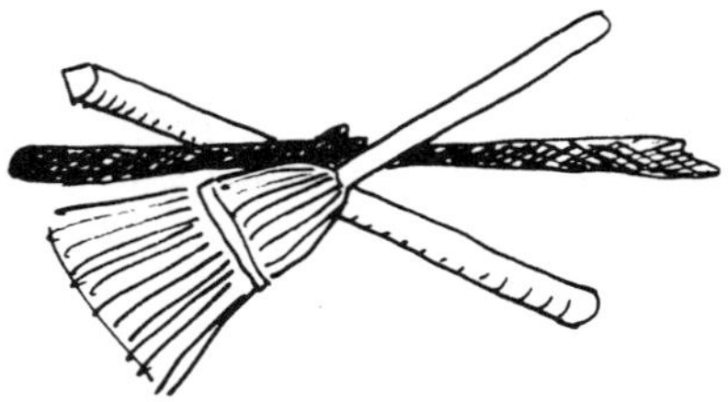

1. If you are using a branch, peel off the bark. This is easy to do with dead branches. The wood will probably be satiny-smooth but sand any rough spots. If you are using purchased wood, round off any sharp corners and sand the wood smooth.

2. Attach the washers to one end of the branch with the screws. Place them on either side of the wood like eyes. These serve to weight the stick so that it travels faster.

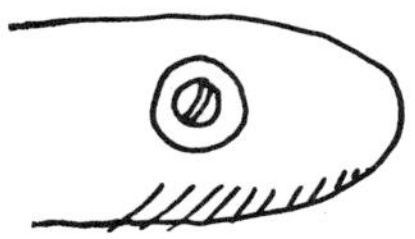

3. Paint designs on your snake. This isn't strictly necessary, but it makes it easier to identify your own snake. Some of the traditional Iroquois Indian designs used in their art are shown on this page.

4. The rules of the game are simple. Find a nice, steep, snow-covered hill. First prepare a track by dragging a log through the snow; pack the snow down firmly. Make a lip along the sides so the snakes won't fly off the track. One by one, send the snakes down the hill. The one that travels farthest wins.

Many scientists believe snakes evolved from lizards millions of years ago, as snakes resemble lizards more than any other of the reptiles. Unlike lizards, snakes lack legs, movable eyelids, and outer ears. There are 2,700 kinds of snakes worldwide.

The Iroquois Indians were comprised of many tribes, including the Mohawk, Oneida, Onondaga, Cayuga and Seneca. The Iroquois name for themselves was *Ongwanonhsiono* which means "we long house builders."

For another Iroquois Indian craft you can make, see the felt moccasins on page 148.

Did you know?
Because snakes are cold-blooded, they are unable to survive in the polar regions and in higher elevations. There are no snakes, however, in Ireland and New Zealand.

THE PORTRAIT GALLERY

It was a long time before artists learned to draw people. It's not that the human figure is hard to draw, it's just that our superstitious ancestors were afraid of capturing their own spirits if they drew themselves! Luckily, people figured out that portraits didn't cast spells. And because of this, we know how the Egyptians, ancient Greeks, and Chinese people looked, how they dressed, and what they did for work and play. We also have an idea of how they felt about themselves. Portraits have helped us understand people from long ago right up to the present day.

ME, MYSELF & I

When you're looking for someone to draw or paint, you can always choose yourself. Work from memory or set up a mirror and seat yourself in front of it.

SELF–PORTRAIT
Paper or canvas
Pencils, paint, or markers
Mirror

Note Keep in mind that a mirror reverses images. This doesn't matter much in portraiture, but you may be surprised when you look at your self-portrait to discover that your hair is parted on the wrong side!

1. Think about what you want your self-portrait to "say" about you. Do you want to make a realistic rendering of your face or are you interested in painting a picture of yourself at work or play? You can work out the details by spending some time sketching yourself in different poses or from different angles.

2. Lightly sketch in the outlines on the paper or canvas itself. Paint or color in the portrait as you like. Add some detail to the background or highlight your face against a dark, plain background.

PENCIL POINTERS

Pencils are an indispensable tool for artists. They are perfect for everything from marking measurements to sketching with.

Pencils come in varying degrees of hardness. You are probably familiar with the different hardnesses writing pencils come in, such as No. 2 and No. 3. Artists' pencils are graded on a different system. They range from 8B, the softest, to 10H, the hardest (some manufacturers use yet another numbering system). There are at least 18 different hardnesses!

The softer pencils make a darker line that is easy to erase, but also smudges easily. (Drawings done in the softer leads should be sprayed with a fixative.) The harder leads hold a sharp point better, so they are good for detailed work. They make a grayer line that doesn't erase easily, especially when you press down hard when you're drawing.

Soft and hard pencils used in combination, can create a variety of effects. For instance, a landscape might work well using soft pencils for the foreground, and hard ones (using light pressure) for the distant background. (See page 108 for more on creating perspective.)

The Story of Art
Many artists throughout history have painted their own portraits, but none are as amazing as those painted by Rembrandt, a Dutch artist.

Rembrandt Harmenszoon van Rijn was born in 1606, and by the time he was in his twenties, he was a well-established artist. While he painted other people's portraits to make a living, he found time to paint over 60 of himself before he died in 1669.

For hints on proper proportion in figure drawing, see page 69.

PENCIL POINTERS, CONT.

Experiment with a medium-soft pencil such as a 2B (perhaps the most common for sketching) on different paper surfaces. Slightly textured paper works well, but you can have fun drawing on very rough paper, such as watercolor paper, as well as smoother stock.

One of the nice things about pencils, of course, is that lines can be erased and reworked. The standard rubber eraser (the kind found on the ends of writing pencils) is good for general erasing, but you can get better results erasing small areas, if you use a kneaded eraser or the relatively new plastic or vinyl erasers.

Artists traditionally make detailed pencil drawings of paintings they later execute in oil. The pencil drawings are every bit as expressive and beautiful as the full-color, finished paintings.

ALL TOGETHER

Before the camera was invented, artists were commissioned to paint portraits, and many of these were group portraits. You be the artist and paint a portrait of your schoolmates, your family, or any group you want.

"There is nothing in the world as interesting as people . . . one can never study them enough."
Vincent van Gogh

GROUP PORTRAIT
Long roll of wide paper, such as newsprint
Pencil, paint, or markers

Note If you don't have a continuous sheet of paper, tape individual sheets together at the back, to make a piece as long as you need.

1. Think about how you want to group all the people in your portrait. If you have the space to show each full-figure, you can have everyone lined up single file.

If you'd rather show a group assembled around a table, for instance, or a campfire, or on the playground, plan your composition to include everything you want.

2. Make plenty of sketches of the group before setting out to make a final portrait. You don't want to forget anyone! Spend some time planning the picture so that it is balanced (not everyone should be huddled on one side of the paper, for instance), and so that each person is clearly defined.

3. Complete the portrait by painting all the large areas and then all the details. If you are painting a lot of people, emphasize the notable details only, so the painting won't be too busy.

The Story of Art
Group portraiture was very popular in the Netherlands in the 17th century. Many artists used hired models to pose for the portraits—the real faces of those who had commissioned the portrait would be painted in later.

Everyone pictured in the portrait was expected to pay his share of the cost of the painting. Those people who were only partly shown in the background, paid less.

In the 18th century, family portraits were very popular in England. The entire family, or a small group of friends, were usually shown enjoying each other's company outdoors or in a finely furnished room.

WELL-PROPORTIONED

Here are a few tricks you can use to make your portraits a little more realistic. These proportions work for figures seen from the front (change the proportions slightly for figures seen from different angles, to make them appear more natural).

The human head can generally be divided into three parts. From the top of the head to the top of the eyebrows is one; from eyebrows to bottom of the nose another; and from nose to the bottom of the chin a third.

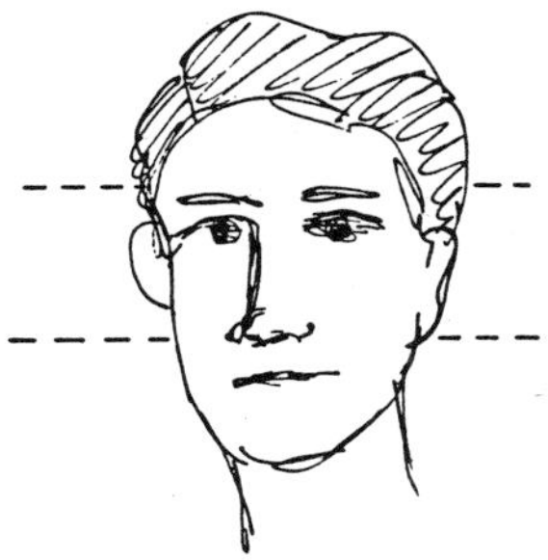

The width of the nose is roughly equal to the width of one eye, and the mouth is just a bit wider.

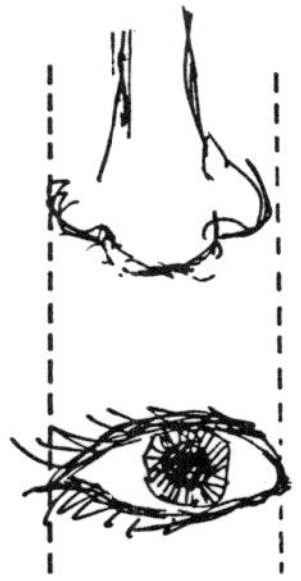

Children's heads can be divided into just two parts. Their eyes appear larger, while their noses and mouths seem smaller.

The body, too, can be marked off into sections. If you count the head as one, an adult figure is about seven heads tall. But a 1-year-old is only four heads tall; a 4-year-old, five heads; a 9-year-old, six heads.

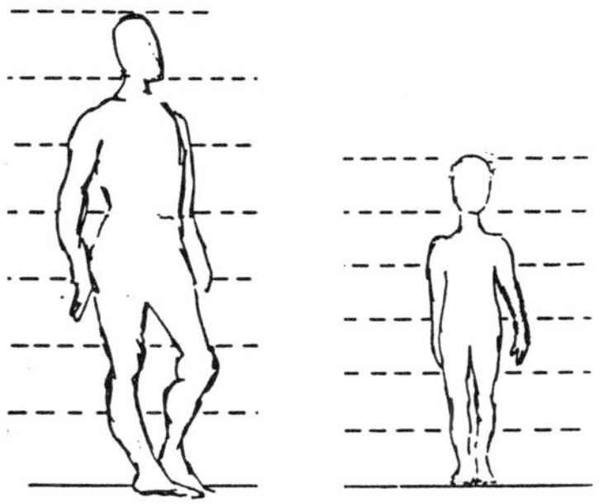

Similarly, a young child's arms might be about two heads long, but a full-grown man's arms are easily three heads long.

The Story of Art
The sandpaintings the Navajos make are not permanent paintings. A patch of bare ground is cleared inside a hogan, the traditional Navajo adobe building, and sand is carefully poured into intricate designs right on the ground. The sandpaintings are always destroyed as part of the healing ceremony.

The Navajos are thought to have learned the art of sandpainting from the Pueblo Indians. They, in turn, are said to have learned it from the Spanish who first came upon the southwestern part of the United States in the mid-16th century.

MR. SANDMAN

The Navajo Indians of Arizona and New Mexico create sandpaintings that often include figures from their religion as part of healing rituals. You can make your own sand portraits using a similar technique.

SANDPAINTING
Clean, sifted sand, about 1 shovelful
Colored powders, such as powdered poster paints, ground spices, corn meal, crushed charcoal
Stiff cardboard, about $8\frac{1}{2}'' \times 11''$
White glue

Note Some of the finely-ground spices and powdered paints can make you sneeze! Mix them with the sand carefully, so that the fine particles won't irritate your nose.

1. Make an assortment of colored sands by mixing various powders with small amounts of sand. (You can use some of the coarser powders, such as corn meal, by themselves.) Real Navajo sandpaintings are made with earth colors, such as tans and browns, brick red, soft yellow, and turquoise. Leave a portion of the sand untinted for the background.

2. Brush slightly watered-down glue over the entire piece of cardboard, and sprinkle it with plain sand. Give the cardboard a tap to shake off any loose grains.

3. "Paint" designs directly on the background with glue. Squirt it from the bottle for fine lines; use a brush to fill in larger areas. Do one color at a time, sprinkling the sand in place while the glue is still wet.

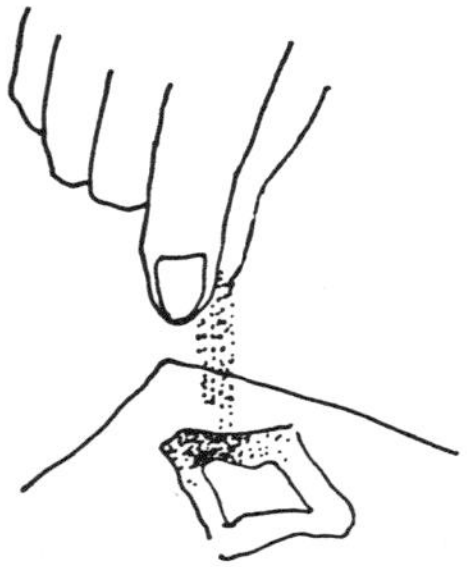

Use the picture here to guide you or make up your own designs.

Tip With normal handling, some of the sand may work loose and fall off. To prevent this, you can spray the painting with a matte fixative. Be sure to do this outdoors to avoid breathing the fumes.

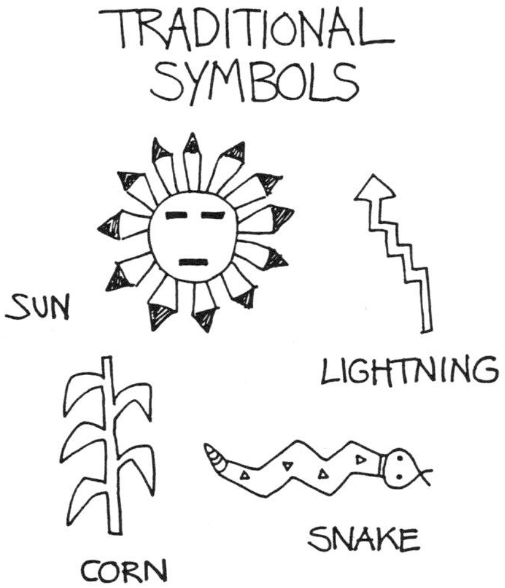

Instead of preparing your own background, use a sheet of purchased sandpaper. This comes in a variety of colors, from the charcoal gray of emery paper to the reddish sand of garnet paper.

You can dig your own sand down by the beach (if it's your own property), or you can purchase it from a sand and gravel pit or a lumberyard (the latter sells it by the bag).

SHADOW SHOW

People have been making puppets for thousands of years, and shadow puppets are among the oldest. Simple silhouetted figures can be glued to long sticks or straws, but puppets with movable parts are even more fun to use.

SHADOW PUPPETS
Poster board, about 9″ × 12″, per puppet
Scissors
X-acto knife
Hole puncher
4 paper fasteners, per puppet
2 wire coat hangers, per puppet
Wire cutters
Pliers
Tape

Note The instructions here are for a male figure with arms that bend at the shoulder and elbow. Adapt the instructions to make other figures, including animals that have moving arms, legs, or heads.

1. Sketch the outline of your figure on the poster board. (You can do this on a separate piece of paper first, if you prefer, and transfer the outline to the poster board.) It must be large enough so that the shoulder and elbow joints are at least ½″ wide (to accommodate the paper fasteners). Notice how the shoulders of the figure shown here are very broad, and how the arms are made in two parts.

2. Cut the figure out with a pair of scissors. Use the X-acto knife to cut out any interior sections, such as the eye, ear, and buttons of this figure.

3. Punch holes in the shoulders and in the shoulder and elbow joints of the two arms. Fasten them together with the paper fasteners. Make sure the fasteners aren't pressed down too hard against the poster board—there should be a little play so that the joints bend easily.

Cut the paper fasteners with the wire cutters, so that they don't show when the arms are moved about.

4. Cut a wire coat hanger (snip off the bent hook completely) the length of the puppet plus about 8″. Bend it with the pliers so that it conforms to the figure. Tape the wire in place with short lengths of tape.

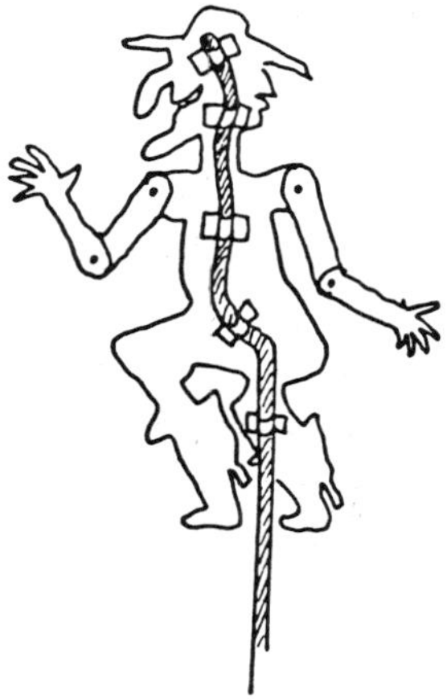

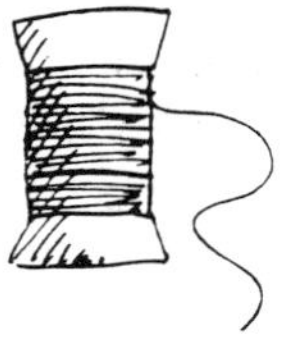

Instead of taping the wire to the back of the puppet, you can sew it in place. Use strong thread such as carpet or buttonhole thread, and stitch right through the poster board and around the wire to hold it in place.

The Story of Art
The best known shadow puppets and plays are those from Java. There are over 600 different characters used to tell various legends and stories that have been handed down for centuries.

The Javanese puppets are called *wayangs,* and they are made from thin buffalo skins, chiseled and punched into intricate designs. The puppets are brightly colored on both sides. Size plays an important part in identifying characters. The ogres are large with rounded eyes and blunt features. The heroes are always small, slender figures with downcast eyes. In the enacted stories, the heroes always conquer their larger foes by means of cunning and thoughtful actions.

5. Cut two wires for the arms from the other coat hanger. They should be about 18″ long, or long enough so that you can raise the puppet's arms high, but still have your hands hidden. Wrap some tape around one end of each wire several times; then tape the wires to the puppet's hands.

6. Use the puppet behind a lit screen. See *Shadow Screen* for hints on making your own.

Variations on a Theme
If you would prefer to use a traditional open puppet stage instead of a lit screen, color the puppets on the side that faces the audience.

SHADOW SCREEN

Shadow puppets are most effective when they are lit from behind, so that the silhouettes really stand out. For the large, jointed figures, stretch a white sheet across a doorway. Create a barrier to hide behind, out of cardboard or an overturned table. Place a lamp or a powerful flashlight at puppet-level; put it on a table or pedestal far enough behind you so that you have room to manipulate the figures.

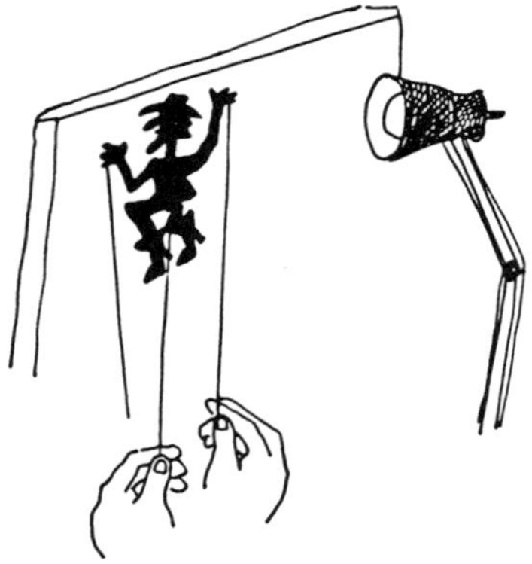

Smaller figures can be placed behind a table-top screen made from cardboard and translucent paper such as parchment (ask for large sheets of parchment at an art store). Use a small lamp to light the screen.

TABLE-TOP SCREEN

Put on your shadow plays in a darkened room for the best results.

Make a stand to hold several puppets when you are putting on a show. Stick the body wires into a thick piece of styrofoam, or drill some holes in a block of wood to stand the puppets in.

A SHOW OF HANDS

Hand puppets are great fun to use, but have you ever made your own puppets with papier-mâché heads? With this simple paper pulp method, you can model the heads for a whole cast of characters!

PAPIER–MÂCHÉ HAND PUPPETS
Papier-mâché pulp (see page 74)
Poster board, about 3″ × 5″
Tape
Narrow-necked bottle, such as a ketchup bottle
Acrylic paints
Felt or other sturdy fabric, about 1/4 yard
Needle and thread
White glue

1. Have a batch of papier-mâché pulp ready. Tape the piece of poster board into a tube (along the 5″ side). Make it so it fits over the neck of the bottle you are using. The tube is the neck support for the puppet's head, and the bottle becomes a handy holder.

2. Using the pulp like clay, mold a head right onto the poster board neck. Build out features such as a nose, eyebrows, mouth, and chin. Attach ears and hair, if you like. Make the features prominent for the best results. Set aside in a safe, warm place to dry for 5–7 days.

3. When the head is completely dry, paint it with acrylic paints. Cover the entire head to protect it from moisture. Add painted features and hair, or make hair from yarn or fake fur.

4. Make a glove for the puppet's body. First make a pattern. On a piece of paper, place your hand in the position shown. Draw the outline of a glove around it. See how your thumb and littlest finger fit into the arms, and your index finger extends up into the neck. Make the outline 1/2″ larger all the way around for the sewing seam. Cut out the pattern.

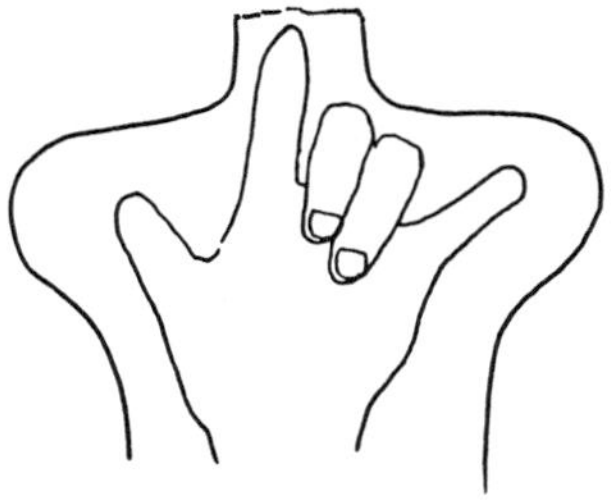

5. Pin the paper pattern onto a piece of felt folded in half. Cut out two glove pieces. Remove the pattern and sew the glove together (right-sides facing), leaving both the neck and the bottom open. Turn the glove right-side out.

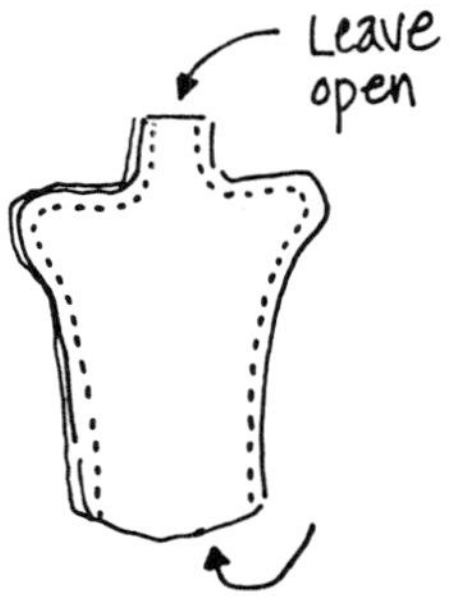

You can use sandpaper to smooth any rough edges on your puppet's head. Give the entire head a sanding for a different look.

Did you know?
Papier-mâché is French for "chewed-up paper"!

The Story of Art
Hand puppets date from about the 17th century. Most had carved wooden heads and hands, and cloth bodies. Traveling puppeteers set up mobile stages or performed from the backs of wagons. The plays usually poked fun at local gossip or politics. Some puppet shows featured Punch and Judy, a quarreling husband and wife who often came to comical blows.

6. Insert the head into the glove neck and glue it in place. Add fabric trims, buttons, and felt hands to the puppet body, if you like.

PAPIER–MÂCHÉ PULP

Papier-mâché pulp, or mash as it is sometimes called, is a terrific modeling material. Use it to make puppet heads and to add dimension to papier-mâché masks. The recipe here makes about 1½ cups pulp.

Fill a medium-sized bowl about half full with scrap paper torn into small pieces. You can use newspaper, computer printout paper, old letters and envelopes—any paper that isn't shiny. Pour boiling water over the paper (have an adult help you with this), so that the paper is completely covered. Let soak for 1 hour.

Meanwhile, measure 2 heaping tablespoons flour and put it into a small saucepan. Add ½ cup water and stir until well blended. Cook this mixture on the stove, stirring constantly, for about 3 minutes, or until it has come to a boil and is thick (have your adult friend help you again). Set aside to cool.

When the paper has soaked long enough, put small handfuls of it into a blender, adding plenty of extra water to each batch. Blend on high for about 15 seconds. Pour the pulp into a colander. Continue in this way until all the paper has been reduced to pulp.

Squeeze as much water from the pulp as you can. Measure 1 cup of the pulp (pack it into the measuring cup) and place it in a bowl. To this, add the cooled flour paste. Mix well with your hands.

HARVEST HELP

In England, where corn refers to any grain, such as wheat, rye, or oats, good luck harvest figures called corn dollies are made each year. You can make your own from what we call corn in this country.

So what do English people call what we know as corn? Maize.

CORNHUSK FIGURE
Corn husks, fresh or dried, about 6–8 pieces
String
Cotton balls, about 4
Scraps of cloth, yarn, beads, and pipe cleaners (optional)

Note If you are using dried husks, soak them in water to soften them. Fresh husks need no special preparation.

1. Take a strip of husk and place a few cotton balls in the middle, twisting and tying it with string to make a head.

Make some arms by folding another husk and tying it near each end to make hands. Slip the arms between the husks that extend under the head. Tie the waist with string.

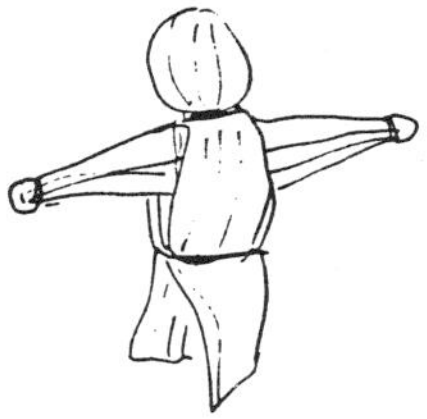

2. Arrange enough husks around the figure's waist so that they overlap slightly. Tie them in place with string.

3. Fold the husks down carefully. For a woman wearing a long skirt, cut the husks straight across at the hem. To make a man, divide the skirt husks in two and tie each half at the ankles. Let the figure dry completely.

4. You can leave your figure as is, or give it a face, hair, or even some fancier clothes. Use a fine-tipped marker to draw facial features. Glue some fuzzy yarn on for hair. Add some tiny beads for buttons, and bits of fabric for aprons or vests. A pipe cleaner staff or cane will help the man stand upright.

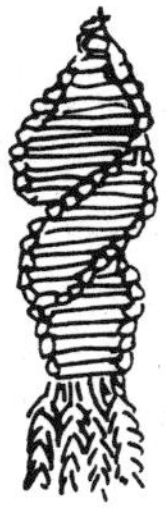

Although they are still called corn dollies, many English harvest decorations are made in shapes such as spiraling ribbons or braided strips.

GOOD SPIRITS

Not all dolls are meant to be played with. The Kachina dolls made by the Pueblo Indians of New Mexico are used to teach religion. Real Kachinas are carved from wood, but you can make your own from cardboard tubes and glue.

KACHINA FIGURE
Cardboard tubes, from paper towels, toilet tissue, mailing tubes, and coat hangers (see *Note*)
Handsaw or serrated kitchen knife
Scissors
White glue
Paint
Fabric scraps and feathers

Note Make your own tubes, if you like, by rolling up pieces of thin cardboard, such as poster board, and gluing or taping them.

1. The Kachina figure shown here is just one of many different types that are made. Some carved Kachinas have movable arms; others wear cloth kilts or blankets over their shoulders. Use the design shown here or come up with your own (study the pictures in books for authentic designs—your library should have some books).

2. Make the figure's body from one of the larger tubes. Use the handsaw or the serrated knife to saw it to the size you want. To make the legs, cut out two narrow panels, front and back, on one end.

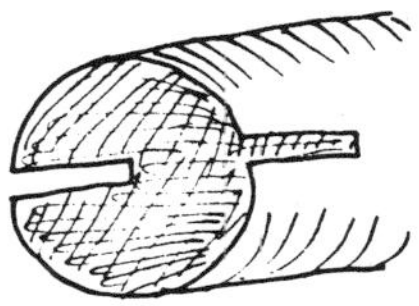

Kachina dolls represent male dancers known as Kachinas, who themselves represent supernatural beings in the various Pueblo religions.

Traditional Kachina dolls are carved from the dried roots of cottonwood trees.

3. Use the narrower tubes for the arms, ears, and nose. Glue these in place. Cut a headdress from a flat piece of cardboard and attach it by fitting it into small slits, cut into the body tube at the head end.

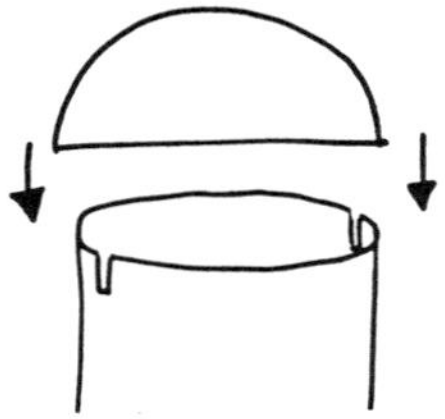

4. Paint the Kachina figure in traditional earth colors or any way you like. Glue on fabric pieces and feathers, if you wish.

Some traditional Pueblo symbols include

OTHER SELVES

You can be anyone (or anything!) you like when you're hiding behind a mask. Here are two ideas for masks you can make. The first is a quick, colorful mask meant to be worn; the second looks like it might have come straight from a tribal ceremony.

Some masks are simply painted on. In many cultures, face-painting is used to identify tribes, but it is also used to work magic. Of course, painting one's face is also a way to beautify it.

CARDBOARD MASK
Corrugated cardboard, about 7″ × 11″
Poster board, about 5″ square
Scissors
X-acto knife
Paint, colored paper, yarn, glitter, feathers
White glue
Hole puncher
1/4″ elastic, about 8″ long

Note For best results, cut the corrugated cardboard so that the corrugated channels run the short way. That way you can easily bend the cardboard to conform to your face.

1. Ease the cardboard into a gentle arc by bending it inch by inch along the channels.

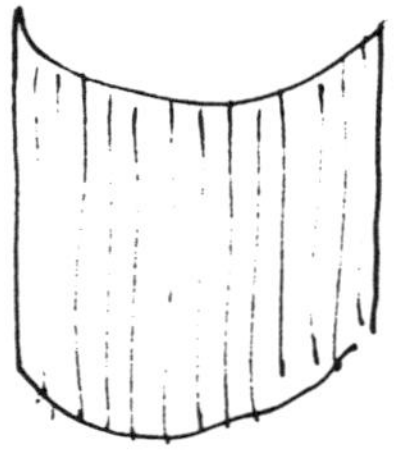

2. Have someone measure the distance between your two eyes, from pupil to pupil. Mark where the eye holes should go on the cardboard, placing them about 2″ from the top edge. Cut out the holes.

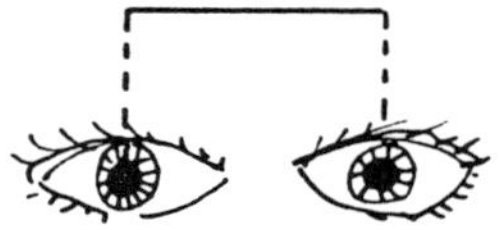

3. Make a triangular hole for your nose. Then cut a nose out of the poster board, in the shape shown here. Fold the nose down the center, fold in the tabs, and glue the nose in place on the mask. Cut a hole for your mouth.

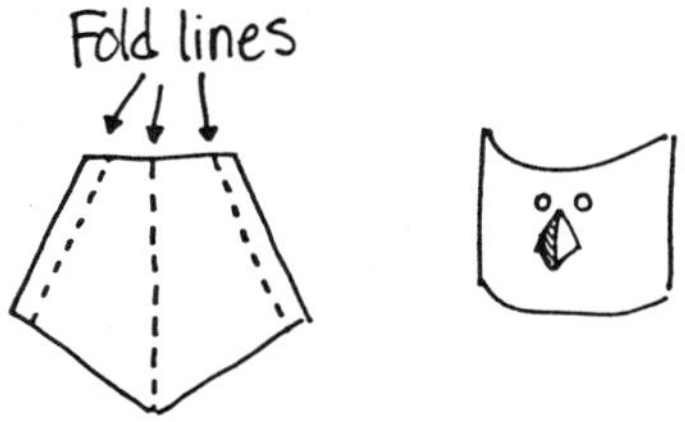

4. Decorate the mask any way you like. Use the paint, paper, yarn, and assorted trimmings to create a colorful mask. Punch holes for the elastic on either side, tie on the elastic, and try on for size.

PAPIER–MÂCHÉ MASK
Corrugated cardboard, about 3″ × 24″
Stapler
Newspaper
1/4 cup flour
Saucepan
Paint
Yarn, beads, and other trims

Note This mask can be made to be worn, if you make the oval ring large enough to fit around your face and poke holes for your eyes and nose, and for an elastic band.

1. Ease the strip of corrugated cardboard into an oval shape and staple the ends together. Crumple up some newspaper and stuff it into the oval, up to the level of the cardboard.

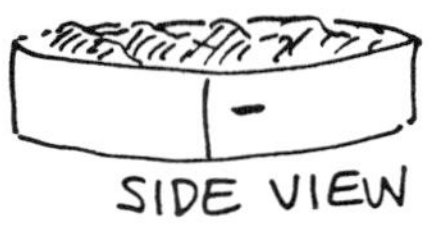

2. Make the flour and water paste. Mix 1/4 cup flour with 4 cups of water in a medium-sized saucepan. Bring to a boil on the stove (ask an adult to help you), stirring until the mixture is smooth and the consistency of cream. Set aside to cool.

3. Meanwhile, tear some newspaper into short strips. Save some whole sheets to crumple and twist into shapes to build up the features of your mask. When the paste is cool enough to work with, paste down the strips and twists to make the mask's face. Overlap the strips, and smooth them out with your hands as you lay them down to avoid wrinkles and bumps.

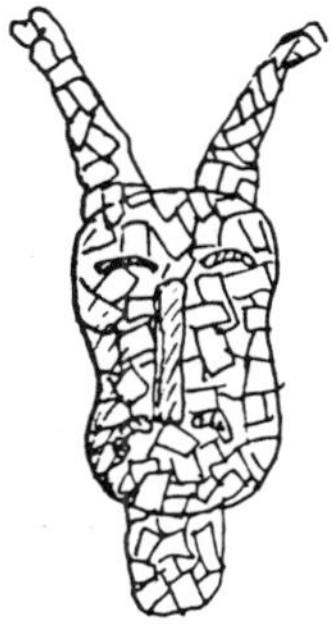

4. The entire mask should have four to five layers of strips. It's a good idea to put down two layers and let them dry before adding the next two. The final layer can be made with tissue paper or another thin paper, if you like.

5. Remove the crumpled-up paper that is stuffed inside the oval. Let the mask dry for an additional few days, until there is no hint of moisture. Paint the mask a rich brown to look like wood, or paint it any way you like. Add some extra touches, such as a tongue and matted hair made from yarn.

Masks have long been used in theater. Ancient Greek actors wore masks to convey emotions as well as different characters. Today, masks are still used in traditional Japanese Noh plays, and actors in India and China paint their faces to resemble masks. Can you think where you might have seen painted face-masks? The circus, that's where!

In some cultures, masks are used for special ceremonies and dances. A mask is sometimes used to hide the wearer from evil; it is sometimes used to frighten away ghosts. Sometimes masks are used as disguises so that people can summon spirits without being recognized.

THE THIRD DIMENSION

What makes a sculpture different from a painting or a print? The fact that it is not flat but has a third dimension that you can touch gives sculpture its own place in the art world. You can view some sculpture from all sides, either walking around large pieces on the ground, or holding the smaller ones in your hand. Some sculptures are meant to hang on a wall and be viewed from the front and sides only. Some pieces even hang from the ceiling, and others, like kites, know no bounds!

WHITTLE AWHILE

Have you ever pared an apple with a knife? Then you can carve soap to make a sculpture. A bar of soft soap is perfect for beginning whittlers and advanced ones alike.

SOAP CARVING
Bar of soft soap, such as Ivory®
Paring knife or jack knife (see *Note*)
Pencil

Note You can also use a table knife for carving, but the sharper knives, such as those listed above, are easier to work with. Handle any knife with care.

1. Make several sketches of your sculpture on a piece of paper, before you begin carving. Draw what you want the sculpture to look like from the front, back, top, and sides. Make your sketches the actual size of the bar of soap. The sketches shown here are for a bear.

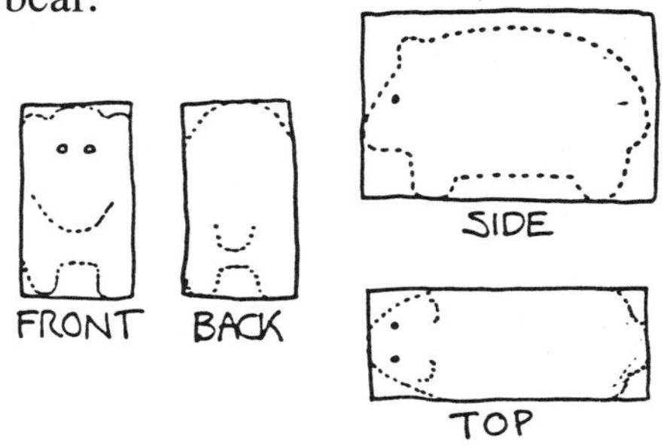

2. With the pencil, carefully draw the outlines directly on the soap.

3. Holding the soap firmly in one hand, start carving the soap outside the outlines. Brace your thumb against the soap, and cut slowly and carefully towards yourself. This really is the safest way to handle the knife. You have more control, and if you take small slices, there is little danger you will cut yourself.

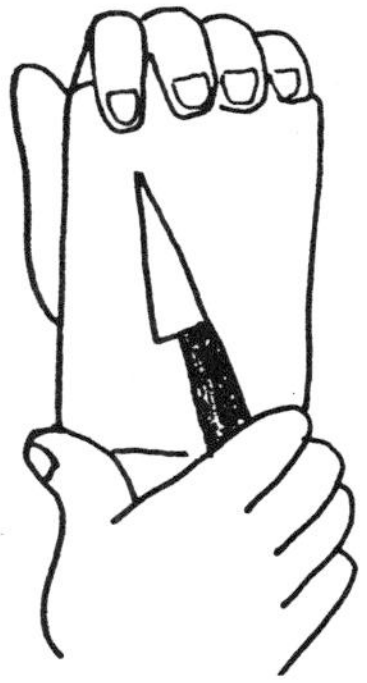

4. Take your time. Remember you can always take away more of the soap, but you can't replace what you've already carved. Whittle away the soap from all the different angles. Use a pencil, or linoleum cutting tools to add various textures or to gouge out parts of the soap. To smooth the surface, hold the knife blade at a 90° angle and scrape the soap by pulling the knife towards yourself.

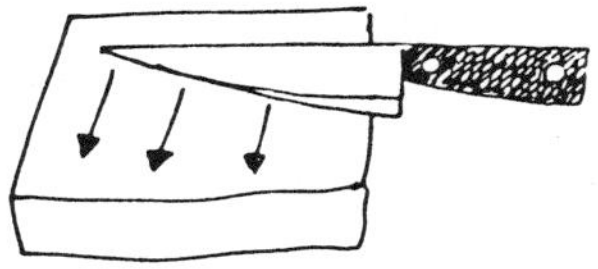

5. For a final smoothing, wet the soap and rub it gently with a soft cloth. Let the sculpture dry for several days before handling it.

Tip Keep your knife as clean as possible. The soft soap slivers will cling to it, making carving difficult. Scrape the soap off now and again with another knife or against a piece of scrap wood.

Sculptors who carve their work have many materials to choose from. There's wood, ivory, and any number of types of stone, from marble to jade.

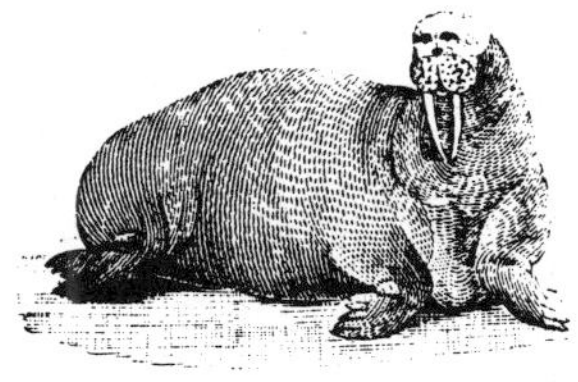

This small animal figure is very similar to the carved pieces made by the Eskimos. The Eskimos make their carvings out of a soft stone called soapstone (steatite). This is a recent trend in Eskimo art. Originally, the Eskimos carved only walrus tusks and bone.

Did you know?
Marble sculptures made in ancient Greece and Rome were painted with bright colors. It's hard to imagine what they looked like because we are so used to seeing the marble statues unpainted.

CHIP OFF THE OLD BLOCK

For something a little different, you might want to try your hand at sculpting with plaster of Paris.

Plaster of Paris comes as a powder that you mix with water (follow the instructions on the box) and pour into containers such as milk cartons or shoe boxes. You can also pour it into plastic bags or in holes made in sand to create free-form pieces.

Vary the texture of the plaster by adding such things as coffee grounds or vermiculite (ask for this at a garden center) to the mix. These happen to make the plaster a little easier to carve as well.

Plaster of Paris sculpting is a messy business. First of all, it's best to mix your plaster in disposable containers, and never, never dump any plaster down the drain. It will harden and clog the drain. Secondly, the plaster raises a lot of dust while you're carving and chipping away at it, so make sure to cover your work area and clean up after yourself. Dipping the block of plaster in water every now and again helps to keep the dust down and may make carving a bit easier. Use a chisel or a flat-head screwdriver and a hammer to chip away at the block. Other workshop and kitchen tools you can use include metal files, nails, and old kitchen knives.

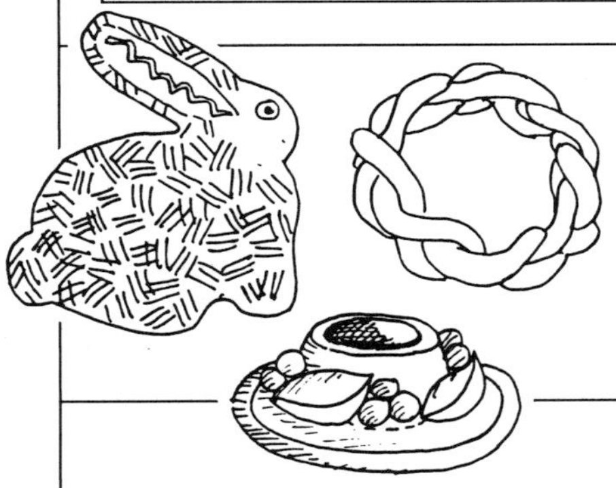

PAT IT & PRICK IT

Salt dough is one of the easiest materials to model with, and it doesn't require any special equipment to make it hard. Just pop your sculptures in the oven, or let them air dry.

SALT DOUGH SCULPTURE
Salt dough (see page 81)
Acrylic paints
Clear nail polish or other varnish

1. Have a batch of salt dough ready. Keep what you aren't using at the moment in a plastic bag or covered bowl.

2. The items shown here are just a few of the possible things you can do with salt dough. The rabbit is made by rolling out the dough and cutting it with a cookie cutter. The eye is simply a tiny ball of dough placed in position and poked with a toothpick. The fur is made by pressing the tines of a fork into the dough in a random pattern.

The earliest sculpted pieces we know of were carved ivory and stone figures, known as fertility figures. These were supposed to bring good luck to women of child-bearing age.

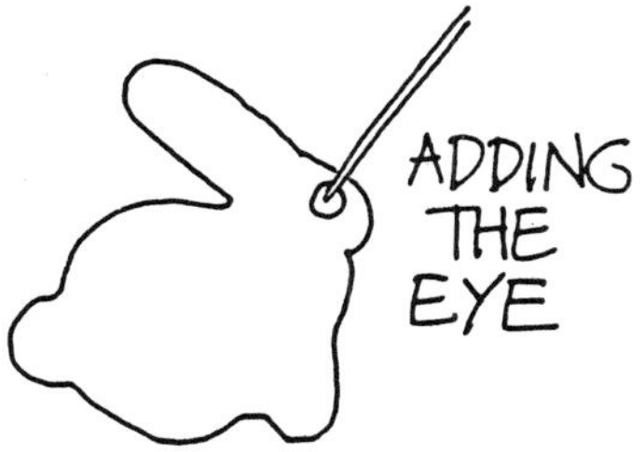

The braided napkin ring is made by braiding three ropes of dough together and wrapping them around a paper towel roll. The ends are wetted slightly and pinched together to secure them.

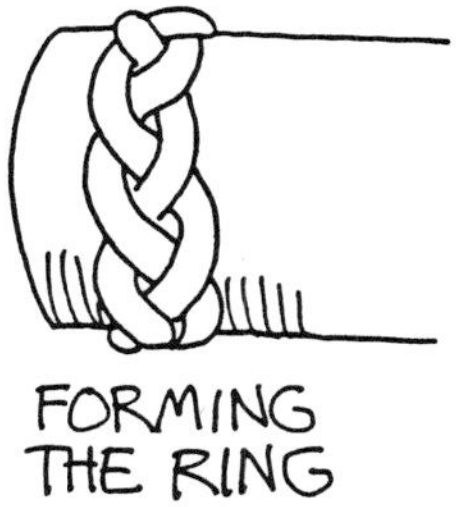

The candle holder is made by cutting a circle of rolled-out dough and adding modeled pieces of dough all around it to build up the sides. Each little piece is brushed with water to help make it stick.

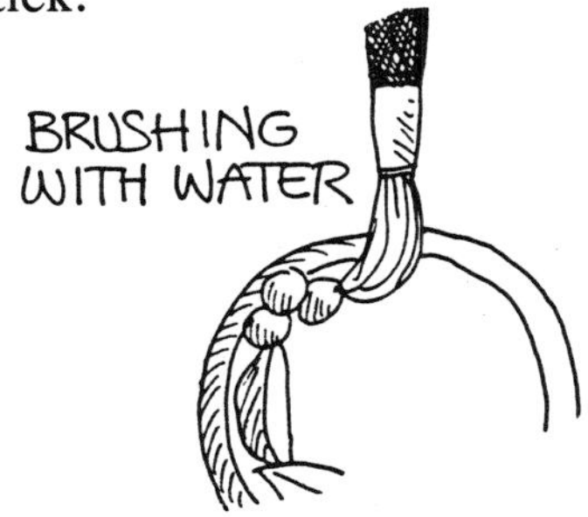

3. You can let your sculpted pieces air dry, or you can bake them in the oven. Air-drying takes about 2–3 days, depending on how thick the sculpted pieces are. The pieces stay white when you dry them this way.

If you prefer to speed things up, you can bake the pieces in a 300°F oven for about an hour. The dough will turn a light brown. The dough should be firm when done, so check it after an hour and let it bake longer, if necessary. Let the pieces cool completely before handling them.

4. Seal your sculptures to protect them from moisture. You can paint the pieces with acrylics, in which case they need no other sealer (just make sure to cover the entire piece with the paint). Or you can varnish the salt dough sculptures with clear nail polish or another waterproof varnish.

For another use for salt dough, see *A-Tisket, A-Tasket* on page 131.

Variations on a Theme

Salt dough sculptures can be "finished" in a number of different ways. If you are baking your pieces, brush them with some egg yolk before putting them into the oven. This gives the pieces a golden brown color. Experiment with other finishes, such as staining the pieces with shoe polish or wood stain. (First seal the dry dough with a couple of coats of clear varnish, then stain the dough; rub off any excess with a soft cloth and brush on another coat of varnish.)

SALT DOUGH

This recipe makes enough salt dough for a dozen ornaments, several napkin rings, plenty of candle holders, and then some! You can make half as much dough for starters, if you like, by using just half the ingredients.

Mix 2 cups flour and 1 cup salt in a bowl. Slowly add 1 cup water, mixing it thoroughly. Knead the dough with your fingers for about 5 to 7 minutes. It shouldn't stick to the table; if it does, sprinkle a little flour on your work surface.

Keep the dough in a plastic bag or covered bowl, so that it won't dry out. The dough will keep for about 5 days.

Not all carvings are freestanding. Have you ever seen examples of *relief* work, perhaps as part of a building? This is done by cutting away parts of a flat surface so that the figures stand out from the background, but are still part of it. Depending on how deep or shallow the carving is, the relief is known as high or low (low relief work is usually known as *bas-relief*, after the French word for "low"). Much relief sculpture tells a story. The Egyptians used this story-telling technique, as did the Greeks.

HANG UPS

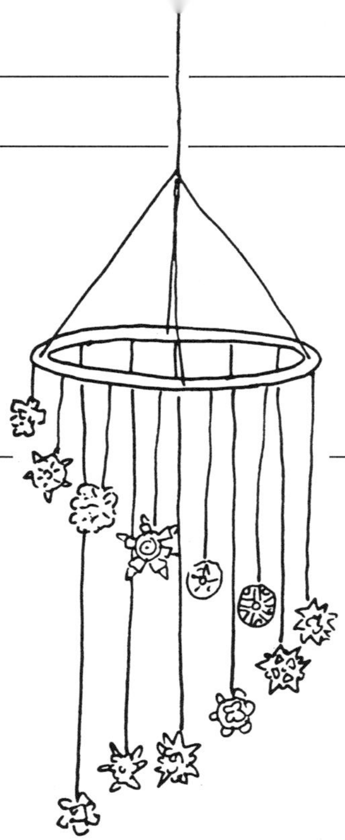

Not all sculptures are meant to sit solidly on the ground. Mobiles are hanging sculptures that move freely with the breeze or with the touch of your hands. Here are two types of hanging art you can make.

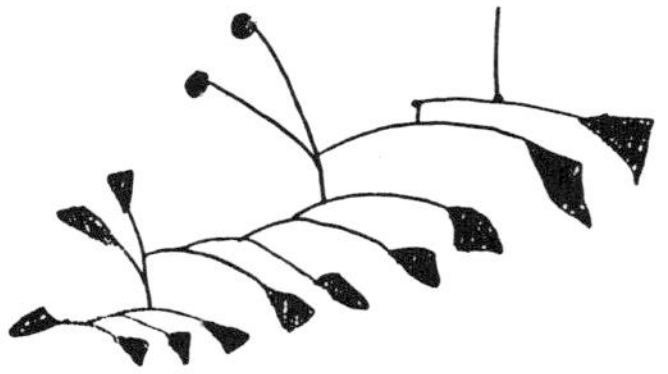

The Story of Art
In the 1930s, an American artist named Alexander Calder had an idea to hang a wire sculpture from the ceiling. He had seen how Chinese wind chimes moved with the breeze or with a push of the hand, and he wondered if large sculptures made from bent wires would do the same. The mobile was born!

SPIRAL MOBILE
Poster board, about 11″ square
Thin paper, 12 pieces about 4″ square
Pencil
Compass
Scissors
Needle and thread

Note The instructions here are for a mobile of hanging paper snowflakes. See *Variations on a Theme* for other things you might hang in this fashion.

1. Cut a 10″ circle out of the poster board. Use a compass to draw the circle or trace around a dinner plate with a pencil. Make a circle inside this one, about 1/2″ smaller. Cut it out. You now have a flat ring.

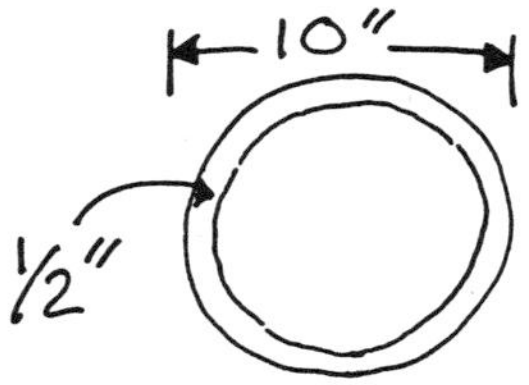

2. Pencil 12 dots around the ring, evenly spacing them. Poke four holes in the ring (placed between the pencil dots) and attach four pieces of thread to the ring. Make the threads about 18″ long; tie them together at the top so that the ring hangs level. Tack the ring up where you can reach it easily.

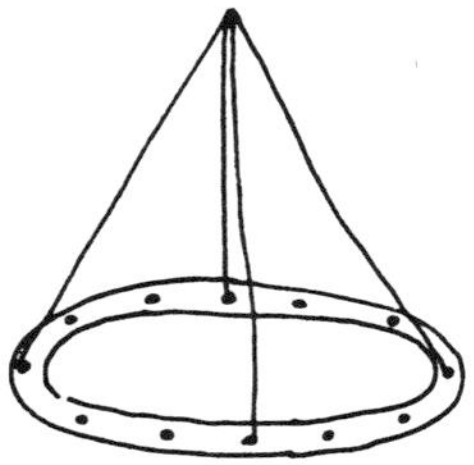

3. Cut 12 circles from the 12 pieces of thin paper. Use a compass to draw the circles or trace around a mug or drinking glass.

4. Fold one circle in half, then in thirds, and in half again. Use the scissors to snip little bits from the paper, on both sides, at the top and at the point. Open the paper, and there you have a 6-sided snowflake. Make 11 more snowflakes, altering the cuts so that each is slightly different.

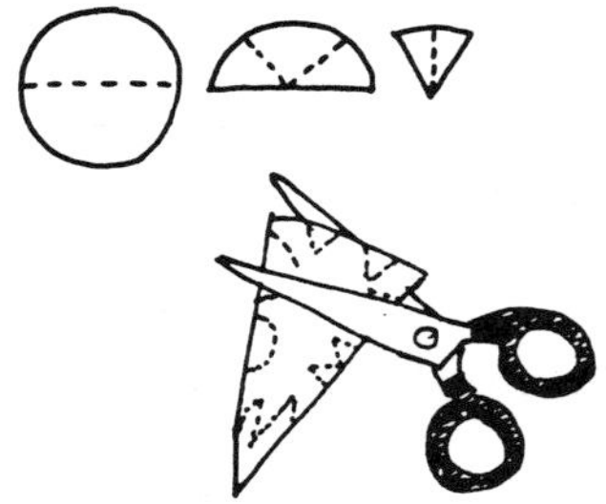

5. Hang the snowflakes from the ring. Place one at each of the 12 dots. Let the first snowflake hang down about an inch from the ring. Have the second flake hang down about 2″ below the first; the third 2″ below the second, and so on. Hang the mobile high up.

Variations on a Theme
Hang other things from the ring, such as tiny birds made with tissue paper wings or stars cut from paper. Origami figures are also very effective grouped like this (see how to make flower blossoms from origami paper on page 94). You can also hang heavier items, if you start out with a sturdier ring. Look into using an embroidery hoop or a large plastic ring (the kind used for handbag handles) for this mobile.

The spiral is well represented in natural forms. From the unfurled fronds of ferns (these are called fiddleheads because they resemble the peg heads of violins!) to the inner chamber of the nautilus shell, there are many examples of spirals in nature.

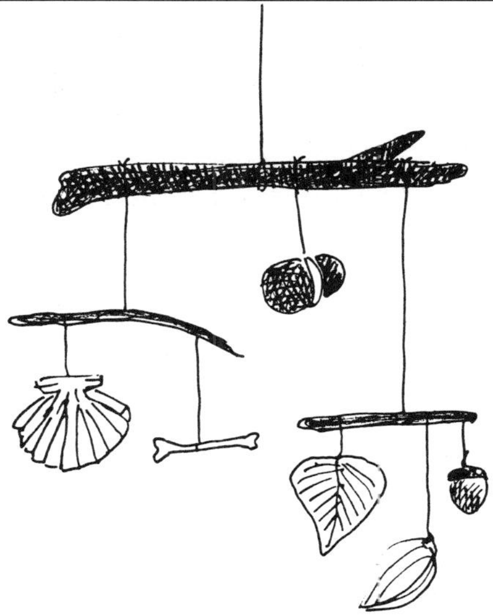

FOUND TREASURE MOBILE

Feathers, shells, pieces of wood and bark, rocks, anything you can find!
Branches and twigs
Strong thread or fishing line

Note The mobile shown here is made from items collected outdoors, but you can also use bits and pieces of old toys, kitchen utensils, or what have you.

1. Gather up all your treasures to see what you have to work with.

2. Select a thick branch for the main cross piece, or use several thinner branches. Putting together a balanced mobile is an exercise in trial-and-error. You can't really know how everything will balance until you try, but that's part of the fun. Hang the mobile in a spot where you can easily reach it while you are working on it.

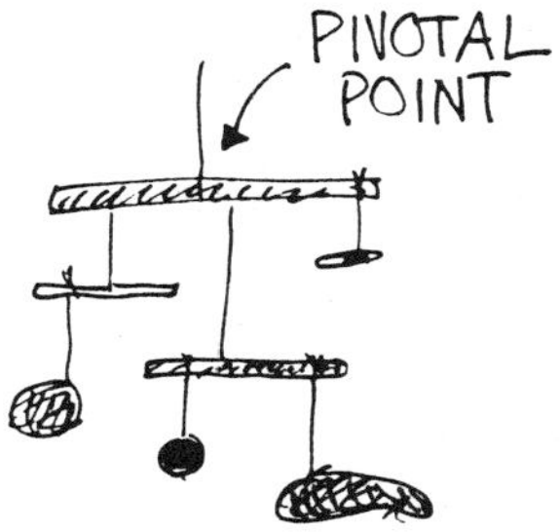

Balance the mobile by adding (or taking away) weight from one part of a branch, or by moving items closer to (or farther from) the pivotal point.

3. Make sure all the knots you make in the string or fishing line are nice and tight. Hang the mobile in its permanent home, well out of the way of heads or leaping pets.

Make your own wind chimes using natural materials. Shells are a natural (no pun intended!). There's even a shell found on Atlantic beaches called the jingle shell, because it has such a nice tinkling sound. String up some hollow reeds or bamboo pieces for deeper sounding chimes. Just make sure you hang your material close together so that a slight breeze will set the chimes in motion to create the sound.

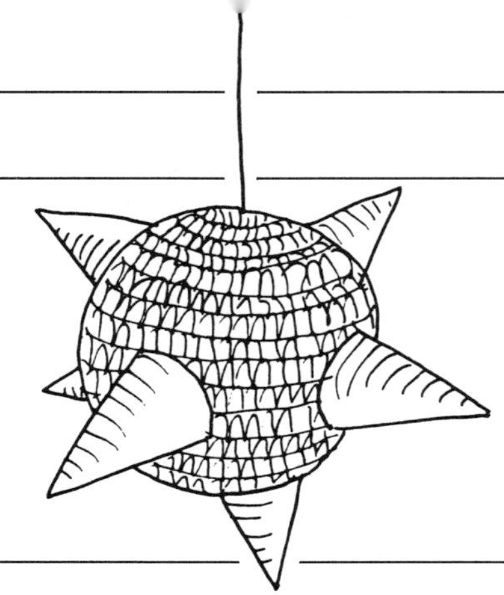

PARTY FAVORS

Piñatas can really liven up a party! Here's how to make your own in the traditional star shape. Fill it with candy or with individually-wrapped packages for all the guests at your next party.

The piñata originated in Italy in the 16th century. Just for fun, an earthenware pot called a *pignatta* was hung from a rope and swung at by a blindfolded person. The pot was not decorated nor did it have anything in it.

The custom made its way to Mexico, where the piñata became part of the Christmas celebration. It was only in this century that the piñata was gaily decorated with tissue paper and that papier-mâché was used as an alternative to an earthenware pot. Some Mexican piñatas are still made with a pot.

STAR PIÑATA
Large, round balloon
Newspaper
Flour, 1/4 cup
Saucepan
Strong string
Poster board, 6 pieces about 9″ square
Tissue paper, about 6–10 sheets
White glue
Candy or other treats

1. Blow up the balloon and tie it. Make some flour and water paste by mixing the 1/4 cup flour with 4 cups water in the saucepan. Stir well; bring to a boil on the stove (have an adult give you a hand), and cook until it is smooth and the consistency of cream. Set aside to cool.

2. Meanwhile, tear the newspaper into short strips. When the paste is cool enough to handle, paste the strips to the balloon. Overlap them slightly. Cover the entire balloon with a single layer of strips.

3. Make a harness for the balloon. Tie two lengths of string into a cross and lay the balloon on top of it. Bring the four strands up over the sides of the balloon and tape them in place. Tie the strings together at the top.

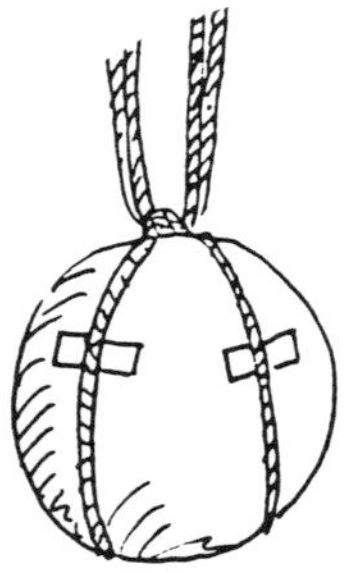

4. Cover the balloon with at least three more layers of newspaper strips. Hang the balloon to dry. This takes about 3–5 days.

5. Cut six shapes from the poster board, following the diagram shown, to make six cones. Glue the cone edges together.

Glue the six cones to the balloon.

6. Cut the tissue paper into strips 3″ wide. Fold each strip in half length-wise, and make cuts in the folded edge every 1/4″, to within half an inch of the cut side. To speed things up, you can cut through four or five folded strips at a time.

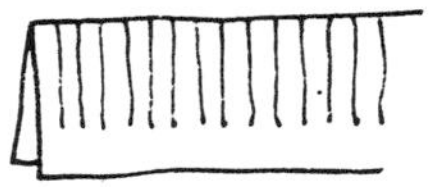

7. Unfold each strip and refold it inside out so that the ruffles stand up. Glue the ruffles to the hanging piñata, making the strips conform to the piñata's shape (and working around the cones). Start at the top and work your way down. Place each row so that the ruffles cover the glued portion of the previous row.

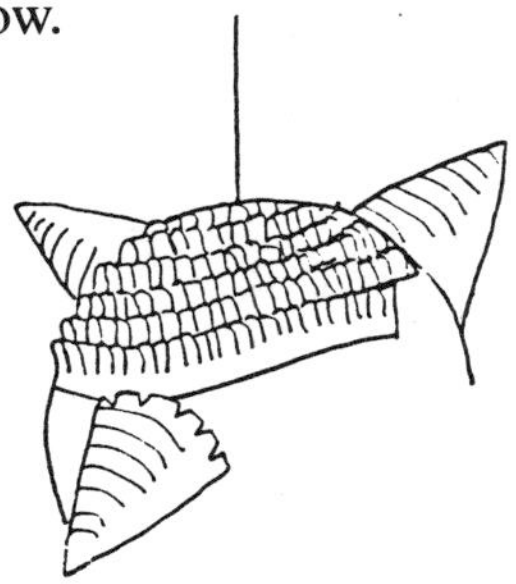

8. Cut a small triangular trap door in the piñata by making two cuts and folding down the flap.

Pop the balloon and remove it. Fill the piñata with goodies; push the flap back in place.

Variations on a Theme

Piñatas come in all shapes and sizes. You can turn a round balloon form into a face (just add some papier-mâché features) or an animal (attach some legs).

Instead of covering the piñata with tissue paper ruffles, you can make the final layer of your piñata from white paper towels and finish it with whole sheets of tissue paper glued down. Or paint the piñata with poster paints or acrylics.

Use your imagination to create some other piñata shapes. How about making a snake from a couple of long balloons laid end to end? For something really easy that would be perfect for your next birthday party, try this: wrap a square box with wrapping paper to look like a big present!

Tissue paper bleeds when it gets wet, so make sure you wear a smock or an apron when you are gluing the tissue ruffles in place.

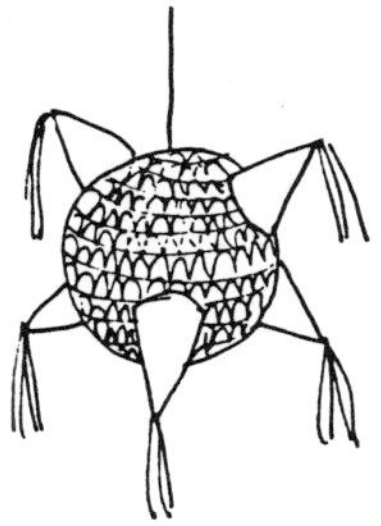

For added decoration, glue or tape some long strands of tissue paper to each of the cones.

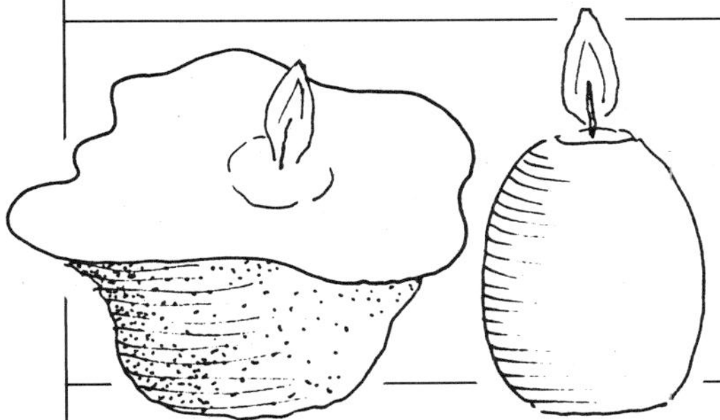

LET THERE BE LIGHT

Candles add a festive glow to the dinner table. Here are two simple candles you can make with ingredients found at your local supermarket or hardware store.

SAND-CAST CANDLE
Paraffin wax or old candles, about 1/2 pound
Crayons
Stub of an old candle
Sand, enough to fill a large bowl
Double boiler, or a saucepan and a bowl that fits over it

Note Wax is highly flammable. It must be melted over boiling water, and *never* directly in a pan set on top of the stove. Make sure you have an adult help you with this.

▶

The Story of Art
Tallow (fat from sheep and cows) and beeswax have been used in candlemaking since Roman times. Paraffin, which is distilled from wood, coal, and petroleum, was developed in the 19th century. Today, many candles are made from a combination of paraffin and beeswax.

This would be a great project to do down at a beach. Bring along a portable cookstove, but don't bother with the sand. You should find plenty there already!

1. In a large bowl (or in a sandbox), dampen some sand slightly so that you can dig a hole that keeps its shape. A hole about 4″ deep and 4″ across holds about half a pound of melted wax.

2. Place the candle stub in the hole so that the top is level with the top of the hole. Cut the stub shorter, if need be, or build up a little sand in the center of the hole to rest the candle on.

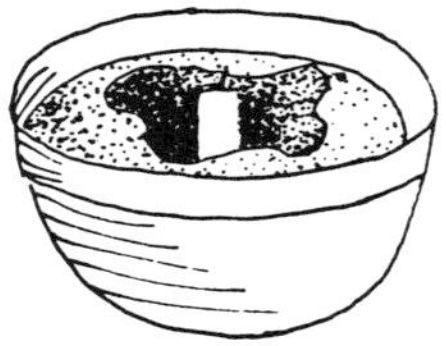

3. Cut the paraffin into small chunks and melt it in the top of the double boiler. Bring the water in the base to a boil. Keep an eye on the wax at all times (it may take as long as 15 minutes to melt ½ pound of wax). Have an adult help you at the stove. Color the wax with pieces of broken crayons (stir in only one or two to keep the color from getting muddy).

4. Carefully pour the wax into the hole. After about 15 minutes, poke a hole in the center of the candle, and pour in some more hot wax (wax shrinks as it cools, so you may have to do this again). Let the candle harden for several hours or overnight. Dig the candle out of the sand; brush off any loose grains. Level the bottom of the candle with a paring knife, if necessary.

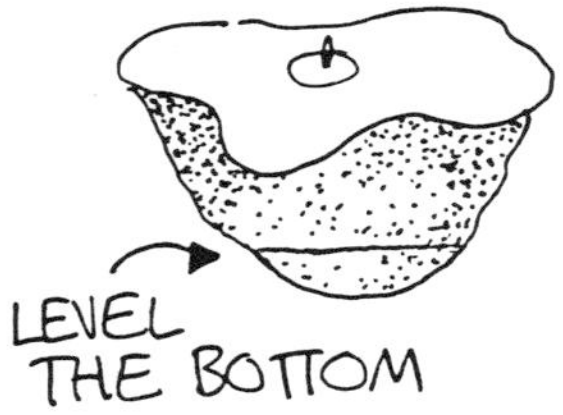

EGG CANDLES
Eggs, as many as you like
Egg carton
Sharp pin
Nail scissors
Cooking oil
Small brush
Paraffin wax or old candles (see *Note*)
Crayons
String
Toothpicks
Double boiler, or a saucepan and a bowl that fits over it

Note A pound of paraffin fills about a dozen large eggshells.

1. First blow the eggs. To do this, poke a small hole at each end of an egg with a sharp pin. Thrust the pin deep into the holes to break the membrane. Holding the egg over a bowl, blow through one hole; the yolk and the white will come out the other.

2. Enlarge the hole at the narrow end of the egg with the nail scissors. Make the opening about 1″ wide. Do as many shells as you need in this way. Wash the shells carefully and place them upside-down to dry. When they are dry, brush the insides of the eggs with cooking oil. Set the eggs in the egg carton.

3. Break the paraffin into small chunks and melt it in the top of the double boiler. (Have an adult help you at the stove, and remember that paraffin is flammable—see page 85). Color the wax with pieces of crayons (use only one or two crayons, or the wax will get muddy looking).

4. Cut the wicks for your candles. Cut the string into pieces about 5″ long. Lower the string halfway into the hot wax, one at a time; lift the string and wait a few seconds. Pull the string out straight while the wax is still soft.

5. With one hand, hold the wick upright in the shell. Carefully fill the shell up to the top with wax (have an adult pour the wax for you to make it easier). Anchor the wick between two toothpicks. Let set for 15 minutes.

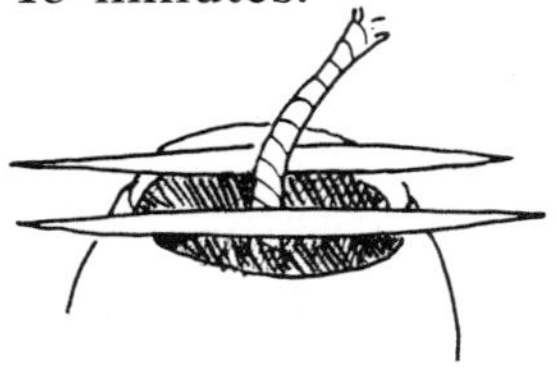

6. Pierce a hole in the top of the candle and pour in more hot wax. (You may have to do this again as the candle cools.) Leave the candles for several hours or overnight, then peel away the shells. Trim the wicks, and level the bottoms of the candles with a paring knife.

Variations on a Theme

Give your candles a striped look. This is easily done. Fill the eggshells a third of the way up with one color. Let the wax harden for 15 minutes, then pour in more wax in a different color. Do this again with a third color.

You can either melt separate batches of wax for each color, or try this trick. Color the wax initially with just one light-colored crayon. Fill the shells part way. Then add a second crayon in a deeper shade to the wax in the double boiler. Stir well and pour a layer of this into the shells. Finally, add a dark crayon to the remaining wax and top off the shells with this color.

Tilt the eggshells slightly when you pour the first two layers. This gives the candles an interesting wavy look.

Put one of your egg-shaped candles in a pierced tin can lantern. See page 135 to learn how to make your own.

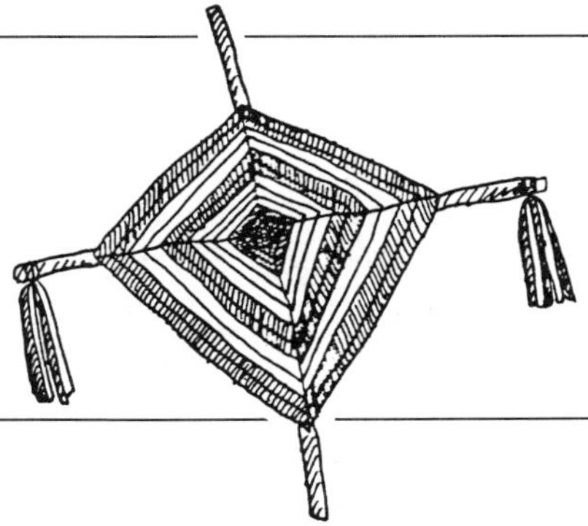

OJO DE DIOS

The *Ojo de Dios,* or God's Eye as it translates to English, is a traditional Mexican decoration that is thought to bring good luck. Maybe it will work for you!

GOD'S EYE
Yarn, in a variety of colors
2 straight twigs, 6″ to 10″ long

1. Make a cross with the twigs by placing one over the other. Lash the twigs together by wrapping yarn around them, first one way and then the other, until there's a nice, rounded hump that covers the twigs where they cross. This is the "eye."

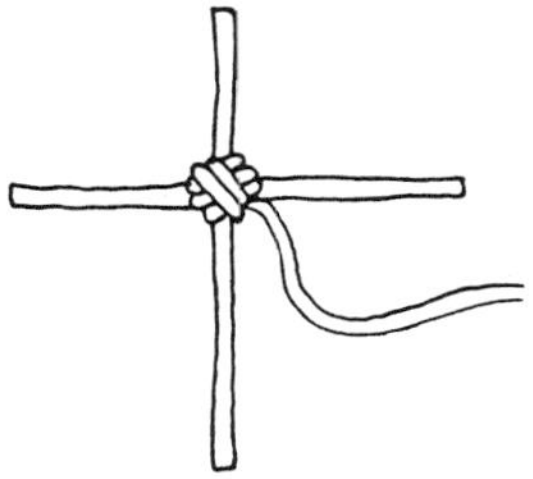

The *Ojo de Dios* is traditionally displayed during the Green Squash Festival each October in Mexico.

Make an *Ojo* from variegated yarn, which is already dyed several different colors. Or make your *Ojo* from short lengths of yarn you've dyed yourself. See page 147 for all you need to know to dye yarns with leaves, berries, and bark.

2. Bringing the yarn from behind, wrap it completely around one of the spokes of the cross. Carry the yarn to the next spoke and do the same. Continue in this way until the *Ojo* is as big as you like.

Change colors as you go, by tying new lengths of yarn. Try to make any color changes at the spokes, so that the knots are hidden at the back.

3. Finish the *Ojo* with a knot near one of the spokes. Add some tassels to the ends of the horizontal spokes, if you like. Tie a short length of yarn to the back for hanging the *Ojo*.

Variations on a Theme
For a more elaborate *Ojo,* add short twigs to the ends of any or all of the spokes, and make miniature *Ojos* at these points.

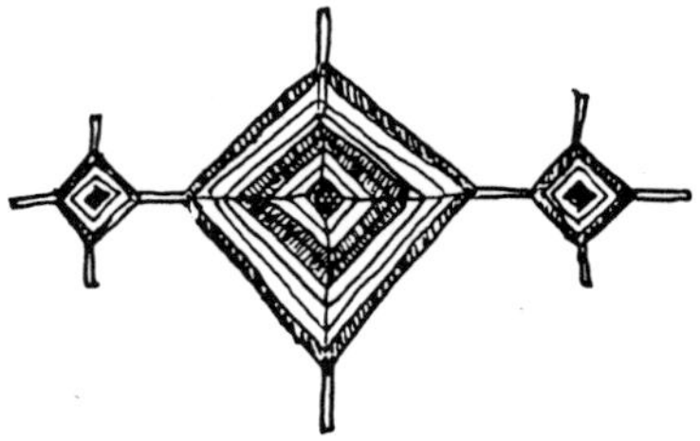

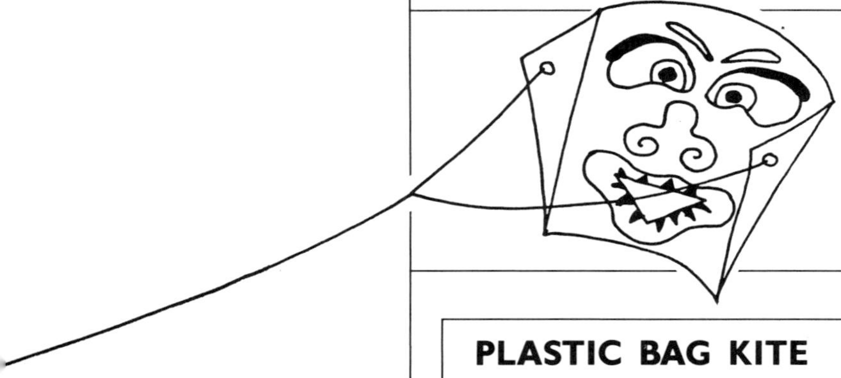

HIGH FLYER

You don't need to wait for a forecast of "high winds" to get this kite off the ground. This kite is as easy to launch as it is to make.

Kites are thought to have originated in China about 3,000 years ago.

PLASTIC BAG KITE
Plastic garbage bag, large kitchen size (13 gallon)
Scissors
Two 3/16″ dowels, 29″ long
Tape
Permanent markers, in assorted colors
String

Note You can use any plastic bag that's at least 23½″ × 29″.

1. Spread the garbage bag flat on your work surface. Measure and mark the cutting lines as shown in the diagram (use any felt-tipped pen to mark the lines).

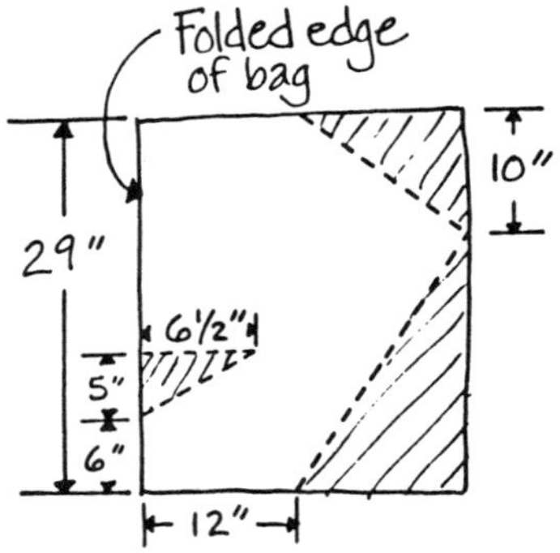

Cut along the lines, cutting away the shaded areas.

2. Open up the bag. Draw some features on the bag with the permanent markers. Take care not to smudge the markers before they have a chance to dry. Draw the traditional Japanese face shown here or decorate the kite any way you like.

3. Turn the kite over and tape the dowels in position. Use six pieces of tape for each dowel, as shown. Reinforce the corners of the cut-out and the wing tips with tape.

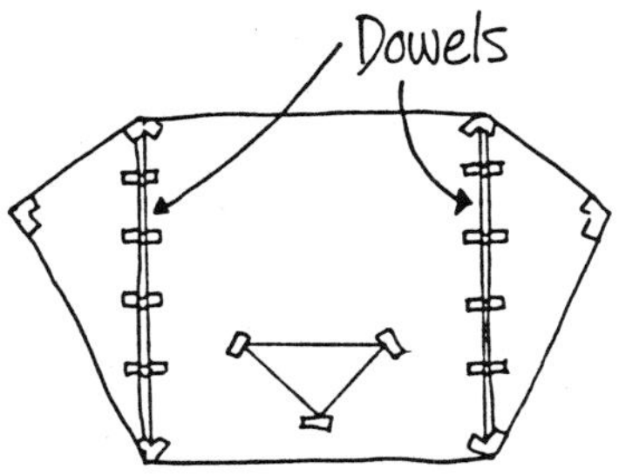

4. Poke a tiny hole in each wing tip. Cut a piece of string ten feet long. Tie each end through the holes in the wing tips. This is the kite's bridle. Tie a loop at the end of the bridle. Attach the flying line (wrap lots of string around a piece of wood) to this loop.

MARK MAKERS

Felt-tip markers are very popular because they come in a rainbow of colors and are very easy to use.

There are two basic types of markers—permanent or waterproof markers, and water-based (sometimes called watercolor) markers. Permanent markers have the disadvantage of being slightly toxic and of staining clothes and skin. They are useful, however, wherever a waterproof drawing is needed. They do smear before they dry, especially when used on slick surfaces such as the plastic bag kite, so keep this in mind.

Water-based markers are safer to use but finished artwork must be protected from moisture. These markers won't work on certain surfaces that repel the watery ink.

It's always a good idea to test your markers on a scrap of your material first. Permanent markers bleed quite a bit when used on porous paper, so be sure to protect your work surface with newspaper and keep in mind how the ink spreads outwards on the paper itself. If you are using permanent markers to color outlined artwork, save making the outlines until last. That way you can be sure the outlines really are on the outer edges of your drawings! Lightly pencil where the color is meant to go, color in the shapes, then come back with a water-based marker (or pen and ink) and make the outlines.

FLYING TIPS

The plastic bag described here is very easy to fly, even if you're on your own (many kites need two people to launch them, but not this one). All you need is a light, steady breeze (4-7 miles per hour is good—you can tell it's about right if you can feel the wind on your face and the leaves are rustling), and an open place away from power lines and trees.

Stand with your back to the wind and hold the kite up high with one hand. Let the line out as the kite tugs and climbs upward. If the kite dips down, let the line out a little more until the kite rights itself, then reel in the slack. If there doesn't seem to be any wind close to the ground, create your own by running with the kite until it's aloft.

Be sure to put the caps back on your markers when you are done using them; otherwise, they will dry out.

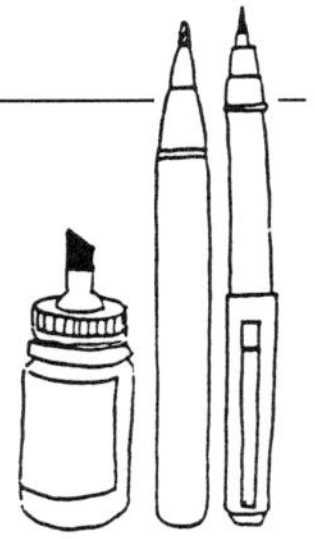

The Japanese make some enormous kites. In Hoshubana, kites are as large as 48 feet by 36 feet, with bridle lines 100 feet long! It takes as many as 50 grown men to get the kites up into the air.

We often refer to March as the kite flying month, but the gentle breezes of summer are often better than the gustier winds of spring.

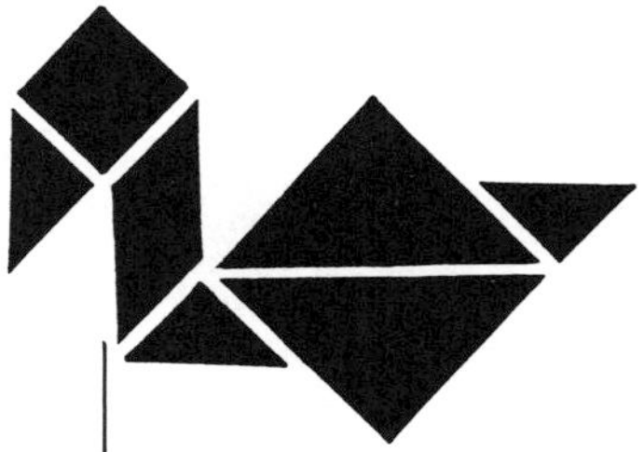

PUZZLE PIECES

Most puzzles form a picture when you put the pieces together. Not this one! You have to break apart this Tangram square before you can make any pictures with its seven pieces.

The Tangram puzzle originated in China, where it's called *Chi-Chiao*. That's Chinese for "the seven clever pieces"!

TANGRAM
Sturdy cardboard, 6″ square
Metal ruler
X-acto knife

Note The instructions here are for a Tangram measuring 6″ square. Follow the instructions to dissect a square of any size.

1. Mark the four corners of the cardboard with the letters A, B, C, and D, as shown.

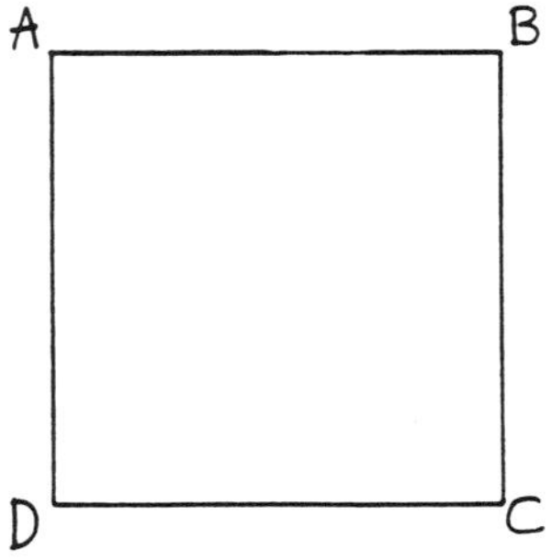

2. Draw a line from D to B.

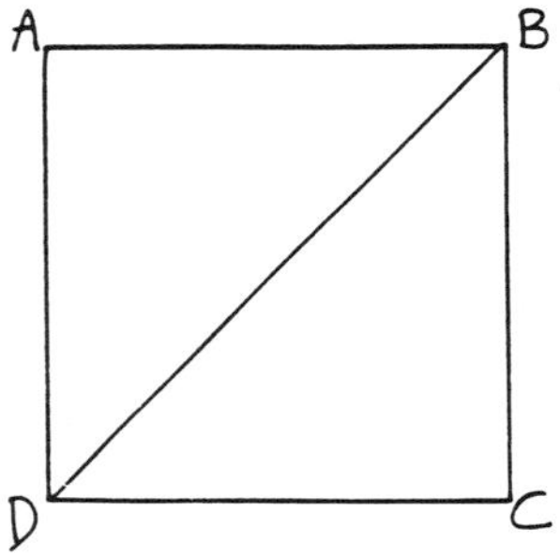

3. Make a mark halfway from A to B, and halfway from A to D. Draw a line connecting those two marks (this line is parallel to the one you made above).

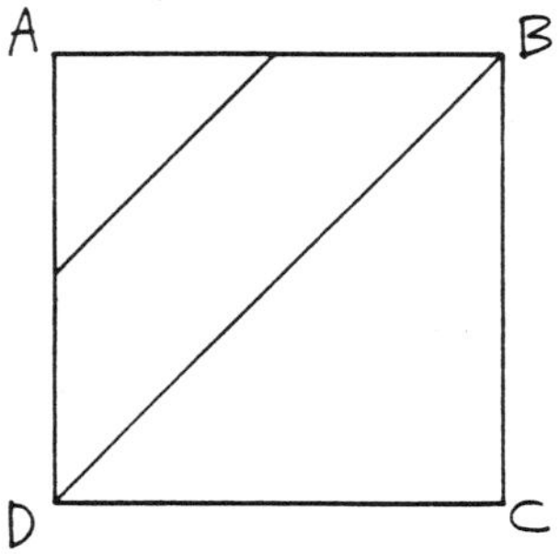

4. Place the ruler across A and C and draw a line from C up to the line you drew in step 3. Mark the very middle of the square with an O.

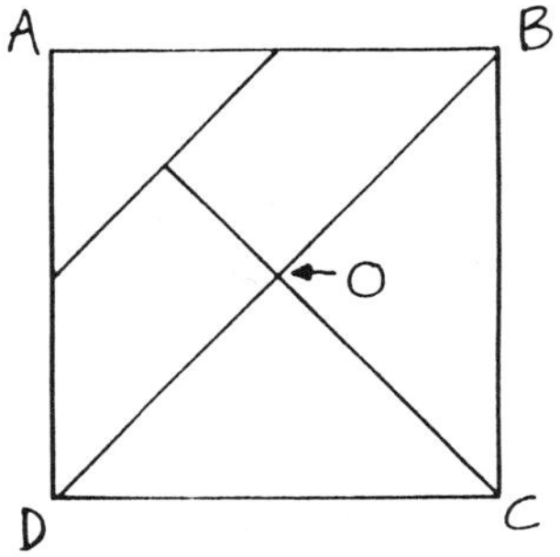

5. Make a mark halfway between D and O. Draw a line connecting that mark to the one halfway between A and D.

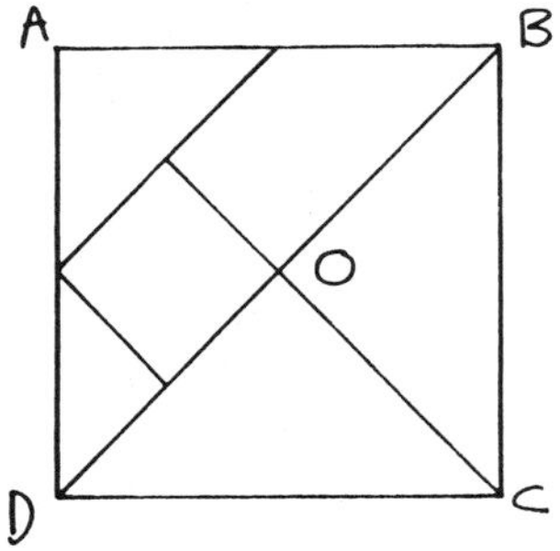

6. Make a mark halfway between B and O. Draw a line connecting that mark to the halfway mark of the line you made in step 3.

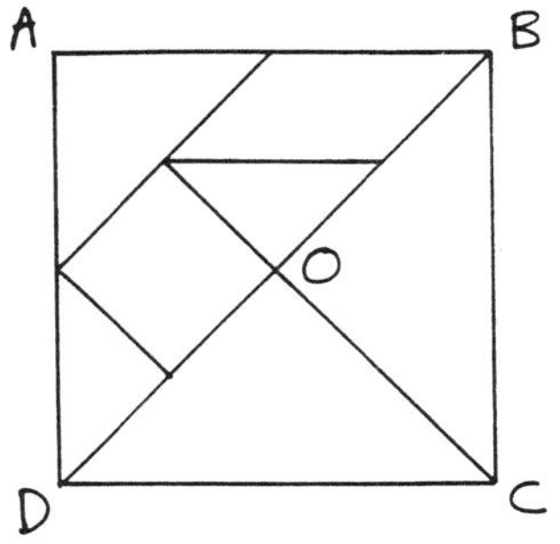

7. Using an X-acto knife, carefully cut along the lines. You now have seven puzzle pieces.

Scramble the puzzle pieces to create hundreds of different figures. Here's how to make a whale.

Here's how to make a sailboat.

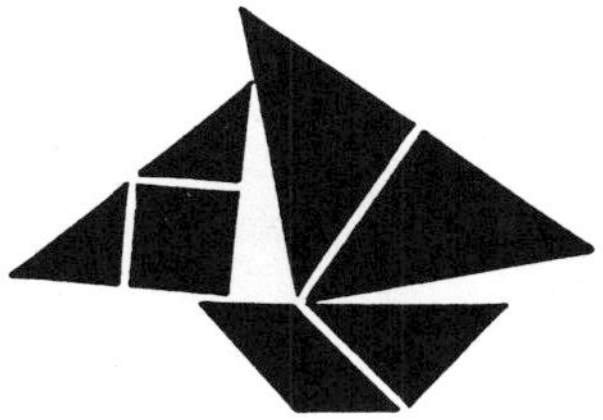

How do you think you might make this dog?

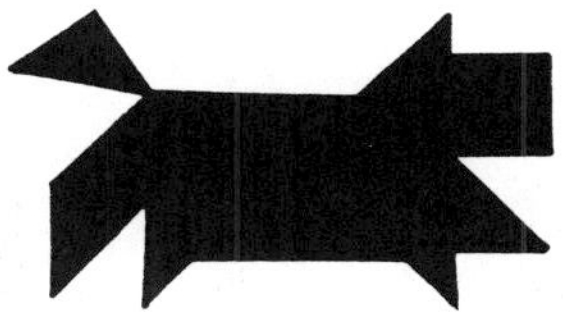

The answer is shown upside-down. What other pictures can you make using all seven pieces?

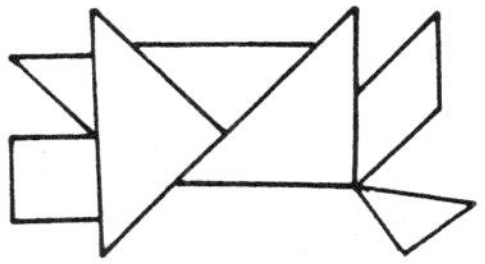

Variations on a Theme

Your Tangram square doesn't have to be made out of thick cardboard. Cardboard is a good choice because the pieces hold up well and are easy to grasp, but experiment with other materials. Make a Tangram out of poster board (this is easy enough to cut with scissors). Or go the other way, and make one out of wood. Quarter-inch plywood or composition board works well. Be sure to sand any rough edges. Paint the wood (black looks nice) or seal it with varnish.

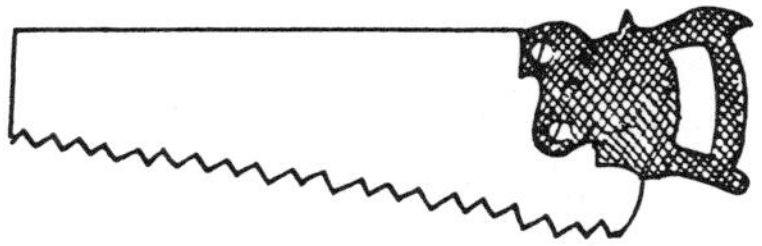

Some people say that long ago in China there lived a man named Tan who dropped a square tile on the floor. It broke into seven pieces. Try as he might, Tan was unable to put the pieces together again into a square. But he was able to fit them together in the shapes of birds, boats, and hundreds of other things! Do you suppose this is a true story?

GARDEN OF DELIGHTS

To an artist, an apple is more than something tasty to eat—it's something beautiful to paint or to sculpt. Artists have been inspired by plants and gardens for thousands of years. Fruits, flowers, and vegetables are well represented in the art world, from centuries-old mosaics of baskets brimming with luscious edibles to modern botanical illustrations.

FOOLING MOTHER NATURE

You can't fool Mother Nature, as the saying goes, but you sure can try! Here are some ingenious flowers made from natural materials that you can "grow" right in your kitchen.

SEED FLOWERS
Seeds of all sorts, such as sunflower, squash, apple, pumpkin, and melon seeds (see *Note*)
Poster board scraps
Needle or awl
Florists' wire
Florists' tape
White glue

Note Save the seeds from fruits and vegetables that you eat. Wash the seeds thoroughly and let them dry. (This takes a few days, or you can speed things up by putting them in a 250°F oven for about an hour.) You can also use garden seeds that come in packets—perhaps some that you didn't get a chance to plant last season.

1. Cut a small circle the size of a quarter out of poster board for each flower. Poke two holes in the center of the circle with a needle or awl.

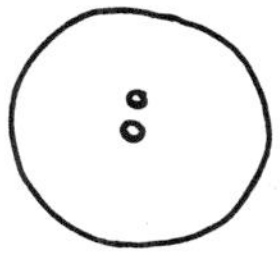

2. Cut a 12″ piece of florists' wire. Stick one end up through one hole and down through the other, twisting it around itself under the poster board circle. Wrap the wire with florists' tape.

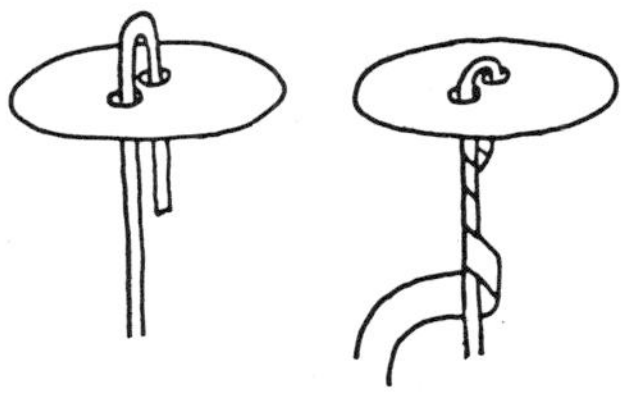

3. Squirt some glue around the edge of the circle. Place a ring of seeds right around the circle, letting them hang over the edge slightly. Add some more glue and make a smaller ring of seeds, inside the first ring. Add another ring inside of that one. Place a single seed right in the middle if there's room.

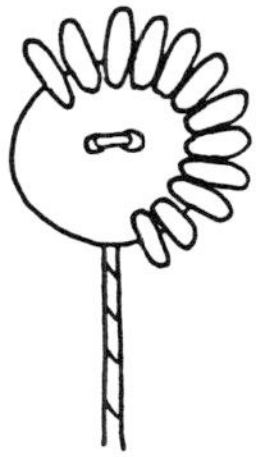

4. Let dry completely. Spray with clear acrylic spray, if you like.

Tip Seeds come in a variety of shades of brown, but you can dye many seeds any color you like with fabric dyes or food colors. Mix some dye with a little water in a small jar, add the seeds, and let sit for a few hours. Drain the seeds and let them dry before using them.

Variations on a Theme

You can make other "flowers" from things you pick up on walks through the woods and meadows. Your garden may also yield some interesting finds.

Dried seed heads from poppies, black-eyed Susans, and teasels are very striking, even on their own. But if you wire some pine needles around the base of a

Seeds come in all sorts of shapes and sizes. They can be as small as finely-ground pepper (many wildflower seeds are tiny) to as large as your fingernail (pumpkin and squash seeds are both quite large).

"Seed money" is an expression referring to money that is invested (planted) with the hope that it will grow!

Did you know?
Tulips originated in the area of modern-day Turkey, Iran, and Afghanistan. Today all the tulip bulbs planted in the United States come from Holland.

teasel, you'll have a very unusual flower unlike any you've ever seen before!

Or attach a handful of seed cases from a luminaria (honesty) plant to the scales of a pine cone (rub the covering off the seed cases first).

A little spot of glue will hold them in place. Slip a wire through the base of the cone as a stem, and cover it with florists' tape.

What other fanciful flowers can you create from natural materials?

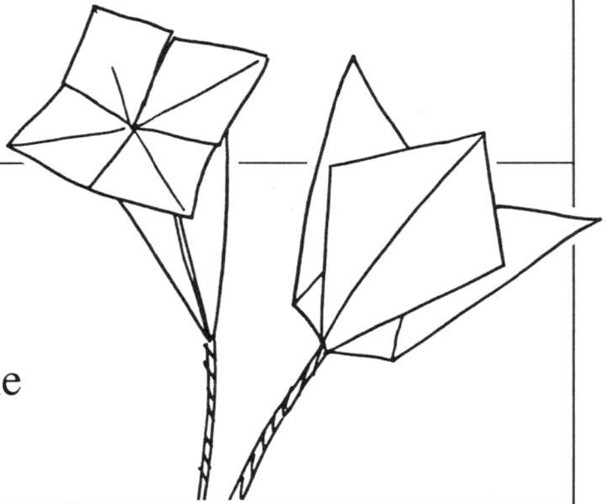

FLORAL FOLDS

Take a piece of paper, fold it this way and that, and presto—a paper flower that's almost as lovely as the real thing. You can make a whole bouquet using this Japanese paper-folding technique.

ORIGAMI TULIP
6″ origami paper (see *Note*)
Florists' wire
Florists' tape
White glue

Note You can use any thin paper cut into squares to make origami flowers (and other figures). Gift wrapping paper is especially nice. Vary the size of the squares to make blooms of different sizes.

1. Place the paper colored-side down. Fold it in half to make a triangle.

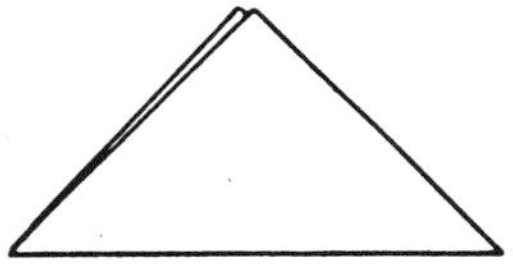

2. Fold the right-hand point over to the left side, so that the top of this fold is parallel to the base of the triangle.

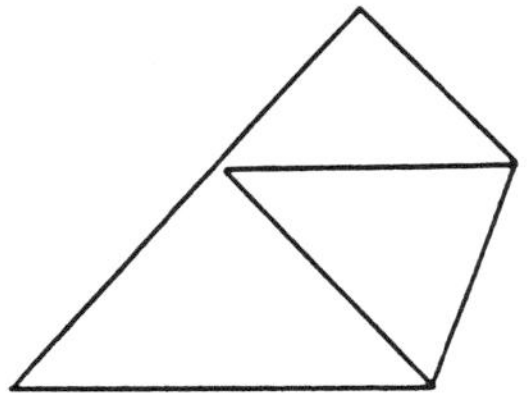

3. Fold the left-hand point over to the right side.

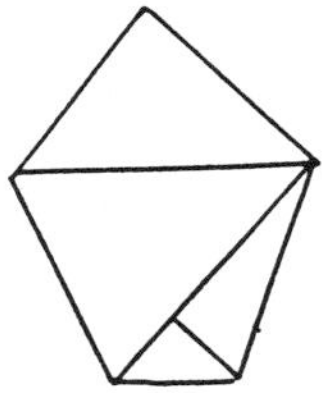

4. Unfold the paper back to the triangle. Slip your finger between the layers on the right, and push the folded part back into a kite shape.

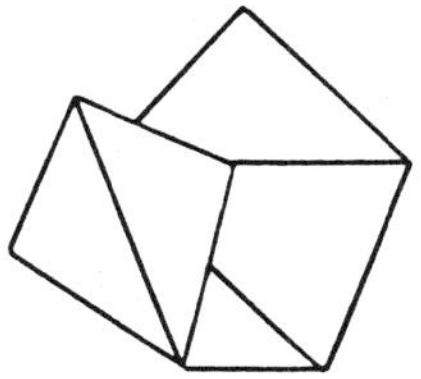

Do the same on the other side.

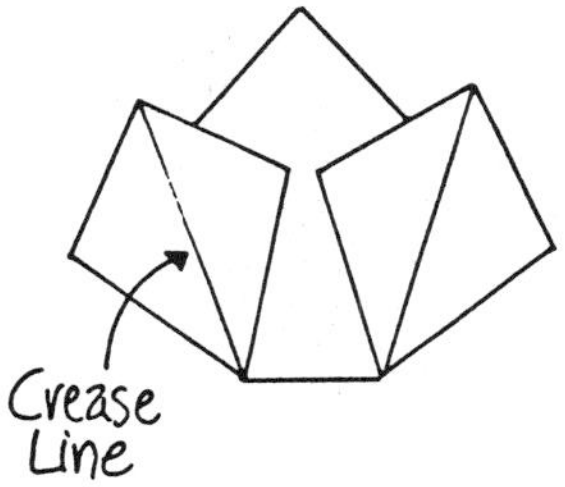

5. Turn the paper over. Fold the edges in at the crease lines. The front and back should look exactly the same.

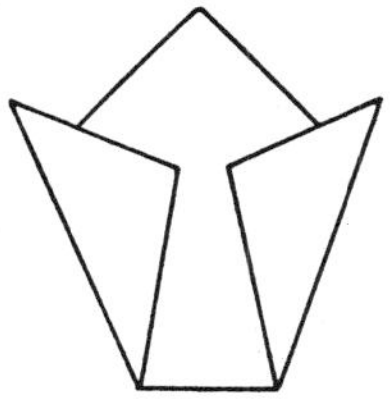

6. Fold in half. Fold up the bottom point (from the fold side). Crease very well.

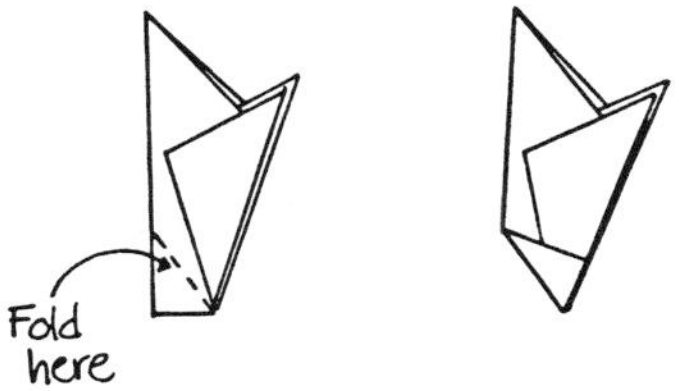

7. Open up the flower so that it looks like it did in step 5. Push the bottom diamond shape up inside the flower—reversing the creases. The flower will pop out to look like this.

8. Cut a 12″ piece of florists' wire, bend down one end into a hook and poke it through the inside of the flower (from the top). Wrap florists' tape around the wire, starting up near the paper flower. Use a little glue to secure the tape to the flower and to hold the flower shut, if necessary.

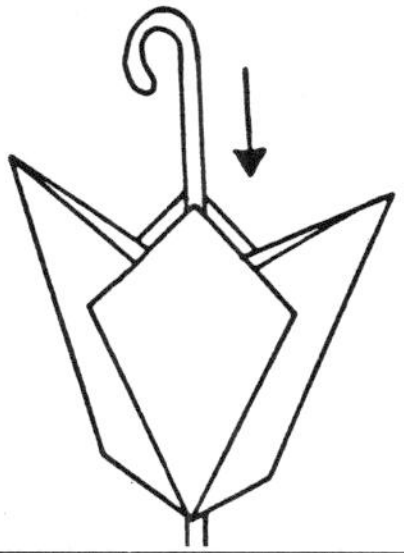

ORIGAMI TRUMPET FLOWER

6″ origami paper
Florists' wire
Florists' tape
White glue

1. Place the paper colored-side up. Fold in half to make a rectangle.

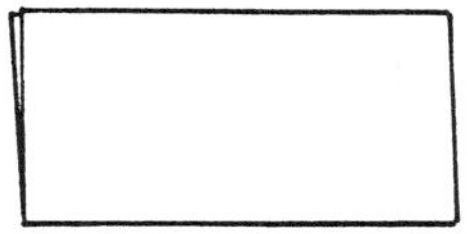

Fold in half again to make a square.

2. Open up the paper (keep it colored-side up) and fold it in half to make a triangle.

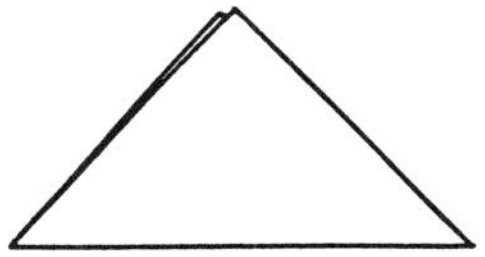

Fold in half again to make a smaller triangle.

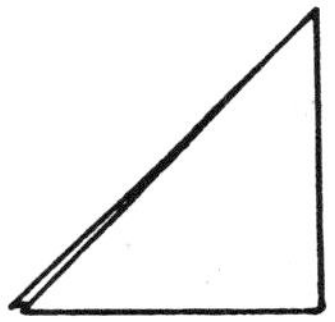

The Japanese learned how to fold paper from the Chinese, some time in the 6th century when the Chinese introduced paper to Japan. Despite this long history, the word *origami* is a recent one. From *oru*, "to fold," and *kami*, "paper," the word was coined in 1880 by a teacher at a Japanese kindergarten.

Several flowers are trumpet-shaped, among them the bindweeds and the Morning Glory.

3. Push the top layer out and up and flatten it into a diamond shape.

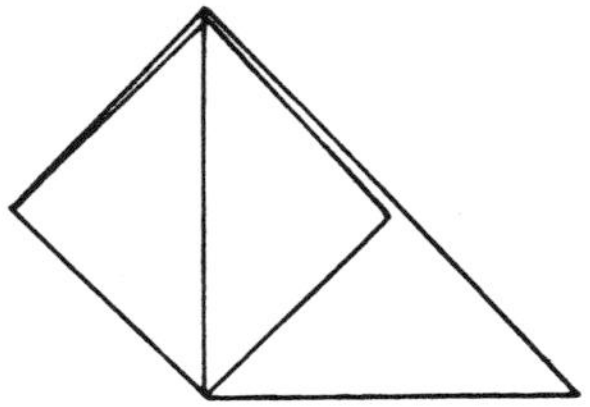

Turn the paper over and do the same to the other side.

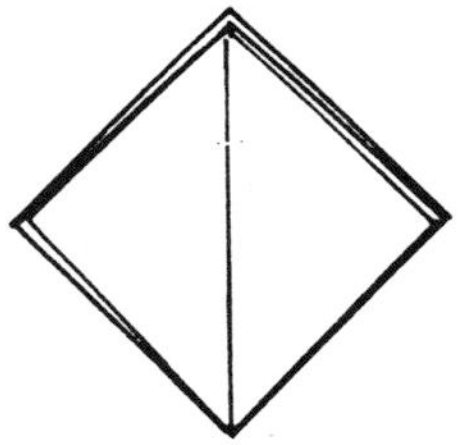

4. Fold the edges of the top layer in to meet at the center line.

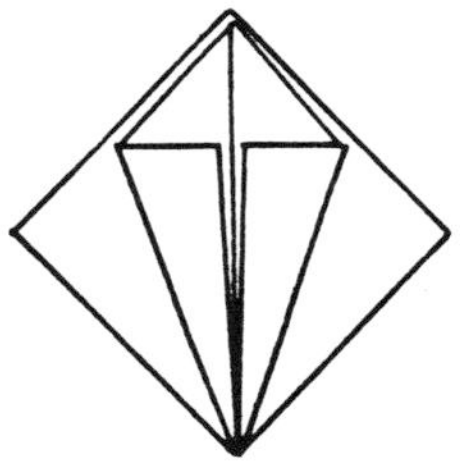

Turn the paper over and do the same on the other side.

5. Fold the top down (all layers) about a third of the way from the top.

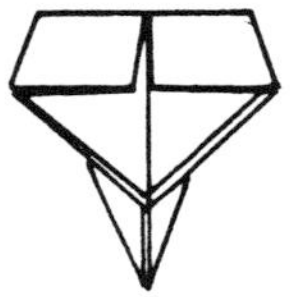

6. Unfold and push the petals down, flattening the two diamond shapes on either side into petals.

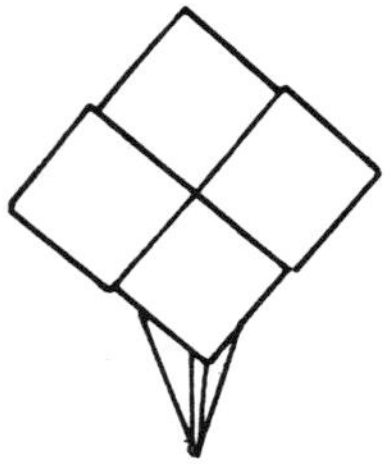

7. Cut a 12″ piece of florists' wire, bend one end into a hook and poke it through the inside of the flower (from the top). Wrap it with florists' tape, starting up near the flower. Use a little glue to secure the tape to the flower.

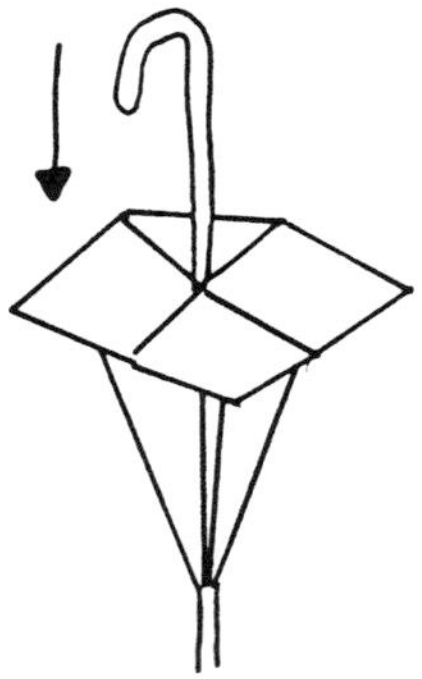

The Japanese are also well known for their distinctive arrangements of real flowers. *Ikebana* ("arrangement of living plant materials") is one style of flower arranging that is used to "illustrate" ideas with color and form, such as the seasons, or a feeling of quiet.

Look for some of the many books containing detailed instructions for origami objects. You'll find everything from seasonal decorations for all of our American holidays to traditional Japanese symbols, such as the crane, the best known Japanese symbol for good luck.

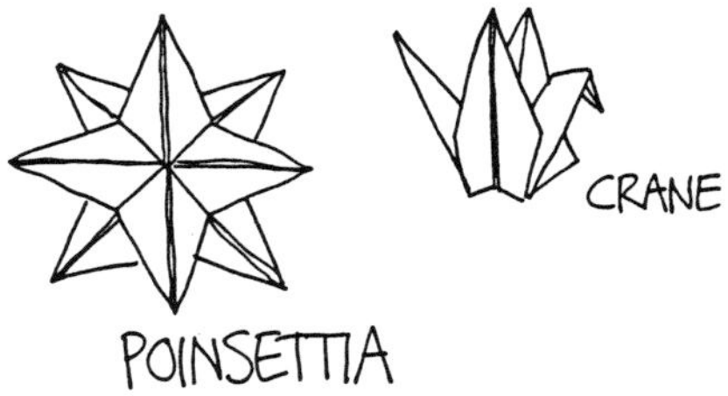

PETAL PRESERVE

Flower blossoms and leaves can be given new life when they are pressed flat and dried. Here are two ideas for using those plants you pick on your walks to your garden, your windowbox, or through the wilds.

PRESSED FLOWER BOOKMARK
Flower blossoms, leaves, ferns, and grasses
Clean scrap paper
Fat book or plant press (see *Plant Press* on page 98 for one you can make)
Heavy paper, about 2½″ × 2½″ × 8″
Clear Contact® paper, enough to cover paper
X-acto knife

Note You can press just about any plant material that isn't too fat. Avoid garden blooms with very hard centers or those that have very fleshy petals.

1. The blossoms and leaves you press should be fresh and dry (wait until the afternoon to pick blooms if they're wet with dew). Sandwich the plants between sheets of clean paper. Place these between the pages of a thick book, or put them in between the layers of cardboard in your press.

Press the plants for 1-2 weeks, or until they are completely dry.

2. Lay all your pressed plant material out so that you can see what you have to work with. Handle the plants carefully as they are fragile. Try to plan an arrangement in your head, so that you can avoid moving the pressed plants around too much.

3. Glue the pressed flowers and leaves to the piece of heavy paper. Use just a spot of glue for each. Let dry for a few minutes.

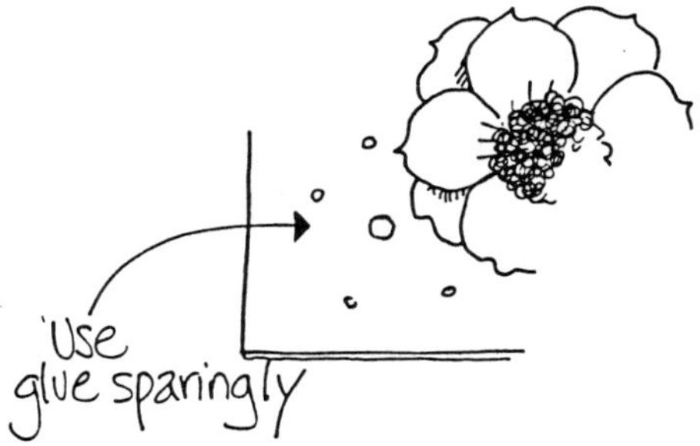

4. Cover the entire bookmark with a piece of clear Contact® paper that is slightly larger than the bookmark. Lay it over the plants, starting at one end. Rub your fingers over the Contact® paper as you lower it to press out any air bubbles.

5. Trim the excess Contact® paper from the perimeter of the bookmark.

▶

For a nice touch, punch a hole in one end of the bookmark and loop a piece of satin ribbon through it.

You can use pressed flowers and other plant material to decorate candles. Glue the flowers directly on the candle with a little white glue; let dry completely. Coat the entire candle with slightly watered-down glue to protect the flowers.

Use pressed flowers to make a border for a favorite poem.

PRESSED FLOWER COLLAGE
Flower blossoms, leaves, ferns, and grasses
Fat book or plant press
Scissors
Thick cardboard, about 5″ × 7″
Frame with glass

Note Make your pressed flower collage in a standard size, such as 5″ × 7″, or 8″ × 10″. That way you can use a purchased frame that already has glass in it.

1. Press your flowers and leaves as described in *Pressed Flower Bookmark* (see page 97). Lay them all out so you can see what you have to work with.

2. Make a pleasing arrangement of blossoms and leaves or use the plant material to create an imaginary scene such as the one shown here. Use the scissors to cut out parts of leaves and thin bark to make the roof of the house. Snip stems into short lengths and lay them side by side to make the fence. The trees in this picture are the tops of ferns and other plants. Use a very small amount of glue to stick the plants to the cardboard.

3. Place the cardboard in the frame. Hang the picture away from direct light. Sunlight quickly fades most dried flowers.

PLANT PRESS

In a pinch, you can always press blossoms and leaves between the pages of a fat book. But a plant press is an even better idea, and this simple press isn't hard to make.

You need two pieces of 1/4″ plywood or masonite cut to size. A 6″ × 8″ rectangle is a good size for a portable press to take along with you on walks; make the press larger, if you like, if you plan to leave it at home.

Drill holes in the four corners of each board and attach them to one another with long bolts topped with wing nuts.

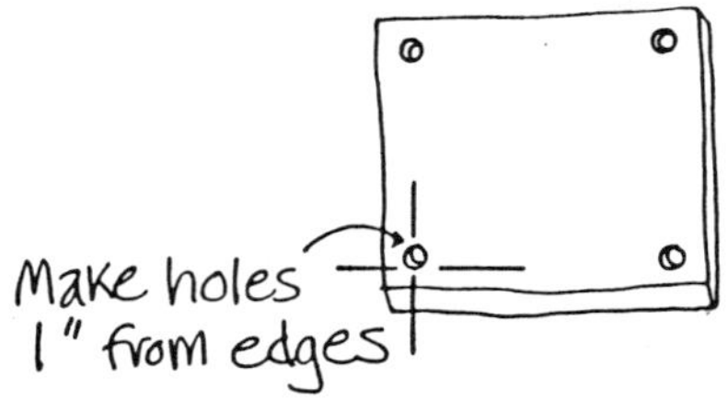

Cut several pieces of cardboard the size of your press. Trim a triangle off each corner where the bolts go.

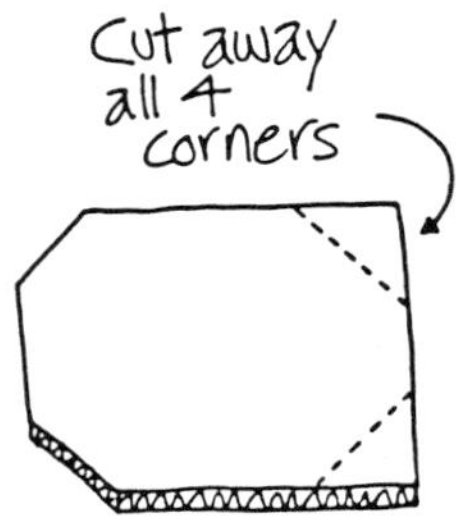

Tighten the nuts evenly at all four corners to put enough pressure on the plants to press them.

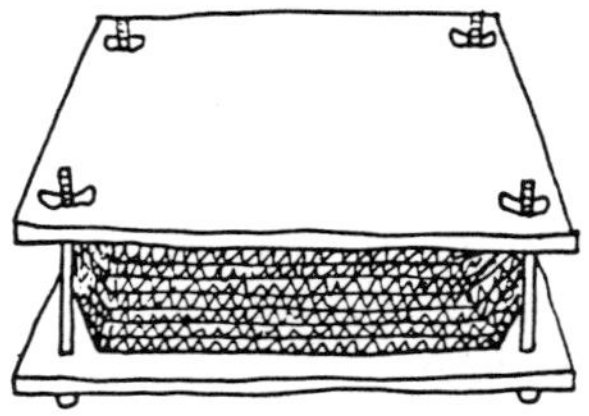

BE STILL

Vases full of flowers and bowls of fruit are often the subject of paintings known as still lifes. You can use these or some of your favorite belongings to create an artful composition.

STILL LIFE
Everyday objects of your choosing
Paper
Paints, markers, or colored pencils

1. Spend some time arranging the objects you have chosen, so that you're happy with the way they look. Play around with clustering the objects together or setting one apart from all the others.

Use a piece of cloth or a towel to cover a plain surface. Drape the fabric in interesting folds. Position a light to shine on your composition to highlight some of the objects and cast shadows on some of the others.

2. Lightly sketch in all the objects. Then make a finished drawing or painting, paying special attention to the shapes, textures, and colors. Add shading to make solid objects look three-dimensional. (See *Shipshape* on this page for hints on drawing three-dimensional objects.)

Tip If you can't complete your painting in one sitting, leave it and come back to it later. That's one of the nice things about a still life—it really does hold still!

SHIPSHAPE

There are four basic shapes that make up just about any object. If you practice drawing these shapes and learn to see how they are a part of everyday objects, drawing is a lot easier. Use a medium-soft pencil and plenty of inexpensive paper for practice drawing.

Start with the cube. A cube is nothing more than a box. It can be square or rectangular in shape. It also looks different depending on the angle from which it's viewed. Here's a tissue box seen straight on at eye level.

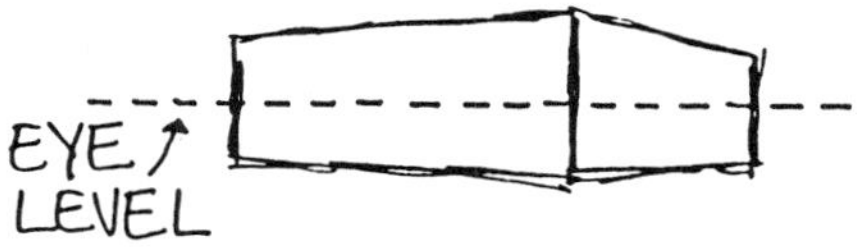

When the French painter, Paul Cézanne, painted people, he had them pose for long hours (because he was a slow and careful artist). If they moved, he would scold, "Sit like an apple!"—a subject he much preferred to paint. Cézanne painted over 200 still lifes during his lifetime.

Tricks of the Trade
There are many ways to create shading when drawing three-dimensional objects. Try cross-hatching—making a series of lines that cross one another.

The more overlapping lines, the darker the area.

Experiment with stippling—creating different tones with tiny dots. Space them far apart for lighter tones; group them densely for darker areas.

Smudging, especially when drawing with a soft pencil, is another way to add shading.

SHIPSHAPE, CONTINUED

Here's what it looks like if you view it from above. Practice drawing a tissue box or a table from different angles.

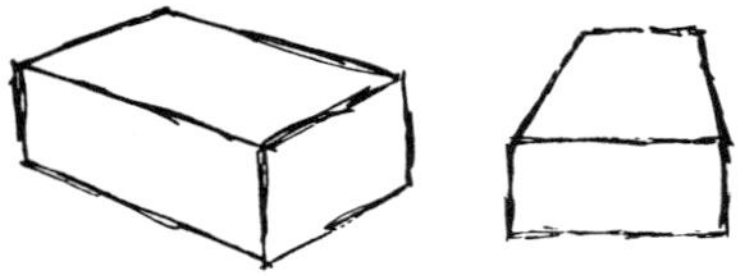

The next shape is a sphere or round ball. A ball is easy to draw—just draw a circle! But an apple is also a sphere, and it's never perfectly round. You also have to remember that you want to give your apple the feeling of roundness, even though you are drawing it on a flat piece of paper. Look how just this one extra line makes the apple appear solid and round.

A cylinder is a sphere with straight sides. Take a drinking glass, for instance. Seen from the side, the sides of the glass are straight lines, but the top and bottom look like squashed ovals. (These are called ellipses.)

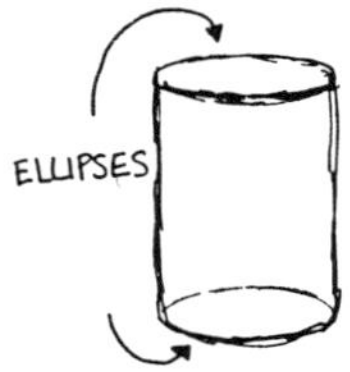

Practice drawing a glass or a flower pot (it, too, is a cylinder with sides that get narrower toward the bottom). The tops and bottoms of these cylinders look slightly different, depending on the angle that you are looking from.

Lastly, there is the cone. An ice cream cone is a perfect example of a cone. Look at how the opening is an ellipsis when the cone is viewed lying down. Practice drawing the cone from different angles.

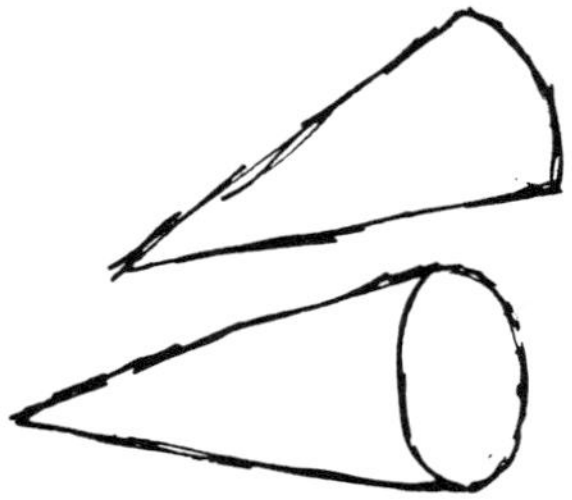

Now draw some objects that are made up of these different shapes. How about a glue bottle? It's a cylinder topped with a cone. A table lamp? This one is made up of several cylinders and spheres.

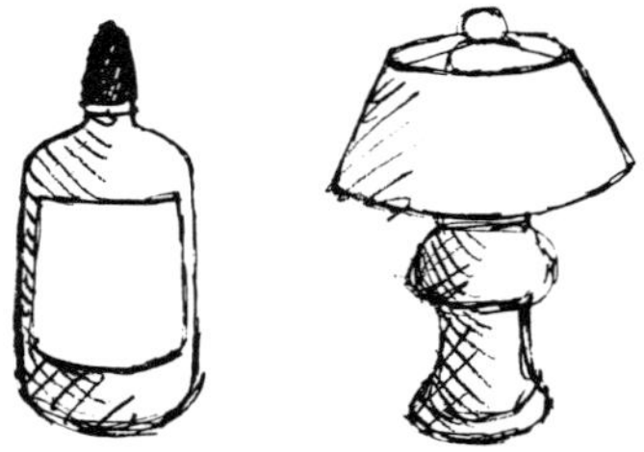

SQUARE ONE

Not all still lifes are painted, of course. Here's one that is made one square at a time, like a mosaic. You can create a dazzling still life with tiny colored paper "tiles."

PAPER MOSAIC
Colored paper in assorted colors
Ruler
X-acto knife
Scissors
White glue
Black paper, about 5″ × 7″
Clear varnish

Note The instructions here are for paper squares 1/4″ in size. You can use larger squares but you won't be able to get as much detail.

1. Cut the paper into 1/4″ squares. The quickest way to do this is to cut the paper in 1/4″-wide strips first, then snip the strips into squares.

To do this, gather up your paper into a stack. Mark a row of lines 1/4″ apart on the top sheet. Using a ruler to guide you, cut along each line with the X-acto knife. Run the knife along each line several times to cut through the whole stack.

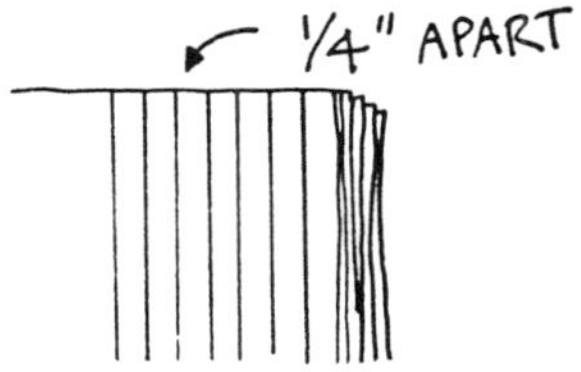

Gather together those strips that are the same color. Cut them into 1/4″ pieces with the scissors. Put each color in a separate bowl or pile.

2. Pencil the outline of your design on the black paper. Keep the design simple because it's hard to get a lot of detail with such a small mosaic.

3. Start by covering the outlines of your design with paper squares. Glue the squares down one by one, leaving a little space around each square. Here's a trick that makes handling the tiny squares easier. Squirt some glue on a scrap piece of paper. Dip just the tip of your finger into the glue. Place your glued finger on a square—it will lift right up. Use your other hand to flip the square over and position it on your paper.

4. Now fill in the design, and the background. Follow the curves of your outline. Cut the squares into smaller pieces to fit into any tight, irregular spots.

The Story of Art
Mosaics originated in the Near East, where they were made as early as 3000 B.C. It was not until around 800 B.C. that they became very popular, especially as floor designs.

The first mosaics were made with rounded pebbles. Later, glass and colored marble chips were used. Still later, specially-made square tiles were made from clay, glazed in every color of the rainbow.

Pick up some paint sample cards (look for these at a hardware store) and cut them into squares. These come in every color imaginable!

5. Brush or spray a couple of coats of clear varnish on the paper to protect the mosaic.

Tip To help your design really stand out, make sure there is plenty of contrast (light versus dark) in your mosaic. For instance, make the background squares much lighter (or darker, for a different effect) than those you choose to use in the design itself.

You can also use colored paper to create a more subtle mosaic. Cut plenty of paper in various shades of the main colors of your picture. Suggest the roundness of the forms in the mosaic by going from light to dark (the darker shades giving the appearance of shadow).

Mosaics were used to decorate churches until the 12th century when stained glass windows took their place.

TILE MOSAICS

Once you've mastered paper mosaics, you may want to go on to make mosaics using real tiles. You can purchase glass tiles made especially for mosaic work, or you can break old ceramic bathroom and kitchen tiles into little pieces (the shapes will be irregular, but that's okay). Place the tiles between some folded newspaper, and hit lightly with a hammer. Wear goggles to protect your eyes from flying pieces.

Make a frame out of plywood and pine molding. Glue or nail the molding around the perimeter.

Draw your design on the plywood. Glue the tile pieces in position with white glue. Leave a little space between each piece of tile. Let dry completely.

Mix some grout (this is available wherever tiles are sold) to a thick, creamy consistency. Spread it over the mosaic, forcing it down between all the tiles by pulling a piece of cardboard over the surface. Before the grout dries, scrape as much off the surface of the tiles as you can. Then run a damp sponge over the tiles and the molding to clean them. Let the grout dry.

Scrub any remaining grout off the mosaic. Sand any dried grout off the frame. You can hang this mosaic or use it as a trivet or table decoration.

A local building supplier may have some broken tiles you can have.

FRUTTI-TUTTI

With a little paper and paste, you can model a whole bowl of fruit that looks good enough to eat.

PAPIER-MÂCHÉ FRUIT
Newspaper
Tape
Paper towels
1/4 cup flour
Saucepan
Tissue paper in assorted colors
White glue
Medium-gauge wire, about 2′ long
Florists' tape

Note The fruit shown here is covered with colored tissue paper, but you can also paint it, if you prefer.

1. Make some flour and water paste. Mix 1/4 cup flour with 4 cups water in a saucepan. Bring to a boil; cook until it is a smooth and creamy consistency. Set aside to cool.

2. Meanwhile, tear some of the newspaper into short strips (leave some of the sheets whole to form into the basic fruit shapes).

3. Crumple up half-sheets of newspaper to make the apples, oranges, and pears. These are basically round balls; make the pear's shape by taping a smaller ball on top of the larger one.

Use a half-sheet to make a banana. Twist the newspaper into a curved crescent, taping it so the curve will hold its shape.

Individual grapes are made from small pieces of paper rolled into balls.

4. Cover the basic fruit shapes with strips of newspaper moistened with the flour and water paste. Overlap the strips slightly. Make at least 3 layers of newspaper strips. For the best results, let each layer dry before adding another (this way there is less distortion). Use torn paper towels for the final layer. Take care to smooth out any wrinkles and lumps. Let dry for 3–5 days.

5. Choose tissue paper colors for each piece of fruit. Smear slightly watered-down white glue over the fruit shapes and cover them with tissue paper cut to size. Experiment with using different shades of one color to suggest natural coloring. Let dry completely.

Don't limit yourself to fruit. Papier-mâché eggplants, green peppers, and pea pods bursting with peas are lots of fun to make, too.

Did you know?
Tutti-frutti is Italian for "all fruits."

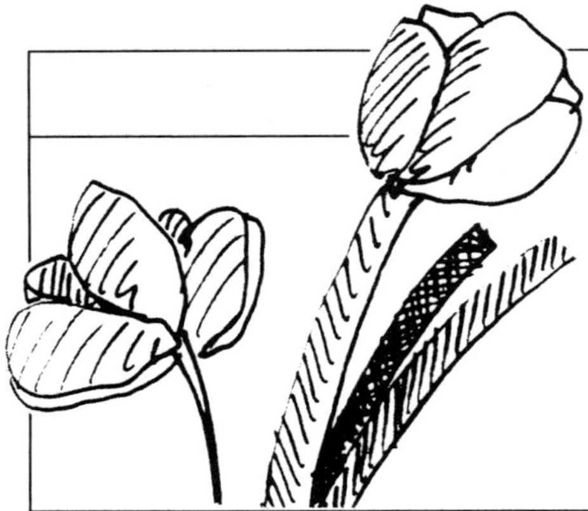

EDIBLE BLOOMS

Presenting food that not only tastes good but looks good, too, is truly an art. Chefs sometimes garnish dishes with flowers and fruit made from unexpected ingredients. You can add an artistic touch to your meals at home, too.

The Japanese are renowned for the visual artistry of their prepared foods. Much attention is paid to color, texture, and the way that foods are arranged on plates. The Japanese are particularly adept at creating unusual garnishes from common vegetables.

VEGETABLE & FRUIT GARNISHES

LONG-STEMMED RADISH ROSES

Red radishes, one per rose
Scallions, one per rose
Thin bamboo skewers, one per rose (see *Note*)
Green cabbage, one small head
Bowl

Note Look for bamboo skewers in the kitchenware section of department stores and supermarkets. They are usually sold in packages of 50 or 100.

1. Cut the root end off each radish. Make a series of vertical cuts in each all the way around. Be careful not to cut all the way through. Place the radishes in a bowl of cold water. Refrigerate overnight.

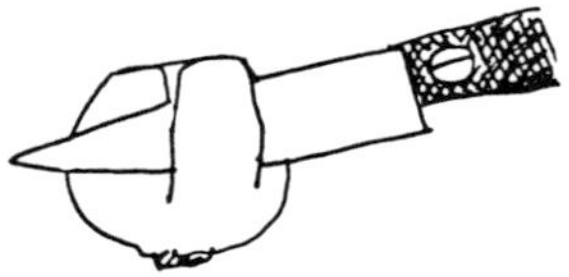

The next day, notice how the radishes have "bloomed" or opened up.

2. Cut the root end off each scallion. Insert a skewer in each scallion, pushing it up through one leafy tip (most scallions branch out into two or three leaves). Cut that leaf back just enough to expose the tip of the skewer.

3. Place an opened radish "bloom" on the tip of each scallion "stem." That completes one flower.

4. Slice the cabbage in half. Place it flat-side down inside a bowl. Stick the "long-stemmed roses" into the cabbage. Shred the remaining half of the cabbage (use a grater or a knife to cut thin slivers). Cover the upturned cabbage base with the shredded cabbage, to look like grass.

Tip For "roses" without stems, omit the scallions and skewers, and place the radishes directly on the serving platter.

CARROT CARNATIONS

Carrot
Vegetable peeler
Sharp knife
Toothpicks

1. Peel the carrot. Cut it into thin slices. Put all the slices in a bowl of cold water and refrigerate overnight.

2. Notice how the slices have curled and become twisted. Spear 3 to 5 slices on a toothpick to make a flower.

CITRUS WATERLILIES
Orange or grapefruit
Sharp knife
Green paper
Scissors

Note One piece of fruit makes two lilies.

1. Cut a zigzag pattern into the orange or grapefruit with the knife. Be sure to thrust the blade well into the fruit. Work your way around the entire fruit, ending right where you began.

Pull the two halves apart.

2. Cut some leaf shapes out of the green paper. Arrange the citrus "waterlilies" on top of the paper "pads."

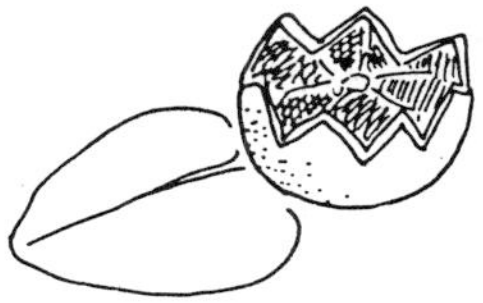

MARZIPAN FLOWERS & FRUITS
Uncolored marzipan (look in the gourmet section of your market)
Food colors
Powdered sugar

Note Marzipan is a confection made from ground almonds, egg whites, and sugar. It is available in tube-shaped packages, the smallest weighing 7 ounces. It also comes pre-colored in kit form.

1. Divide the marzipan into sections, one for each color. (A little goes a long way, so use just half the tube for starters, if you like.) Add a few drops of food coloring to each piece of marzipan; leave one section uncolored. Green, yellow, red, and brown are just a few colors that work well for making fruit and flowers.

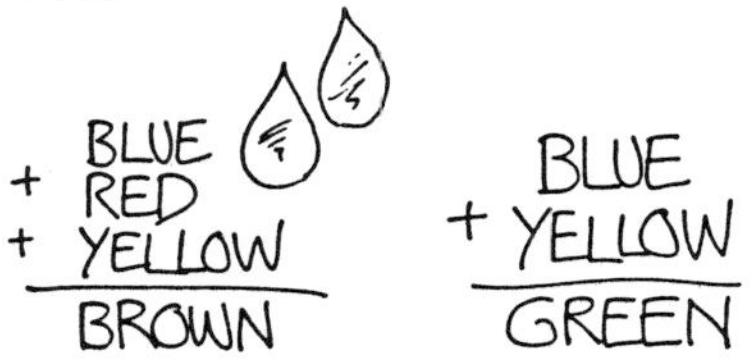

Work the food coloring into the marzipan with your fingers. Make sure the color is evenly distributed. If the marzipan seems sticky, knead in a little powdered sugar to firm it up.

2. Use the marzipan like modeling clay to create flowers and miniature fruit. Roll it between your fingers to make round shapes such as the apple, pear, and banana shown here. Use a tiny bit of brown for stems and the ends of the banana.

Flatten some marzipan on your work table (dust the surface with powdered sugar so that the marzipan won't stick to the table). With a small knife cut out shapes such as petals for the flower and leaves.

Use your marzipan flowers and fruit to decorate cakes, cupcakes, and cookies.

Marzipan can be used to create more than just fruit and flowers. Model little animals from the paste; roll it out and cut out letters from the alphabet to personalize a cake. Use your imagination to create some delicious decorations of your own.

LAY OF THE LAND

Many artists get their inspiration from nature. From the colors of a winter sunset to the trees that shade your street, there is untold beauty in the natural world.

Whether you live in the country or in the heart of a bustling city, just outside your front door is a landscape ready to inspire *you.* Gather up your gear and head outdoors!

ON A CLEAR DAY

Drawing and painting outdoors is a wonderful way to get to know the world around you. Every season—even every day—there's something new to observe.

LANDSCAPE
Paper, large sheets
Colored pencils, markers, or paint
Sturdy cardboard or masonite to put under the paper

Note You may not need a separate support for your paper, if your paper comes in a pad with a cardboard back.

1. Walk around until you find just where you want to view the landscape. Things look very different depending on your vantage point. An outdoor view seen from high up (from a second-story window or from the top of a small rise) is quite different when viewed from ground level.

Draw an imaginary frame around the part of the scene you want to paint. Choose something like a tall tree or a grouping of houses as a focal point.

2. With a pencil, lightly sketch in the main elements of your picture. Leave out anything that doesn't "belong"—anything that makes the picture confusing or that competes with the parts you want to stand out. You can do this because it is your drawing, and not a photograph.

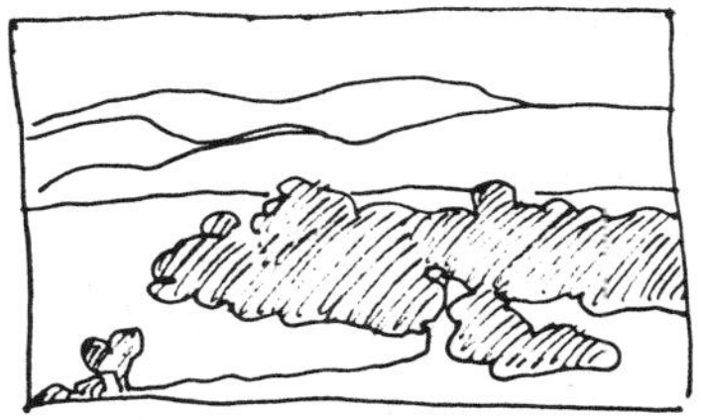

Pay attention to perspective. See *Distant Relations* on page 108 for some perspective pointers.

3. Color the landscape. Make the background colors lighter than those in the foreground or front of the picture. This helps to give your drawing depth and makes it look more like a real landscape.

Painters who live in towns and cities sometimes paint "townscapes" and "cityscapes."

Artists in Japan and China were painting landscapes as long as 1,000 years ago. It was not until the mid-17th century, however, that artists in Europe thought to paint landscapes for their own sake.

Before this, landscapes were found only as backgrounds for paintings of other subjects. It was the Dutch who first took up landscape painting. They were interested in showing nature realistically and became very skilled at painting large areas of sky.

The Story of Art
In the 1870s a group of French artists became interested in painting outdoors in natural sunlight. In order to capture the effect of the light before it changed, they painted quickly with loose brushstrokes. One of the painters, Claude Monet, exhibited a painting entitled *Impression: Sunrise.* From this painting's title came the name given to the style of painting these artists perfected—impressionism.

Did you know?
Trompe l'oeil (trawmp LOY) is French for "fool the eye."

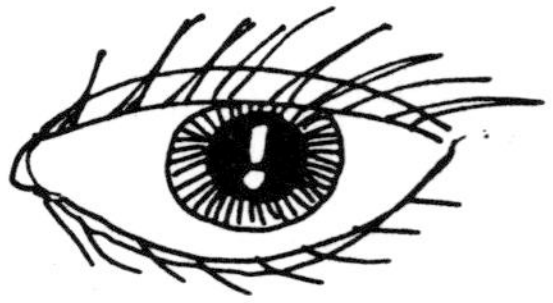

DISTANT RELATIONS

There are a few tricks you can use to give your landscapes a feeling of depth and to make them more realistic looking. Draw objects and lines the way they appear rather than the way they really are.

Objects appear smaller the farther away they are. They also usually appear higher up the farther away they get.

Parallel lines appear to be closer together as they get farther away. They look as if they come together at the horizon.

Objects in the foreground or front of a picture are more distinct and vivid than those objects in the background. Foreground objects are brighter in color; objects in the background are lighter and hazier looking.

FOOLED YOU!

Windows not only let in light but offer a glimpse of the world outside. Here's a way to make the view from a window anything you want!

TROMPE L'OEIL WINDOW
Sturdy cardboard, about 20″ × 30″
Colored pencils, markers, or paint
Yardstick or long ruler

Note This type of painting is especially effective painted directly on a wall. Check with your parents before you ever paint on walls, however. If you do intend painting it on a wall, it's a good idea to make a cardboard version first as a practice piece.

1. Draw the outlines of the window frame on the cardboard. Match the size and style of those windows near where you will hang the painting, or make the window any way you like.

Give the illusion of depth by drawing the bottom half of the window as it might look if viewed from above.

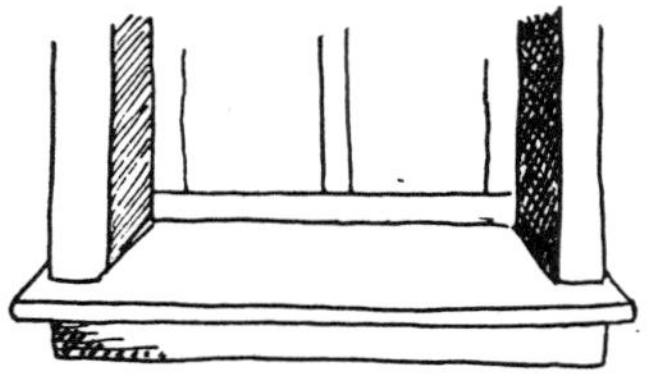

2. Pencil in the landscape or outdoor scene as it would be seen from the window. For fun, add an object sitting on the inside window sill, such as a potted plant.

3. Color in the painting. Paint the window frame with two shades of the same color. Use the darker shade to suggest shadows cast by the frame.

Make the outdoor scene lighter in color, so that it appears to be in the distance. Paint the object on the windowsill, paying special attention to how it would look lit with the bright light from the window.

4. Hang the picture, either level with the other windows in the room, or at a logical height.

Variations on a Theme
Paint a picture directly on an interior door. Paint a door slightly ajar, showing a glimpse of what is going on in the room beyond.

GLORIOUS GARDENS

With some printed and patterned paper, a pair of scissors, and glue, you can make a garden that's in bloom all year long.

The Hanging Gardens of Babylon were one of the Seven Wonders of the Ancient World. According to legend, they were built by King Nebuchadnezzar II (604–562 B.C.) for his mountain princess bride so she wouldn't feel homesick in Babylon. The gardens weren't actually hanging, but were instead built on a terraced pyramid. The garden, full of rare and exotic plants, was watered by man-made fountains and waterfalls on the pyramid.

CUT–PAPER COLLAGE
Sturdy cardboard, about 9″ × 12″
Assorted printed and plain papers, such as geometric and floral gift wrap, note cards, and wallpaper
Scissors
White glue

1. Cut out individual flowers and leaves from the printed paper you have collected. Cut your own flower shapes from the smaller over-all patterned paper. Cut stems, tree trunks, lawn, and sky from plain colored paper.

Have on hand various patterned and colored papers to add to your picture as you make it.

2. Plan your picture around the paper you have cut out. Play with color combinations and contrast (light versus dark) to make the most of the different scale patterns and prints. Don't glue anything down yet.

▶

Artist's Profile
Claude Monet, a French painter living from 1840 to 1926, was an avid gardener. Many of his later works were inspired by the vast gardens at his home in Giverny. Monet painted 48 canvases of water lilies alone from 1904 to 1908. Some of these paintings are enormous. Up close all you see is thick paint and brushstrokes. Only when you stand well back can you make out the flowers themselves.

3. When you are happy with the picture you have made, glue the paper in place. Paste down the large areas first, such as the sky or the expanse of lawn.

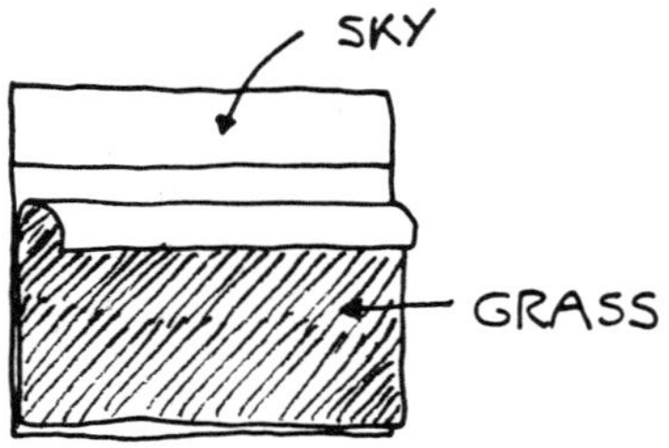

Cut them so they butt up to one another, or so they overlap slightly. Build up the picture by gluing down the flowers and foliage, and other elements, one by one.

Tip Brush on a coat of clear varnish or polymer medium, if you like, to protect the collage and give it a soft sheen.

Variations on a Theme
Use printed fabrics instead of paper for this collage. Use an iron-on bonding material such as Stitch Witchery® to adhere the fabric pieces to either a cardboard or fabric background.

Study a real garden to see how flowers are interplanted for effect. Some gardeners strive for harmony, planting flowers in one or two related colors. Other people prefer the more exciting look of flowers in complimentary colors planted next to one another.

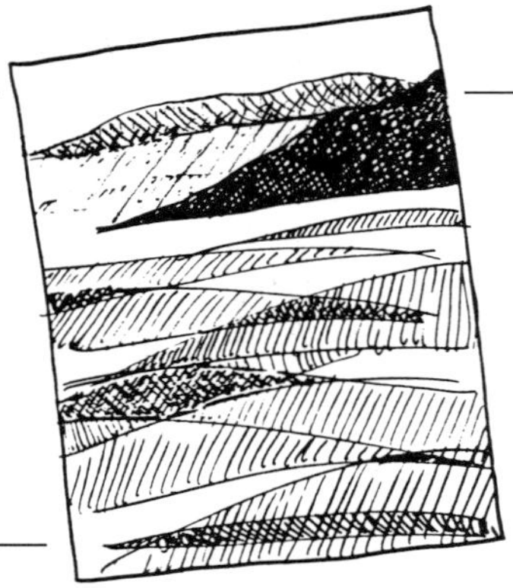

SURF'S UP

A painting of the ocean and its shoreline is often called something other than a landscape. It's known as—you guessed it—a seascape. Here's an interesting way to capture the majesty of the sea on paper.

Some heavier colored-papers are made by printing the color onto white paper. When you tear one of these types of papers, the ragged edges show up white.

TISSUE PAPER SEASCAPE
White poster board, about 9″ × 12″
Colored tissue paper, in blues, blue-greens, and tans
White glue
Brush

Note If you don't have any white poster board on hand, glue a sheet of white paper onto any piece of sturdy cardboard.

1. Mix some white glue with a little water in a small bowl or glass.

2. Tear the tissue paper into irregular pieces. Brush some glue onto the poster board and place the paper over it, one piece at a time. Brush more glue over the paper to make it lay flat. Arrange the torn tissue pieces so that some overlap; leave some white space between some of the pieces to suggest waves.

3. Add some land (perhaps an island in the distance), if you like, and some sky. Let dry completely. Trim the ragged edges of the picture with a pair of scissors or an X-acto knife.

Tip Tissue paper "bleeds" when it gets wet. Take advantage of this for some interesting effects. Glue a piece of tissue paper down; lift it off before the glue dries. Some of the dye is left behind. Notice how the glue becomes slightly tinted. Use it to paint with, like watercolors, wherever you want some subtle color.

Colored tissue paper is also perfect for more abstract collages. Overlap two colors to create a third color.

Winslow Homer, an American artist living from 1836 to 1910, is best known for his coastal and country scenes. He once said, "Never put more than two waves in a picture: it's fussy."

LIGHT OF THE MOON

Just imagine what things would look like if colors were as bright at night as they are by day. Do you suppose this is what you'd see on a walk through the jungle on a moonlit night?

WAX RESIST NIGHTSCAPE
Medium-weight paper, about 9″ × 12″
Crayons in assorted colors
Black poster paint or watercolor
Large brush

Note Fluorescent crayons work especially well with this technique.

1. Draw a picture of the outdoors using crayons. Draw the jungle scene shown here or make up one of your own. Press down hard as you outline and color in the picture. Use plenty of bright colors (and white, too) for the best effect.

2. Brush the poster paint over the entire drawing. The wax in the crayons "resists" the paint, making the drawing show up clearly against the black background. Let dry.

Variations on a Theme
Make this drawing using what's known as a scratchboard technique. Cover the entire surface of a piece of paper with areas of solid color using different colored crayons. Press down hard on the crayons. Now cover all these colors with a thick layer of black crayon.

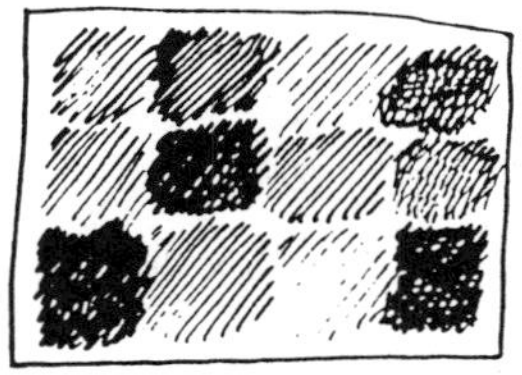

One of the best known night landscapes is Vincent van Gogh's *The Starry Night.* Instead of pinpoints of light in a dark sky, Van Gogh's stars are huge, swirling orbs of light.

Because oil pastels smudge easily, it's a good idea to protect pastel drawings with a spray fixative.

Scratch through the top layer of black with an instrument such as a pencil point, nail, or screwdriver. The colors underneath will appear as you draw the picture.

PASTEL PASTIMES

You're probably very familiar with crayons, but there's a similar drawing medium you might like to try that offers even more possibilities. Oil pastels (you may find these under the name Cray-pas®, a brand that takes its name from *cray*ons plus *pas*tels) are even brighter than crayons and are softer and easier to use.

Like crayons, oil pastels can be used with light or heavy pressure. Because they are so soft, however, they can be blended with your fingertip. When they are layed down thickly, they cover the paper completely.

Oil pastels can be thinned with turpentine or mineral spirits to create watercolor-like effects, too. Try dipping a cotton swab in turpentine and rubbing it on parts of an oil pastel drawing. Those parts will be lighter in color, and a little hazier looking, perfect for the backgrounds in landscapes, for instance.

A SAMPLING OF STARS

One star, our sun, dominates the landscape each day, but millions of distant stars bring the night sky to life. Here are two stars you can make. The first is a five-pointed star cut from a folded sheet of paper; the second is an eight-pointed version made from long, narrow strips of paper.

Stars have been depicted throughout history with three, four, five, six, seven, and even eight points!

FIVE-POINTED CUT STAR
Lightweight paper, 8½″ × 11″
Scissors

1. Fold the paper in half crosswise. With the fold at the bottom, bring the lower right-hand corner up to the halfway point on the left side. Crease well.

2. Fold the right-hand edge over to the left and crease. Fold the remaining section on the left over to the right and crease.

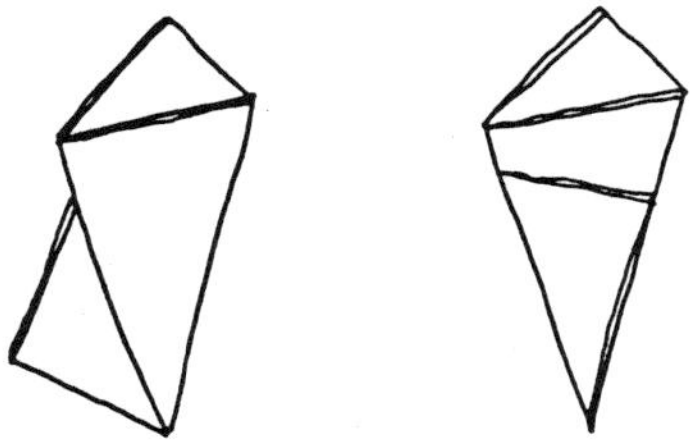

3. Cut along the imaginary line indicated by the row of dots. The smaller portion is the star. Unfold it and see!

Tip Before you unfold the star, snip little bits out with the scissors. Your star will have an intricate lacy pattern just like snowflakes cut from paper.

EIGHT-POINTED WOVEN STAR
4 strips medium-weight paper, 3/4″ × 24″
Scissors
Thread or thin string
Needle

Note Three-quarter inch strips make a star that is 3¼″ across. Use thinner strips for a smaller star; wider ones for a larger star.

1. Fold each strip in half and cut the ends at an angle.

2. Weave the 4 strips together as shown. Pull the strips so they are snug.

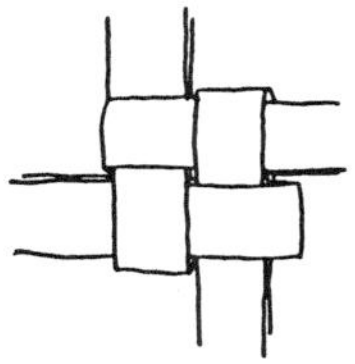

3. Bend one of the top left-hand strips down. Bend one of the strips on the left over to the right. Bend one of the bottom strips up. Bend one of the right-hand strips over to the left, weaving it under the first strip to hold them all in place.

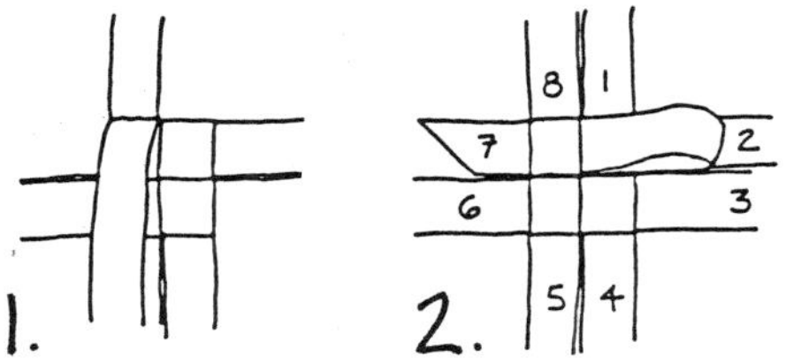

There are now 8 strips radiating from the central square. They are marked 1 through 8 in the drawing above to make the next steps clearer.

4. Fold strip 1 down at an angle as shown. Wrap the strip around to the back, bringing it to the front again and inserting it under the woven strip below it.

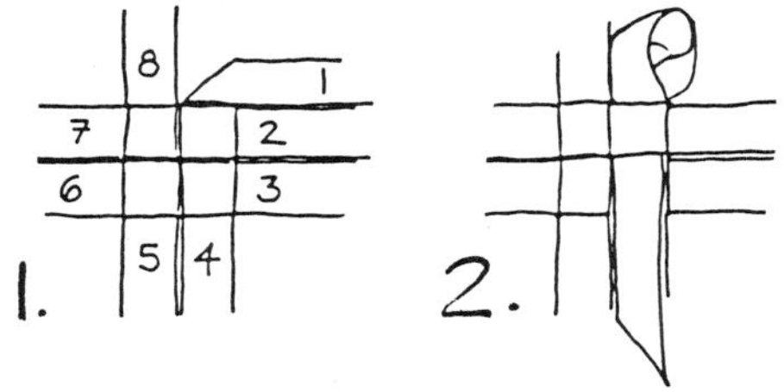

Pull the strip carefully, as far as it will go. A triangular point will form. Trim the strip flush with the woven section of the star.

5. Do the same with strips 7, 5, and 3, in that order. Trim the excess off each.

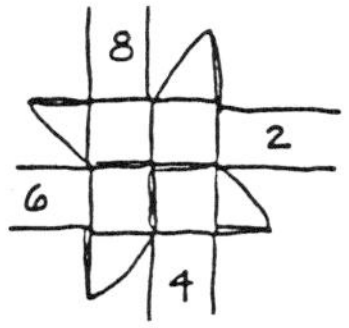

6. Turn the star over. Fold and tuck strips 8, 6, 4, and 2 (in that order), the same way you did the first four strips.

7. Poke a small hole in the star with a needle. Thread a piece of string through the hole and tie.

Variations on a Theme
Use two colors for a checkerboard look (be sure to alternate them in step 2 of the instructions). Weave together four different colors for a very festive star.

Star light, star bright,
First star I see tonight:
I wish I may, I wish I
  might,
Have the wish I wish
  tonight.

Many national flags have stars on them. The flag of the United States has fifty which represent the fifty states. What other countries have stars on their flags? Are they all five-pointed?

PLANT PARADISE

You can create your own landscape indoors with living plants. Make a terrarium out of an old aquarium or glass bottle for a landscape that will practically take care of itself.

Terraria were all the rage in the 19th century when Victorian households were not considered complete without a glass case planted with ferns.

The first botanical garden in Europe was founded in Padua, Italy in 1545.

TERRARIUM
Glass aquarium, at least 10-gallon size
Gravel
Charcoal
Potting soil
Humidity-loving plants, such as ferns, mosses, and small flowering species like miniature African violets
Mister

Note Your local garden center will have everything you need for your terrarium (except the container).

1. Wash the aquarium with soap and water; rinse well. Place a ½″ layer of gravel on the bottom of the aquarium. On top of this sprinkle a layer of charcoal. Put about 2″ of damp potting soil over this.

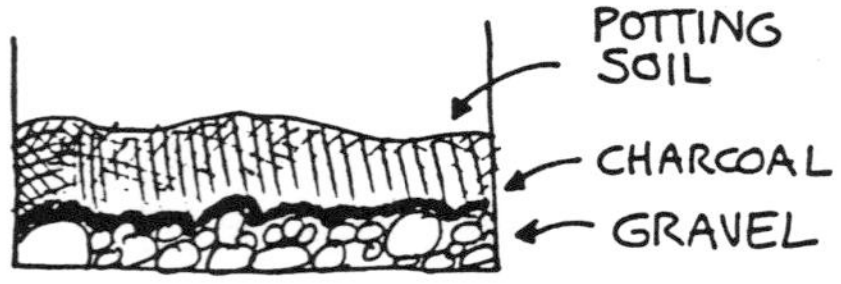

2. Remove each plant from its pot by holding it upside-down in one hand and giving the pot a sharp tap. The plant should fall right out into your hand.

3. Make a shallow depression for each plant in the potting soil. Place each plant in position, spreading its roots out horizontally and packing potting soil around it. (This helps to slow the growth of the plants somewhat.) Arrange the plants so that there is a focal point (a tall plant) and an interesting mix of colors and textures, just as you would if you were planning a drawing.

4. Spray the plants with the mister. Cover the top of the aquarium with a sheet of glass or with foil. Place the terrarium in indirect light, away from a heater.

Tip Terraria thrive with minimal care. Remove the lid for a short time if condensation collects on the inside of the glass; sponge away any algae that forms. Remove any dead leaves and blossoms, and trim those plants that are growing fast.

Variations on a Theme
For a different type of indoor landscape, plant a desert garden. Cacti and succulents can be grown together in a shallow container, even one without drainage holes. Put down a layer of gravel followed by a two-to-one mix of potting soil and sand.

Wear thick gloves when you transplant the cacti, or wrap a strip of folded newspaper around the plants to protect your hands from the sharp spines.

X MARKS THE SPOT

If you wanted to tell someone the way to your house, say, from your school, how would you go about it? You could give verbal directions, or you could make a map. This is a great way to get to know your neighborhood.

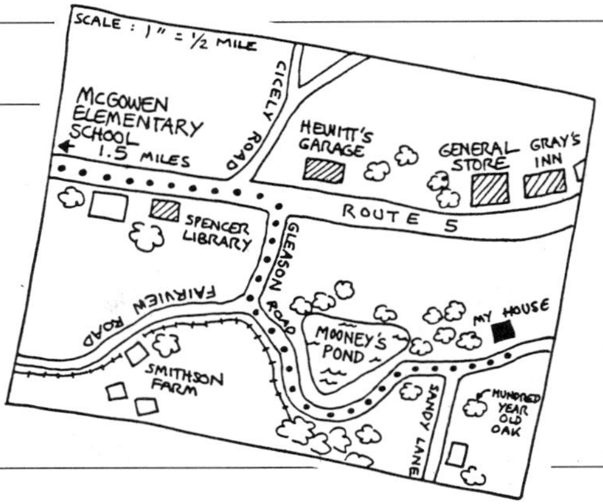

BIRDS' EYE VIEW MAP
Lightweight paper, about 12″ × 18″
Fine-point markers or colored pencils
Compass (optional)
Pedometer (optional)

Note You may already have a map of your general area, such as a topographical map or a map put out by your town or city. Use it to help you orient yourself, if you like.

1. Decide on the area you want to map. The map shown here is part of a rural school bus route, but you can make your map of your backyard, a nearby park, or anywhere you like.

2. To make your map as accurate as possible, measure the distance between major landmarks, such as turn-offs, crossroads and easy-to-identify buildings. If you are mapping a small area, walk the route, orienting yourself with a compass and counting your strides. (Or use a pedometer, a device that measures walking distances.)

If you are mapping a large area, ask your parents to drive the route with you. Use the odometer in the car (stopping frequently to make readings) to measure distances between landmarks.

Sketch a rough map of your route, penciling in all pertinent information.

3. Decide on the scale of your final map. The map shown here is drawn on the scale of 1″ to one-half mile. For mapping a backyard, a scale of 1″ to 1 yard (3 feet) might be a good choice. Be sure to indicate the scale and any other features that you are showing with symbols in a legend or key.

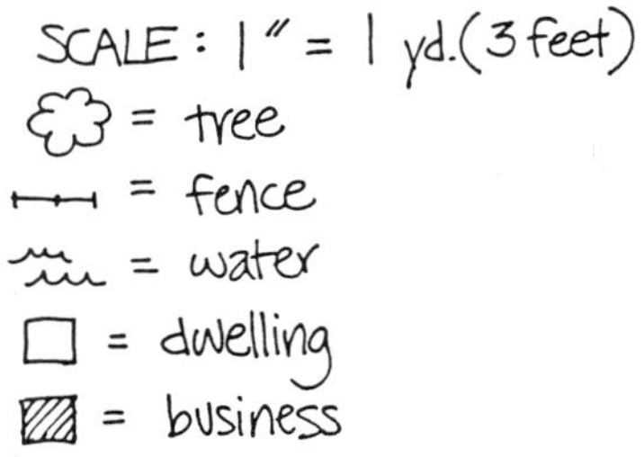

4. Draw the final map. Color it with felt-tip markers or colored pencils. Add as much detail as you like. Let dry, then fold for easier carrying (see page 116 for a first-rate way to fold maps).

Tip Give your map a protective coating of spray varnish. Have an adult help you with this and be sure to do the spraying outdoors.

The United States Geological Survey was organized in 1879 for the purpose of making large-scale topographical maps.

The Story of Art
The oldest known map dates from 2300 B.C. It's a small Babylonian clay tablet showing a wealthy estate.

The oldest known folded map is an ancient Egyptian map drawn on papyrus. Its grid of creases indicates that it was folded much the way maps continue to be folded to this day.

The study of maps and mapmaking is called cartography.

The maps used by pilots and sea captains are known as charts.

FOLDING A MAP

In order to fit in a pocket or the glove compartment of your car, most maps are folded. There are lots of ways of doing this, but none so as ingenious as this unusual method. Practice on a spare piece of paper before you fold your map in this way.

Start with a rectangle of paper. Fold the paper in half from the top to the bottom.

Fold the two top corners down so they meet in the middle. Crease well.

Return the corners to their original positions. Slip your fingers between the layers of the left side and push in and over so the paper is now folded as shown.

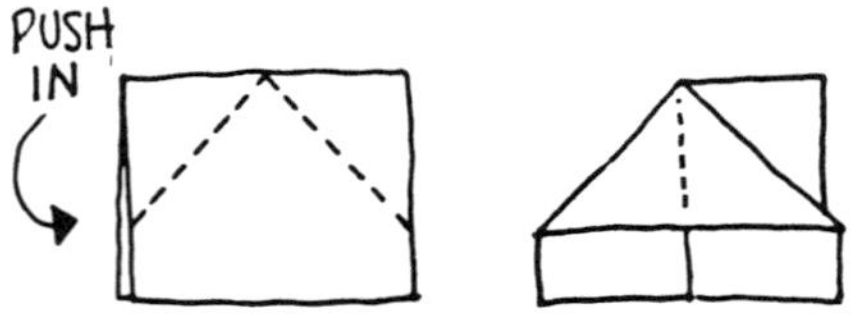

Turn the paper over and do the same on the back. The paper looks like this.

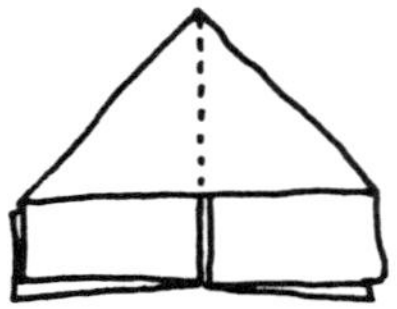

Push the top layer of the bottom left-hand corner in so that it overlaps the center slightly and looks like this.

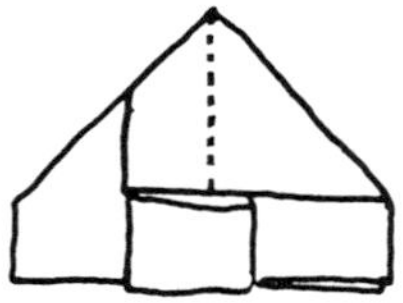

Do the same on the right-hand side of the top layer.

Turn the paper over and repeat these last two overlapping folds. The map should look like this. Crease all the folds well with your fingernails.

To open the map, slip one thumb under the uppermost fold; slip the other thumb under the fold at the back. Pull apart and the map will magically open.

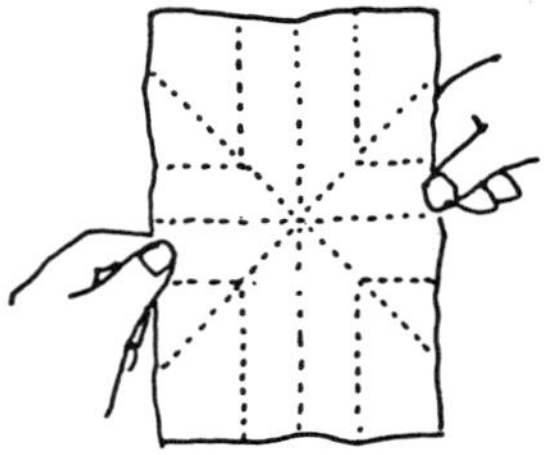

Maps can be made to show a variety of information. General reference maps are used to indicate the lay of the land, as well as roads and political boundaries such as states and countries.

Thematic maps are used to emphasize a topic or theme such as rainfall, population density, or natural resources.

HOME, SWEET HOME

As the saying goes, "Home is where you hang your hat"—or your baseball mitt or your ballet slippers! People throughout the world live in all sorts of houses. From grass huts to high-rise apartment houses, buildings for living in and for working in are designed with native materials, climate, and population density in mind.

Building styles are constantly evolving as fashions and customs change. Some buildings are always "in style" in their particular locale. What type of house do you live in?

NESTING INSTINCT

For a bird, home is where you build your nest. Many birds are finding it harder each year to find good nesting spots. You can help our fine-feathered friends make themselves at home with a sturdily-built birdhouse.

Supply the birds in your area with some nesting materials. Fill a mesh bag (the kind that onions come in) with short lengths of yarn and string, dried grass, even stuffing from old furniture and hair from a hairbrush. Hang the bag where the birds can find it, and watch them helping themselves to these materials.

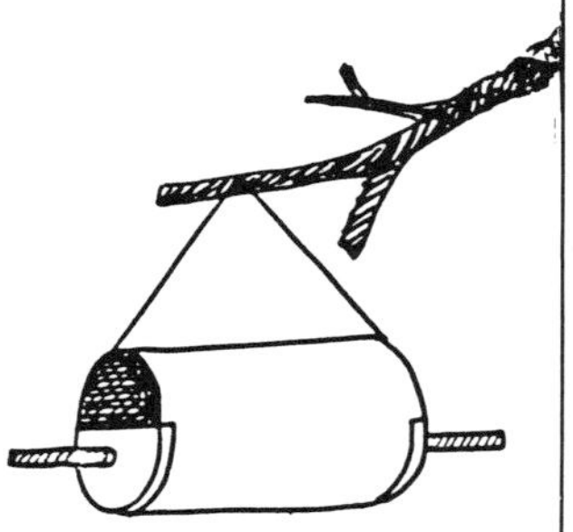

WOODEN BIRDHOUSE
1″ × 6″ pine, 5 feet long
Pencil
Ruler
Screws or galvanized nails, about 2 dozen
2″ hinge
Saw
Drill, with 1/4″ and 1 1/2″ bits
Screwdriver or hammer

1. With a pencil and a ruler, mark the length of pine following the diagram shown here.

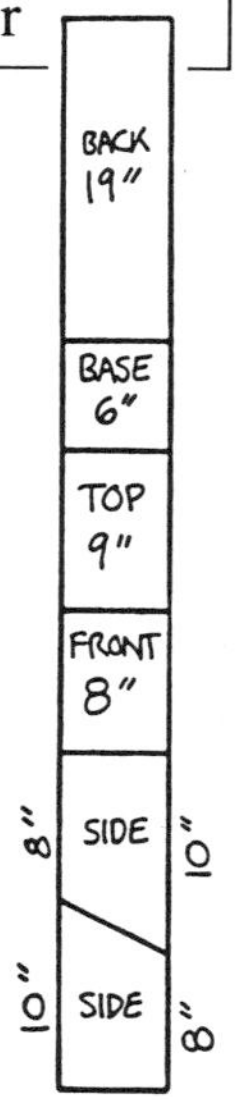

Another way to help out birds is to feed them in winter. Make a flat feeding table from some wood scraps, or fashion your own feeder from an empty milk carton or coffee can.

2. Cut the wood into six pieces. Make the cut separating the top and front pieces at an angle, as shown.

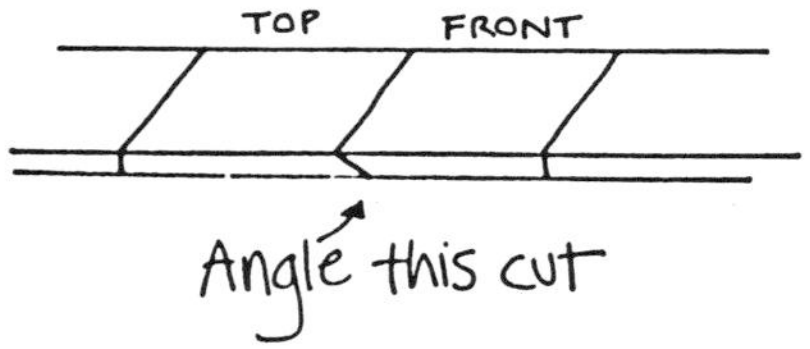

3. Drill a 1/4″ hole near the top of the back piece for hanging. Drill 5 or 6 1/4″ holes in the bottom piece for drainage. Drill a 1 1/2″ hole in the center of the front piece, about 1 1/2″ from the top.

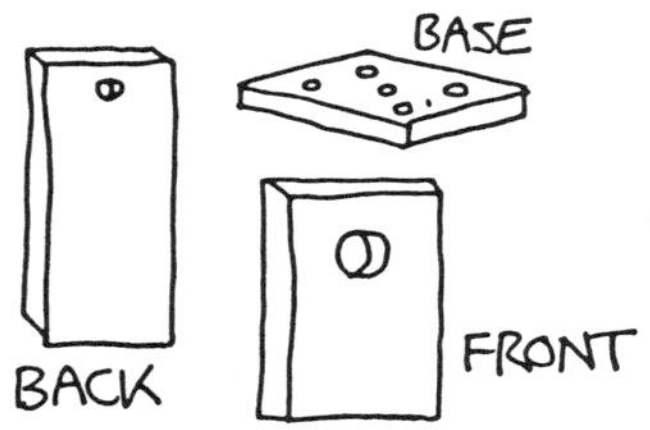

4. Screw or nail the front and two sides to the bottom. Screw the back in place, positioning it so that it hangs a couple of inches below the house base. Lay the top in place; attach it to the back with the hinge.

5. Hang the birdhouse away from direct sun and out of reach of cats. It should be 5-10 feet off the ground. Many birds prefer to make their nests in dead trees, so hang the house away from dense shade.

ENTRANCE HOLE SIZES

This basic birdhouse appeals to a number of birds, but you can encourage certain species to nest in the house by changing the size of the entrance hole.

Bluebirds prefer the 1 1/2″ opening called for in the instructions. Make the opening a little smaller for titmice and downy woodpeckers, say 1 1/4″ in diameter. Chickadees and house wrens like an even smaller hole—1 1/8″ will do nicely for them.

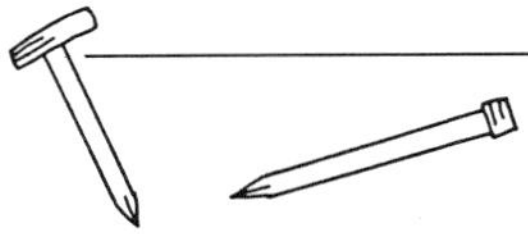

IF I HAD A HAMMER

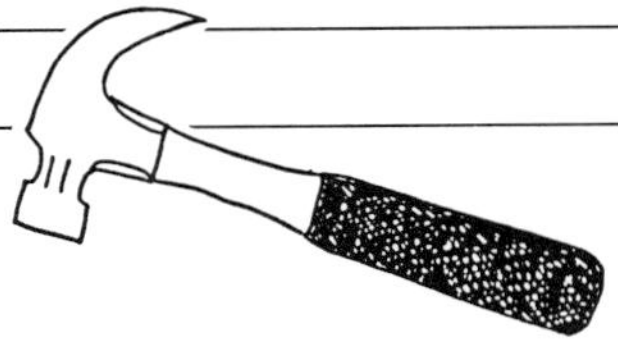

You don't need many tools to get started in woodworking. You can get by with just a saw (a good choice is a compass or keyhole saw which is easier to handle than a crosscut or ripping saw), a claw hammer (look for a lightweight adult model) and a supply of nails.

There are certain times, however, when you'll want to hold wood together with screws.

Match the screwdriver to the type of screw (Phillips-head or regular). It's a lot easier to screw in a screw, if you first make a pilot hole. Bang a nail partly in and pull it out, or drill a hole with a slightly smaller bit.

It's also a lot easier, and safer, to have something to hold your wood while you're working on it. A vice is like a second pair of hands, and strong ones at that!

There are both portable vices and those that clamp to worktables.

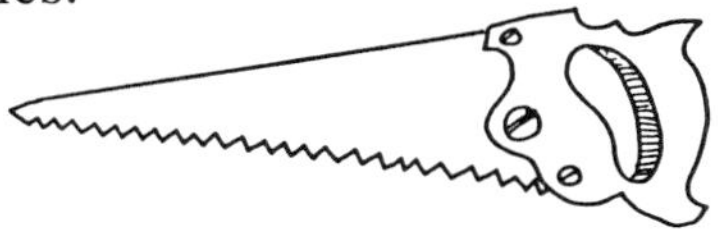

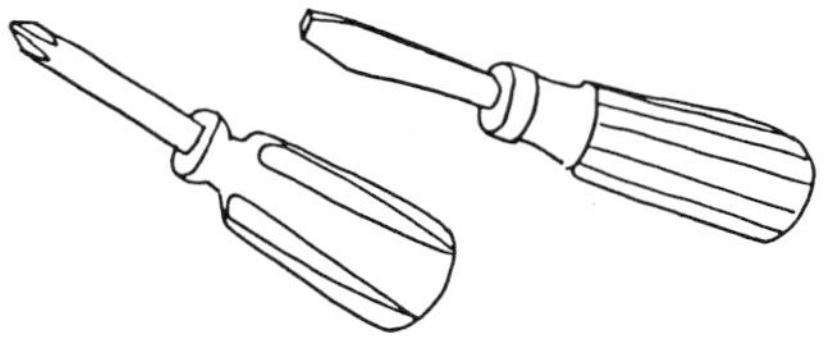

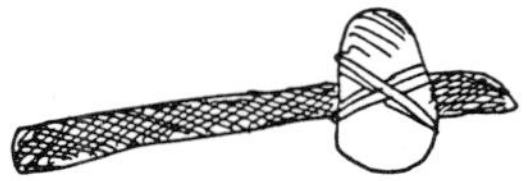

The earliest tool was probably the axe, made of flint or stone in Neolithic times (4000–5000 B.C.).

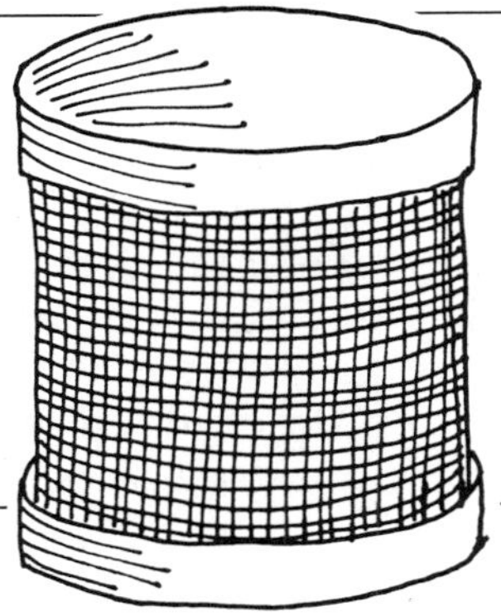

BUG BUNGALOW

Many insects make interesting guests in your home, especially when you provide them with comfortable lodgings. Here's a roomy cage you can make from a few things you may already have on hand.

INSECT CAGE
Round cake pans, 2 the same size
Metal screen, about 12″ × 30″
Masking tape
Non-hardening modeling clay

Note You can also use pie plates for the top and bottom of this cage.

1. Cut the screen 12″ wide and a couple of inches longer than the circumference of the cake pans. (The circumference is the measurement around the outside or perimeter.)

2. Roll the screen into a tube that fits snugly into the cake pans. Tape the seam with the masking tape. Cover any raw edges with tape, too.

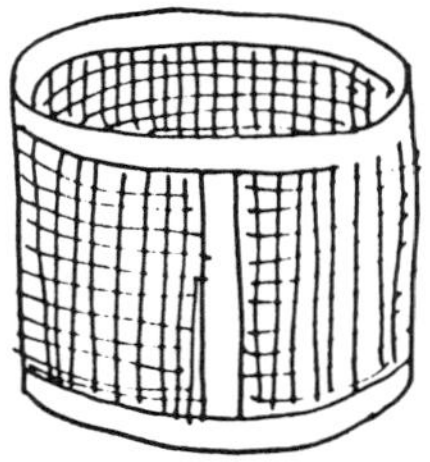

Many nature centers and museums have insect zoos. Look for one near you. If you have any questions regarding the care and feeding of insects, one of the zoo's staff will be happy to help you.

Your house is probably already home to a number of insects. Flies spend the winter in a dormant stage inside many homes. Spiders live year-round high up in the corners of rooms (you've probably seen their webs). All sorts of other creatures make themselves at home in wooden furniture, rugs, and woolen sweaters!

The first coins were issued around 700 B.C. in Lydia, an ancient country bordering on the Aegean. They were made from electrum (a gold and silver alloy) and had a picture of a tortoise on them.

3. Press some modeling clay along the inside perimeter of one of the pans. Place the screen tube in the pan. Pinch the clay all around the screen to secure it. Place the other pan on top of the screen.

Tip Provide food and water for any long-term insect residents. Put a sprig of the plant you found the insect on in a glass of water to keep it fresh. (Be sure to cover the glass with a piece of foil so that the insect doesn't drown). Sprinkle a few drops of water on a cotton ball to quench your insect's thirst. Don't forget to let your guest go when you have finished watching it.

SAVINGS INSTITUTION

The bank is the safest place to keep your money, but here's a good place for all your loose change until you make a deposit.

CARDBOARD BOX BANK
Poster board, about 12″ × 28″
Medium-weight paper, about 3″ square
Ruler
X-acto knife
White glue
Paint

Note The bank shown here is about 5″ square by 6″ high.

1. Draw the cutting outline of the bank on a piece of poster board. Use the dimensions shown here, or change them to suit the building you have in mind.

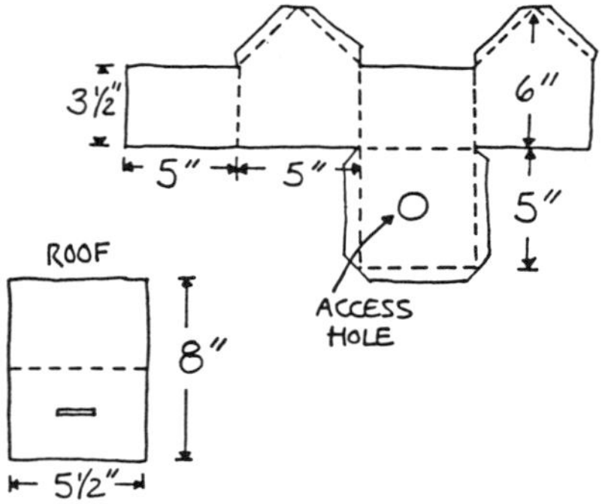

Be sure to mark the dotted fold lines.

2. Cut out the bank and its roof with either scissors or the X-acto knife. Score along the dotted lines by cutting only part way through the cardboard with the knife. Cut out the coin slot in the roof and the circle in the base of the bank.

3. Paint the cardboard. This is easiest to do before the bank is assembled. Let dry completely. Glue a circle of paper over the access hole in the base of the bank.

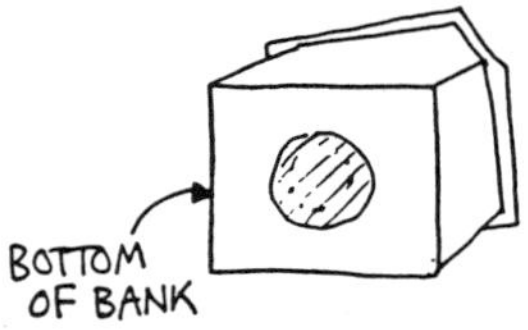

4. Fold the cardboard along the scored lines. Glue the tabs to the inside walls so they don't show. Glue one at a time; hold the joint together for a minute or so until the glue bonds. Attach the roof to the four gable tabs.

5. To remove money from the bank, tear off the paper covering the hole in the base. Glue a new piece of paper back on when you want to fill the bank again.

Variations on a Theme

Use your imagination, and any materials at hand, to create your own architectural bank. Give your bank a flat roof or a gambreled roof (the kind you see on a lot of barns). Make a pyramid from cut and scored corrugated cardboard. Use an empty oatmeal box to make a tower bank. Make it a free-standing tower or part of a building. Make a whole castle to hold the royal coffers!

A penny saved is a penny earned.
Poor Richard's Almanac

In the United States, the terms "dollars" and "cents" refer to money. Some money words from other countries include *peso* (Argentina), *pound* (England), *franc* (Belgium), *guilder* (Holland), and *schilling* (Austria).

DELICIOUS DWELLING

Here's an edible cookie house that's made up of all sorts of goodies that are good for you. Be sure to take a photograph of your house, because it's guaranteed not to last long!

COOKIE HOUSE
Peanut butter sugar wafers, 12 per house
Graham crackers, 3 per house
Royal icing (recipe on page 122)
Assorted nuts and dried fruits
Shredded wheat cereal, 1 large piece
Sturdy cardboard, about 8″ square

1. Make four walls for the house from three peanut butter wafers placed horizontally. Hold them together with some icing piped along the edges. Join the four walls at the corners with more icing.

Some real houses have ornately carved wooden decorations along the edges of their roofs and porches. This is sometimes known as gingerbread style!

Remember Hansel and Gretel? It seems they may have been responsible for the birth of the gingerbread house. In the 1800s, the Brothers Grimm told the tale of two children who happen upon a wicked witch living in a gingerbread house. The story was turned into a popular opera by Engelbert Humperdinck, and everyone who saw it wanted to make a gingerbread house of their own.

2. Cut a graham cracker in half diagonally for the gables. Pipe some icing along two ends of the house; attach the gables. Pipe icing along the gables and place two double graham crackers on them to form a peaked roof.

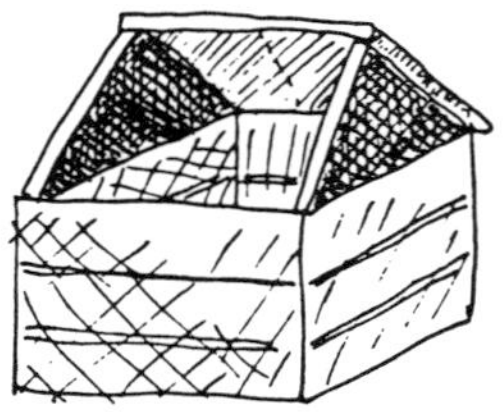

Place the house on the cardboard and set aside to dry.

3. Decorate the house and yard. The house shown here has a shingled roof made from whole almonds stuck on with just a little bit of icing. The door and windows are made from strips of dried apricot "glued" in place with icing. Raisins are used for the door handle and to line the path up to the front door. The grass is shredded wheat sprinkled over some piped icing that has been spread about with a knife. Decorate your house any way you like.

Variations on a Theme

To make a larger dwelling, make a batch of gingerbread cookie dough. Roll it out and cut it into the walls and roof of a house. Look for a gingerbread recipe in a cookie cookbook or in an all-around basic cookbook.

You can decorate your house with candy, too, of course.

ROYAL ICING

Royal icing is perfect for decorating cookies and assembling cookie houses, because it dries hard. The following recipe makes about 2 cups, which is plenty for decorating 3 or 4 peanut butter wafer houses.

Combine 1½ cups sifted powdered sugar, 1 egg white, a pinch of salt, and 1 teaspoon lemon juice in a medium-size bowl. Beat with an electric mixer for at least 5 minutes, until the mixture is fluffy and stands in peaks when you lift out the beaters. Add more lemon juice if it seems too thick; more powdered sugar if it's too runny.

The easiest way to decorate with royal icing is to pipe it out of a decorating bag. If you have one, use it with a small plain tip. Otherwise, make your own from a heavy plastic bag. Fill the bag with about half the icing, squeezing it so it flows down into one corner. Cut the very tip of that corner with scissors. Twist the bag closed, squeezing the icing out with one hand while guiding it with the other hand.

Royal icing can be tinted with food colors. Add more powdered sugar, if the food coloring makes the icing too thin.

Use royal icing to decorate cookies and cakes any time of year. With a fine "writing" tip, you can personalize confections, as well as draw designs and pictures on rolled cookies and cake tops.

CITY LIMITS

Want to be a town planner? With a bagful of wood scraps, you can build a whole town of houses and shops the scale of miniature cars and trucks. They are perfect for playing with both indoors and out.

SCRAP WOOD TOWN
Assorted wood scraps (see *Note*)
Saw
Sandpaper
Waterproof glue
Permanent markers or paint

Note You should be able to round up all sorts of interesting wood scraps. Ask a local carpenter for the scraps that accumulate at the end of a work day. Look for molding at a lumberyard. Check under *Wood Products* in the Yellow Pages. You can often purchase whole bags of turned wood scraps from the businesses listed.

1. Study the wood pieces you have collected. Some of the shapes may already look like buildings (or parts of buildings).

2. Glue the wood pieces with waterproof glue. (If you plan to play with the town indoors only, you can use white glue.) Let dry.

3. Paint the houses and shops, if you like. Add details with the permanent markers.

Variations on a Theme

Larger buildings can be made from cardboard cartons and other containers. Cut out windows and doors with scissors or an X-acto knife. Paint the boxes with thick poster paints or cover them with construction paper.

Settlements of houses and other buildings go by different names depending on how many people the settlement supports. Village, town, city, and metropolis are just some of the names used. What other ones can you think of?

Some cities are built in a regular grid with streets crossing one another at right angles. Much of New York City is arranged in this way. Other cities have evolved along different lines. Paris is one city that has avenues radiating from a central point.

The city

St. Augustine, Florida is the oldest city in the United States. It was settled by the Spanish in 1565.

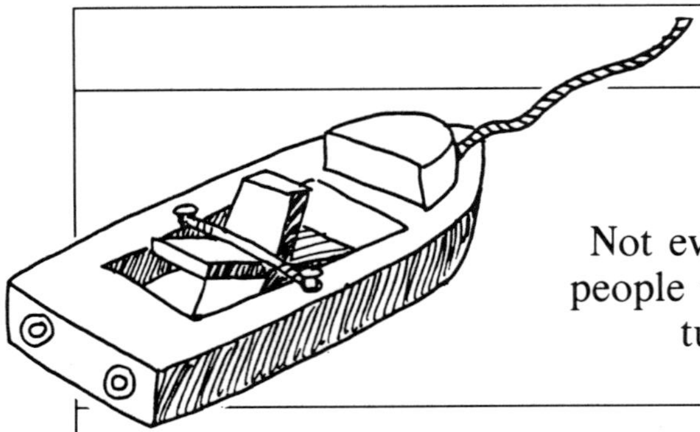

A HOME A-FLOAT

Not everyone lives in a house built on solid ground. Millions of people worldwide make their homes on the water. Here's a miniature houseboat you can make that is paddle-powered.

In Europe, canals were once used for transporting goods. There was room on the barges not only for the boatman, but for his whole family as well. Today many of these boats are used as vacation homes.

WOODEN PADDLEBOAT
1″ × 6″ pine, about 12″ long
1/4″ × 2″ pine, about 6″ long (see *Note*)
Saw
3 small nails
Hammer
Rubber band
String
Assorted wood scraps (optional)

Note Look for pine molding at a lumberyard that is close to 1/4″ × 2″ in size, or slice a thin piece from a larger board to these dimensions.

1. Draw the outline of a boat on the 1″ × 6″ pine, as shown. Cut the shape out with the saw.

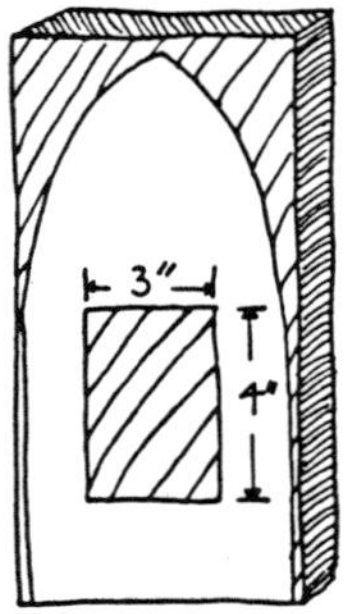

2. Cut the 1/4″ × 2″ pine into two pieces about 3″ long. Carefully cut a notch in the middle of each piece, about halfway through, as shown.

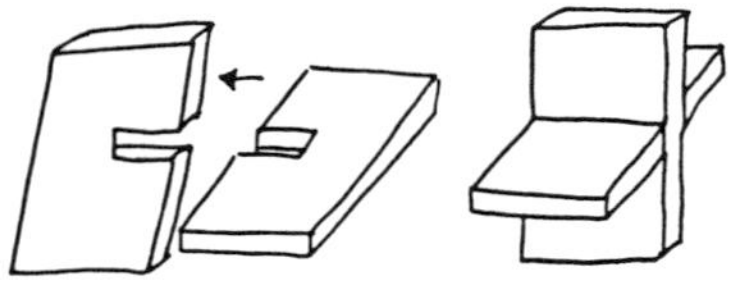

Fit the two pieces together to make a cross. This is the paddle wheel.

3. Hammer two small nails on either side of the opening at the back of the boat. They should stick up about 1/2″ or so. Wrap the rubber band around the paddle (so that it straddles it) and hook the ends of the rubber band over the two nails.

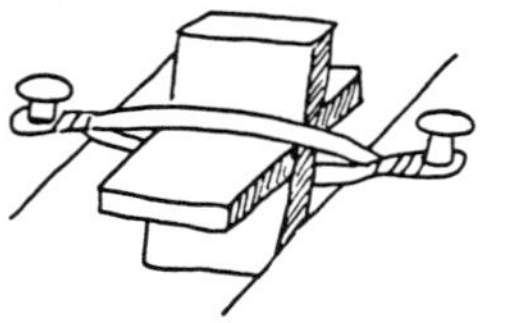

4. Hammer the third nail to the front of the boat, again leaving the nail sticking up about 1/2″. Tie a length of string to this nail (this is so you can easily retrieve the boat if it floats far from shore).

5. Use the assorted wood scraps to give the boat a little cabin, if you like. Another option is to simply string a railing around the perimeter of the boat.

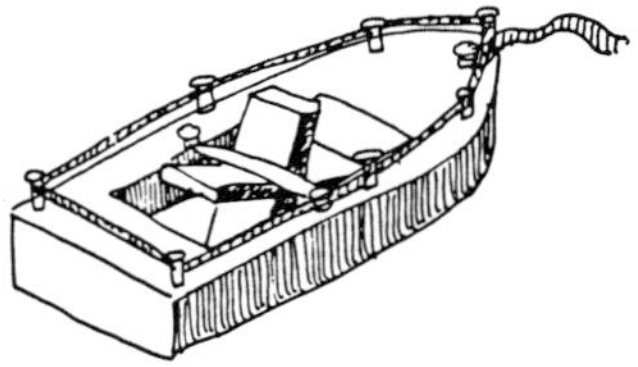

6. To make the paddleboat go, simply wind up the rubber band nice and tight and release the boat in water.

In many harbors in Southeast Asia, thousands of houseboats are anchored next to one another. Families cook, eat, and sleep on their boats.

THE PLAY'S THE THING

With this simple wooden set-up and a few blankets or pieces of fabric, you can create a house, a shop, a puppet theater, or even a secret hiding place! Make the three frames as shown, or add on more for even larger structures.

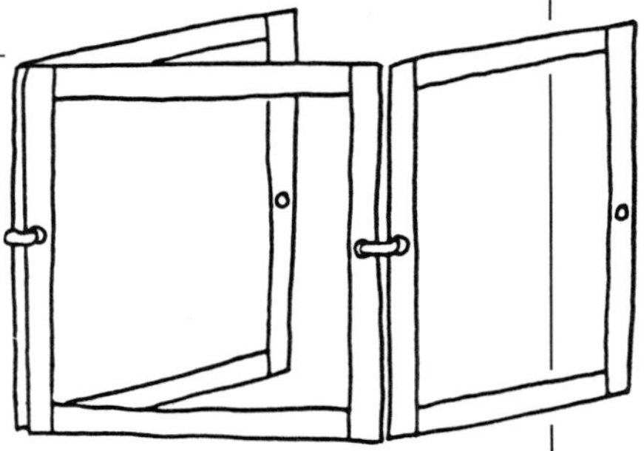

WOODEN PLAY FRAMES
36 feet of 1″ × 1″ pine
12 L-shaped corner braces (with screws)
Saw
Drill, with 1/4″ bit
Screwdriver
Sandpaper
3 leather strips, each 12″ long

Note If you can't find 1″ × 1″ lumber, have a lumberyard rip 1″ × 3″ pine boards down the middle.

1. Cut the lumber into six pieces 36″ long, and six pieces 32½″ long. Sand any rough spots off the ends of each piece.

2. Make a square with two 36″ pieces and two 32½″ pieces, as shown. Screw the wood together at the corners with the braces. Drill pilot holes first with the drill; then screw in the screws.

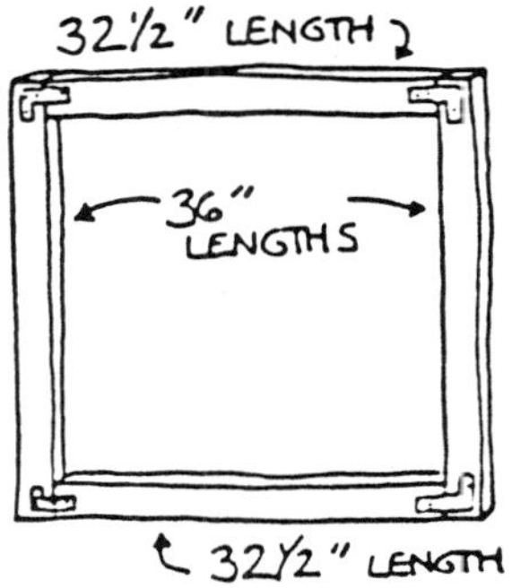

Make two more frames the same way with the remaining lumber.

3. Drill a 1/4″ hole in the very center of each vertical side of each frame. Lace a leather strip through the holes of two frames to hold them together (lace them loose enough so the frames can be placed at right angles to one another).

To make a square house, lace the three frames together (the fourth side of the house is left open). To make a triangular structure, lace all three frames together. Remove one of the frames when you want to use the set-up as a partition in front of a doorway, for instance.

Tip Use sheets and lightweight blankets to drape over the frames to create houses and other play places. Place one or two frames in front of a doorway or other opening to make a puppet theater. Lash branches that have leaves on them to the frames to create a blind from which to watch wildlife.

There are other play structures you can make. Do you have a low-branching tree on your property? Make a tree house! If you'd rather keep your feet on the ground, use brush and fallen branches to construct a secret hide-away. Don't let winter and heavy snowfall keep you from enjoying house-building. Build a snow fort or an igloo using a bread pan to mold the snow into stackable bricks.

FINE FURNISHINGS

Since the beginning of time, people have taken pride in their surroundings. Comfort and utility always come first, but most home furnishings are decorated with meaningful and imaginative designs.

Potters, tinsmiths, basketmakers, and weavers are sometimes considered artisans rather than artists, but there's no question *artistry* plays a very important part in the making of household goods and furnishings.

A BANNER YEAR

Flags and banners are used to represent nations, communicate information, and add decoration. Design your own banner to hang in your room. Make it purely decorative or include some of your interests in the design to make it more meaningful.

FELT BANNER
Felt or burlap for the background, about 24″ × 36″
Felt squares in assorted colors
Fabric trims, such as rick rack, lace, braid, sequins, beads, and buttons
White glue
Needle and thread

Note Felt is the perfect choice for both a banner background and its decorative elements, because it doesn't ravel and can be glued. It also comes in a rainbow of colors. There are plenty of other fabrics you can use, however, but you should turn under any raw edges to prevent raveling.

1. Think about what you want to include in your banner. Sketch your ideas in color. Make a scaled-down version on graph paper, or cut out full-size pieces of paper colored with crayons or markers. Then, pin them on the fabric to see how size, placement, and color work together.

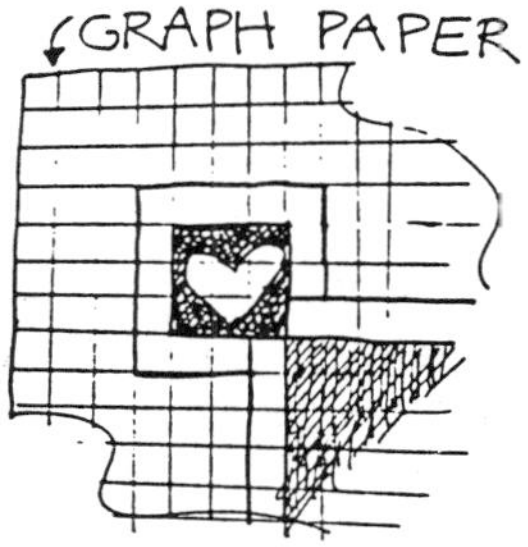

2. Cut and assemble your banner, either gluing the pieces to the background or sewing them on. Use as little glue as possible, placing a series of dots over the back of each piece. Press glued pieces under weights such as a pile of books or bricks, until dry.

3. Hang the banner. You can do this in a number of ways. Simply tack it to a wall (or door) with pushpins or thumbtacks. For something a little fancier, fold over the top edge of the banner (you should have included a little extra in the length to do this) and glue or stitch a long pocket. Slip a dowel or section of a broom handle through the pocket. Tie some cord to either end of the dowel and hang.

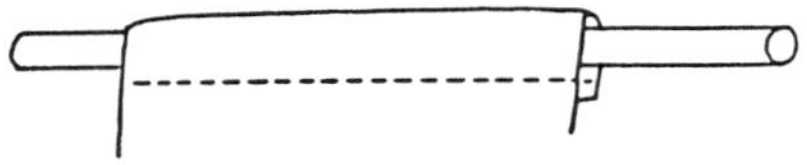

Variations on a Theme
The banner described above is best hung indoors or in a well-protected spot. To make a banner that is meant to hang outdoors, it's best to use fabrics that will stand up to the weather. Nylon is a good choice, as it dries quickly (so it won't mildew), but sturdy cotton and cotton blends, sprayed with a protective coating used on upholstery fabrics, work well, too. To make a Japanese carp windsock that is hung like a banner, see page 58.

You may have heard the story about Betsy Ross, and how she made the first flag for the United States. There is no historical evidence that she really did so. The first public mention of the fact was made by her grandson almost one hundred years later. He had no proof, unfortunately.

Did you know?
The word *banner* means "distinguished from others, especially in excellence." So that means a banner year is a very good year indeed!

THE MAGIC CARPET

Rugs and carpets are popular floor coverings because they are warm, muffle sound, and add color to a room. Here's a painted floorcloth you can make that has one other purpose—you can play checkers on it!

The Story of Art
Floorcloths were popular in both Europe and the United States during the 18th and 19th centuries. They were used not only as a way to duplicate extensive rugs, but they were popular as warm weather rugs, when the woolen ones were put in storage for the summer.

CHECKERBOARD FLOORCLOTH
1 yard 36″-wide canvas
Gesso (optional)
Ruler
Masking tape
X-acto knife
Latex housepaint or acrylic paints, in at least 2 colors
Brush
Polyurethane
White glue

Note There are many grades of canvas available. Artists' canvas made from linen or cotton fibers is very expensive. Look for a thinner canvas at your local fabric store. It is reasonably priced and works just as well.

1. Iron the canvas to smooth out any wrinkles. Find a place to lay it out flat, where it won't be disturbed. Place it on a layer of newspaper to protect the floor or work table.

2. Paint the canvas with gesso (an acrylic medium that is meant to be used under acrylic paints to make them brighter and hold up longer) or a coat of latex housepaint. If you are using housepaint, make it the lighter of the two colors you have chosen for your checkerboard pattern. Let dry.

3. Mark off the checkerboard grid with a ruler and pencil. A 36″-square piece of canvas can be marked off into 4″ squares. (There are 64 squares in a checkerboard—8 going one way, and 8 the other.)

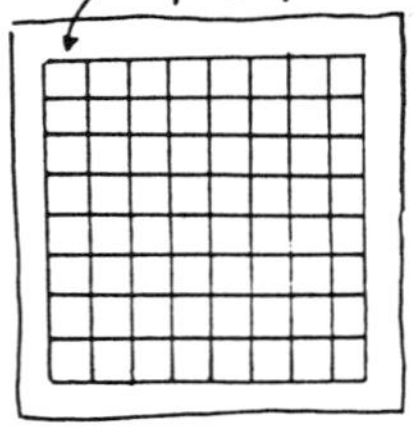

4. Carefully lay down strips of masking tape to mask off those squares that aren't painted the second color. Use the X-acto knife to trim the ends of the masking tape precisely. Use just enough pressure to cut through the tape, and not into the canvas. Press down hard on the tape to make sure the bond is good.

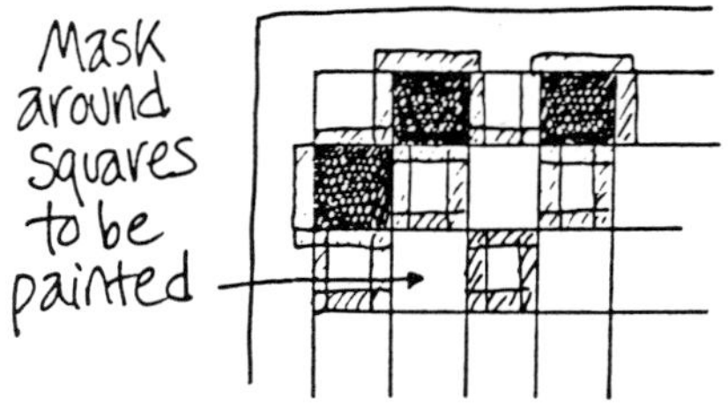

5. Paint the squares you have masked around with the second color. Work from the outside in to avoid getting paint under the tape. Let dry.

6. Peel away the masking tape. Place more tape along the outside edge of the checkerboard, and again about an inch from that, to mask off a border to be painted in the second color (or a third).

Paint the border; let dry. Remove the tape.

7. Turn the hem of the cloth under all the way around. Glue it in place. Put weights around the hem, such as books or bricks, until it dries.

8. Paint one or two coats of clear polyurethane on the cloth to protect it from wear. (This is best done outdoors where there is plenty of ventilation. Ask your parents to help you with this step.) Let the first coat dry; then lightly sand it with fine sandpaper before painting on the second coat.

PLAY PIECES

You can use the checkers that come with a regular checkerboard to play the game on your floorcloth, but if you'd like the checkers bigger, here's a simple idea for making your own.

Cut 24 2½″ circles out of cardboard. Paint the fronts and backs of 12 of them in one color; paint the remaining 12 with another color (use the same colors you painted the checkerboard with or choose 2 different colors). On the backs of all 24 checkers, paint or draw a crown. When a piece is "kinged," simply turn the checker over to display the crown.

Variations on a Theme

Instead of painting a checkerboard pattern on a floorcloth, paint a design typical of other types of rugs. Paint the canvas in the earth colors of Navajo rugs (see *Mr. Sandman* on page 70 for some American Indian motifs you can use). Create an intricate Asian design or an abstract design typical of a Swedish rya rug. Copy a design from a book or from a rug in your house.

Checkers is an ancient game. It was popular in China, Java, and Borneo for hundreds of years before it made its way to Europe, and later the United States.

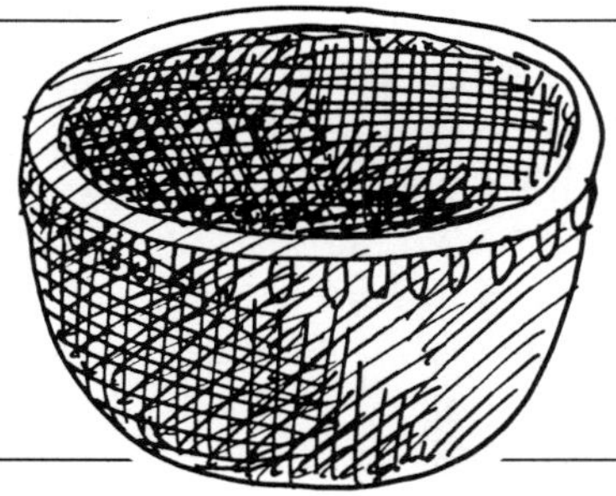

BOWLED OVER

You can make a very sturdy bowl with papier-mâché pulp and an open mold such as a colander or shallow bowl. Add decorative touches by modeling the pulp with your fingers or with paint.

PAPIER-MÂCHÉ PULP BOWL

- Papier-mâché pulp (see page 74)
- Mold, such as a colander or shallow bowl
- Petroleum jelly

1. Have the papier-mâché pulp ready. Smear petroleum jelly on the inside of the colander or bowl you are using as a mold.

The first pottery bowls were probably made by accident. Archaeologists speculate that clay was originally used to line woven baskets to make them watertight. It wasn't long before someone ventured to make a vessel just out of clay itself.

2. Press the pulp into the mold, patting it with your hands or the back of a wooden spoon to make a compact, even layer. Make sure the pulp is not too wet; squeeze out some of the moisture first to help speed up the drying.

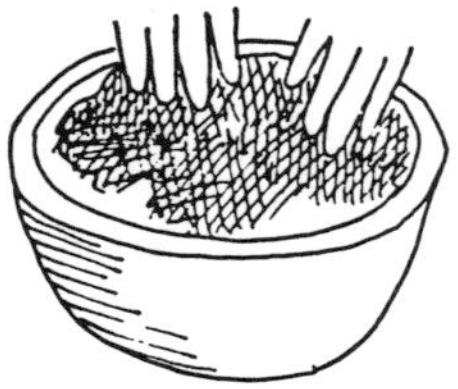

Bring the pulp right up to the top of the mold and flatten it or taper the pulp at the top for a different look. You can also add a decorative rim to your bowl, by pinching the pulp with your fingers or pressing down on it with the tines of a fork (like a piecrust is decorated).

3. Let the pulp dry. This takes from 4 to 7 days, depending on how warm it is. Slow drying is necessary to keep the pulp from drying unevenly and distorting.

4. Remove the bowl from the mold. (Insert a knife blade under the rim to ease it away from the mold.) Paint the bowl with acrylics, if you like, or cover it completely with a coat of clear varnish.

Variations on a Theme
Instead of using the inside of a bowl as a mold, invert the bowl and pat the pulp in place on the *outside* of a bowl. Be sure to coat the mold with petroleum jelly first. This gives your papier-mâché bowl a smooth finish on the inside and a rough one on the outside.

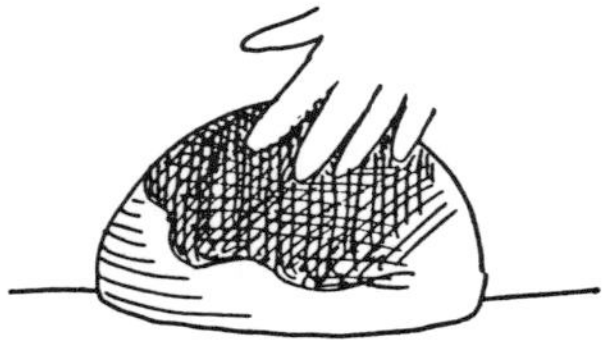

The earliest surviving objects made from papier-mâché are two Chinese helmets dating from the 2nd century. They were painted with many coats of lacquer which served to strengthen the helmets, so that they were effective protection.

MISH MASH

You can alter the finished look of papier-mâché pulp (mash) in a number of ways. You can start out with a finer pulp by chopping up the paper in the blender for a longer time. You can also sand the dried pulp with sandpaper to change the look.

The color of the pulp can also be varied. You can simply use colored paper scraps when you start out (try adding some colored tissue paper—it "bleeds" freely), or you can dye the pulp with fabric dyes (be sure to protect your hands with rubber gloves). Add a little liquid dye to the pulp and work it in with your hands. Keep in mind the color will be lighter when dry. Experiment by combining some dyed pulp with some undyed pulp for a mottled look.

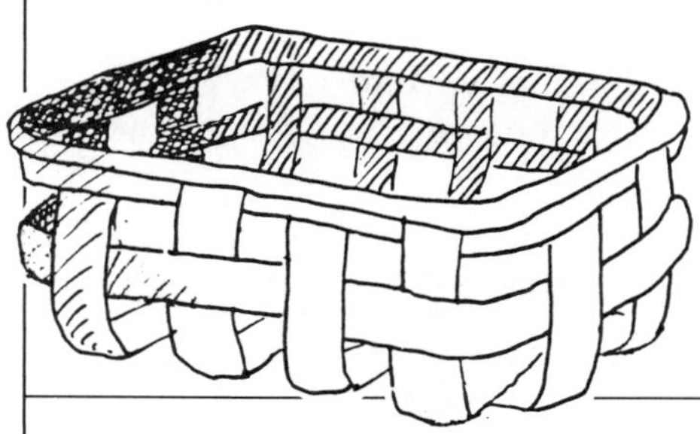

A-TISKET A-TASKET

This woven salt dough basket is surprisingly tough. With normal care it will hold up for many years. Use it to hold rolls and sliced bread at the dinner table or odds and ends around the house.

SALT DOUGH BASKET
Salt dough (see page 81)
Bread pan
Cooking oil
Rolling pin
Ruler
Knife
Varnish

Note You can use any ovenproof pan or bowl as a frame for this basket. Use it inverted as described in the instructions or form your basket in the inside of the pan or bowl.

1. Have the salt dough ready. Most dough baskets require about half a batch of dough as made on page 81.

2. Turn the bread pan upside down. Rub cooking oil all over the outside.

3. Roll the salt dough out about 1/4″ thick. (Sprinkle a little flour on your work surface, if it is sticking.) Cut the dough into 3/4″ strips using the ruler and the knife.

4. Lay 5 or 6 strips across the bread pan as shown.

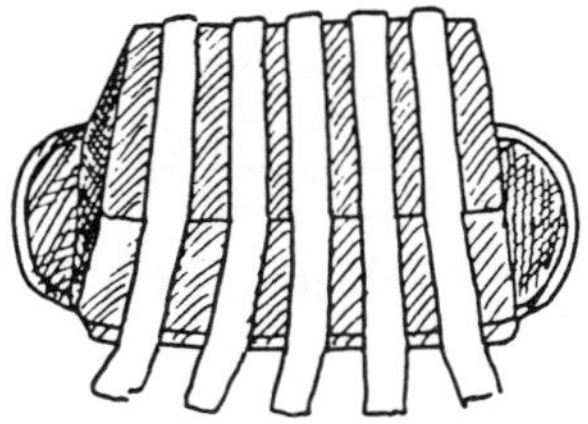

Then lay 2 or 3 strips lengthwise, weaving them over and under the crosspieces.

Weave two strips around the sides of the pan. Hold the strips in place by wetting the dough with a very small amount of water where two strips meet. Press the dough together firmly but gently. If your strips are not long enough to go all the way around the sides, splice them together. Join the new strip right next to the old, preferably under a crossing strip for added stability.

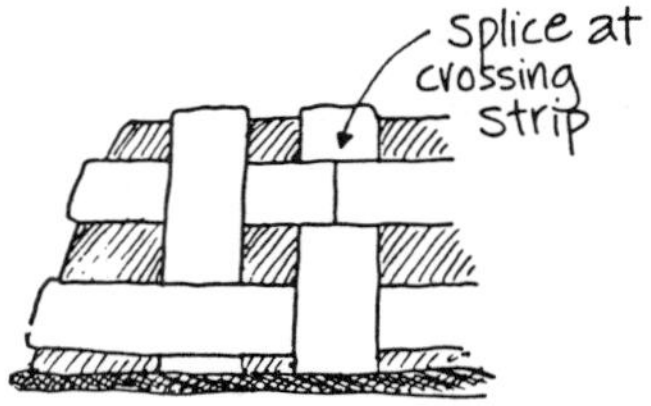

5. Cut the excess off all the strips at the lip of the bread pan. Roll some dough into a long rope and wind it around the pan right at the lip. Moisten the ends of the strips to help them stick to the dough rope.

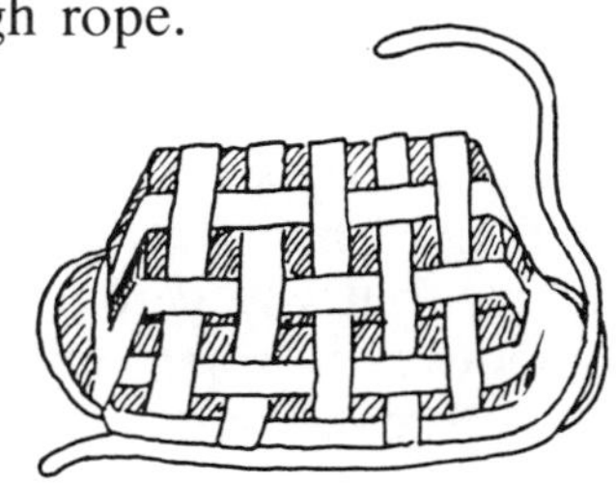

6. Let the basket dry at room temperature (this takes about 3 days), or bake it in a 325°F oven for about an hour. Let cool completely before carefully

Baskets are made from every imaginable material. Most are made from cane and reed, but they can be made from everything from pine needles to cloth coils. While many former handcrafts are now machine-made, baskets continue to be made only by hand.

The oldest known baskets were unearthed in Faiyum, Egypt. They are thought to be between 10,000 and 12,000 years old.

lifting the dough basket off the bread pan.

7. Seal the basket with a coat of varnish to strengthen it and protect it from moisture. Brush on an acrylic varnish or spray the basket with artists' fixative.

Tip Give the basket a textured look by poking holes in the soft dough with a toothpick or the tines of a fork. Experiment with other textures using other utensils.

Give the basket a golden-brown color by brushing it with a beaten egg yolk mixed with a little water before baking it in the oven.

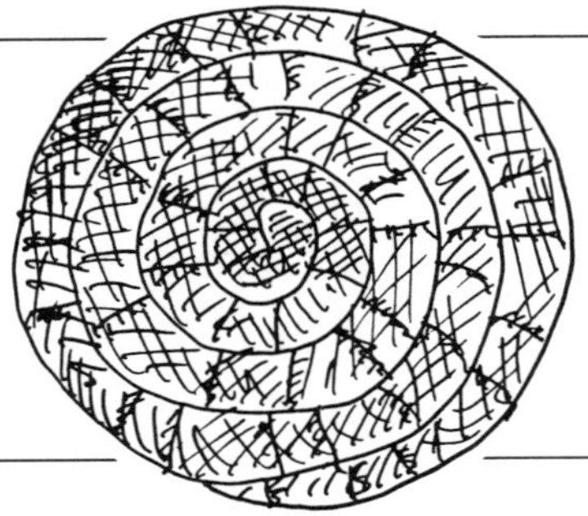

HOT SPOT

Cloth-covered craft cord or rope can be shaped into circles, ovals, and even baskets. This simple circle made from cord and torn fabric strips makes a perfect trivet for hot dishes.

Some trivets are three-legged iron stands. That's what the *tri* in trivet stands for— three, like the *tri* in triangle, tripod, and triple.

CLOTH COIL TRIVET
1/2″ craft cord or rope, about 7 feet long
1/4 yard cotton or cotton-blend fabric
Scissors

Note Fabric stores carry 1/4″ and 1/2″ craft cord made for covering with fabric, but you can also use thick, lightweight rope. Seven feet of 1/2″ cord makes a circular trivet about 7 1/2″ in diameter.

1. Cut each end of the cord at an angle.

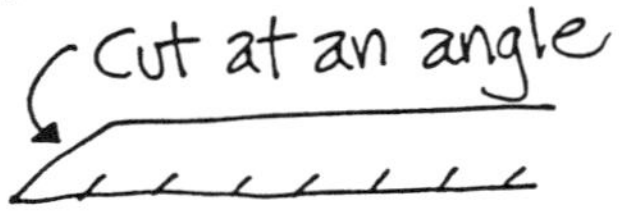

2. Tear the fabric into 1″ strips. Do this by cutting slits an inch apart at one end of the fabric and tearing the fabric at each slit.

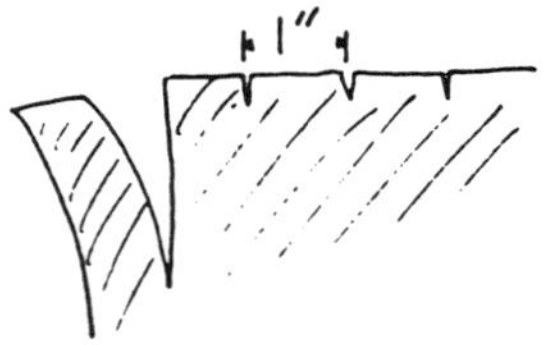

3. Place one end of a fabric strip along one end of the cord, as shown. Reverse direction and wrap the strip around the cord. As you wrap, overlap each previous strip so that no cord shows.

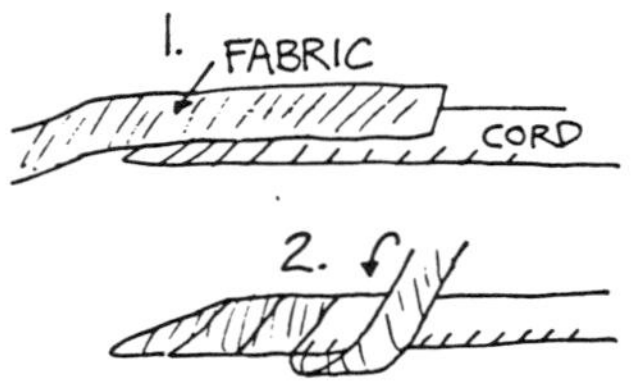

4. When you have wrapped about 4″ of cord, bend the wrapped portion into a tight circle. Secure it in place by wrapping the fabric strip in a figure-eight that loops through the circle and back out to the yet unwrapped portion of the cord.

5. Continue wrapping the cord and coiling it, holding the coils in place with figure-eight twists every 2 or 3 inches. When you have used up one fabric strip, wrap the start of another under the last few inches of the first, and continue.

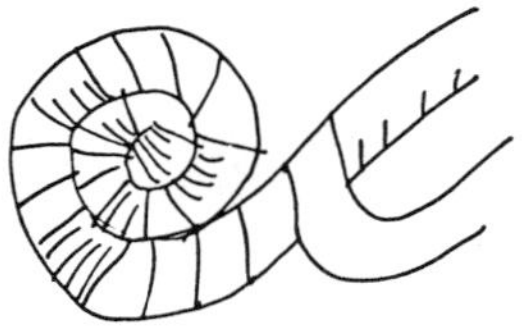

6. Finish the coil by wrapping the tapered end of the cord together with the previous coil, as if they were one. Pull the end of the strip through the final wraps and trim off the end.

Tip You can thread the end of the fabric strip through a large-eye tapestry needle to help you pull the strip between the coils.

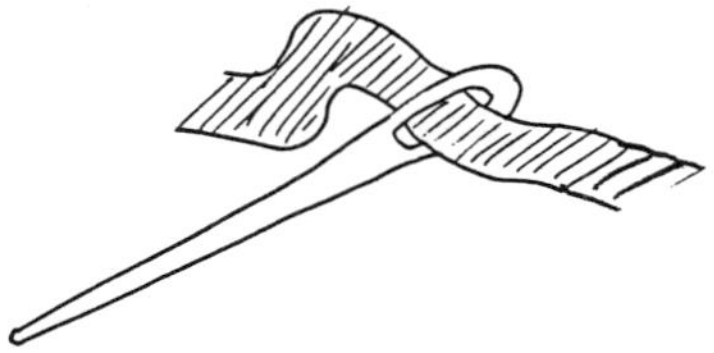

Variations on a Theme
Change colors as you coil by using different colored strips. Experiment with different shapes. Make an oval trivet by shaping the first bend in the cord into an oval. Make a basket by coiling straight up, angling out the coils a little as each circle is completed..

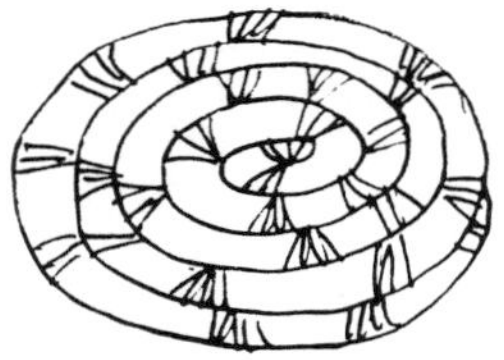

Many Native Americans make coil baskets. Intricate designs are incorporated into the baskets as they take shape.

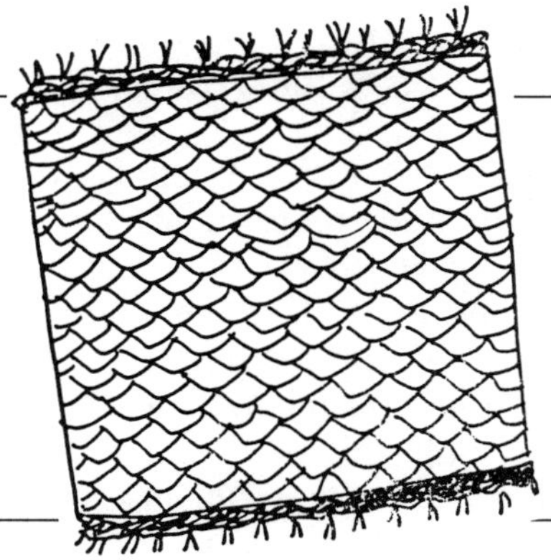

HANDLE WITH CARE

Weaving is easy with a simple frame loom you can make yourself. Use torn fabric strips to make thick, cushiony potholders. With this same technique, you can also weave placemats, handbags, and even rugs.

WOVEN RAG POTHOLDER
Cotton or cotton-blend fabric, about 1/2 yard
Cotton yarn or thin string
Medium-weight yarn
Paper, about 8½″ × 11″
Flat stick, such as a stir stick used for painting
Frame loom (see page 134)

Note The instructions here are for a potholder measuring about 7″ square. Make yours larger (or smaller) by changing the number of warp threads on your loom.

1. Tear the fabric into 1″ strips. Do this by cutting slits at one end of the fabric an inch apart and tearing the fabric at each slit.

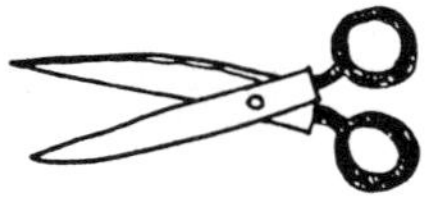

2. Wrap cotton thread around the loom as described in *Frame Loom* on page 134. Wrap enough yarn to make 28 warp threads.

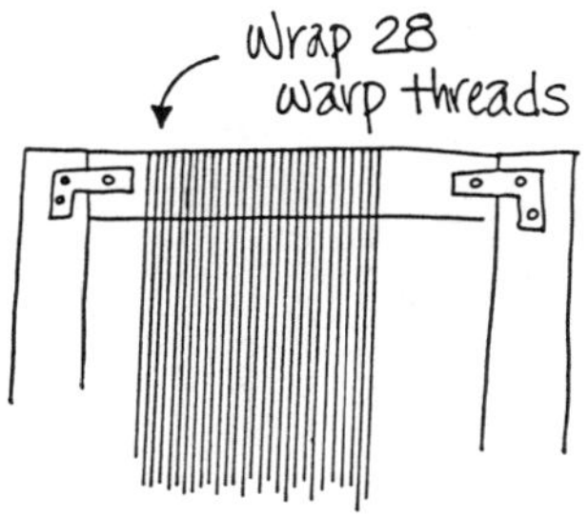

Weaving is closely related to basketry. The main difference is the need for a loom, because the fibers used for weaving cloth and tapestries are more flexible than the fibers used in making baskets.

The Story of Art
Perhaps the most famous woven tapestry is the one popularly known as the Bayeux Tapestry after the name of the town where it was discovered. It is actually a woven strip decorated with embroidery, illustrating William the Conqueror's invasion of England in 1066. The piece is 20″ wide and an incredible 230 feet long! It is not known who made the tapestry, nor how long it took.

3. Place the piece of paper over the warp threads that are wrapped around the back of the loom to block them from view. (This makes it a lot easier to concentrate on the warp threads you're working with.) Slip the painter's stir stick under the warp threads at the front of the loom.

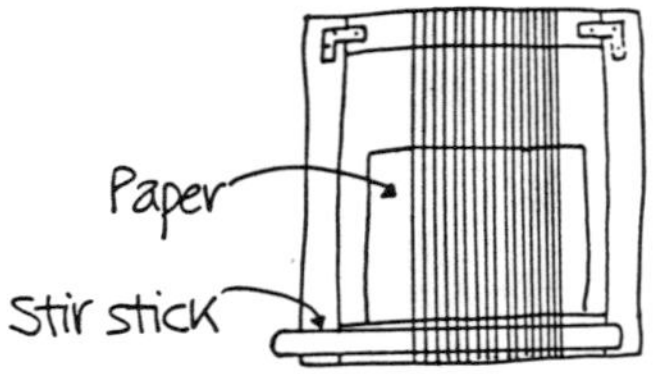

4. Wrap about 12 feet of medium-weight yarn into a small bundle. Weave about 3″ of the loose end through the warp threads. Now weave over and under the warp threads from side to side. Push the yarn down against the stir stick with your fingers, each time you reach a side. To prevent the far warp threads from being pulled inward, gently arch the yarn before you push it down.

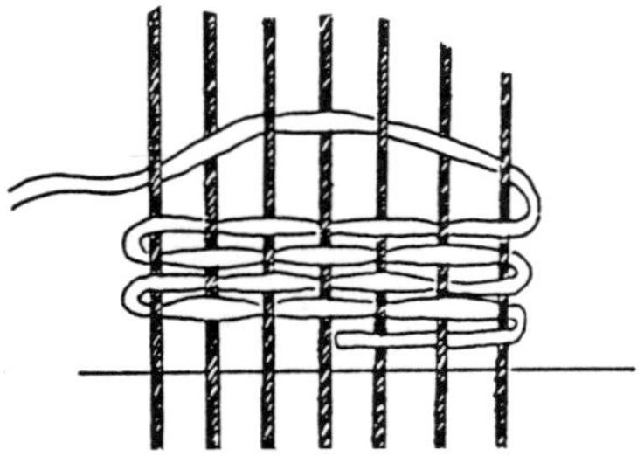

Weave about a 1″ band with this yarn.

5. Wrap about 9 feet of cotton yarn into a bundle, and weave a narrow band (1/4″–1/2″) with it. Start the weaving the same way you did the medium-weight yarn; finish it by back-weaving the last few inches.

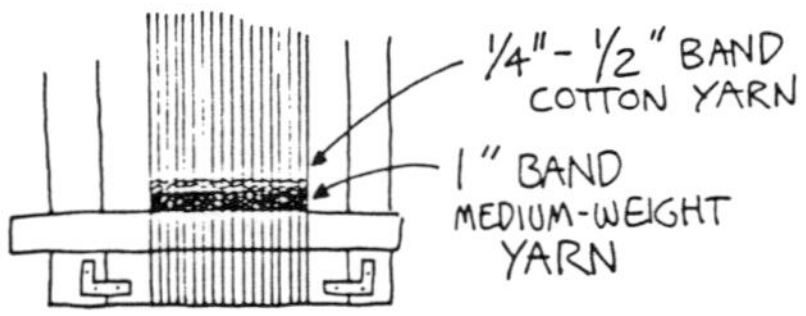

6. Now weave with the torn fabric strips. Start and finish as before. Fold the strips in half to make them a little more manageable. When you finish with one strip, simply continue with another (overlap them slightly so there aren't any gaps). Continue until the weaving is about 7″ long. End with another narrow band of cotton yarn.

8. Cut the warp threads about 2″ beyond the end of the potholder. Cut them the same distance from the beginning. Remove the medium-weight yarn that was woven at the start. Knot the warp threads together right up close to the narrow bands at either end of the potholder. Trim the excess with a pair of scissors.

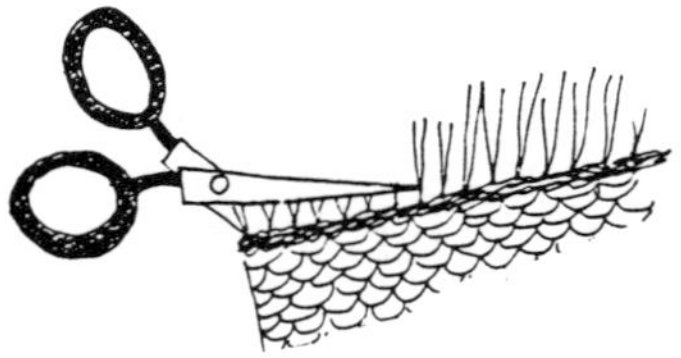

Tip Weave another potholder (or another item) on the reverse side of the loom *before* you cut the warp threads, if you like. Block off the first weaving with a piece of paper to make it easier to see what you're doing.

Variations on a Theme
Experiment with different materials. You can weave with just yarn, of course, to create some striking tapestries and useful articles. You can also incorporate such things as feathers, straw, and twigs into woven pieces to make them three-dimensional.

Experiment with changing the over-and-under pattern. Instead of always weaving over one warp thread and under another, try going over two and under one, for instance. Play around with changing colors in the middle of a row, and weaving shapes into your tapestries.

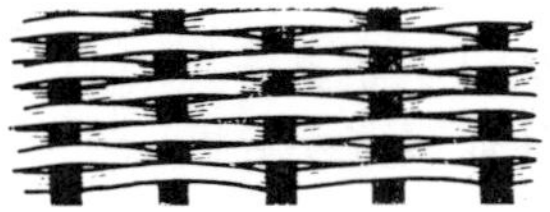

FRAME LOOM

Frame looms are among the easiest to use and to make. There are several types of frame loom. The version shown here has notches at either end to hold the warp threads, although you can also tap in a row of tiny nails (take care the wood doesn't split).

Make your loom out of pine (have a lumberyard rip 1″ × 3″ pine boarding down the middle) or from an old picture frame or stretcher strips. A 12″ × 18″ frame is a good size to start with. If you are using pine, saw the wood into four pieces and attach them at right angles with corner braces or irons. If you are using an old frame or stretcher strips, reinforce the frame at the corners.

Carefully measure and mark lines 1/4″ apart on both ends of the frame. Use a thick knife blade (such as a pocketknife blade) to make a notch at each mark.

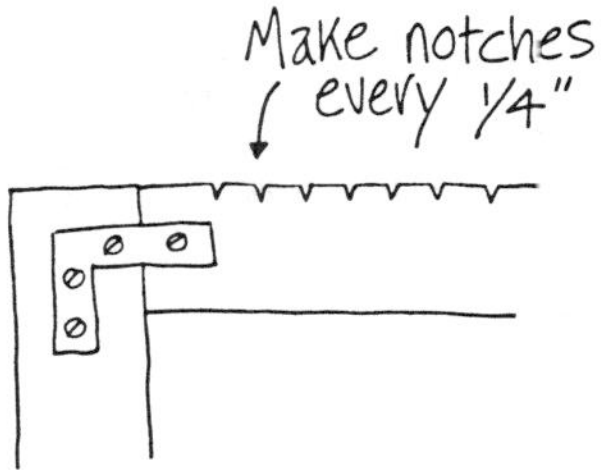

All woven pieces are made up of the *warp* (the threads that run vertically, and are usually hidden) and the *weft* (the horizontal yarn or fabric strips that are woven in and out of the warp). Warping the frame loom is very simple. It is best to use a strong material such as cotton crochet yarn or other thin but strong string. Wrap the string from one end of the loom to the other, pressing the string into the notches to keep the warp evenly spaced. A notched frame loom can be woven on both sides (one at a time), or the extra warp threads can be cut away and discarded when you are done weaving just one side of the loom.

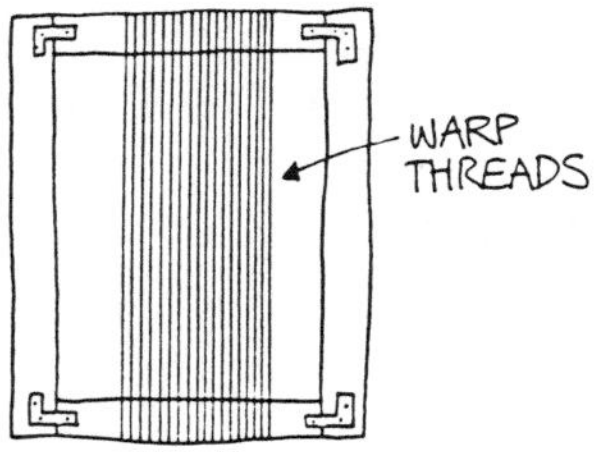

The oldest picture of a loom is on a pottery dish that was found in a tomb at El Badari, Egypt. The dish is thought to date from about 4400 B.C.

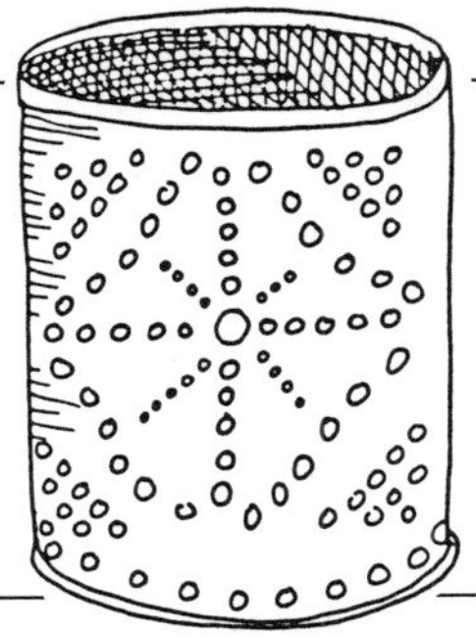

NIGHT LIGHT

The candlelight shining through the holes of this tin can lantern makes an interesting pattern on walls and ceilings. Make several lanterns for an even more dramatic effect.

PIERCED TIN CAN LANTERN
Empty metal food can (with removable paper label)
Permanent marker
Assorted nails
Hammer
Towel

Note Look for cans that have plain sides without any ridges. These make the nicest lanterns.

1. Remove the label from the can. Scrape any remaining glue off the can by chipping it off with a knife while holding the can under running cold water.

2. Draw a pattern of dots on the outside of the can with the permanent marker (be careful not to smudge the dots before the ink dries). Use the patterns shown here, or come up with your own ideas.

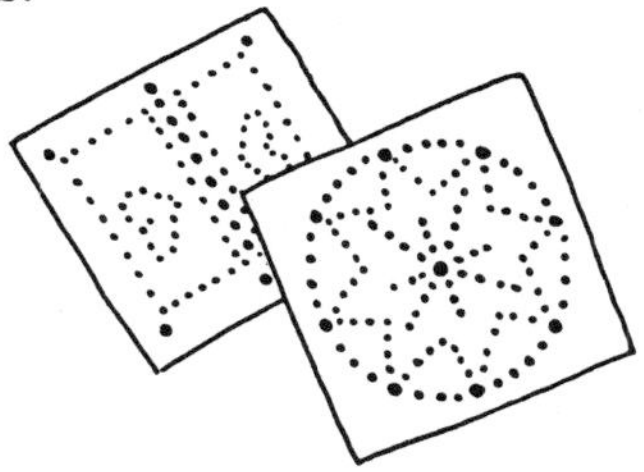

Indoor lighting probably originated about 50,000 years ago when Cro-Magnon man placed a fiber wick in a saucer-like depression that held animal fat.

▶

Tin is a valuable commodity in Mexico, where it is used to make beautiful trays, pitchers, mirrors, and candelabras. Originally, the native Mexicans used silver and gold to make metal objects, but when the Spanish invaded Mexico and took these precious metals, the Mexicans improvised and used tin because it was inexpensive and easy to work with.

Did you know?
Warm air is constantly being drawn towards colder air. When your parents warn you not to let in any cold air, they really mean not to let any warm air out.

3. Fill the can with water and place it in the freezer. Leave for at least 24 hours in order to freeze solid.

4. Place the can on its side on a folded towel. Use the assorted nails to pierce through the pattern of dots you've drawn. Hammer the nails in just far enough to pierce the metal. Return the can to the freezer for a few hours, if the ice is melting too quickly.

5. When you are done, place the can in the sink and let the ice melt. Dry the lantern (take care not to cut or scratch yourself on the jagged edges inside the can), place a small candle in it, and light. (Have an adult help you with lighting the candle.)

Variations on a Theme
Pierce a pattern of holes in the metal top from a frozen juice can (the kind that is held in place with a plastic strip that has nice, smooth edges) to make a hanging ornament. Place the lid on a wooden work surface you can bang nails into, such as a scrap

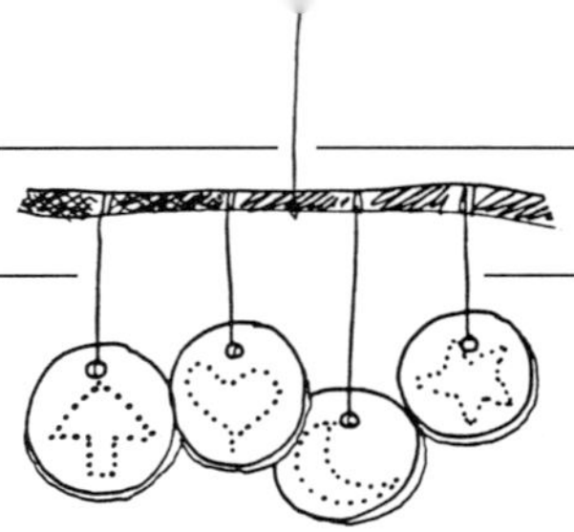

of soft pine. Hang several pierced lids together in front of a light source for a dramatic nighttime mobile.

You can also pierce holes in paper. Make your own note cards or lamp shades using this technique. Place the paper on top of a piece of foam or several layers of felt. Poke the holes with a sharp needle, taking care to space them evenly.

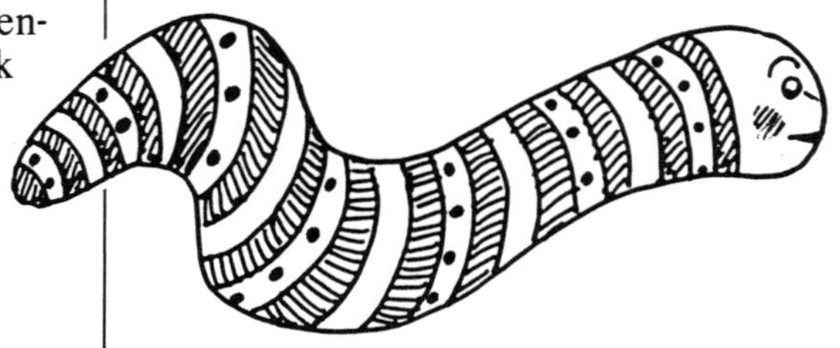

THE ARTFUL DODGER

This whimsical snake will liven up a room while keeping cold drafts at bay. It's also hefty enough to keep doors propped open, or it can be used as a book end when it's coiled.

DRAFT STOPPER
1/4 yard tightly-woven fabric, such as cotton or a cotton-blend
Fabric paints or acrylics
Sand, about 2 shovelfuls
Needle and thread
Funnel

Note A 36″ snake spans most doorways. Make your snake longer, if your doors are wider than usual.

1. Fold the fabric in half lengthwise. Make a mark 37″ from one end; cut off the excess fabric. (If you are using 36″ fabric, omit this step.) Round off the corners at one end for the head; taper the fabric slightly at the other end for the tail.

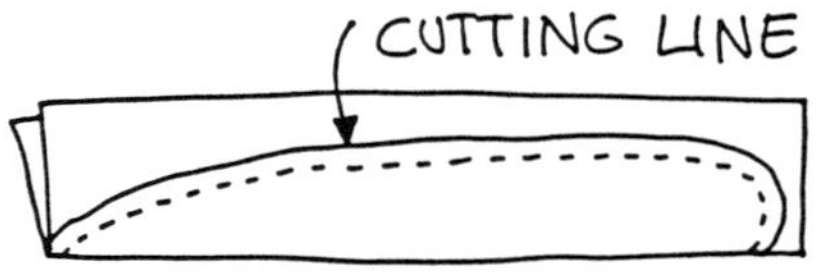

2. Open up the fabric and lay it on some newspaper. Paint it to look like a snake (remember the top of the snake is where the fabric was folded). Paint crazy patterns in bright colors or make the snake more realistic looking. Let dry.

3. Fold the fabric in half again, this time with the painted side facing in. Sew the fabric together leaving a 1/2″ seam. Leave an opening at the tail end. Turn the fabric right-side out.

4. Place the funnel in the tail end of the snake and pour in enough sand to fill out the snake's form. Sew the tail opening shut.

Variations on a Theme
You can stuff your snake with fiberfill instead of sand, if you don't plan on using it as a draft stopper.

Embellish the snake with buttons and other decorative trims for a different look.

Add some felt legs to your snake to turn it into a caterpillar. Turn it into a "bookworm" with a pair of glasses painted at one end!

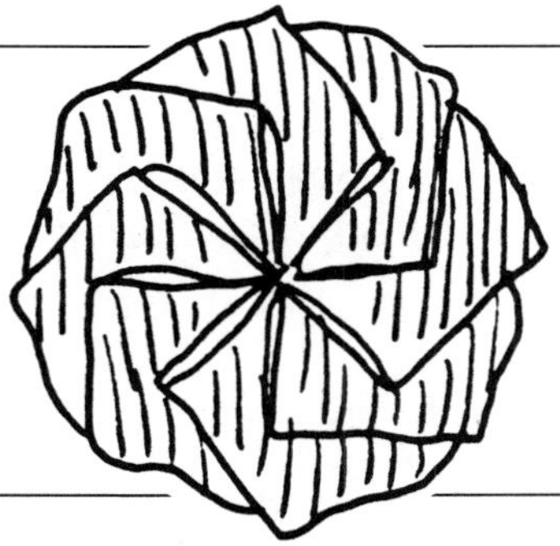

CASE CLOSED

This ingenious cushion cover for a round pillow is so easy to make that you can re-cover your cushions whenever you like. The cover is folded and tied in place instead of being sewn.

FOLDED CUSHION COVER
Round pillow or pillow form
Felt, about 1¼ yards of 72″ felt
Measuring tape
String
Needle and strong thread

Note One-and-one-quarter yards of felt will cover a 16″ round pillow that is about 4″ thick. For a larger pillow (or one that is plumper), use a longer piece of felt.

1. Place the end of the measuring tape in the center of the pillow and measure from there to the center of the other side.

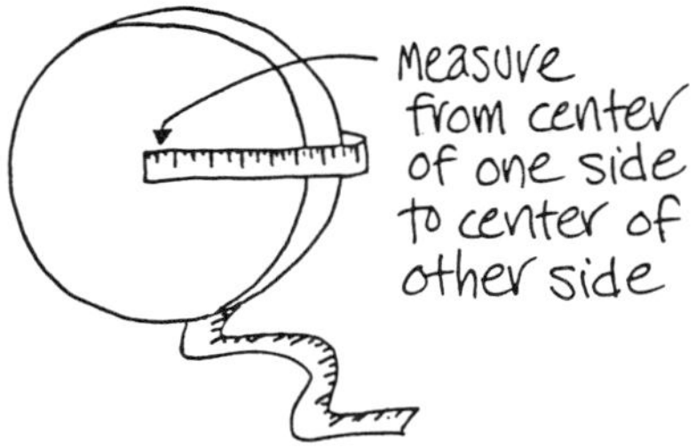

2. Spread the piece of felt out flat on a firm surface. Cut a piece of string 2″ longer than the measurement you made in step 1. Tie the string to a felt-tip marker. Holding the end of the piece of string in the very center of the piece of felt, pull the string taut and carefully draw a circle on the felt. (You may find this is easier to do with two people—one to hold the end of the string, the other to draw the circle.)

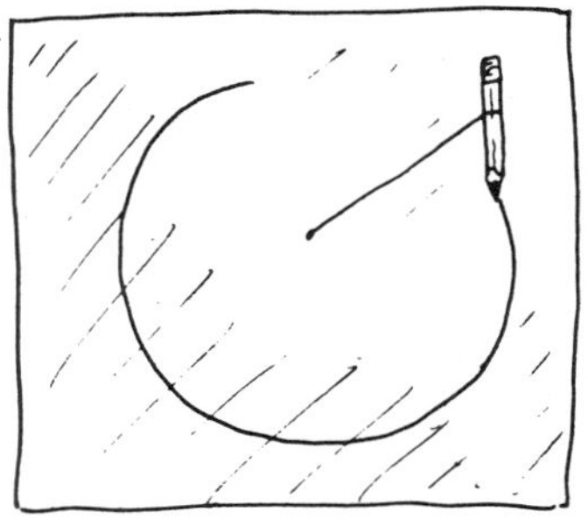

In ancient Greece and Rome, cushions and pillows were the only form of upholstery in homes.

There was a time when only the very wealthiest people slept with soft pillows. Throughout history, however, hard pillows were sometimes preferred because they were thought to be better for your health. The ancient Chinese slept with their heads elevated in porcelain "cradles."

3. Cut out the circle. Fold the circle in half. Thread the needle with the strong thread and tie an 8″ length to either end of the fold.

Open the circle and refold it in the opposite direction; tie thread to both ends of that fold. Unfold and refold the circle two more times, so that there are 8 pieces of thread evenly spaced around the circle.

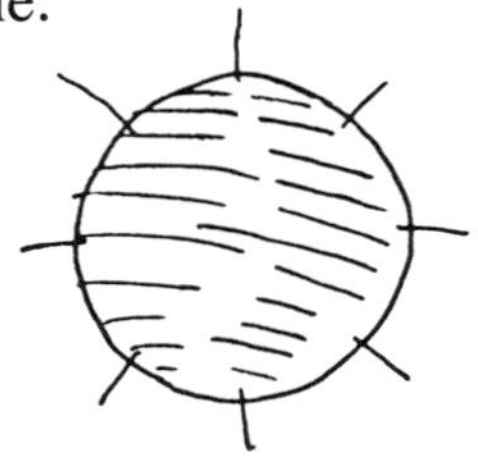

4. Place the pillow in the center of the circle. Tie together any two pieces of thread that are opposite one another. Knot them securely. Now bring together and tie the pair of threads that are in the opposite direction.

Knot the remaining two pairs of thread. Arrange and smooth out the folds.

Tip Sew a button in the center of the pillow to hide the knots, if you like.

Variations on a Theme

You can cover a square pillow with a similar technique. Measure around the pillow starting and ending at the very center of one side. Cut a square out of felt that is that size.

Tie the strong thread to each corner of the felt square, and to the mid-point on each side. Place the pillow in the center of the felt square. Bring two opposite mid-point threads together and knot them; do the same with the other mid-point threads.

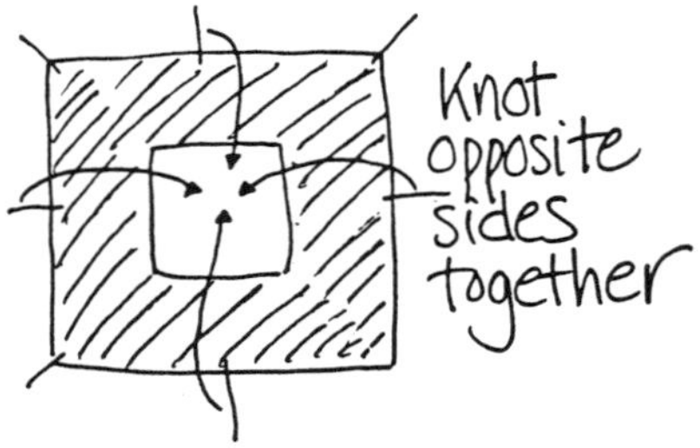

At one time, there were as many as 20 different spellings of the word "pillow" in English. Among them: plye, pele, pilewe, and pylow.

Pull the four corners of the felt square out, folding them to look like a pinwheel.

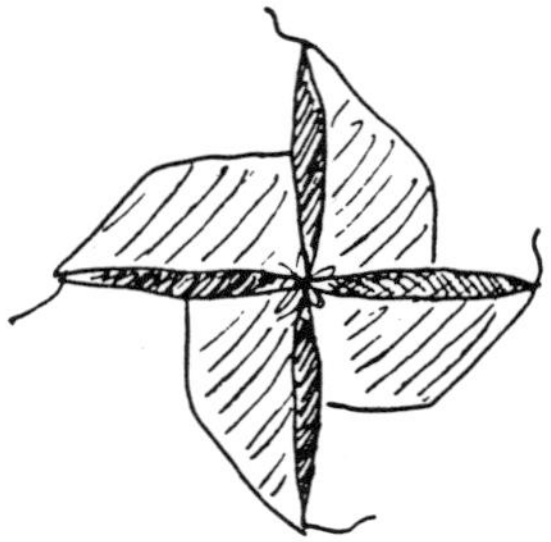

Turn the pillow over and tie the threads of the opposite corners together.

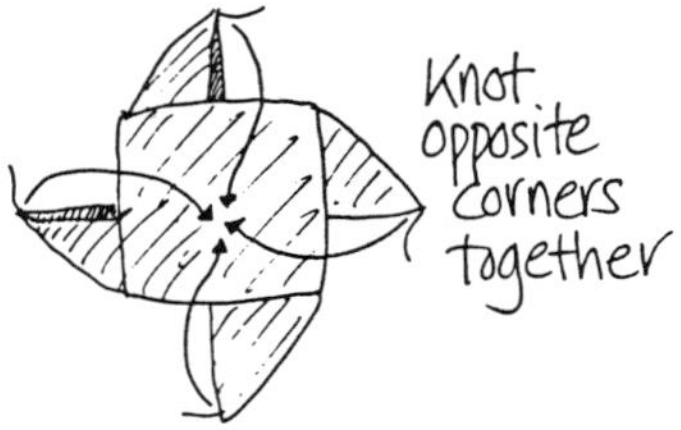

The phrase "to consult with one's pillow" was once a common expression. It meant to take a night to consider a matter of importance—in other words, "to sleep on it."

FRAMED!

Special artwork and cherished photographs deserve to be framed. Here are two simple frames without glass that you can make. Use them to frame some of your own work or give them as gifts.

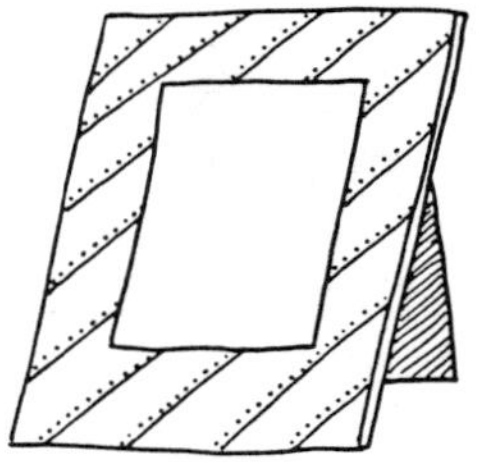

FOAM-CORE FRAME

FOAM-CORE FRAME
Paper, 8½″ × 11″
Scissors
Foam-core board, about 8½″ × 11″
X-acto knife
Blunt tool, such as the end of a paintbrush
Metallic paint
Clear acetate (optional)

Note The frame shown here is an ornate old-fashioned looking oval. Make your frame any shape and style using the same technique.

1. Make a template for the frame's outline and opening. Fold the 8½″ × 11″ paper in half, and in half again. Draw two curved lines on the paper, making sure the folds are on the left-hand side and bottom, as shown.

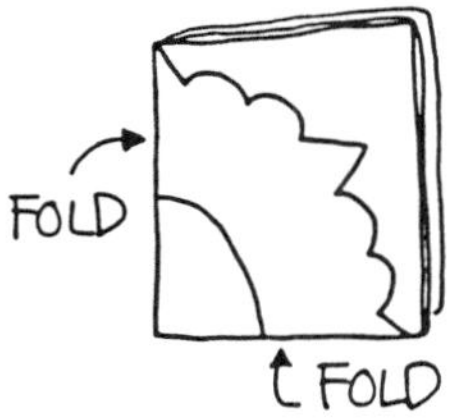

Make the frame outline scalloped as it is here or any way you like. Cut along the two lines. Open the paper.

2. Lay the template on the piece of foam-core board. Trace around the outline and the opening. Cut along these lines with the X-acto knife. Hold the knife as straight as possible to make the cuts level.

3. With the blunt end of a paint-brush or other tool, "draw" patterns and designs on the frame as decoration. Go over the lines if necessary to make them deep enough to really stand out. Make rows of dots by gently pushing the end of the paintbrush straight down (take care not to push too hard or you might break through the board).

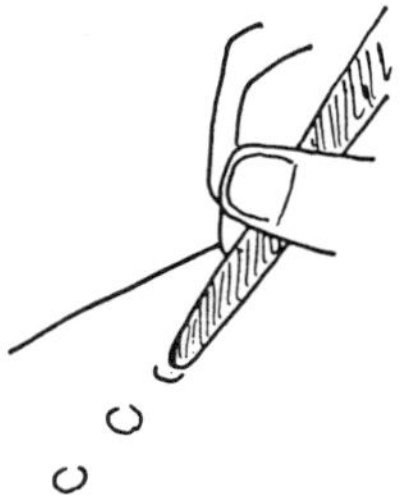

4. Paint the frame with metallic paints. Spray paint is best for over-all painting (be sure to get the edges); brush on the kind of paint that comes in a jar to further emphasize the incised lines. Let dry.

Tip Protect whatever you are framing with a piece of clear acetate cut slightly larger than the frame's opening. Tape it to the inside of the front of the frame.

The Story of Art
The first paintings were painted directly on walls and ceilings. Artists often "framed" them with painted lines to give them definition and a finished look. When paintings became portable (when they were done on canvas or wood), frames were used not only to enhance them, but also to act as a deterrent to thieves.

Tricks of the Trade Consider your artwork carefully when you choose a frame for it (homemade and store-bought alike). A frame should complement, but not overwhelm, a drawing or painting. Choose simple wooden or metal strip frames for abstract pieces, for instance. More ornate frames are more in keeping with classic still lifes and portraits.

Choose your mat board in a color that complements the art, as well. Pick up one of the colors in the art itself, or choose a neutral shade such as off-white or beige.

PAPER–COVERED FRAME
Sturdy cardboard, 2 pieces about 8½″ × 11″ plus a 2″ × 7″ piece
Wrapping paper or art paper
Medium-weight paper, about 2″ × 8″
X-acto knife
Rubber cement
White glue

Note The instructions here are for an 8½″ × 11″ frame. Alter the dimensions of all the materials to suit any other frame size.

1. Draw the outline of an opening 2″ in from all sides on one of the pieces of cardboard. Cut out the opening with the X-acto knife.

2. Cut two pieces of 10½″ × 13″ wrapping paper. Place one piece face down. Brush rubber cement over the entire back of the paper and on one side of the cut out frame. Let dry; then carefully position the frame in the center of the paper.

Rub your hands over the frame to bond the paper to the cardboard and to smooth out any wrinkles.

3. With the X-acto knife, cut an "X" in the frame's opening, from corner to corner. Trim the paper at the outer corners.

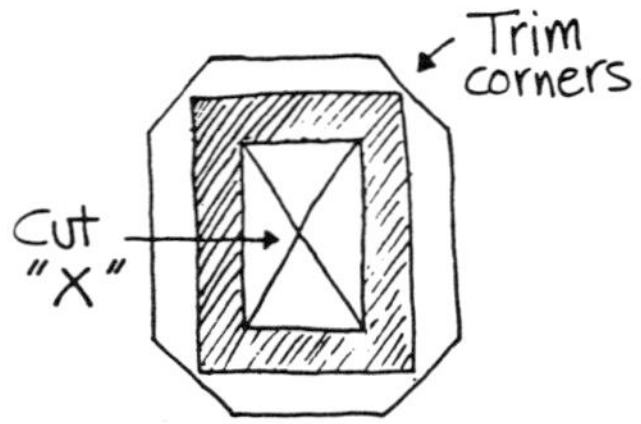

Fold the flaps back around the opening; glue them down (brush some rubber cement to the back of the frame where the flaps touch). Glue down the excess paper around the frame.

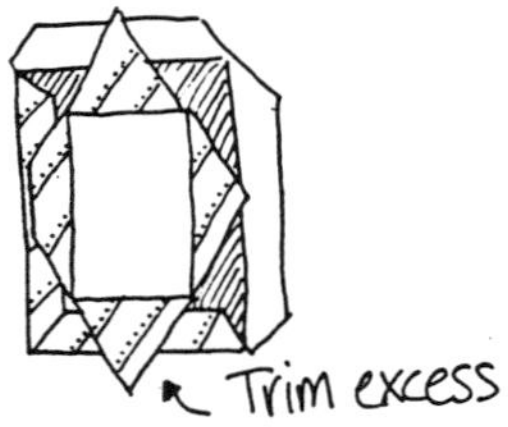

4. Cover the other 8½″ × 11″ piece of cardboard with the remaining piece of wrapping paper.

5. Lay the two pieces of cardboard end to end, face down. With the white glue, glue the 2″ × 8″ paper strip so that it spans the two pieces as shown.

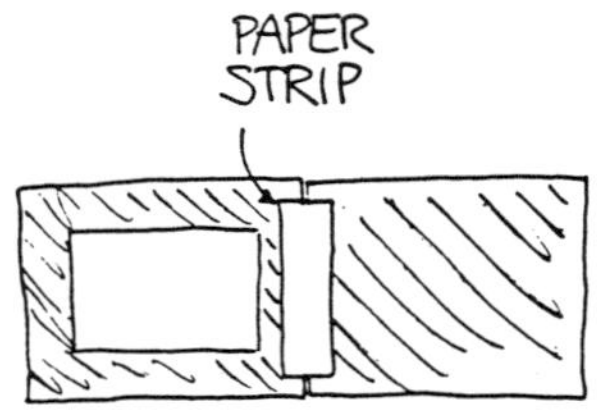

Let dry; fold the frame at this "hinge."

6. Cut one piece of wrapping paper 4″ × 9″, and one 1¾″ × 6¾″. Cover the 2″ × 7″ strip of cardboard with the larger paper. Use the smaller piece to cover the flaps on the back side. This is the support to hold up the frame.

7. Score a line 1½″ from the top of the support with the X-acto knife. Bend it back slightly. Glue it to the mid-point of the back of the frame with white glue. Let dry.

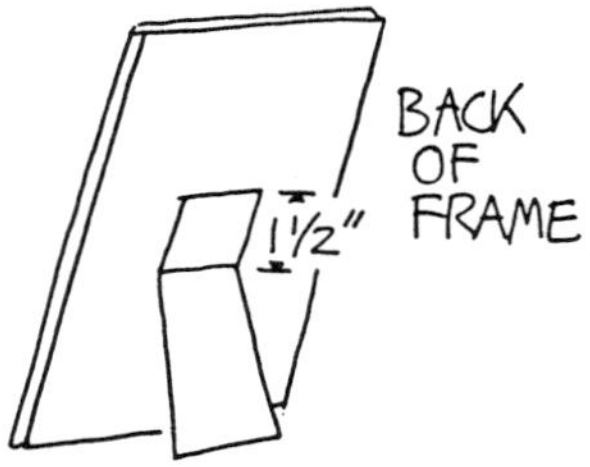

8. Lift the front of the frame and position your artwork so that it shows through the opening. Tape the artwork to the frame back. Lower the front of the frame and adjust the angle of the support, so that the frame stands on its own.

EYE OF THE BEHOLDER

The way people dress throughout the world is as varied as the languages that are spoken. While some fashions come and go, many clothes are designed with climate and function in mind and change little over the years. Traditional clothes such as these go back a long, long time.

In some cultures, such as our own, there are few rules of dress, and clothing is a form of self-expression. Fashions borrow freely from various periods in history as well as from other cultures. Such clothing really is wearable art!

GOTCHA COVERED!

Not all art is messy, but in the excitement of discovering new techniques and things to make you can sometimes forget what you're doing. It's a good idea to wear a cover-all of some sort, because, if nothing else, it makes cleaning up that much easier.

The smock gets its name from *smock frock,* a yoked shirt or loose blouse made from coarse linen that was worn by field laborers in Europe. Originally it was smocked, a method of pleating and stitching fabric in a honeycomb design that cinches in the fullness of a garment at the yoke and cuffs.

OVERSIZED SHIRT SMOCK
Man's long-sleeved button-front shirt
1/4″ elastic, 2 pieces 8″ long
Large-eye tapestry needle
Needle and thread
Fabric paint or acrylics

Note Ask your dad if he has an old shirt that's too worn to mend. Even clothes can be recycled!

1. Put on the shirt. Stand up straight with your arms hanging by your side. Have someone cut off the sleeves about 2″ below the tips of your fingers.

2. Take off the shirt and turn it inside out. Turn back 1″ at the bottom of one sleeve. Sew around the sleeve to make a 3/4″ casing for the elastic. Leave a 2″ opening.

3. Thread the elastic through the large-eye needle and insert it in the casing. Take care not to pull it all the way through. Adjust the elastic so that it fits snugly around your wrist; sew the ends together.

4. Sew the opening in the casing closed. Insert the elastic in the other sleeve in the same way.

5. Turn the shirt right-side out and decorate with paint. Make large free-hand brush marks all over the shirt, or spatter it with paint in an over-all pattern. (Put it in a large cardboard box if you are spatter-painting, to protect yourself and your work area from spatters.) Let dry.

Variations on a Theme
Instead of sewing casings for the elastic, you can simply tie the elastic into tight bands to slip over the ends of the shirt sleeves to keep them from flapping about.

Many professions require protective clothing. Cooks, for instance, wear aprons (so do carpenters, but theirs are meant as holders rather than as protective garb). Scientists wear lab coats. What other cover-all garments can you think of?

TO A TEE

These cheerful T-shirts are as sunny as summer itself. With fiber-reactive dyes, you can tie-dye shirts in as many colors as you like. Best of all, you don't even need a stove—this type of dyeing is done in cold water.

TIE-DYE T-SHIRT
White, or light-colored, 100% cotton T-shirt
Fiber-reactive dyes, 2 or more colors (see page 144)
Fixer solution (see page 144)
Rubber bands, about 4
Rubber gloves
Plastic sheet (see *Note*)
Plastic bag, 1-gallon size

Note Protect your work table with a plastic sheet or a couple of plastic garbage bags opened up and overlapped on the table. (Save these bags to use again whenever you need to protect your work surface.)

1. Wash the shirt in warm, soapy water; rinse well. (You must do this even if your shirt is new, to remove any sizing that might affect the fabric's ability to accept dye.) Place the shirt in the container of fixer solution. Let soak 30 minutes.

2. Remove the shirt from the fixer; wring it out. Lay the shirt on the plastic-covered table. Smooth out the big wrinkles and bumps.

3. Fold or gather the shirt to create the pattern of your choice. To make stripes, like on the shirt shown here, fold the shirt from hem to neckline in inch-wide accordion folds (back and forth folds).

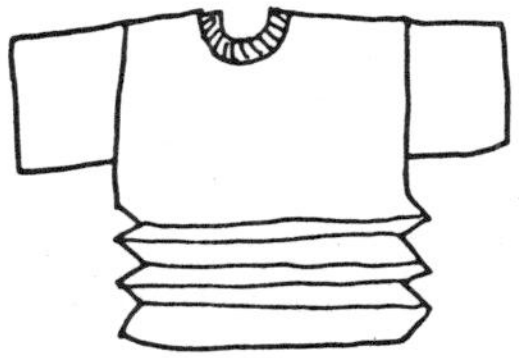

Evenly space four rubber bands around the bundle to keep it in place.

4. Set the bundle on its side. Put on the rubber gloves to protect your hands. Dribble a little dye along the fold lines—use a different color for each fold, or dye each section of the bundle a different color.

Turn the bundle over and do the same on the other side.

5. Place the bundle in the plastic bag. Leave it for 1 to 3 days (the longer you let the dyes set, the brighter the colors).

6. Remove the bundle from the plastic bag. Rinse it under running water until the water is nearly clear. Remove the rubber bands. Rinse a few minutes more under running water.

7. Fill the sink with a squirt of dishwashing liquid and the hot-test water from the tap. Put the shirt into the sink; let soak for 10 minutes. Rinse in clean water until ▶

Tie-dyeing originated in Asia around the 6th century. It is still commonly used to decorate fabrics in such places as India, Africa, Japan, China, and various Southeast Asian countries.

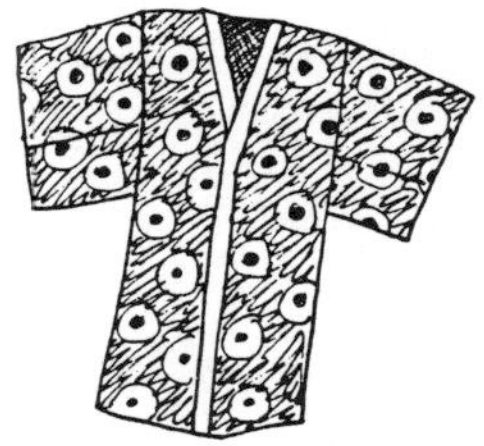

Make diagonal stripes by folding the shirt diagonally.

Most people agree that T-shirts get their name from their shape. Some historians, however, feel that the name comes from the "tea shirts" worn by 17th century dock workers in Maryland. They wore the special shirts to keep loose tea leaves from collecting under their collars when they were unloading the ships.

the water runs clear. Wring out the shirt and lay flat to dry.

Variations on a Theme
Traditionally, tie-dyeing was done in one color using hot water dye. You can do it this way yourself, too.

Get a dye bath ready (using a dye such as Rit®) following the instructions on the package. Crumple, fold, twist, knot or stitch the fabric, binding it together tightly with rubber bands, string, or a needle and thread. Wherever you bind the fabric, no dye can penetrate. Dye the fabric, then cut away the bindings and open it up to reveal the pattern you have created.

FIBER–REACTIVE DYES & FIXER

Fiber-reactive dye is available at many fabric and yarn stores, as well as art and craft suppliers. It is sold in both powdered and liquid form, often in small amounts that include a separate packet of fixer.

Follow the directions on the package or use this general rule. One teaspoon of powdered dye is enough to make 1/2 cup of dye solution. Place the dye in a disposable container, and add 1 tablespoon warm water to the container; stir with a Popsicle stick to make a thick paste. Pour in the rest of the water.

Dyes can be mixed together to create new colors. Covered, they can be stored for several weeks in a cool, dark place.

Make a fixer solution from a chemical called sodium carbonate (not to be confused with sodium bicarbonate, which is baking soda), salt, and water. (If you can't find sodium carbonate where you purchased your dyes, you can buy it from a swimming pool chemical supplier. Ask for soda ash. Mix 4 teaspoons sodium carbonate and 1/4 cup salt per shirt in a bucket. Add enough water to cover the shirt completely.

Handle these chemicals with care. It's a good idea to wear rubber gloves whenever you are working with dye (and put on a smock, too, in case of splashes). Measure the powdered dyes carefully, so you don't send the fine particles flying. When dyeing, use only disposable containers or old pots and jars reserved only for dyeing purposes.

Make a sunburst on your shirt. Start with the shirt flat; pinch the fabric near the center of the shirt; lift up. Twist the shirt into a tight spiral, then roll it into a doughnut shape. Place a rubber band around the outside to hold it in place. Dribble dye on the top; then turn the bundle over and do the same on the other side. Proceed as usual.

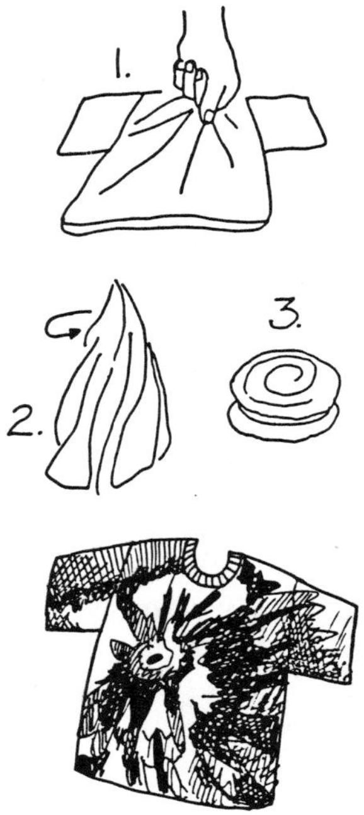

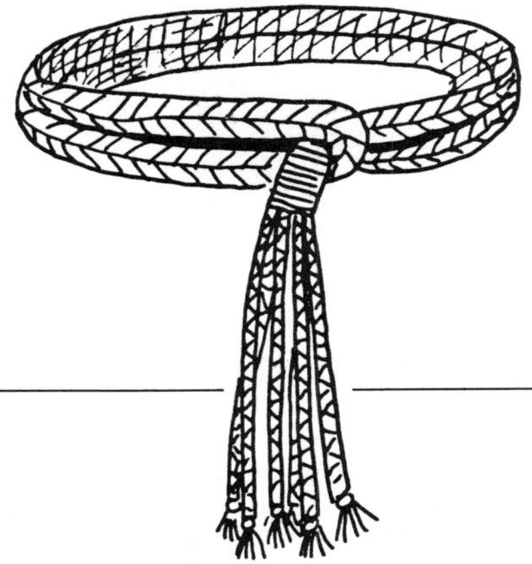

WHAT A CINCH

Long belts that tie are perfect for cinching in costumes as well as wearing with "real" clothes. Here are two belts you can make yourself. The first is braided from long pieces of yarn; the second uses a technique known as spool knitting.

BRAIDED BELT
Yarn in assorted colors, 24 strands about 10 feet long
Scissors

Note Use as many colors as you like. The belt shown here uses 4 different colors (6 strands of each) which produce a nice, colorful effect.

1. Tie the strands of yarn together, with a loose knot, about 20″ from one end. Anchor the yarn in a drawer by placing the yarn—up to the knot—in the drawer and closing it as far as it will go.

2. Divide the yarn into 3 sections of 8 strands each. Loosely knot the ends of these 3 bundles of strands. Braid the 3 bundles of strands until the braided part measures about 48″, or about twice the measurement around your waist.

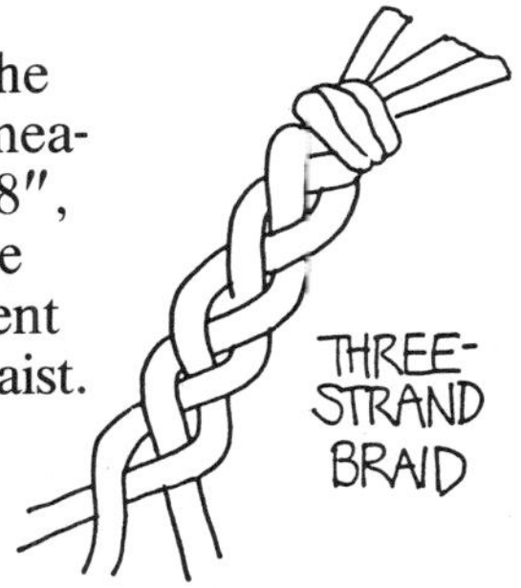

As you braid the long strands, stop and shake the yet-to-be-braided yarn every few inches or so. The extra yarn has a way of getting tangled as you braid; shaking the strands loose makes the job a lot easier.

3. Remove the yarn from the drawer and untie the knot holding all the strands together. Double over the braided part and join the two ends by wrapping yarn around them as tightly as possible. Tie this yarn to itself to keep it from unraveling.

4. Loop the belt around a chair. Finish off the belt by braiding the loose strands into small braids (using 3 pairs of strands per braid). Choose the colors for these small braids randomly, or pair off the strands of any one braid in 3 colors. Tie the end of each braid with a secure knot. Trim the excess yarn evenly with the scissors.

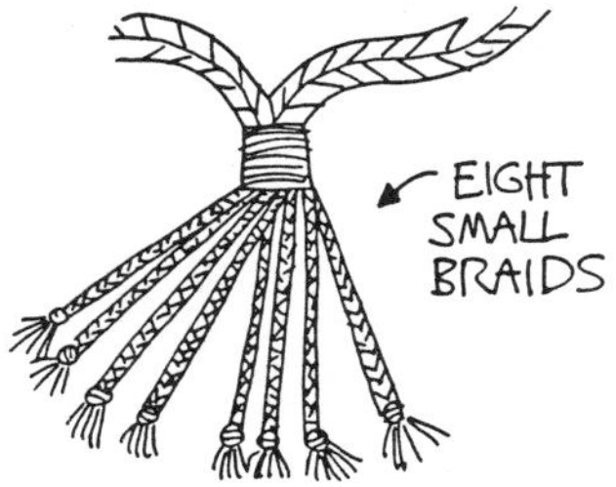

5. To wear the belt, place it around your waist and slip the wrapped portion through the loop.

Belts come in all sorts of styles. Some are threaded through belt loops of trousers and skirts. Wider sashes are simply tied around the waist. Still others go over the shoulders and clip on to whatever they are holding up. We call this last type suspenders, of course!

Spool-knitting is perhaps more closely related to macrame than to the knitting that is done with long needles. Both macrame and hand knitting are ancient crafts.

SPOOL-KNITTED BELT
Yarn, 1 or more colors, about 60–75 feet
Knitting spool (see below)
Blunt tapestry needle

Note This belt, which measures 36″, is meant to be tied with a loose knot. Make your belt longer (or shorter), if you want to tie it differently.

1. Drop one end of the yarn through the hole in the spool. Let about 6″ hang below the bottom of the spool.

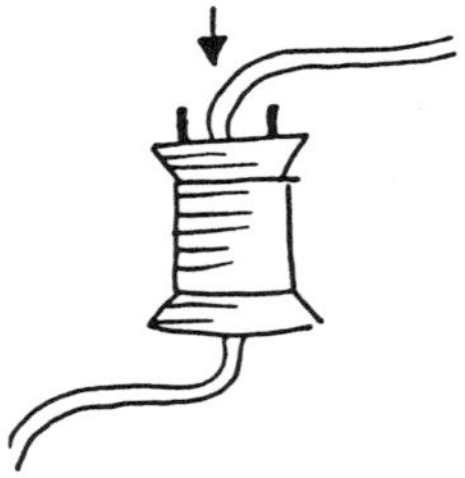

2. Loop the yarn around each nail once. This is what the loops should look like from above.

3. Loop the yarn over the first nail again. Slip the first loop up and over this second loop, letting the first loop come right off the nail completely.

Continue doing this all the way around the spool (be sure to follow the order of the original loops). Every few rounds, pull on the yarn that is hanging through the hole to keep the knitting from bunching up inside the spool.

4. Change colors by cutting the yarn you are using and tying on a new color. Trim the excess yarn near the knot. The knot itself will be hidden in the knitted cord.

5. Keep knitting the belt until it is the desired length. Finish off by cutting the yarn about 6″ from the top of the spool. Slip the loops off the nails one at a time, carefully pulling the yarn through each loop. Make a final knot.

Variations on a Theme
Spool-knitted cord can be made into all sorts of items. Coil a long piece to make a trivet (sew it together as you coil it). Make a necklace using metallic thread. Fashion some miniature rugs for a dollhouse.

KNITTING SPOOL

To make your own knitting spool you need an empty wooden thread spool, 4 finish nails (these are the kind that have no heads) and a hammer.

Carefully nail the nails into one end of the spool, spacing them evenly around the hole. Leave the nails sticking up about 1/2″. These are the posts you wrap the yarn or string around as you knit the cord.

European children enjoy making spool-knitted items using a purchased tool that has a face painted on it. It is affectionately known as Knitting Nancy.

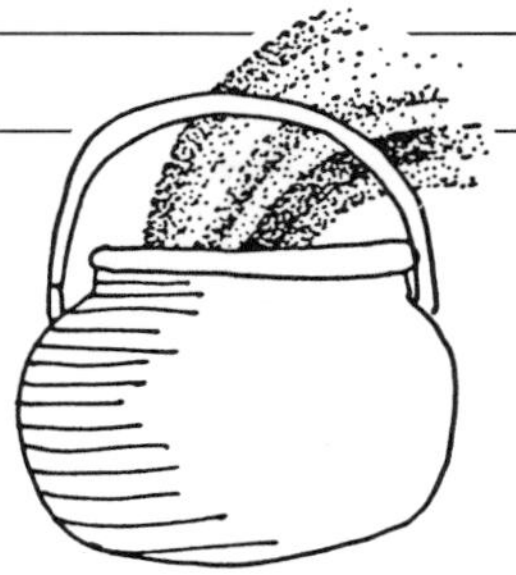

DYED IN THE WOOL

Make the belts described on pages 145 and 146 from yarn that you've dyed yourself using natural dyes. Natural dyes yield subtle colors quite different from chemical dyes. The process is easy to do and a lot of fun.

Gather a variety of dyestuffs, from your kitchen as well as from outdoors. Onion skins, herbs and spices, nutshells, and vegetables such as beets all yield dyes, as do flower blossoms, the leaves, berries, and bark of trees, and lichen. If you divide a skein of wool (use 100 percent wool, because it takes dye better than cotton or synthetic fibers) into small hanks, you can experiment with all sorts of dyestuffs and have plenty of different colored yarn on hand to weave, knit, and craft with. To form hanks, wind some yarn around your outstretched fingers in a figure-eight and tie loosely in two spots with a short piece of yarn.

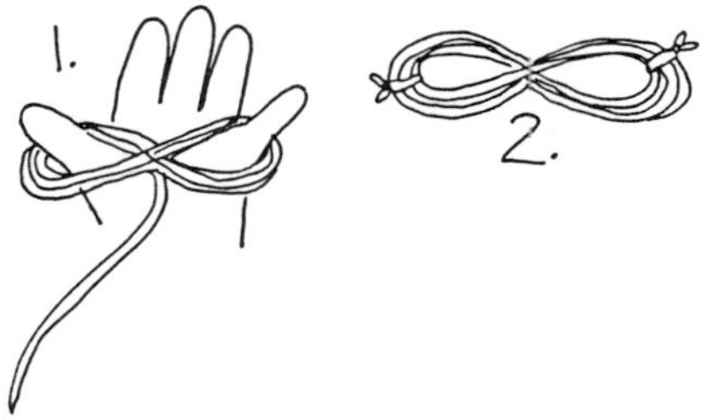

You'll get the best results if you first mordant your wool to make it fade-resistant. Alum is one of the most common chemicals used as a mordant. The day before you plan on dyeing (or well before, in which case let the mordanted wool dry), fill an old pot with enough water to cover all the yarn, and add 4 ounces of alum mixed with 1 ounce cream of tartar. Bring to a boil and cook for one hour. Let cool overnight in the mordant bath.

Look for alum at your local pharmacy. Cream of tartar can be found in the spice section of your supermarket.

The next day, boil up your plants or kitchen scraps to extract the dye. For the small amounts of yarn you are going to dye, you only need a couple of handfuls of dyestuffs for each color. Put the plants and a little water into another old pot. Simmer for about 30 minutes. Strain the dye and put it back into the pot with enough cold water to cover the yarn you are dyeing.

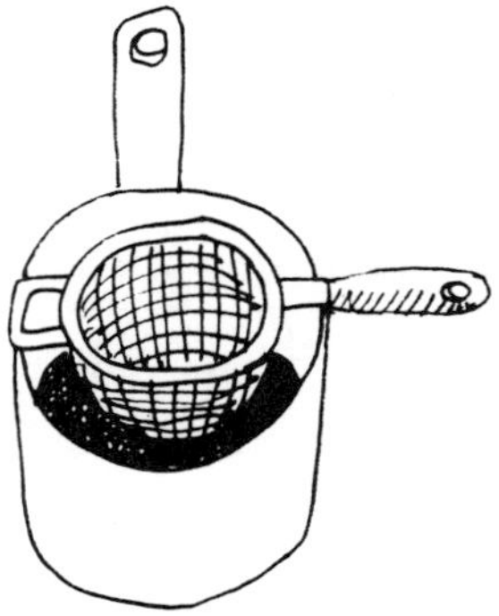

Place the pot on the stove. Poking the yarn gently with a spoon, cook until it turns the shade you want (remember the yarn will look lighter when it's dry). Let the yarn cool in the pot. Rinse it with cool water until the rinse water runs clear. Gently squeeze the yarn and hang it to dry in a shady spot.

Here are some plants you can use as dyestuffs. Using alum as the mordant, these are the colors they yield.

Dandelion flowers—Yellow

Elderberries—Violet

Marigolds—Yellow-tan

Nettles—Greenish yellow

Red onion skins—Reddish orange

Yellow onion skins—Yellow to burnt orange

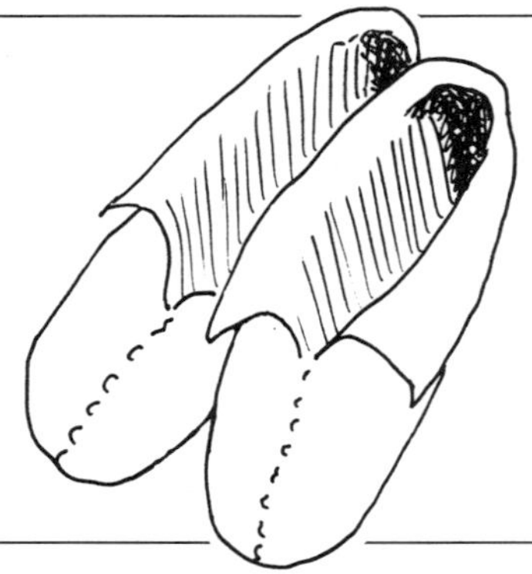

TREAD SOFTLY

No one really knows when our ancestors first made footwear, but it is likely that the shoes were similar to many of the moccasins still made by Native Americans today. Make your own pair of soft-soled moccasins from felt using a traditional Iroquois design.

Did you know?
The word *moccasin* comes from an Algonquin Indian name for footwear.

CENTER-SEAM MOCCASINS
Paper, about 11″ × 14″
Felt-tip marker
Scissors
Measuring tape
Felt, about 1/2 yard 72″ felt
Stitch Witchery®, about 3/4 yard
Iron
Needle and embroidery thread

1. Place one of your feet (with or without socks) on a separate piece of paper and trace around it. Cut out the tracing.

2. Wrap the measuring tape around the widest part of your foot. Make a note of the measurement.

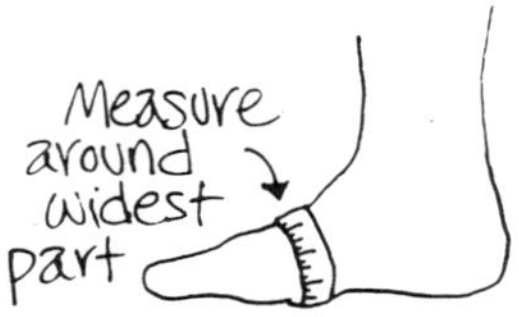

3. On the large sheet of paper draw a pattern for one of the moccasins. It should look like the diagram below. Use the foot tracing to help you determine the size. Trace around it right-side up for one foot; flop it over for the other foot. Make the distance from the outside of one foot to the outside of the other equal the measurement you made with the tape.

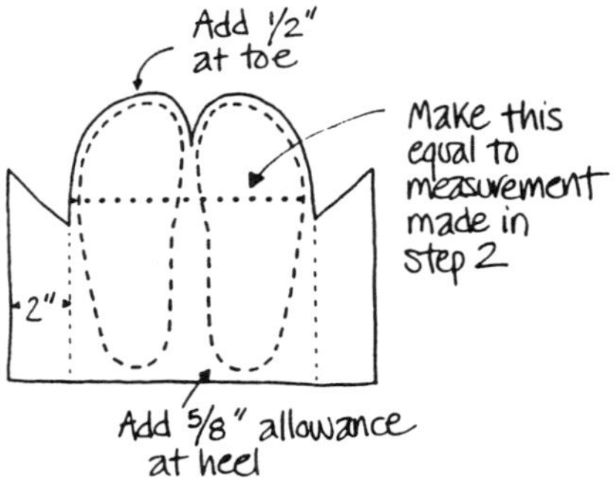

Add 1/2″ at the top of the moccasin, and 5/8″ at the heel, as shown. Note the other measurements in the diagram. Cut the pattern out along the outline.

4. Set the iron on "wool." Cut two 18″ × 24″ pieces of felt. Sandwich the Stitch Witchery® between the felt. Following the manufacturer's directions, iron the felt pieces together to bond them. Let cool.

5. Place the pattern on the felt and trace around it with the felt-tip marker (make two tracings, one for each moccasin). Cut the two moccasins out.

6. Fold one felt piece in half. Sew the front half with a whip stitch, spacing the stitches about 1/4″ apart.

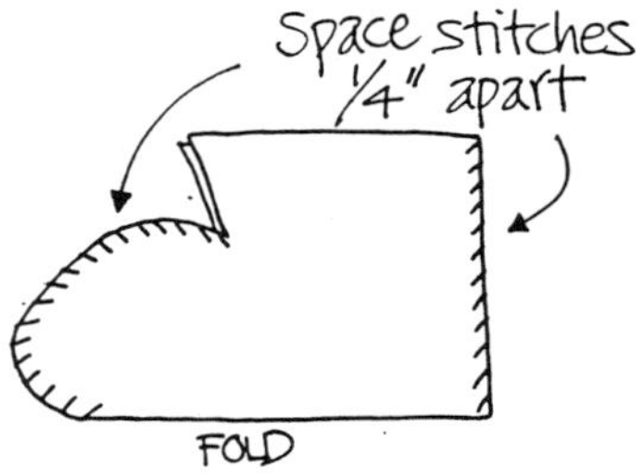

Sew the back of the moccasin the same way.

7. Turn the moccasin inside out. Fold down the side flaps and try it on for size. Make the other moccasin in the same way.

Variations on a Theme
Make these moccasins out of leather, if you like. Follow the instructions above with one exception—don't bother to bond two pieces of leather together. A single layer will do.

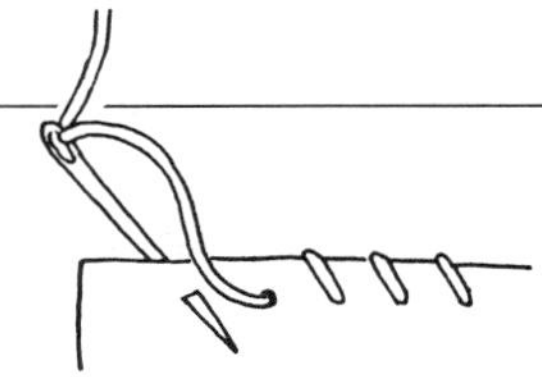

To whip stitch the felt for these moccasins, place the raw edges of the felt together and sew them with diagonal stitches that go right over the edge, as shown here.

Stitch Witchery® is the brand name of an iron-on bonding mesh. Ask for it at a fabric store or in the sewing section of a department store.

FIT TO BE TIED

The country of Java is famous for its fine batiks. These wax-resist-decorated fabrics have a very distinctive look. You can create your own using a much simplified method. Start small and make a scarf or panel for a wall-hanging.

BATIK SCARF
White 100% cotton fabric, about 16″ square
Newspaper
Waxed paper
Paraffin, one slab
Double-boiler
Old paintbrush
Liquid Rit® dyes, 2 or more colors
Rubber gloves
Bucket
Iron
Needle and thread

Note The scarf shown here is dyed with two colors, red and blue. The completed scarf is white (the color of the fabric), red, and purple (red and blue make purple). When you choose your colors, keep in mind how they mix to make new colors.

1. Put a thick layer of newspaper on your work surface. Lay waxed paper over this. Place the fabric on the waxed paper (it should be washed—and dried—to remove any sizing that might affect the dyeing).

2. Prepare the first dye. You should always start with the lightest color. (Using one bucket, you can make one dye bath now, then clean out the bucket and make the other while the fabric is drying from the first dyeing.) Mix a gallon of hot tap water with 1/4 cup liquid dye and 1 tablespoon salt in a bucket. Stir well; let cool.

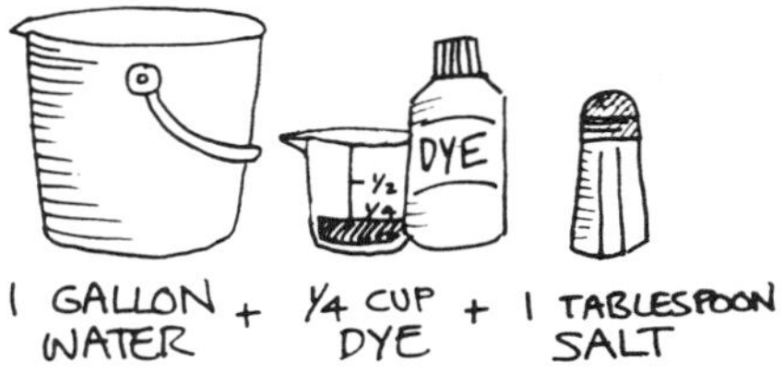

3. Place the paraffin in the top of the double boiler. Heat it over boiling water until it melts. (*Caution:* Paraffin can ignite. Be sure to ask an adult to help you here.) Watch it carefully so that it doesn't overheat. Remove the double-boiler from the stove.

You can also use a prehemmed man's cotton handkerchief for this project.
Experiment with various light-colored fabrics for different effects.

The Story of Art
While many countries decorate fabric with a wax-resist technique, the batiks of Java are the best known. The Javanese invented a tool called a tjanting (CHAHN-ting) that allows the artisans to make very fine lines with the liquid wax. Traditionally, Javanese batiks were made in three colors—the creamy, off-white color of the fabric (made by soaking it in coconut oil), dark blue (from indigo) and brown (from soga bark). Today many other colors are used, as well.

4. With the melted wax, paint the part of your design that is meant to stay the color of the fabric. (You can sketch a design on the fabric with a piece of chalk first, if you like, or paint freehand.) The wax should saturate the fabric for best results. Reheat the paraffin if it starts to solidify. Let the wax harden on the fabric.

5. Put the fabric in the dye bath. Make sure it is completely immersed. Leave it there for 30 minutes, or until it is a little darker than you want (it will dry lighter).

6. Remove the fabric and rinse it in lukewarm water until the water runs clear (protect your hands with rubber gloves). Hang to dry. Empty the dye in the sink, clean the bucket, and mix the next dye bath.

7. When the fabric is dry, carefully reheat the wax and paint the fabric wherever you want the first color to remain.

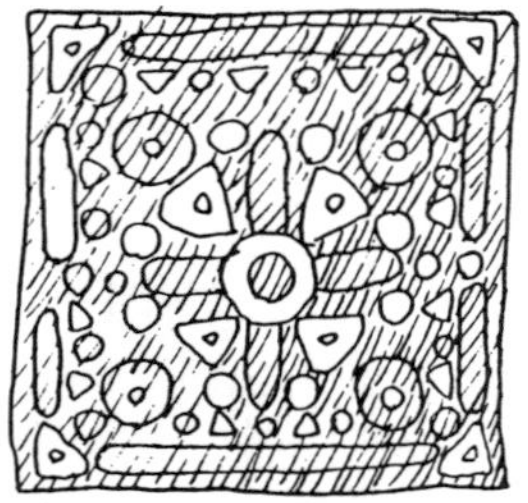

Let the wax harden, then dye with the second color. Rinse; hang to dry. (Repeat this sequence with any additional colors.)

8. To remove the wax, place the fabric between two sheets of old newspaper (the ink is liable to rub off fresh newspaper). Iron over it with a hot, dry iron. Keep the iron moving. Replace the paper as it gets saturated with wax, and continue until no more wax is absorbed by the newspaper.

9. Wash the fabric in soapy water, as hot as you can stand it. Hang to dry. (If the fabric is still stiff with wax, have it dry cleaned.) Hem all the way around to make the edges neat.

CITIZEN BAND

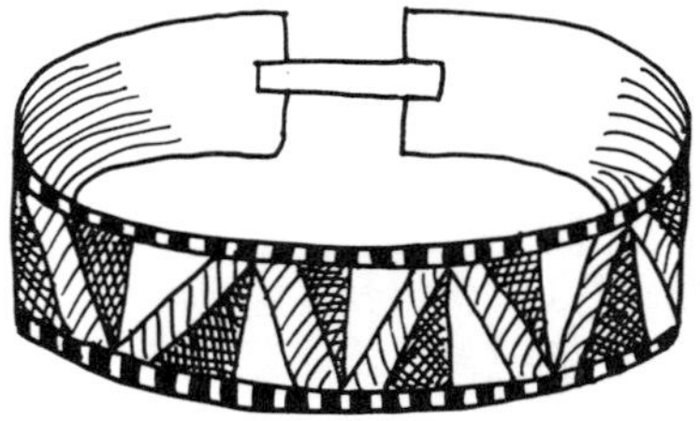

These headbands can be worn by boys and girls alike. Place them on your head, or use them to keep your hair from your face.

Native American Head-Dress Designs

FELT HEADBAND
Felt strip, about 1″ × 16″
Assorted felt scraps
Sequins, buttons and other trims
3/4″ elastic, about 4″ long
White glue
Needle and thread

Note The headband shown here is inspired by the feathered bands worn by a number of American Indian tribes. Design your headband any way you like.

1. Cut the felt scraps into various shapes. Glue them to one side of the long felt strip, using the glue sparingly, so that it doesn't bleed through the felt.

2. Add other trims, if you like, such as fabric trims, sequins, buttons, and beads (the latter two items you'll have to sew on).

3. Sew the elastic to the inside of the headband at both ends.

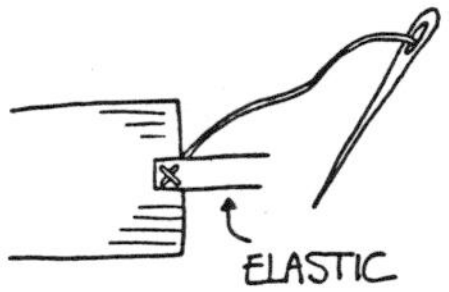

Turn your headband into a tiara with the addition of lots of sparkly trims and sequins.

Instead of a felt strip, you can use a length of wide fabric trim for the background of your headband.

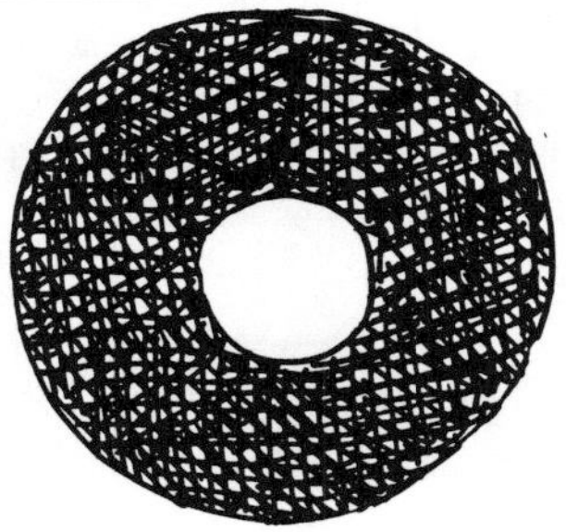

HATS OFF!

This unusual felt ring doesn't really look like a hat until you start twisting and folding it into various hat shapes. It's the perfect addition to your costume box because it's so many "hats" all rolled into one.

FELT CHAPEAU RING
Heavy-weight paper, about 16″ square
Black felt, about 1/2 yard 72″ felt
Stitch Witchery®, about 1 yard
Scissors
Iron

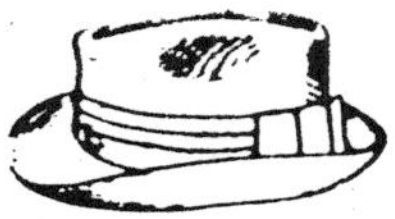

Note You can also use a sewing machine to stitch the layers of felt together, rather than bond them. Criss-cross the surface of the ring with stitches to make the ring fairly stiff so it will hold its shape.

1. Cut a 16″ circle out of paper (trace around a round platter or rig a compass from a pencil and piece of string—see page 137). Cut a 5″ hole in the middle of the circle. Place the ring on your head to check for size. You should be able to pull the ring down onto your head easily. Adjust the size of the hole if necessary.

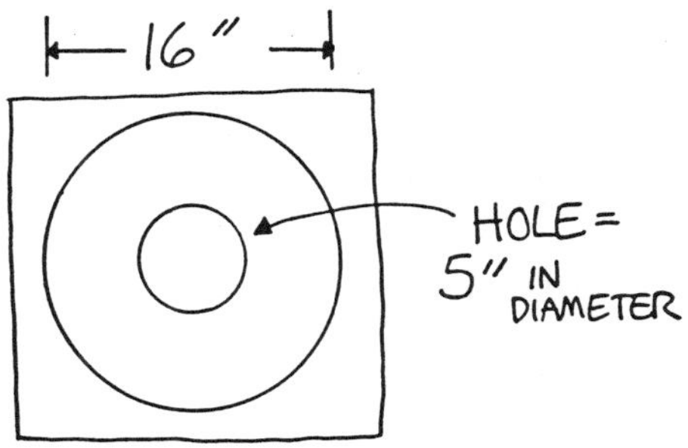

The Story of Art
Manipulating a felt ring to create a variety of "hats" originated in France in the 18th century. By the 1900s, chapeaugraphy ("hat-writing") was a popular entertainment in both Europe and the United States.

Did you know?
Chapeau (shah-PO) is French for "hat."

2. Using the paper ring as a pattern, cut three identical rings out of felt. Bond them one on top of the other, following the manufacturer's directions that come with the Stitch Witchery® (or stitch them as described in the *Note* on page 151).

3. Place the ring on your head. Experiment by folding, twisting, and pulling the outer rim through the ring, to create various hats.

While some hats are worn as a fashion statement, most hats serve a purpose. Some are used to shade the head and keep it cool (loosely woven straw is a common material used); other hats are designed to keep the head warm (wool, fur, and down are good choices for these hats). Some hats are molded into shape with steam; others are nothing more than a long piece of cloth wrapped around the wearer's head.

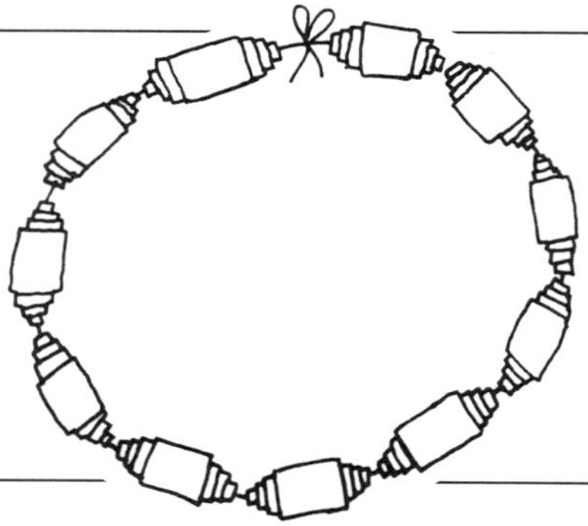

BAUBLES & BEADS

People have been adorning themselves with jewelry for thousands of years. Our prehistoric ancestors probably wore necklaces strung with shell and ivory beads. You can make your own beads to string from rolled paper.

Glass beads thought to be 4,500 years old were found in the Near East. These beads are one of the earliest examples of glass that have been found to date.

ROLLED PAPER BEAD NECKLACE

- Colored paper, such as Canson paper, origami paper, and wrapping paper
- Ruler
- X-acto knife
- White glue
- Knitting needle
- String or yarn
- Needle

Note Rolled beads are made from narrow strips of paper that are tapered at one end and wrapped around a uniformly-thick rod. How long each strip needs to be, depends on how thick both the paper and the rod are. Make the strips longer if you are using thin paper; shorter for heavy paper.

1. The beads shown here are made from heavyweight Canson paper wrapped around a No. 9 knitting needle (you can use a pencil or a straight paint brush shaft, if you like). Cut each strip 6″ long. It should be 1″ wide at one end, tapering to 1/2″ at the other end.

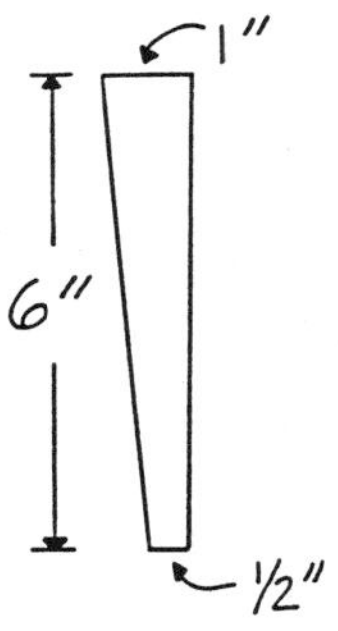

2. Starting with the wide end, wrap the strip around the knitting needle. Squirt a small amount of glue at the beginning to hold it in place. Wrap the paper as tightly as possible, and as evenly as you can, so that the bead is built up evenly on both sides.

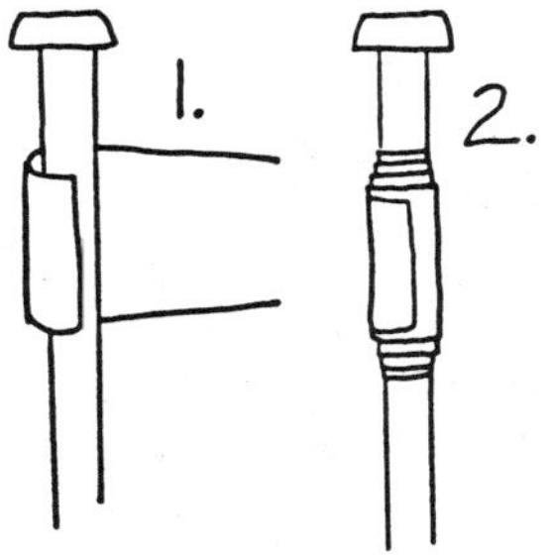

Finish the bead by gluing down the narrow end with a spot of glue. Hold until the glue sets.

3. String the beads on a length of string, heavy thread, or yarn.

Tip Here's a trick for making short work of cutting lots of tapered strips the same size and color.

Draw two lines on a large sheet of paper 6″ from one another. Mark the dimensions for a series of strips that alternate wide ends and narrow ends, as shown.

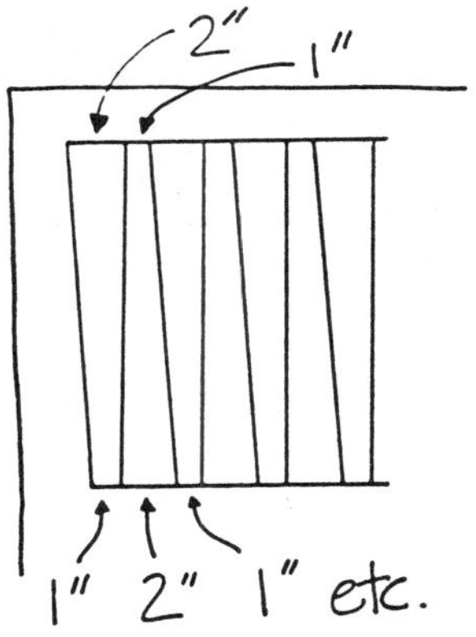

Cut the long straight lines at top and bottom first. Then cut each strip apart.

Laotian women often wear silver bands and coins as jewelry. These literally represent their family's wealth.

Some of the oldest surviving jewelry that is intact dates from 2500 B.C. Necklaces, bracelets, earrings, and rings belonging to Queen Paubi of Ur, in Sumeria, were found in her burial tomb. Stone animal figurines dating back to 3000 B.C. have also been found.

A

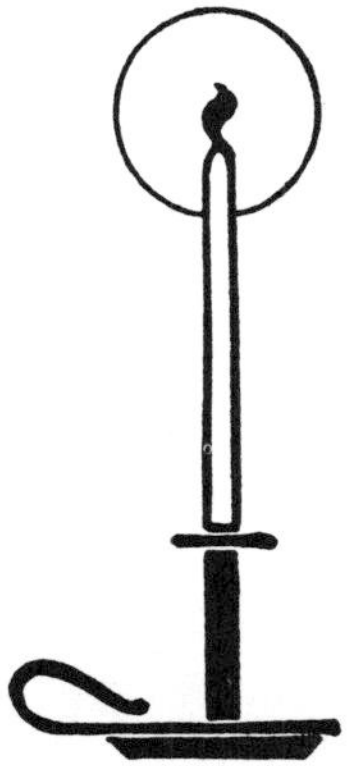

B

C

D

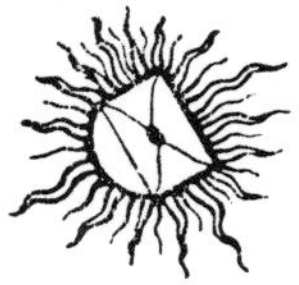

E

F

P

R

S

T

V

W

Y

MORE GOOD BOOKS FROM WILLIAMSON PUBLISHING

Kids Can!®

The following *Kids Can!*® books for ages 4 to 10 are each 160–178 pages, fully illustrated, trade paper, 11 × 8½, $12.95 US.

HAND-PRINT ANIMAL ART
by Carolyn Carreiro ($14.95)

CUT-PAPER PLAY!
Dazzling Creations from Construction Paper
by Sandi Henry

Early Childhood News Directors' Choice Award
VROOM! VROOM!
Making 'dozers, 'copters, trucks & more
by Judy Press

COOL CRAFTS & AWESOME ART!
A Kids' Treasure Trove of Fabulous Fun
by Roberta Gould

Oppenheim Toy Portfolio Best Book Award
American Bookseller Pick of the Lists
Benjamin Franklin Best Nonfiction Award
SUPER SCIENCE CONCOCTIONS
50 Mysterious Mixtures for Fabulous Fun
by Jill Frankel Hauser

Dr. Toy Best Vacation Product
Parents' Choice Gold Award
Parents Magazine Parents' Pick
THE KIDS' NATURE BOOK *(Newly Revised)*
365 Indoor/Outdoor Activities and Experiences
by Susan Milord

Benjamin Franklin Best Multicultural Book Award
Parents' Choice Approved
Skipping Stones Multicultural Honor Award
THE KIDS' MULTICULTURAL COOKBOOK
Food & Fun Around the World
by Deanna F. Cook

KIDS' COMPUTER CREATIONS
Using Your Computer for Art & Craft Fun
by Carol Sabbeth

Parents' Choice Approved
Dr. Toy Best Vacation Product Award
KIDS GARDEN!
The Anytime, Anyplace Guide to Sowing & Growing Fun
by Avery Hart and Paul Mantell

Oppenheim Toy Portfolio Best Book Award
American Bookseller Pick of the Lists
THE KIDS' SCIENCE BOOK
Creative Experiences for Hands-On Fun
by Robert Hirschfeld and Nancy White

Parents' Choice Gold Award
American Bookseller Pick of the Lists
Oppenheim Toy Portfolio Best Book Award
THE KIDS' MULTICULTURAL ART BOOK
Art & Craft Experiences from Around the World
by Alexandra M. Terzian

Parents' Choice Gold Award
Benjamin Franklin Best Juvenile Nonfiction Award
KIDS MAKE MUSIC!
Clapping and Tapping from Bach to Rock
by Avery Hart and Paul Mantell

American Bookseller Pick of the Lists
KIDS' CRAZY CONCOCTIONS
50 Mysterious Mixtures for Art & Craft Fun
by Jill Frankel Hauser

Oppenheim Toy Portfolio Best Book Award
Skipping Stones Nature & Ecology Honor Award
EcoArt!
Earth-Friendly Art & Craft Experiences for 3- to 9-Year-Olds
by Laurie Carlson

KIDS COOK!
Fabulous Food for the Whole Family
by Sarah Williamson and Zachary Williamson

THE KIDS' WILDLIFE BOOK
Exploring Animal Worlds through Indoor/Outdoor Crafts and Experiences
by Warner Shedd

HANDS AROUND THE WORLD
365 Creative Ways to Build Cultural Awareness & Global Respect
by Susan Milord

KIDS CREATE!
Art & Craft Experiences for 3- to 9-Year-Olds
by Laurie Carlson

Parents Magazine Parents' Pick
KIDS LEARN AMERICA!
Bringing Geography to Life with People, Places, & History
by Patricia Gordon and Reed C. Snow

American Bookseller Pick of the Lists
ADVENTURES IN ART *(Newly Revised)*
Arts & Crafts Experiences for 8- to 13-Year-Olds
by Susan Milord

Little Hands®

The following *Little Hands®* books for ages 2 to 6 are each 144 pages, fully illustrated, trade paper, 10 × 8, $12.95 US.

MATH PLAY!
80 Ways to Count & Learn
by Diane McGowan and Mark Schrooten

American Bookseller Pick of the Lists
RAINY DAY PLAY!
Explore, Create, Discover, Pretend
by Nancy Fusco Castaldo

Parents' Choice Gold Award
FUN WITH MY 5 SENSES
Activities to Build Learning Readiness
by Sarah A. Williamson

Children's BOMC Main Selection
THE LITTLE HANDS ART BOOK
Exploring Arts & Crafts with 2- to 6-Year-Olds
by Judy Press

Parents' Choice Approved
Early Childhood News Directors' Choice Award
SHAPES, SIZES, & MORE SURPRISES!
A Little Hands Early Learning Book
by Mary Tomczyk

Parents' Choice Approved
The Little Hands BIG FUN CRAFT Book
Creative Fun for 2- to 6-Year-Olds
by Judy Press

Parents' Choice Approved
THE LITTLE HANDS NATURE BOOK
Earth, Sky, Critters & More
by Nancy Fusco Castaldo

OTHER BOOKS FROM WILLIAMSON PUBLISHING

American Bookseller Pick of the Lists
PYRAMIDS!
50 Hands-On Activities to Experience Ancient Egypt
by Avery Hart & Paul Mantell
96 pages, 10 × 10
Trade paper, $10.95

Benjamin Franklin Best Juvenile Fiction Award
Parents' Choice Honor Award
Stepping Stones Multicultural Honor Award
TALES ALIVE!
Ten Multicultural Folktales with Activities
by Susan Milord
128 pages, 8½ × 11
Trade paper, $12.95

Benjamin Franklin Best Multicultural Award
Benjamin Franklin Best Juvenile Fiction Award
Parents' Choice Approved
TALES OF THE SHIMMERING SKY
Ten Global Folktales with Activities
by Susan Milord
128 pages, 8½ × 11
Trade paper, $12.95

To see what's new at Williamson and learn more about specific books, visit our website at:
http://www.williamsonbooks.com

TO ORDER BOOKS:

You'll find Williamson books at your favorite bookstore or order directly from Williamson Publishing.
We accept Visa and MasterCard (*please include the number and expiration date*), or send check to:

Williamson Publishing Company
Church Hill Road, P.O. Box 185
Charlotte, Vermont 05445

Toll-free phone orders with credit cards:
1-800-234-8791

E-mail orders with credit cards:
order@williamsonbooks.com

Catalog request: mail, phone, or E-mail

Please add **$4.00** for postage for one book plus **$1.00** for each additional book.

Satisfaction is guaranteed or full refund without questions or quibbles.

Prices may be slightly higher when purchased in Canada.

ECOART!

Library of Congress
Cataloging-in-Publication Data

Carlson, Laurie M., 1952 -
EcoArt! : earth-frientlly art & craft experiences for 3- to 9-year-olds / Laurie Carlson; illustrated by Loretta Trezzo Braren.
p. cm.
"A Williamson kids can! book."
Includes index.
Summary: Presents art and craft projects that benefit the environment through such activities as recycling.
ISBN 0-913589-68-3
[1. Handicraft – Juvenile literature. 2. Nature craft – Juvenile literature. 3. Recycling (Waste, etc.) – Juvenile literature. (1. Handicraft. 2. Nature Craft. 3. Recycling (Waste)]
I. Braren, Loretta Trezzo, ill. II. Title.
TT160.C35 1992 92-21347
745.5 – dc20 CIP
AC

Cover design: Trezzo–Braren Studio
Illustrations: Loretta Trezzo Braren
Project diagrams: Laurie Carlson
Printing: Capital City Press

Williamson Publishing Co.
Box 185
Charlotte, Vermont 05445
1-800-234-8791

Manufactured in the United States of America
20 19 18 17 16 15 14 13 12

Notice: The information contained in this book is true, complete, and accurate to the best of our knowledge. All recommendations and suggestions are made without any guarantees on the part of the author or Williamson Publishing. The author and publisher disclaim all liability incurred in connection with the use of this information.

Laurie Carlson is also the author of Williamson Publishing's ***Kids Create!*** Art & Craft Experiences for 3- to 9-Year-Olds.

ECOART!

Earth-Friendly Art & Craft Experiences for 3- to 9-year-olds

Laurie Carlson

Illustrated by Loretta Trezzo Braren

A Williamson *Kids Can!* Book

Williamson Publishing • Charlotte, Vermont 05445

ECOART!

"Every genuine work of art has as much reason for being as the earth and the sun."
Ralph Waldo Emerson
ART SPEAK

1.

Pollution is nothing but the resources we are not harvesting. We allow them to disperse because we've been ignorant of their value.
Buckminster Fuller

ECOART

TAKE CHARGE!

Use it up,
Wear it out,
Make it do,
Or do without!

That wise, old saying was probably around when your grandparents and great-grandparents were the same age as you are now! In those days, people made a great effort to be frugal which means they took care of their few possessions and made them last, and last, and last. Everyone — rich or poor, young or old — took pride in not wasting anything, and reusing clothes and tools was a way of life. "Buying new" was done carefully and thoughtfully, and more often than not, families made what they needed, or did without.

Well, for many of us, all that has changed now. People tend to buy whatever they can afford, and as we all know, throw a lot of "stuff" out, only to go to the store and buy something else "brand new." But where do all of the materials come from to make toys, and gadgets, and stationery, and packaged frozen foods? And where does all the energy come from to run the factories and power the trucks that carry these things to the stores? And what happens to all the trees and wildlife that must be removed to build shopping centers and malls for the stores that sell these things? And what happens to our forests, and plants, and animals, and fresh water, and fresh air in the process?

You already know the answer to that, don't you! Many of us around the world are using up our natural resources at a very, very fast rate, and along the way we are creating big problems — endangered species like the giant panda, quickly disappearing forests like the tropical rain forests, dirty air and water that aren't fit to breathe and drink, and overflowing landfills because we have so much garbage!

You can make a difference!

Even though it sounds pretty bleak, and you may wonder what is to become of our wonderful earth, there is some really good news! You can make a difference! You and I, and our friends, and our family — can make a difference that will count and will help the earth. We're the ones who will do it. We will set up a home recycling center (see page 148), we'll keep a rag bag (see page 154) and an art inspiration box (see page 145). We'll learn to treat nature's wonders with respect and care (see page 89). We'll avoid products that are overpackaged, and always choose to buy things that aren't made with styrofoam or other materials that will clog our landfills.

Best of all, we will learn to make things just like people did years ago, and in the process we will discover just how creative and imaginative we can be. We can make our own paper, pastes, and dyes (see pages 13 to 30). And then, we can make everything from vases to sculptures, to games and dolls, to castles and jewelry, to cornhusk wreaths and bird feeders. *We don't need brand new; homemade is better — especially when we are reusing and recycling!*

Let's get specific

Things won't change overnight. It will take some thinking about what we do every day. If we think about the choices we make, then we can leave the world even better than we found it. Attitude is everything, so don't feel that you are sacrificing enjoyment by being more environmentally aware. Change must come through consuming less, reusing and recycling, and shopping smart. Kids like you will become the teachers to the grown-ups who have never had to recycle or reuse before now. As you ask your parents and grandparents to please recycle, and as you set a good example for your younger sisters and brothers, we will all learn to be better citizens of the earth, together. You will make a difference!

The best way to save the earth is to just not use up so much of it. You and I have to stop buying useless things that we really don't want or need. Shop for things that will last and can be repaired or refilled, instead of being disposable. People have always reused things in order to save money. Now we have to think about reusing things in order to save the open spaces, forests, and water.

Practice *precycling* by looking at items from an environmental viewpoint — *before* buying them. Select the items that have less packaging, use up less of the environment, and have lasting value.

Many things can be *recycled*, using the materials from existing products to create new ones. Newspapers can be recycled into new paper. Aluminum cans, glass, and some plastics can be brought to recycling centers where they will be used to make new aluminum cans, glass jars and bottles, and some plastic containers, thereby saving natural resources and energy.

Reusing means getting as much wear and tear out of every item you have for as long as possible, and then thinking up new uses for the old parts. All of us can reuse materials in our everyday lives, and we never have to leave our houses or use any additional natural resources. There are lots of fun and interesting items you can make from things that would usually go in the garbage. Start an art inspiration box right now, for things you can save. It will provide a ready source of supplies when you are working on projects.

What is EcoArt?

My guess is that you can already figure out what EcoArt is, because you already understand so much about our earth. *Ecology*, as you know, is the study of how plants and animals and people interact with their environment. A lot of scientists are concerned about the *balance of nature* which is the idea that nature, when left to its own, will take care of itself, but when humankind starts polluting the air and water, for example, the balance is thrown off and some creatures begin to die while others become too plentiful.

So what does this have to do with art? Well, that is a good question. All of the art and craft projects in this book relate to good ecological practices — respect for nature and a love of nature, good recycling efforts, and reusing everything that you possibly can. As you look to nature for inspiration, you will be strengthening your commitment to do your part to save the earth. As you create treasures out of trash, you will open your eyes to all sorts of possibilities for using things that would otherwise end up in our landfills. There really is an art to safeguarding our ecology — in more ways than one!

The projects in this book will help you look at the world around you with different eyes. Begin noticing

the tiny signs of life around you: plants, insects, birds, shells, the variety of leaves, and bark, and flower petals. Be alert to your surroundings, listening to bird calls, watching a daddy long legs gracefully and silently walk across some pebbles, and smelling the fragrance in weeds. Begin to look at nature's bounty — nuts, weeds, pods, moss, twigs, shells — as gifts to you that you can make into wonderful decorative and useful items. Watch for things to renew and reuse: paper products, discarded toys, empty boxes. As you begin to create with natural and reusable materials, you will begin to respect and appreciate everything around you more. Go ahead — with wonder, and questions, and imagination — and have a great time!

Be a recycling sleuth! You can tell if paper is made from recycled paper by the tiny flecks of fiber showing in it. Recycled cardboard is gray, like the inside of cereal boxes.

SAFETY FIRST!

To ensure your safety and well-being, please observe these safety measures. They really are important.

Paraffin: Wax and paraffin should be melted in a can placed in the top of a double boiler (water in both parts of double boiler). ***A grown-up must always do this part of a project. Paraffin is flammable.***

Hot glue gun: These are very handy, but must be used by grown-ups. If a grown-up isn't around, use a tacky-type glue instead, and press very hard until glue holds.

Balloons: Balloons may seem safe to play and create with, and they are, but they can be very dangerous for little children who still put things in their mouths. Be sure to pick up any pieces of popped balloons and deflated balloons so that little children won't pick them up. Thank you.

Craft knives: Grown-ups should use the craft knives and sharp scissors. Ask them to show you correct methods for safe use and handling.

Ventilation: Proper ventilation is necessary when using rubber cement and many fixatives. Acrylic sprays are extremely flammable as well as toxic. (Non-aerosol hair spray is a good substitute.) Grown-ups should apply fixatives, not children.

Wild plants: Wild plants are beautiful to look at and to collect, but never eat them. As you know, many of them are poisonous.

Thank you for being so careful.

• A NOTE TO PARENTS, TEACHERS, & CARE-GIVERS •

Today's child is in danger of losing touch with nature. The natural world is far from our apartments and lifestyles. For many, the natural play in woods, streams, mud puddles, and snowbanks that past generations so enjoyed, is but an image from a picture book. Yet, children gravitate to anything in its natural state. They enjoy working with all kinds of natural materials: pine cones, pods and weeds, shells, moss, driftwood, smooth stones, wildflowers, feathers, and vines. They are intrigued by the feel of these items in their hands, by the process of collecting materials while feeling the wind in their hair, and by the earthy scent of the forest.

It is this natural world that our children are in danger of never experiencing and never appreciating; it is not found in stores, nor advertised on television. It does not draw attention to itself artificially. Sadly, what once was common, has now become unusual.

Given the opportunity, children from all walks of life respond to the excitement and warmth of the natural world. They quickly come to respect its wonder and its fragility. Every child becomes a nurturer when placed in a natural setting. Every child discovers an inner peace and hidden creativity when given the chance to interact with nature.

It is my hope that children using this book will awaken this creative impulse, will experience nature with all of their senses, and will treasure that experience, for it is only through a personal sense of awe that our children will make the monumental effort to put our earth first. I ask of you as parents, and teachers, and care-givers to encourage their efforts; let them awaken in you the energy and interest to share in their efforts to save their earth.

Toward a Positive Experience

Each project is identified as to the approximate degree of difficulty involved to confidently complete it. Look for the leaves to identify the suggested range of ability or dexterity each project might involve.

🍁 = Few fine motor skills needed. Adults may need to help very young children by preparing some of the materials ahead of time. With very little adult assistance, these projects should delight most children.

🍁🍁 = Skills such as cutting, folding, using a template, or painting may be required. Young children need practice with these skills, but adults should avoid creating frustrating experiences for those truly too young to handle them. Most children enjoy these projects and will want to experiment with the wider range of mediums and tools.

🍁🍁🍁 = More involved projects that require manual dexterity and a variety of steps to completion. Most children will do just fine with these, especially if they are left to improvise and use their own creative approaches.

These indicators of skill level are quite arbitrary. Don't let them limit your choice of project. If a project is interesting, fun, and appropriate, work around any part that seems beyond a child. Most projects have at least some part that all children can participate in. Collecting materials and thinking about new uses for old objects will tantalize even the youngest creator. Kids are extremely versatile, especially when they really want to do something. Usually they are very willing to stretch their abilities or find clever shortcuts.

Clock Watchers

Most projects in this book can be completed in twenty to thirty minutes, or less. Because time allowances are necessary for using some mediums and completing some of the projects, I've identified those projects requiring more than one hour to complete. Look for the little clock which is your signal that the project takes more than one hour. Read through these projects because many of them have convenient stopping points. If you can leave your materials out and come back later, the time may not be a factor.

In some cases, materials must be prepared ahead of time, or drying or baking time is required. This is not included in the estimate. Allow extra time for drying which varies with the medium used, as well as thickness of the project, humidity level, and temperature.

2.

MAKING YOUR OWN ART & CRAFT SUPPLIES

NATURAL ART

Nature provides many gifts. The brilliant colors of autumn leaves, the intricate symmetry of a bird's feather, the glistening beauty in a chunk of rock, the cracked patterns in mud as it dries — all nourish our creativity. Nature surrounds us with its beauty and strength. If we stop and look closely, we see that nature has given us inspiration for our own art. The musical trill of a bird call, the feel of a rabbit's downy coat, the patterns in clouds above us — everywhere is inspiration for our eyes, our ears, and our fingertips.

Artists, musicians, and poets have been inspired by nature in many ways. Let it inspire you, too. As you look for the perfect pebble for a project, or choose an interesting leaf or branch, you will be joining with nature to shape your creations.

Natural art can be found in the tiniest rock, the simplest shell. It inspires us and gives us encouragement. But natural art is fragile and can be easily lost. To find the twig, you must have a tree. To smell a wildflower, there must be meadows for them to bloom in. To watch a creature, there must be space and nourishment for it to survive. If we protect and preserve the natural world, the quiet path or cooling creek will always be there for us.

QUILL PEN

MATERIALS

- Feather
- Ink or tempera paint
- Scissors or knife

You can make a pen like those used by writers from the sixth century until the mid-nineteenth century, when the steel pen point was invented.

Feathers from geese were most commonly used. Swan feathers were more expensive. Crow's feathers were best for creating fine lines.

In order to make your own quill pen, you need to find or purchase a feather. Look outside and see if you can find any feathers in your yard or along the beach. (Wash your hands after handling.) Chicken or turkey feathers are sold in most craft supply shops, if you can't find any.

With scissors or a sharp knife, snip off the end at a slant. Dip the cut end into ink or paint and write just like your ancestors might have!

When the tip wears down, snip it off a bit more, to create a fresh sharp tip. Now that is really recycling!

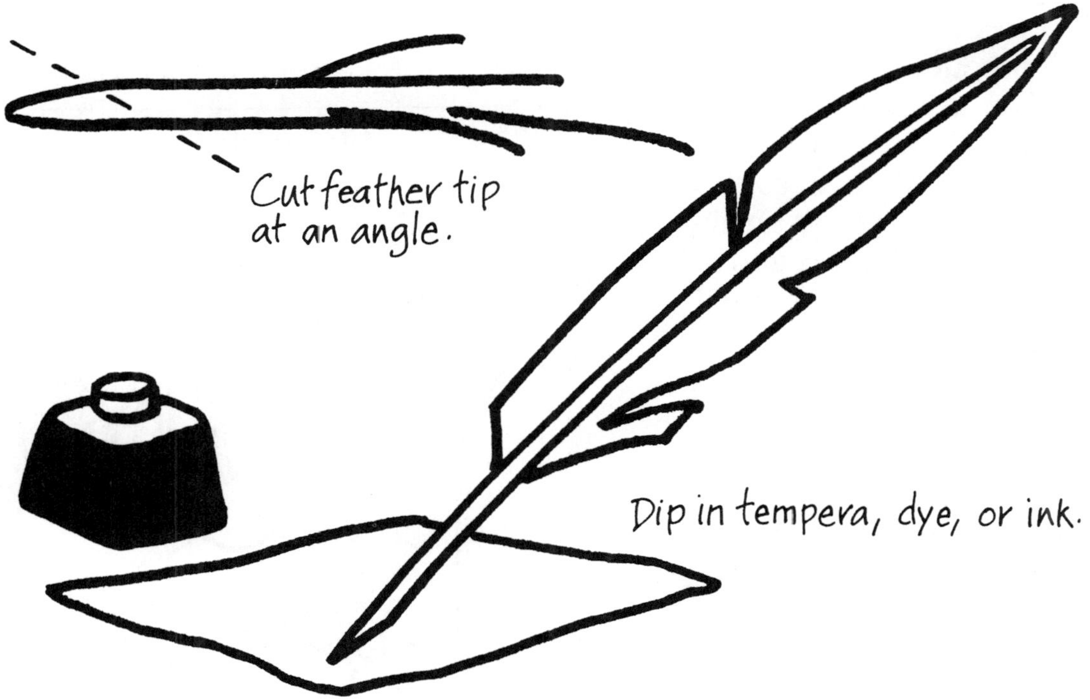

NATURAL DYES

MATERIALS

- Plant materials
- Cloth or paper to dye
- Large pot and water
- Wooden spoon

Creating dyes from natural plant materials is fun and interesting. Put on your old clothes and go gathering and collecting. You'll be so surprised to see what colors your gathered materials will produce. You can use your natural dyes to color cotton, or wool yarn, or fabrics. Use your dyes to paint on paper or fabric, to color cornhusks, feathers, straw, egg shells, and, of course, cotton T-shirts and socks. You can even use your natural dye to color eggs, or just pour the dye into jars and paint with water-color brushes.

The colors you can make are soft, natural, and sometimes muted. To get a stronger color, let items soak for a longer time or redye in freshly gathered materials.

Here's what to gather to make a variety of natural dyes:

For this color:	*Use one of these materials:*
Yellow	Goldenrod, sassafras flower, pomegranate rinds, onion skins, willow tree leaves, marigolds, orange peels
Red	Cherries, birch bark (gathered from the ground only)
Rose	Willow bark (gathered from the ground only)
Purple	Blackberries, elderberries
Blue	Red cabbage leaves, sunflower seeds
Green	Carrot tops, grass clippings, spinach, moss
Tan	Walnut shells, tea leaves, instant coffee

If you are unable to gather natural plant materials to make your dyes, you can purchase frozen or canned berries or vegetables to create the dye. To use canned beets, strain the liquid and add 2 teaspoons of vinegar. To use frozen blueberries or blackberries, let them thaw in a bowl and press out the juice.

Experiment with other flowers, berries, and leafy materials you find. Boil them in water to see what color they create. And guess what? Rusty nails can be added to a dye to make the color darker, so you can be cleaning up while gathering, too.

To prepare dyes from any of these natural materials, first cut or tear the plant materials in small pieces and place in a large pot. Add enough water to cover the material. Ask a grown-up to help you boil it for 5 – 20 minutes, until the water reaches the color intensity you want. With help, strain the mixture into a cut-down plastic jug through a piece of cheesecloth, or the foot section of a pair of panty hose. Add a tablespoon of vinegar to act as a *mordant* to the dye bath. The mordant will set, or keep, the color. Now, have a grown-up help you reheat the dye bath in a large saucepan.

Experiment by dipping fabric, yarn, or paper into the dye to check color. If you like the color, let the material you are dying simmer in the dye bath, until it reaches the color you like. Stir or turn it to be sure the color covers evenly.

Tear the plant materials in small pieces & cover with water. Boil for 5 to 20 minutes.

When you like the color of the dyed material, rinse it in water. Keep rinsing in fresh water, until the rinse water is clear. Spread the material out and let dry.

If you want, you can freeze the dye water and use it again at a later time.

Be sure to avoid eating or drinking any of the plant materials or natural dyes because many wild plants, flowers, leaves, stems, and roots are poisonous.

HOMEMADE RECYCLED PAPER

MATERIALS

- Newspaper or other waste paper
- Plant materials: flower petals, leaves, weeds, onion skins
- Water
- Dishpan
- Screening, about 8" x 8"
- Towels
- Bucket
- Pieces of old bedsheet material, about 12" x 12"
- Sponge
- Electric blender or mixer

The first U.S. paper mill was built in 1690. The paper was made from old cotton and linen rags. It was 200 years later when wood pulp from trees was used to make paper.

Paper has been made from a variety of natural materials such as cotton, mulberry bark, hemp, and grass. Today, it is usually made from pulp that is produced by grinding up trees. Because paper is so important to us, and because we use so much of it, we need to be careful not to waste it. Remember that it takes only seconds to use a paper tissue or napkin, but decades for a tree to grow.

Paper is one item that can be completely recycled. Old newspapers can be turned into wet pulp and pressed into fresh paper again and again. You can recycle paper by making your own handmade paper from scraps of waste paper.

Tear the waste paper into small pieces, and soak it overnight in a bucket of water. Place a few handfuls of the soaked paper into a blender and fill it about half full with water. Blend in short bursts to break the material up. Add torn bits of leaves, flower petals, grass, weeds, or whatever. You can put in some natural dyes or food coloring, too.

Now lay the piece of screen in the dishpan, and then fill the dishpan with about 3" of water. Pour the pulp from the blender into the dishpan. Slide the piece of screen back and forth through the mixture, and then lift it straight up. The pulp will be distributed evenly on the screen. Lay the screen on a towel to drain.

Place a piece of old fabric or sheeting on top of the pulp, and press firmly with a sponge to remove the excess water. Continue until all water is removed from the pulp.

Turn the screen over, releasing the paper onto the sheeting material. Lay it on a flat surface to dry. Peel the paper away from the cloth when it is dry.

To hasten the drying process, lay a second sheet of fabric on top of the strained paper and ask a grown-up to press with a heated iron. This also makes the paper flatter and smoother in texture.

STEM PAINT BRUSH & CLAY PAINT

MATERIALS

Soft plant stalk: yucca, iris or cattail stem, or cornhusk
Knife
Rock
Clay (freshly dug or bought)
White glue

Native Americans in the Southwest used to chew the ends of yucca stalks to soften them and then use the "brush" to paint pottery with delicate brush strokes.

To make your own stem paint brush, break or cut a plant stalk to get a piece 8" – 10" long. Break up the fibers at one end to make your brush's "bristles," by cutting them with a knife, shredding in narrow strips, or mashing the end with a rock. Work at it until the fibers are separated and brush-like. *Don't chew on plant materials, as they may be poisonous.*

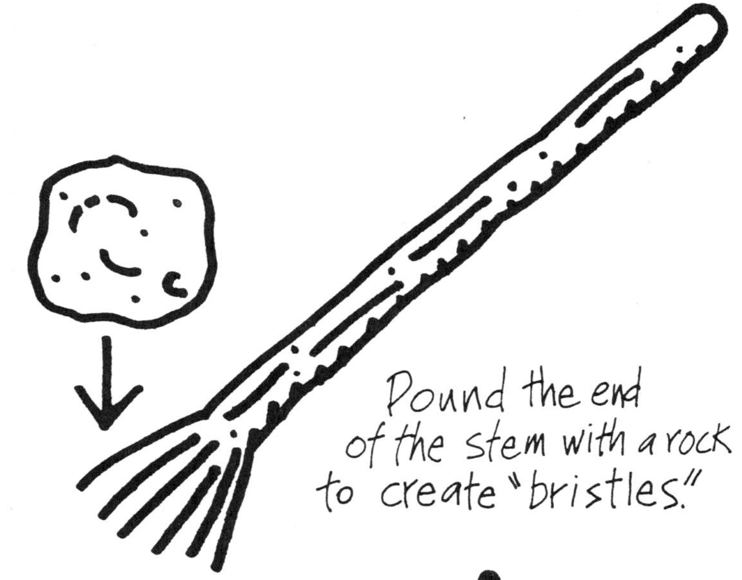

Great! Now you're ready to make some *clay paints* like the Native Americans did (or you can paint with poster paints). Begin looking for some soft clay in your backyard or in your neighborhood. Dig a bit here and there, squishing the clay with your fingers until you find some that sticks together. Depending upon where you live, natural clay can be chocolate brown, light tan, or orange-red.

After you have dug some clay, let it dry; then, pound or break it up into small pieces. Pick out any rocks, sticks, or roots.

Now, add some water and let it soak until the clay is dissolved. Stir and add a bit more water and a squirt of white glue, until the clay paint is smooth. Paint on heavy cardboard or brown paper bags. Crumple the bags, then smooth flat, and they will resemble animal hide.

NATURAL CLAY

If you live in an area where soft, pliable clay is available for the digging, you'll have a great time digging, then shaping and sculpting items that can be dried in the sun. While sun-dried clay pieces aren't waterproof or permanent, if they are carefully stored, they can last for many, many years.

Locate clay that is fine textured, and free of leaves, gravel, and sticks. If you need to clean the clay, dilute it with water, and strain it through a sieve or colander to remove the debris. Let the diluted clay dry in the sun, until it is thick enough to work with. If you add a few tablespoons of white glue to the clay, it will dry harder.

Strain the clay to remove leaves, gravel, and sticks.

To shape objects from clay, you will want to use a clump the size of your fist. To add arms, legs, or a neck, use your fingers to pull the clay into shape. (If you roll tiny pieces and add them to the clay body for arms and legs, they will often break off later.) Remember, pull the sculpture into shape from the larger ball. If you don't like the sculpture, just squish it all back into a ball and start again.

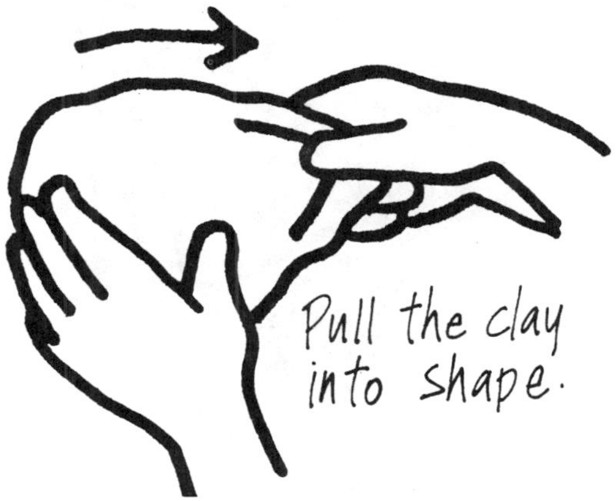

Pull the clay into shape.

When working with clay, have a pan of water handy. Dip your fingertips in it to moisten and smooth the clay as you work it. Use sticks, stones, and tools such as nails or dull knives to trim and decorate your sculptures. You can press bits of twigs, feathers or leaves into the clay to add interesting details, since you will be air-drying your sculpture.

Try your hand at shaping simple clay animals, pots, napkin rings, or potpourri bowls.

PORTABLE BOX EASEL & CLIPBOARD

MATERIALS

- Cardboard rectangle from packaging, and a cardboard box
- Clothespins
- Serrated knife (grown-up use)
- Yarn or string

If you want to take along additional art supplies for sketching or painting, make a simple easel from a box.

Cut away one side of the box as shown. Ask a grown-up to help, using a serrated knife to cut. Angle the cut slightly so the paper will be held at the appropriate angle. Place a larger rectangle of cardboard, or your clipboard, across the opening and clip your paper to it. Your supplies can be kept inside the box.

Make a clipboard for sketching or writing when you go on outdoor hikes. Find a rectangle of heavy cardboard (or get help cutting one from a grocery box). Paint or decorate the cardboard as you wish. You can glue on used gift wrap, paint with left-over latex housepaint, or cover with crayon rubbings over leaves. Fasten your paper to the clipboard with clothespins or heavy clips. To keep your pencil handy, punch a hole in a corner of the clipboard and tie a length of yarn or string from it to the end of your pencil.

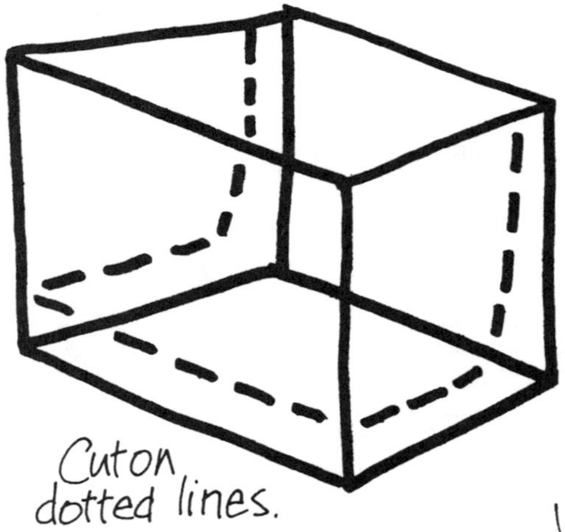

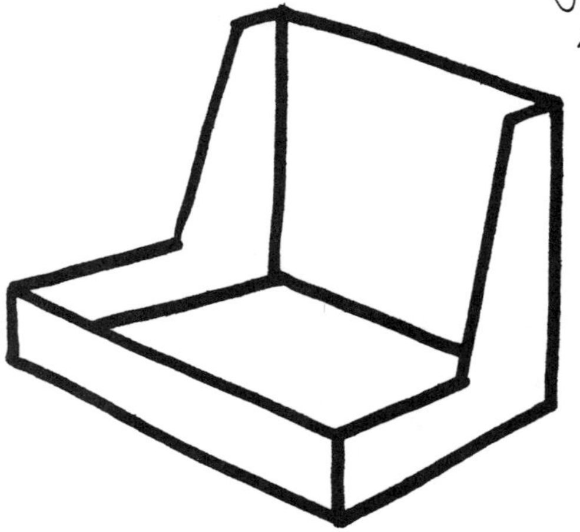

HOMEMADE SUPPLIES

Make your own! If you like to do art and craft projects, you know that the materials often cost a lot or are toxic or hazardous to your environment, if not used properly. To be safe and to save the earth (and some money), why not make some earth-friendly, natural art supplies?

Here are some "art and craft recipes" that you may want to try. Many can be stored for use in other projects throughout this book.

PASTES & GLUES

Homemade pastes and glues are perfect for any project using paper or cardboard. The glues are best for projects needing small amounts of adhesive. They work with most papers, fabric scraps, and yarn. The pastes are best for paper projects, whether you are using brown bags, wallpaper scraps, or old newspapers. If you want to make collages or papier-mache, use the paste recipes, but stir in additional water until the mixture is the thickness of pancake batter. Whatever recipe you choose, it will begin to mold and sour in a few days, unless you refrigerate it or add a natural preservative, such as oil of cloves or oil of wintergreen.

Cornstarch Glue

MATERIALS

- 3 tablespoons cornstarch
- 4 tablespoons cold water
- 2 cups hot water
- Saucepan and spoon

Ask a grown-up to help you use the stove. Mix the cornstarch and cold water in a saucepan. When smooth, begin pouring in the hot water, stirring as you add it. Heat the mixture to medium heat and cook until it begins to thicken. Stir it constantly. When it's thick, remove it from the heat and let cool. Pour into a clean dish detergent squeeze bottle or other type of container, label the bottle "glue," and store in the refrigerator when not using.

Flour and Water Paste

MATERIALS

- 1/2 cup flour
- 3/4 cup cold water
- 3 cups hot water
- Saucepan and spoon

Ask a grown-up to help you use the stove. Put the flour and cold water into a saucepan, stirring to blend smooth. Add the hot water, stirring constantly. Heat and stir until mixture is thick and smooth. Let cool and pour into a squeeze-type container, like one from shampoo or mustard. Label the bottle "paste," and store in the refrigerator.

Library Paste

Makes a thick paste that spreads with your fingers. Use it on paper projects.

MATERIALS

- 1/2 cup sugar
- 1/2 cup flour
- 2 cups water
- 1/2 teaspoon alum (from supermarket or drugstore)
- Oil of cloves, optional (from drugstore)
- Saucepan and spoon

Ask a grown-up to help you at the stove. Mix everything (except oil) together in a saucepan, and heat to medium, stirring constantly. When the mixture thickens, remove from the heat and let it cool. If you want to keep this paste for up to several months, add 15 drops of oil of cloves to keep it from spoiling. Label and store in covered containers, like margarine or cottage cheese tubs.

Crazy Paste

My favorite! This paste uses unusual ingredients to make a smooth paste that dries without flaking or cracking. It dries clear, and works well with most craft materials.

MATERIALS

1/4 cup cornstarch
3/4 cup water
2 tablespoons corn syrup
1 teaspoon white vinegar
1/4 teaspoon oil of wintergreen, optional preservative
Medium saucepan and spoon

Ask a grown-up to help you at the stove. Mix the cornstarch and water in the saucepan. Add the corn syrup and vinegar. Stir and cook over medium heat until the mixture thickens. It will take a few minutes; then it will begin to thicken quickly. Continue stirring as it thickens. Remove from heat. To add a preservative, stir in 1/4 teaspoon of oil of wintergreen. This paste will get thicker as it cools. Label and keep in a covered container (like a cottage cheese container) for about two months. Without oil of wintergreen, store in the refrigerator for about two weeks.

Bookbinder's Paste

Here's an old recipe that professional bookbinders used long ago. It's simple, inexpensive, and uses no chemicals. It works for any type of paper-pasting project. It cleans up with water and the paper dries flat and smooth.

This recipe makes about five cups of paste which will be enough for several projects.

MATERIALS

1 cup flour
1 cup cold water
4 or 5 cups of very hot water
Saucepan and spoon

Put the flour in a saucepan and slowly stir in the cup of cold water. Stir till smooth, breaking up any lumps. Ask a grown-up to help you slowly pour in the hot water, a cup at a time. Place on medium heat. Cook for three minutes, stirring all the time. Let it cool; then it's ready to use. Use a sponge, paint brush, or your fingers to spread it.

This paste will keep for a few days, if covered and refrigerated. If you want to keep it longer, add 2 teaspoons of powdered alum or 3 drops of oil of cloves.

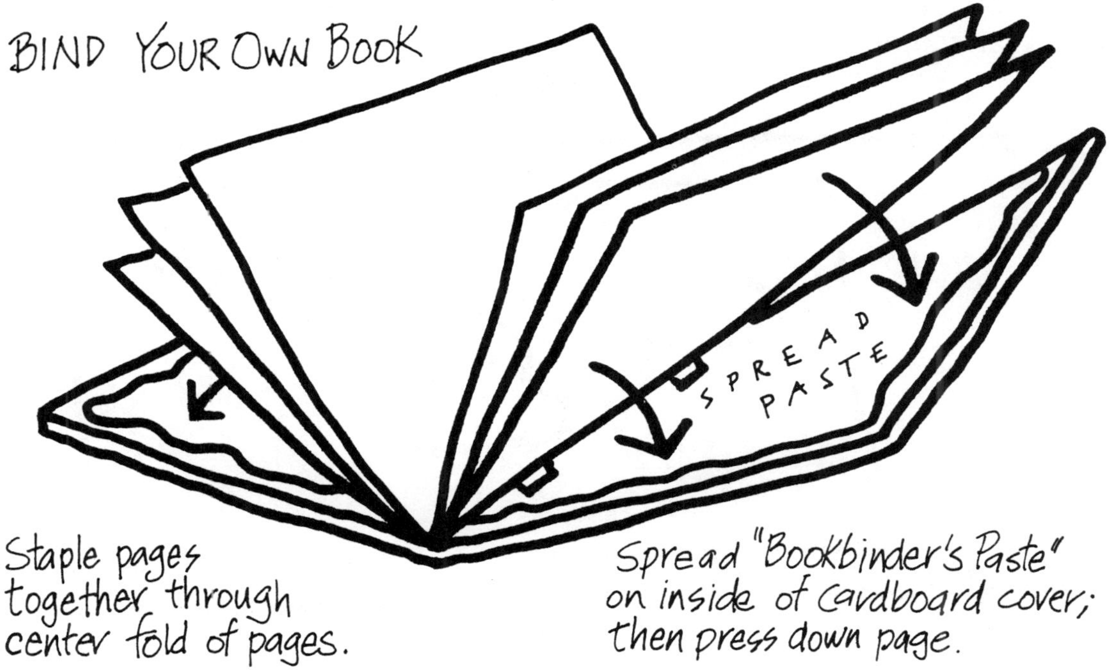

HOMEMADE FINGER PAINT

Finger paints can be made from many things. You can use shaving cream to finger paint on washable surfaces. Liquid starch can be colored with powdered tempera or a squirt of food coloring. In the winter, mix a bit of Bon Ami and water in a jar lid and fingerpaint snowflake designs on windows. Wipe off with a wet cloth to clean up.

MATERIALS

- 1/2 cup flour
- 2 cups water
- Food coloring
- Paper: save used typing and copier paper; use the backside
- Newspapers
- Saucepan and spoon
- Baby food jars, yogurt containers, or similar containers

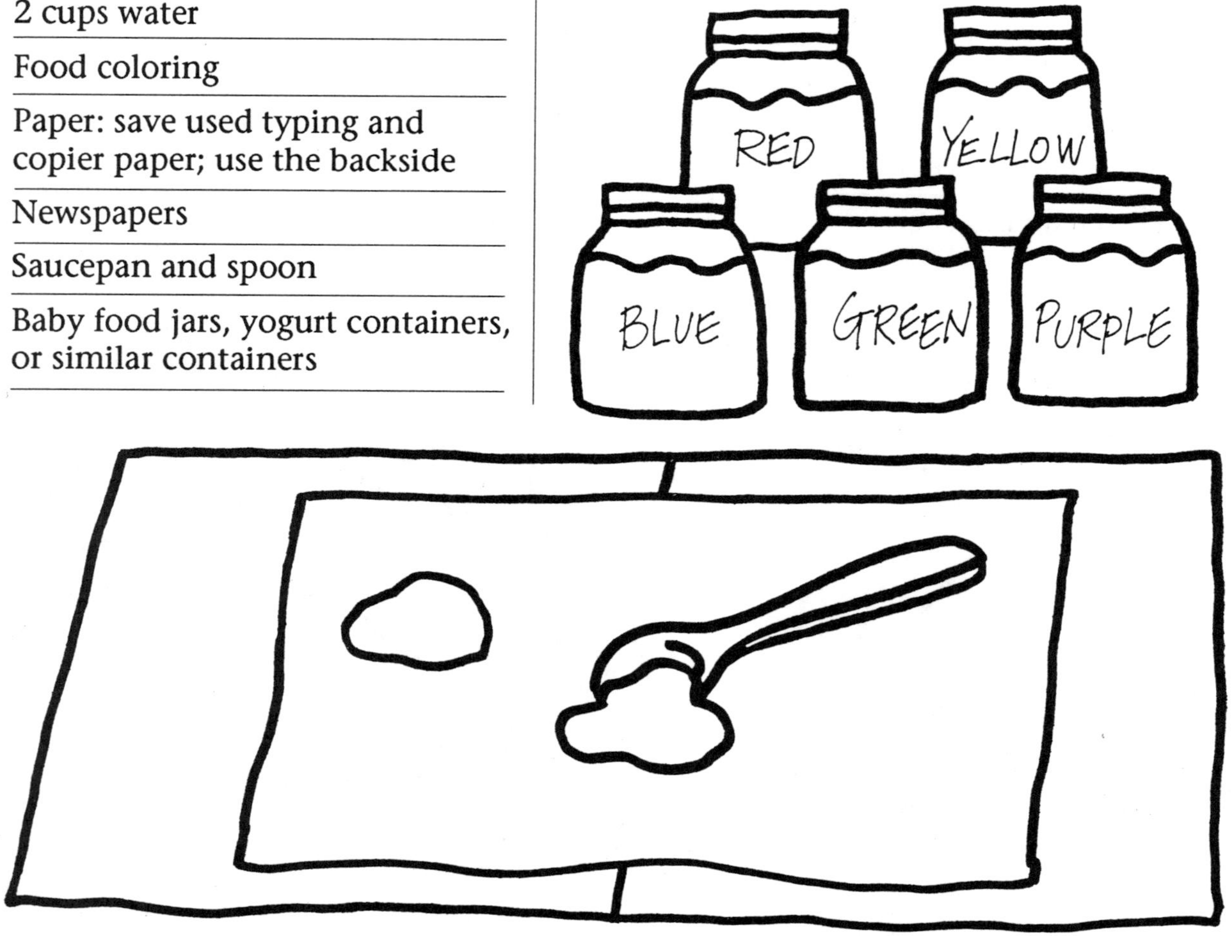

Mix the flour with a little water, stirring out the lumps. When smooth, slowly stir in the rest of the water. Ask a grown-up to help you cook over medium heat, stirring constantly until the mixture gets thick and shiny.

Carefully pour some of the mixture into each jar. (You may want to make a funnel to do this. See how to do it on page 128.) Stir in drops of food coloring until the paint is bright and the color you want. Let cool.

While waiting, cover the table or floor painting area with old newspapers. Wet the painting paper with water, smoothing the wet paper out on the newspapers. Spoon the finger paint onto the paper and get started!

Salt can be sprinkled into the wet paint to create a sparkling effect when dry. Use this technique on dark-colored paper for snow scenes or eerie ghosts.

TOOLS ★★★★★

MATERIALS ✱

Old plastic bottles

Fine tip permanent marking pen

Scissors or craft knife

Nail or hole punch

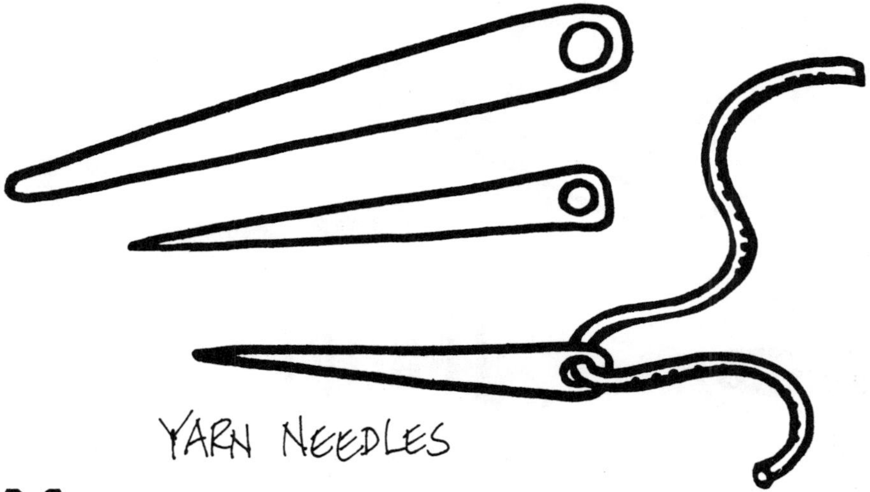

Make some of your own art and craft tools, so you'll have them ready when you need them. You can make brushes (see page 20), remelt crayons (see page 30) and make paper (see page 18).

To make *templates* and *stencils,* cut flat areas from plastic bottles and packaging materials. Draw your design with a marking pen; then, cut it out with scissors or craft knife.

Make simple *yarn needles* for stitching, weaving, and stringing objects by cutting thin needle shapes from a plastic jug. Use a hole punch or nail to make a hole at one end. Thread with yarn or embroidery thread. Cut as many as you need, in several sizes.

HOMEMADE YARN ★

MATERIALS ✱✱

Old T-shirts

Scissors

Use your homemade yarn any time you need a heavy yarn or string — for wrapping packages, weaving, or creating toys and puppets. Remove any pockets, cuffs, or trim from the T-shirt, and cut away the hem and sleeves. Begin cutting at the bottom of the shirt, and cut an inch-wide strip in a continuous spiral around the shirt. When you stretch the yarn, the cut ends will curl under, giving it a tubular shape. Roll it in a ball and save for your projects. You can also obtain yarn for projects by unraveling old knitted scarves, sweaters, or whatever, and saving the yarn in balls.

WEAVING LOOMS & LOOPS

Make the loom by tapping long nails into a board in the shape of a 12" square. Cut the loops about 1" wide from the leg section of old panty hose and colorful tights. Hook the ends of the loops on the nails. Weave loops over and under until the loom is full. To finish the ends, slip one loop end off the nail and through the next loop, until you come to the last loop. Make a slip knot with it and tuck the loop back inside the weaving.

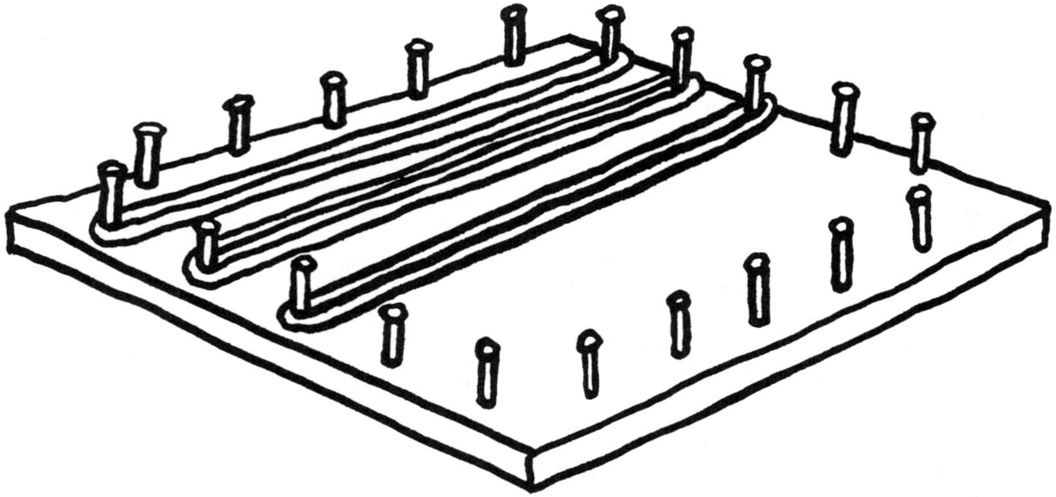

Weave the loops over and under.

To finish the edges, begin at one corner and pull each loop off the nail and through the loop next to it. Knot the very last loop.

Creative Clay

This recipe makes a soft clay that can be cut with cookie cutters or shaped, and then air-dried until hard. It can be painted or decorated with acrylics, tempera, watercolors, or markers.

To give a shiny finish, coat with acrylic floor wax.

MATERIALS

1 cup cornstarch
1 cup baking soda
1 1/4 cups cold water
Saucepan and spoon

Ask a grown-up to help you mix ingredients together in a saucepan over medium heat, stirring constantly. Stir, about 5 minutes until it's very thick — like mashed potatoes. Cool on a plate until you can work with your hands. Roll, cut, or shape as you wish. Let dry for about 2 days. Paint or finish as you like.

If you are making ornaments, press a paper clip into the soft clay for a hanger, or punch holes with a nail before the clay dries.

Baker's Clay

This clay is best made fresh before each work session, because it doesn't keep well.

MATERIALS

4 cups flour
1 cup salt
1 1/2 cups warm water
Used aluminum foil
Bowl and spoon
Cookie sheet

Mix flour and salt in the bowl. Slowly add the water, stirring until it becomes stiff; then use your hands to knead the mixture. Knead thoroughly for at least 5 minutes on the table top, adding more flour as needed. Place the dough in a covered container or old plastic bag, taking out only small amounts at a time as you work.

This dough can be hand-formed into shapes, rolled flat to cut with cookie cutters, or pressed into candy and cookie molds. Avoid making thick projects, as the inside will not cook properly and the outside will crack. Instead, press the dough over crushed foil armatures to make large pieces, and then bake. To attach small pieces of clay to each other, wet the surface a bit so they will stick.

Bake on cookie sheets lined with old foil or coated with non-stick finish. (Be sure to save the foil to use again and again!)

Cookie-type projects bake at 300° F for about 30 minutes. Projects that are 1/2" – 2" thick need to bake at 300° F for at least an hour. If an item browns too quickly, cover with used foil and finish baking.

If you're happy with the warm, light brown color of your baked project, just finish it with a coat of sealer, such as acrylic finishes, acrylic floor wax, or clear nail polish. Tempera, water colors, or marking pens can be used to decorate baked items.

CRAYON REVIVAL

Recycle your old crayons by melting them down and making beautiful new ones — even crayons with swirls of color!

MATERIALS

- Old crayons
- Paper cupcake liners
- Soup can
- Saucepan
- Muffin tin

Peel off all the paper, and sort crayons by color. Fill a saucepan with 1" – 2" of water. Pinch the top of a clean soup can to create a sort of pouring spout. Fill the can half full with broken crayons. Ask an adult to heat the saucepan, never going higher than medium heat. *The wax in the crayons is flammable, so don't let it get too hot. Because of the danger involved in using hot wax, a grown-up must do the melting and pouring of the wax.* Crayons melt at a very low temperature, and if the heat is kept low, everything will go safely and smoothly. You can do the peeling, sorting, and breaking up of the crayons, as well as the testing of the final product!

After heating for a few minutes, the crayons will be melted to a liquid wax. Have a grown-up carefully pour the wax into paper-lined muffin tins. Pour about 1/2" of melted crayon into each paper cup. You can add a swirl of another color wax or let cool and add another layer of a different color. Let cool. You can hurry the cooling by placing the muffin tin in the freezer for a few minutes, or setting it outdoors on a cold day. Peel the paper away when the crayon is cooled and solid.

Candy molds can be used to make all kinds of clever crayon shapes. Many fun shapes are available from the Wilton Company, from dinosaurs to cartoon characters. Better yet, save old plastic wrapping materials from candy, make-up, and toys, to use as molds. The hardened crayons pop out easily and the molds can be used over and over.

3.

CREATING WITH THE EARTH'S BOUNTY

TEXTURES

We enjoy art with more than just our eyes. While creating we can use our senses of touch and smell as well. Natural materials are so much fun to work with because they stimulate our fingers as we work with them. The smooth coolness of a pebble or shell, or the crunchy stiffness of cornhusks feels unusual as we work with them. When collecting or preparing materials, take time to squish the soft mud or to smell the dried grasses. These sensations will come back to you again and again as you enjoy your finished artwork in the months to come. Long after you return from the beach or the mountains, you can take out your creations and relive your nature experience.

Nature provides us with many different textures: smooth like a stone, rough like tree bark, slick like a wet shell, spongy like moss, prickly like a pod, soft like a flower petal. Let your fingers enjoy the feel of natural materials, giving you ideas about how best to create with these earthly treasures.

VINE VASE

This project creates a very unusual vase and recycles glass jars or cans.

MATERIALS

- Clean glass jar, bottle, or juice can
- Vine: several lengths of thin vine with leaves removed (grape, honeysuckle, clematis, or similar vines)
- Sturdy scissors
- Tacky-type glue

Turn the jar upside-down and wrap vine around it.

If you don't have vines, any flexible plant material can be tried: reeds, thick grass or flower stems, straw or cornhusks.

Turn the jar upside-down and begin at the base. With spots of glue, begin wrapping vine around and around the jar. Keep it tight and close together so the jar doesn't show. As you come to the end of a length of vine, snip the end neatly at a slant, glue down, and hold in place until the glue sticks. Then glue down the next piece. Keep going until you have covered most of the jar. Then turn it right side up and finish wrapping.

The top wrap can be decorated by attaching a different color or texture of vine, a ring of nuts or pebbles, or tiny pine cones (hemlock cones are perfect) with glue.

You need to be patient while waiting for the glue to dry. A piece of old pantyhose can be secured around the finished vase to hold the vines in place while the glue dries completely.

To preserve the finished vase, you can brush on a coat of clear acrylic finish, or acrylic floor wax.

Use cans for bases, creating pencil holders or desk sets that are all wrapped with similar plant materials.

BASIC BASKETS

MATERIALS

Assorted natural fibers: grasses, yucca, wheat, willow, straw, jute, cornhusks, weeds, raffia — whatever you can find. Look around the edges of your yard, along the sides of pathways and roads, wherever plants aren't mowed or sprayed. You can purchase materials at craft supply stores, too.

Reusables: yarn, string, ribbon, embroidery threads, fabric strips — any or all can be used.

Box for a base: a round box like an ice cream container is best. Or, you can use the pattern provided; just trace it onto some cardboard and cut it out.

Masking tape

Scissors

If you are using a round ice cream container, discard the top and cut slits on the sides about 1" apart, right down to the base. Be sure that you end up with an uneven number of strips. If you are using the pattern, trace onto paper and cut out; then, draw onto cardboard, flip pattern piece over, and draw again to create one rounded pattern. Cut out. Fold the sections up at the base to make the basket form.

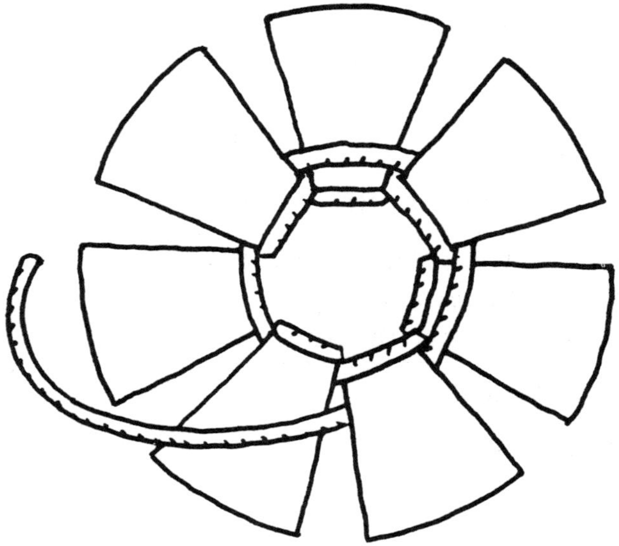

Weave the yarn over and under the basket form.

Shape the sides of the basket as you weave.

Start weaving your fiber strips at the bottom, securing the end of the first piece of fiber inside the basket with masking tape. Weave different pieces of fiber over and under the cardboard strips, adding new or different types of fiber as you go. When you add another piece, weave it over the end of the last piece you used, to hide the end.

Continue weaving over and under, working up the side of the basket as you go. Weave up to about 1/2" from the end of the basket frame. Fold the cardboard ends back and tuck them into the weaving; then finish the last rows, hiding the cardboard ends with them.

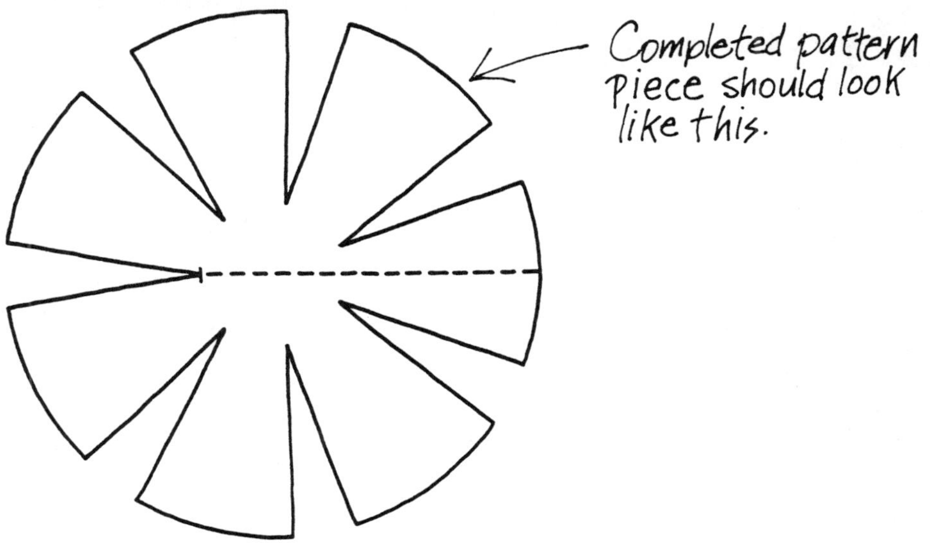

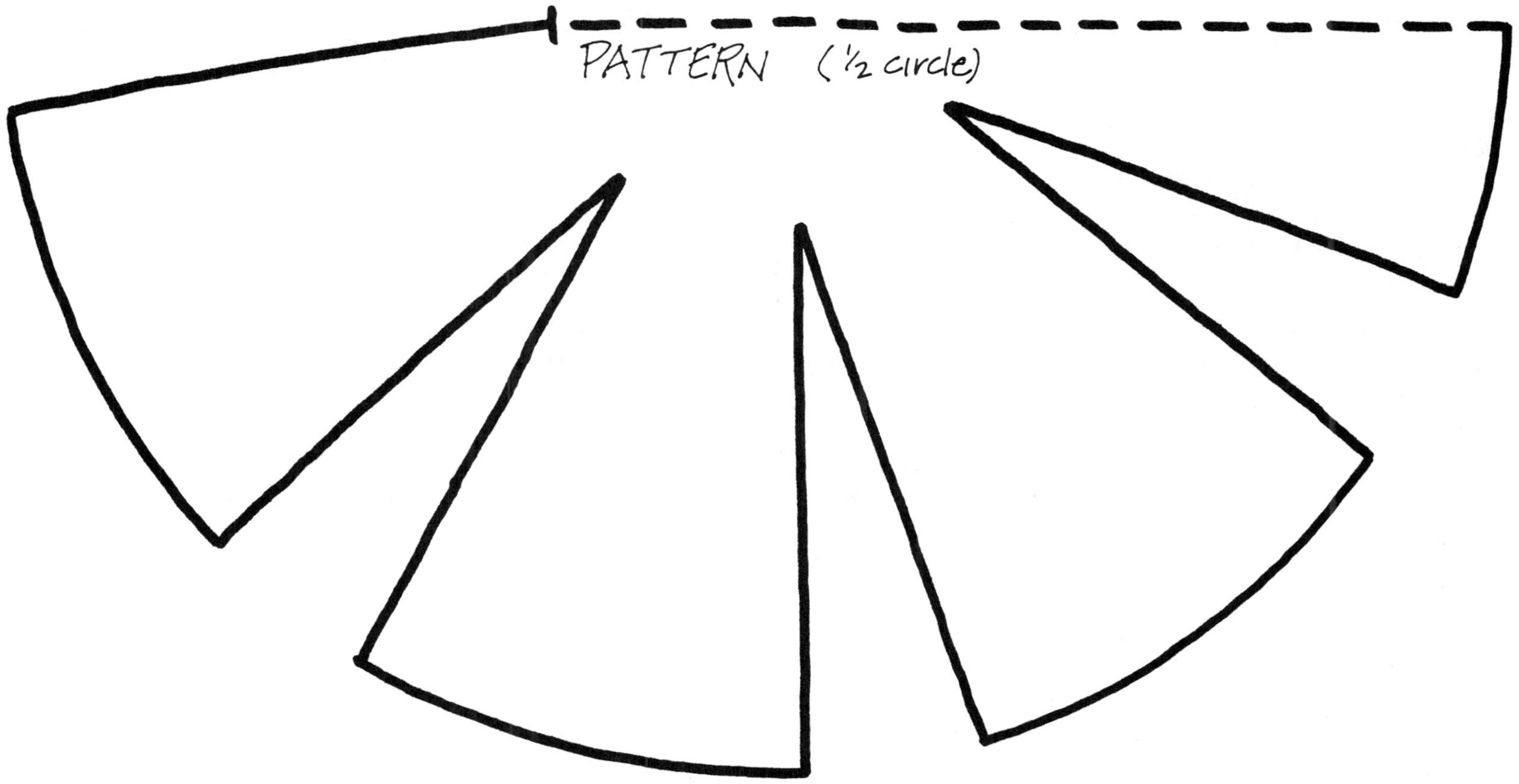

BARK WEAVING

MATERIALS

Slab of tree bark from a log on the ground, or an old weathered board (Don't peel bark off a living tree.)

Nails (1/2" – 3/4" in length, with small heads)

Assorted fibers to weave: cornhusks, grasses, feathers, strips of leather or fabric

Yarn

Scissors and hammer

Have you ever looked very closely at the bark of a tree? Isn't it amazing with all of its bumps and lumps? Now look at another tree. See any differences? Some bark is smooth, some is very rough, and some even looks like it is about to fall off!

A tree's bark acts very much like your skin does for you. It keeps bugs and disease from entering the tree. It protects the tree from the ravages of weather and forest fire. The bark thickens as a tree grows. It provides hiding places for butterflies to lay eggs and nesting holes for small birds. Mosses and fungi grow on it's bumpy surface.

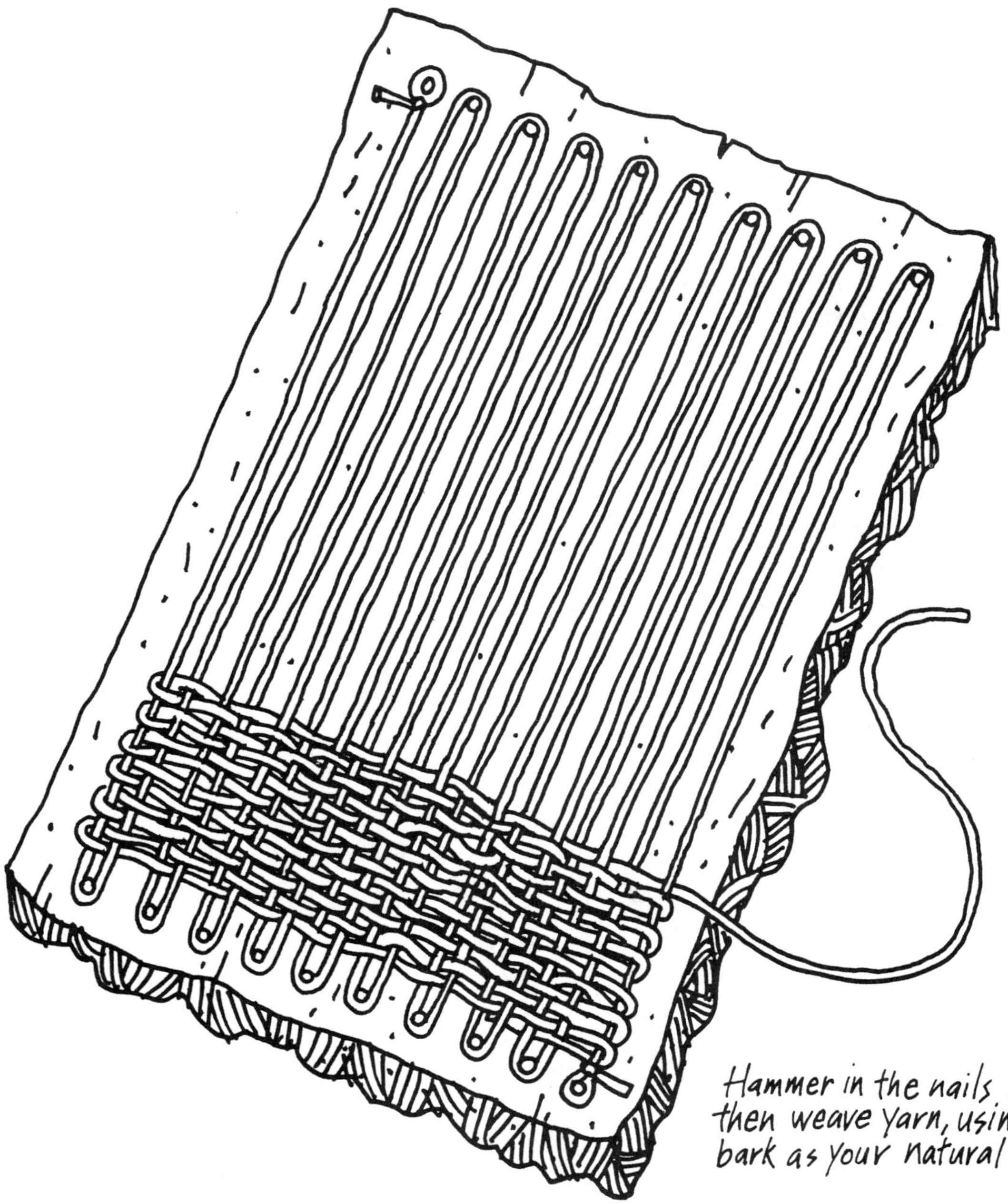

Hammer in the nails and then weave yarn, using the bark as your natural loom.

Work in the natural materials and leave finished weaving on the bark.

When looking for bark for a project, be careful to never pull or cut bark from a living tree. It will let disease enter the tree, and may eventually kill it. Search for your bark on the ground or pull it off a fallen log.

Once you have found a flat piece of bark with an interesting shape, begin hammering a row of nails along one end of the bark. Hammer another row directly opposite at the other end. Knot one end of a length of yarn around the first nail and wind the yarn back and forth between the two rows of nails, looping around each nail. This will be the *warp* for your weaving.

Weave in the fibers (grasses, cornhusks, yarn, etc.) by manipulating the yarn and fibers with your fingers. Continue an over-under pattern across the warp, reversing at the end and returning on the next row.

If working with yarn as your fiber, you might enjoy working with a yarn needle, which makes the weaving much easier. (See page 27 for instructions.) If you choose not to use a needle, the yarn end can be wrapped with tape to stiffen it for easier handling.

Leave the finished weaving in place on the bark or board. Tuck ends of fibers back inside the weaving to hide them. Dried flowers, feathers, and bits of moss can be tucked into the weaving or glued on to make it even more interesting.

CORNHUSKS

Cornhusks are interesting and fun to work with because they can be crunched or stretched into a variety of shapes. They can be rolled and tied, or wet and shaped, or curled. They can be left natural, or painted, or dyed. They act as nature's packaging, keeping the corn moist and sweet. Native Americans used the husks to weave clothing or wrap foods for cooking. Perhaps you have eaten a tamale, a Mexican food steamed in cornhusks.

If you can't obtain husks from a farm or garden, you may want to buy them from a craft supply store. If you purchase fresh corn in the husk, you can save the husks by letting them air dry completely, and then storing in a box in the garage, until you're ready to work with them.

To soften cornhusks for easier working, add three teaspoons of glycerin (from any drugstore) to a dishpan full of water. Soak the husks for a few minutes, and then lay on a folded towel, ready to use.

Cornhusk Dolls

MATERIALS ✱✱✱
12 husks (soak in water a few minutes)
Rubber bands, yarn, or string
Scissors

Lay about 6 husks on top of each other. Gather and wrap a rubber band tightly about an inch from one end. Pull the ends back over the banded area and fasten with another rubber band. This makes the head.

To make the arms, roll 2 husks together lengthwise in a tight roll. Fasten with 2 rubber bands near the ends. Slip this arm section inside the body husks, below the neck. Fasten

Stack 6 husks.

Wrap a band 1" from the end.

Pull ends back over the band and fasten with another band. This makes the head.

the arms in place by wrapping some yarn, string, or a rubber band, in a crisscross across the body top.

Trim the bottom of the husks evenly to create a skirt. If you want legs or pants, separate the husks in 2 sections and wrap each leg section tightly at the ankle with a rubber band or string.

You can glue cornsilk, twine, yarn, or moss to the head for hair.

Roll 2 husks to make arms.

Slide the arms inside the body.

Fasten in place by tying string in a crisscross pattern across the chest.

3-D Cornhusk Collage

MATERIALS

- Cornhusks
- Glue (see page 24)
- Cardboard or tagboard
- Scissors

Draw the image you want onto the cardboard. Trim and shape small pieces of husks, and then glue to the cardboard.

Because cornhusks can be curled on a pencil while wet, or shredded, or twisted, they can become 3-dimensional collages where parts stick out from the cardboard. Tacks can hold pieces in place until the glue dries. Add seeds or beans and let your imagination go.

WALL PLAQUE

MATERIALS

Slab of tree bark (from a log on the ground, not from a living tree)

Assorted decorative items: dry moss, leaves, seed pods, feathers, cones, shells, weeds

Tacky-type glue

Thin wire

Lay the piece of bark on your work area and decide which side is more appealing; then, lay out the leaves, moss, and other things you gathered, until you have arranged something interesting. You may want to create an image, such as a bird or flower arrangement, or you may want to make a collage of the various textures and colors you have gathered.

Glue the items in place. When dry, attach the thin wire to the back for hanging. You can also nail or glue on a loop cut from a soda pop six-pack holder to make a hanging loop.

STICKS & STONES

Stones are one of the natural materials you can find just about anywhere you live. Formed millions of years ago, they were made by volcanic eruptions, or by the settling of ancient ocean bottoms under heat and pressure. Stones have many different textures, from shiny to gritty. If you have a smooth, rounded stone, it was probably worn smooth by the flow of a river or stream for thousands of years. While stones can be found everywhere, some stones are so unusual or have such beautiful colors that they are treasured. We use them for jewelry and call them precious stones. Some stones are very hard and can be cut with a diamond saw into shapes that sparkle when they reflect light. We call these cut stones gems.

Look carefully while searching for stones, and you may find a real fossil which is the remains or imprint of a living creature, left in stone. The actual bone or shell dissolved over time as water and mineral salts filled the imprint and turned to stone. Fossils take millions of years to form.

PEBBLE TRIVET & COASTERS

MATERIALS

Small, smooth, flat pebbles
Quart-jar lid for each coaster (such as mayonnaise jar lid)
Large metal lid for each trivet (ask a restaurant to save one for you or use some other suitable base)
Plaster of Paris and mixing tools

You can make a single trivet or a whole set of matching coasters to set hot or cold drinks on.

Ask a grown-up to help mix the plaster, following package directions. When it begins to thicken, spoon it into the jar lids, filling each lid half full.

Select pretty pebbles and press them into the plaster before it hardens, filling the area inside the jar lid with stones. You may want to create a design, if you have different colors and sizes of pebbles. Plaster may squeeze up and out of the lid, but it can be wiped away later. Let the plaster harden; then use old socks or pieces of old towels to rub away any plaster that covers the tops of the stones.

Brush a coat of acrylic finish or acrylic floor wax over the plaster and stones to give your trivet a shiny finish. You may want to glue some felt scraps to bottoms of the coasters to prevent scratches on furniture.

Make one large trivet or several small ones.

STONE CRITTERS

MATERIALS

- Rounded stones in assorted shapes and sizes
- Acrylic paints or permanent marker pens
- Adhesive: Tacky-type glue, silicone sealer (sold in tubes in hardware stores).

Rinse the stones and let dry. Then lay them out, looking at their shapes and colors to get ideas. You can use them to create paperweights, doorstops, garden sculpture, refrigerator magnets, or interesting designs.

Tiny decorated pebbles can be glued to magnets, pin backs, or barrettes.

To fasten stones together to create animal ears, arms, or legs, dab silicone sealer or tacky-type glue on the stone. Hold stones in place until the glue sets.

Use paints or permanent markers to decorate or draw on eyes and mouth. Glue broom straws, dry grass, or toothpicks on for whiskers. Old leather scraps make good ears or tongues.

Large rocks can be painted like ladybugs or turtles and placed in your garden.

SAND ART

MATERIALS

- Fine sand
- Glue
- White tagboard: good reusable sources are gift boxes, shirt cardboard, and old file folders.
- Cotton swabs

Did you know there is pink sand, pure white sand, along with darker shades of brown and grey sand? Sand is made by wind and water wearing away rocks over many, many years. It is truly one of nature's wonders. Some sand is coarse on your feet and some is as soft as baby powder.

Collect sand, keeping different colors separate, or tint your sand with natural dyes (see page 16) or food coloring. To tint, place sand in separate jars, and then add a few drops of coloring to each jar. Prepare or collect several different shades of sand.

Use the cotton swabs to paint a design with glue on the tagboard. Sprinkle the sand onto the wet glue, using the different colors to get different effects. Let dry and shake off the excess sand.

You can glue on bits of dried flowers and weeds to make your sand art even more interesting.

Sand, shells, and pebbles go together naturally, so if you want to create a frame for your sand painting, collect small shells or pebbles, and glue around the outside edge of your picture. Thick craft glue, or silicone sealer will hold the shells down securely.

SAND CLAY SCULPTURE

MATERIALS

2 cups fine sand
1 cup water
1 cup cornstarch
Saucepan and spoon

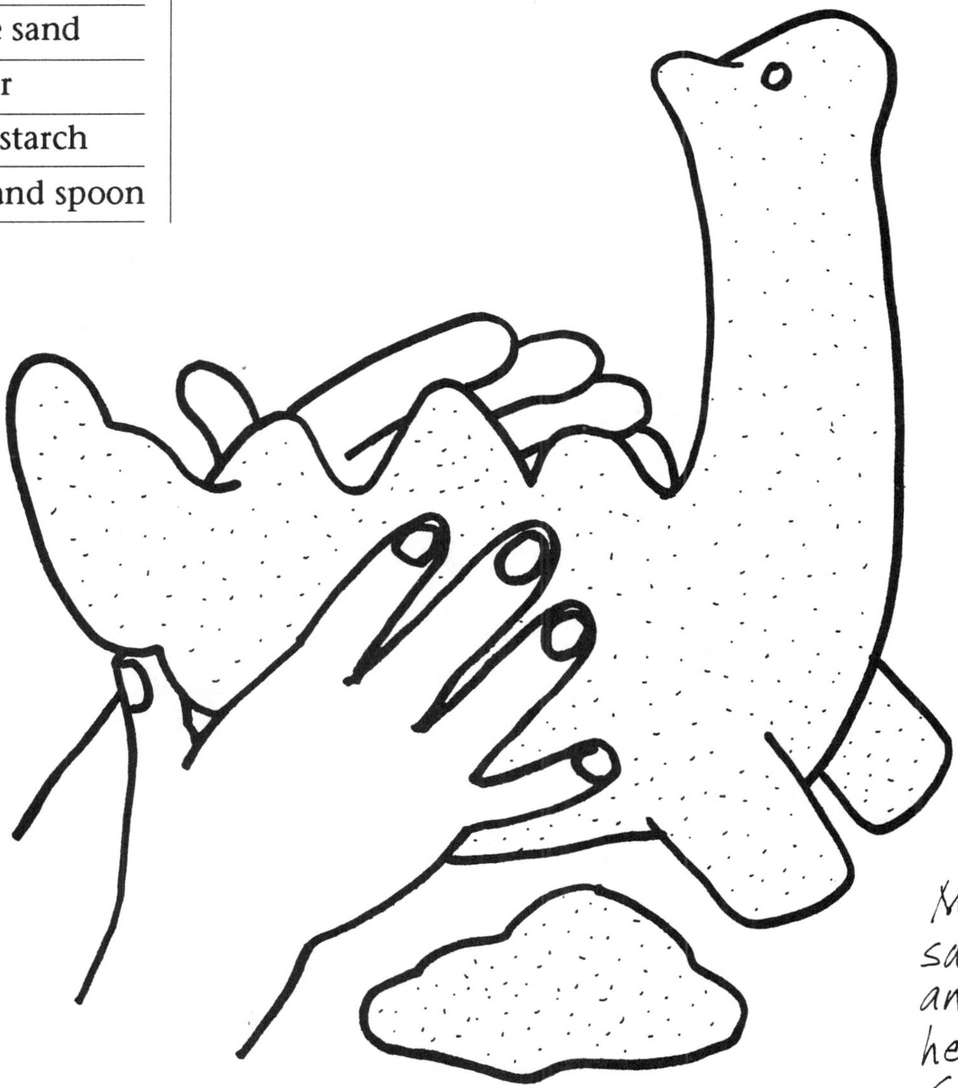

Make clay from sand! Mix sand, cornstarch, and water in a saucepan. If you want to add color, stir in drops of food coloring or natural dyes (see page 16). Ask a grown-up to help you cook over medium heat, stirring constantly.

When your mixture thickens, remove from the heat. Carefully pour it into a dish, and let it cool. If you drape a wet washcloth or towel over the clay, it will cool more quickly. Use your fingers and a stick or spoon to sculpt it into whatever you choose. It will get very hard when dry.

This clay makes interesting small animals or pots. You can also make your own "fossils" by pressing bones (saved from your dinner), leaves, or feathers into the moist clay, then removing them and letting it dry.

Mix together the sand, cornstarch, and water; then heat. Let cool. Sculpt!

LOG PENCIL HOLDER

MATERIALS

- Log or wood block about 4"x 6"
- Sandpaper
- Scrap of felt or other soft fabric
- Glue
- Hand drill (rotary, not electric): Use a drill bit that will make an opening large enough for a pencil
- Hammer and nail
- Scissors

Vermont has approximately 18 billion live trees in its forests. That's 32,000 for each man, woman, and child living in the state.

If you are lucky enough to have access to an old-fashioned hand drill, you can drill the holes yourself. If you have an electric drill, a grown-up must do the drilling, but there is plenty for you to do in making this great pen and pencil holder.

You will need a piece of wood — a block about 4" – 6" in size is good. The most interesting pencil holders can be made from a section of log. Leave the bark on for texture.

Hammer a nail in to create a hole to start the drill. Make as many holes as you like; each will hold a pen or pencil.

Sand the bottom of the pencil holder. Cut the felt to fit the base of the pencil holder and glue it in place to prevent scratches on any furniture.

TWIG ANIMALS

MATERIALS ✱✱✱

Thin willow twigs, about 15" long

Little twig animals like these were made by the ancestors of today's Native Americans. Perhaps the twig animals were associated with hunting. Perhaps they were just for fun! Since archaeologists date them as 2,500 years old, we'll never know for certain.

Now, you can make a collection of your own twig animals from long, thin willow or cottonwood twigs. Isn't it amazing how flexible a twig can be?

Pull the twig apart up to the end, leaving it joined for about 1/2" (1). Bend about 1" from the end to make the back legs (2). Bend the rest of the twig as shown, wrapping the final part around the neck and tucking the end inside the neck.

Make several of these wonderful animals to "roam" a bookshelf or tabletop together.

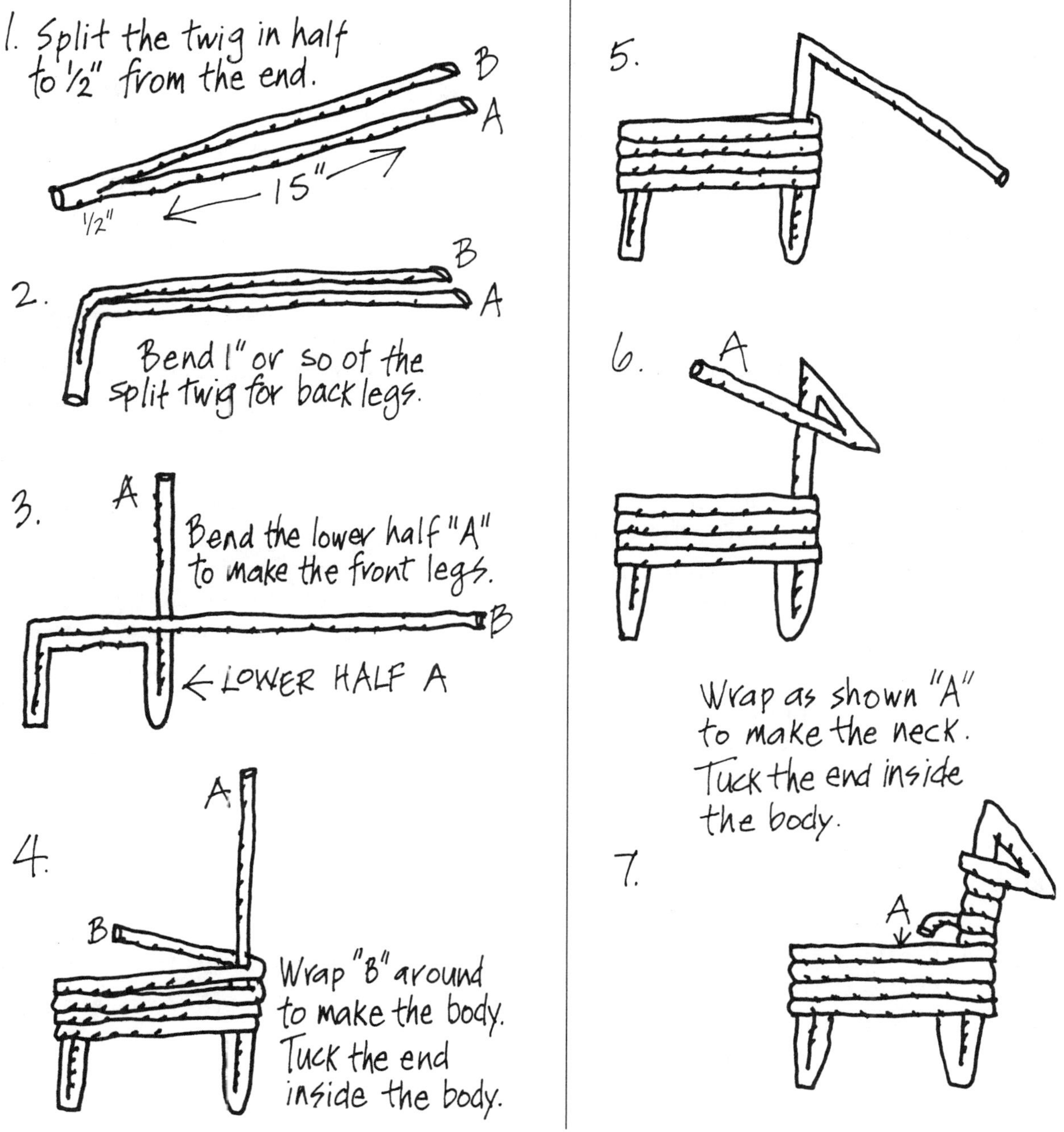

DRIFTWOOD SCULPTURE

MATERIALS

Driftwood in assorted small sizes and shapes

Adhesive: Tacky glue, silicone sealer, or hot glue gun (for grown-up use)

Driftwood is abundant near the seashore, but don't think you have to live near the beach to find it. Look along the banks of a river, lake, or stream, and you will find lots of interesting pieces. While you're out collecting, look for interesting shells, stones, and other things that you can add to your sculpture, or save to use on another project.

Clean the driftwood by rubbing it with an old towel or brush. Select your pieces carefully, looking for unusual twists or shapes in the wood. Some pieces look like animals or pieces of modern art without even adding anything to them — truly nature's work of art!

Choose a flat piece to be the base. Build up from there adding pieces as you like, gluing securely before adding the next piece. Feel free to add other natural objects to your sculpture, such as pebbles, shells, feathers, grasses, or dried flowers.

Sometimes pieces will go together and remind you of a bird, animal, or person. Other times, your sculpture may not look like anything you've seen before! You will have created something out of nothing.

A tree takes in about 20 pounds of carbon dioxide each year. It gives off enough oxygen to keep four people breathing for a year.

Some pieces of driftwood sculpture may look like things you've seen; others will be entirely free-form.

PEBBLE JEWELRY

MATERIALS

- Small pebbles or pretty rocks
- Tacky glue
- Jewelry backings from some old jewelry or craft store

Search around your house for some inexpensive pin backs, earring backs, barrettes, and hair combs. Ask if you can use them first! If not, you can buy backings at craft shops. Button backs from fabric-covered button kits (at the fabric store) can be used to make pebble buttons.

Collect some pretty, small pebbles. Wash them and let dry. Select interesting pebble combinations and glue them to the jewelry backs.

When the glue dries, you can decorate the pebbles with fine-tip marking pens, making designs or faces, or leave them their natural colors.

Brush on a coat of clear nail polish to give the pebbles a shine, as if they just came from the stream bed. What other things can you make by gluing carefully selected pebbles or shells onto backings made from yogurt containers or tissue rolls? What about napkin rings, bracelets, vases for violets, ...

TWIG WEAVINGS

MATERIALS

Small twigs, or branches, with a forked or twisted shape
Yarn scraps
Feathers, leaves, cattails, pods — for trim

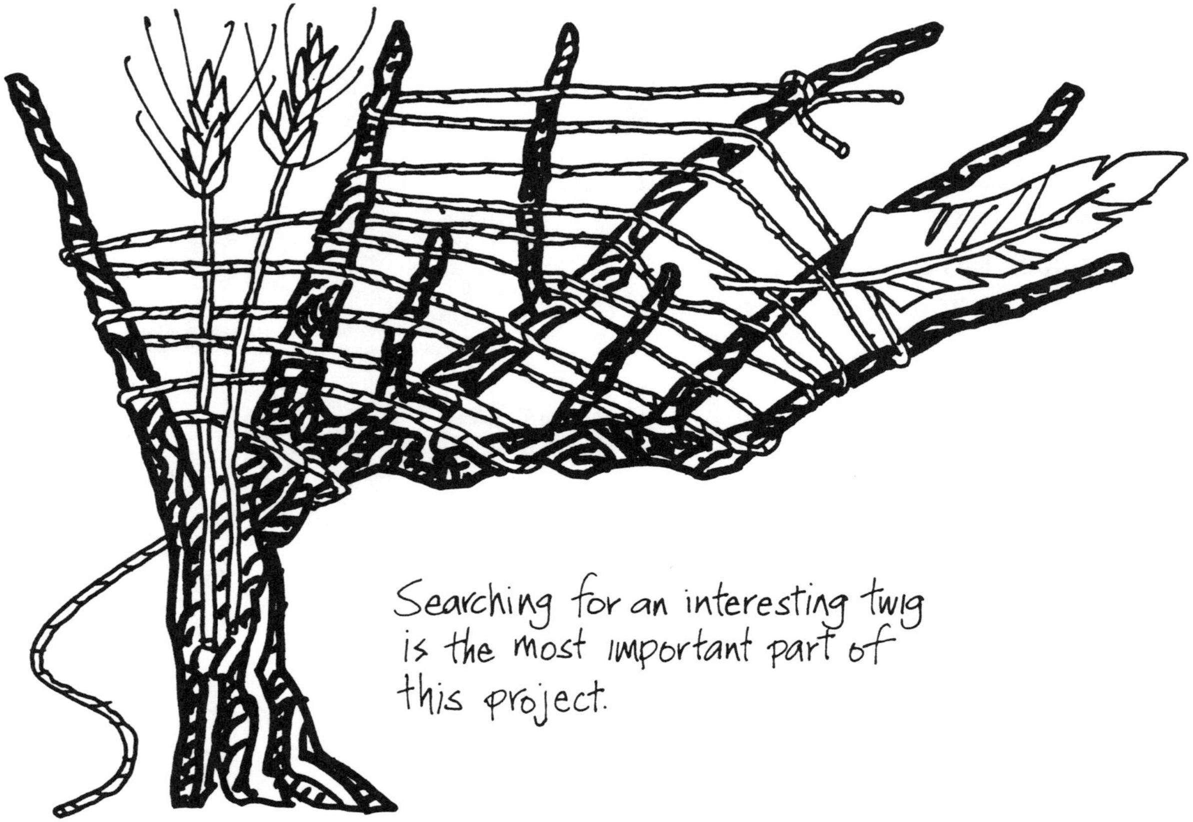

Searching for an interesting twig is the most important part of this project.

Search for an interesting branch to be the loom for the weaving. As you look, you will notice that no two branches are exactly alike. Different types of trees and bushes have different textures and shapes in their branches as well. Some will be slender and delicate, others stubby and chunky. As you search, think about how carefully a bird searches for just the right branch to weave a nest on.

You don't have to break branches from living trees. Just look about you on the ground, especially after a storm when rain and wind have knocked them to the ground.

Weave the yarns back and forth between the branched twigs in a pattern. The yarn will resemble a spider web a bit. Stick feathers, leaves, or pods and cones in between the yarn to make your weaving more interesting. Hang your finished weaving on a wall or lean it against a bookcase or on the mantle.

SAND CASTING

MATERIALS

- Used plastic milk jug or half-gallon milk carton
- Fine sand and water
- Plaster of Paris and stirrer
- Assorted objects to cast: seed pods, stones, shells, leaves, twigs

You can make sand castings right where the sand is — at a beach, a playground, or even your own backyard sandbox.

You will need to wet the sand with water first; then use your hands to dig a shallow hole. Pat the sand to smooth it. Press seed pods, shells, or rocks and driftwood pieces into the moist sand. Leave them in place, making sure the sand is smooth around the base of each object.

Cut the plastic jug or milk carton in half. Mix the plaster in it following the directions on the package.

When the plaster begins to thicken, pour it carefully and gently over the objects to cast. It will be like thick cake batter. Pour on more plaster until it is about 1" – 2" deep. It should be thick enough that it won't spread out on the sand too much. Let it harden and dry.

Go for a walk or clean up the beach while you wait about half an hour. Then, carefully lift up the hardened plaster and gently brush the loose sand away with your hand.

Plaster casts can also be made of designs drawn in the wet sand with your finger or a stick.

Pour plaster over items to be cast.

Wait 30 minutes.

When hard, lift the plaster from the sand and brush off the debris.

TWIG PICTURE FRAME

MATERIALS ✱✱

- Cardboard
- Twigs
- Glue
- Scissors

Cut cardboard to the desired size. Brown cardboard from boxes is best; you can paint it as you desire.

Break twigs to fit the frame and glue in place around the edges. Tiny acorns, pine cones, nuts, and dried flowers can be glued on for accents.

Glue your photograph or drawing into the frame with rubber cement.

To hang the frame from a wall, ask a grown-up to hot glue a pop top from a soda can to the back of the frame.

If you want the frame to stand upright on a table top, cut a support from cardboard, bend it at one end, and glue to the back of the frame.

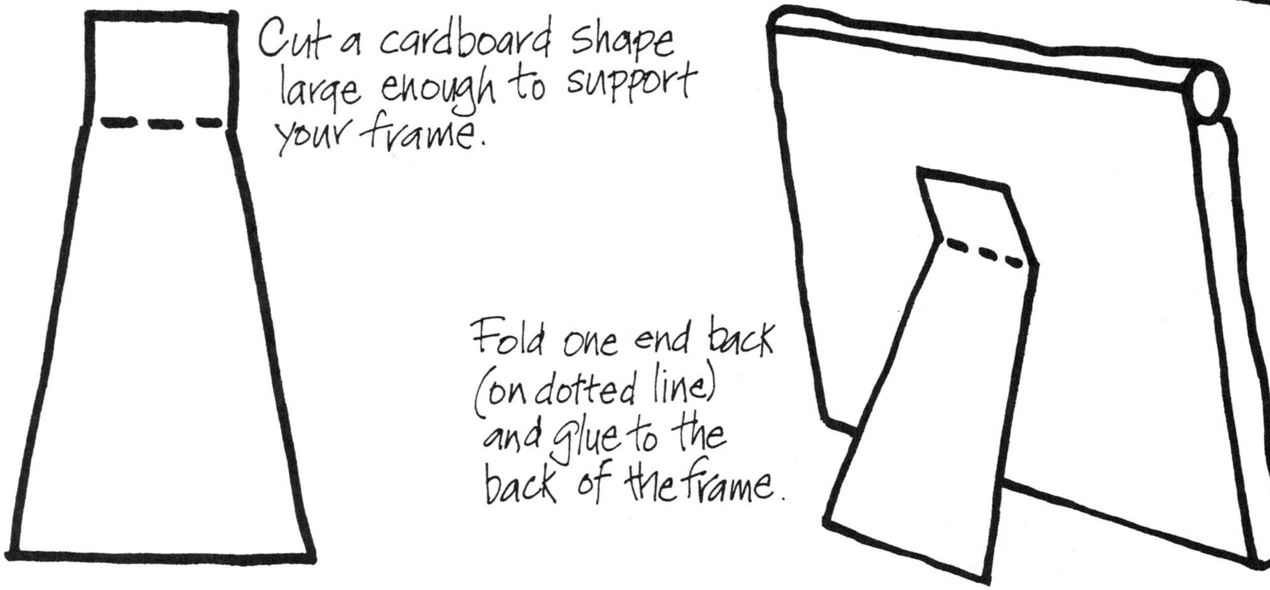

WILD THINGS

BIRD FEEDERS

It's always fun to make something useful, but it's even more fun to watch what you've made being used by a living creature. Birds live all around us, no matter if we're in the city or the country. Making a bird feeder can bring them up close to you for observation and enjoyment. And what a great way to reuse what might have been trash!

Bird feeders can be made from just about anything you have around that can be hung or set out off the ground, ready to hold a supply of birdseed, while hungry birds dig in for a meal!

Birds like to eat where they are safe. You may be feeding ground feeders, such as pigeons or doves. They like to be able to see around them several feet to be certain that nothing is preying on them. Keep their feeders away from shrubbery. When setting your hanging feeders out, take care to place them away from tree branches or fences where cats can position themselves. You don't want your bird feeders to become cat feeders!

Milk Carton Feeder

Materials ★★

Clean milk carton
2' of heavy string
12" long stick or dowel
Scissors

Use the scissors to cut away the carton as shown. Insert the stick in the bottom portion, letting it make a perch on 2 sides for birds to sit on as they dig through the seeds.

Cut or punch a hole to insert the string for hanging.

Jug Bird Feeder

Materials ★★

Gallon plastic jug
Wire, string, or leather strip, 12" long
Stick or dowel, about 12" long
Scissors and nail

Cut away the sides and top of the jug, leaving a base of about 1 1/2".

Poke 2 holes in the plastic with the nail, using scissors or a knife to enlarge the hole if needed. Push the stick through the holes, so it pokes out both sides to give the birds a perch.

Poke 2 holes through the top and insert the wire or string.

Pine Cone Feeder and More

Materials

- Pine cone or tissue tube
- Peanut butter and birdseed
- Corrugated cardboard
- String, about 12"
- Table knife or Popsicle stick
- Shallow pan

Use the knife or stick to spread peanut butter all over the pine cone. Be sure to spread between the scales of the cone, too.

Place a layer of birdseed in the pan and roll the cone in the seed, until all the peanut butter is covered with birdseed. Tie the string around one end of the pine cone and hang it from a tree branch.

If you don't have pine cones, you can do the same thing with a toilet tissue tube. Punch 2 holes in one end (opposite each other), and thread a string through for hanging. Spread with peanut butter and roll in birdseed.

If you want to get even more creative, use old corrugated cardboard boxes to draw clever shapes — perhaps a cat outline. Ask a grown-up to help you cut the shapes out of the cardboard using a serrated knife, like a steak knife, or a craft knife. Punch a hole in the top to tie string through. Spread the cardboard shape with peanut butter and dip in birdseed.

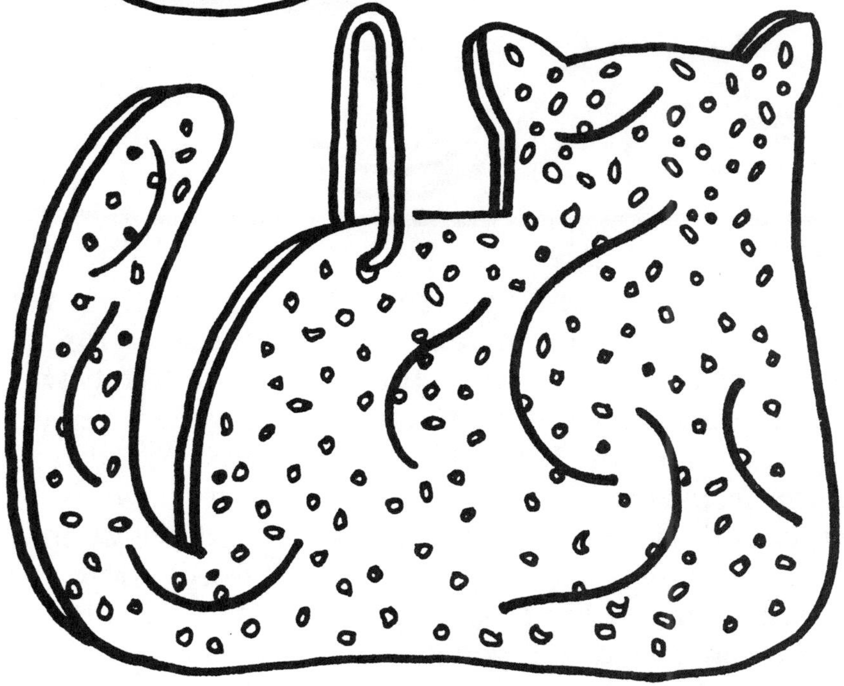

EARTHWORM WONDERLAND

Materials ★★

- Large glass jar: choose one with a wide mouth and a metal lid
- Soda pop can
- Soft, damp soil
- Black construction paper
- Colored chalks
- Tape
- Nail and hammer

This project looks like a beautiful piece of decorative artwork, but lift the decorated paper ring and you can view earthworms hard at work.

Worms help turn garbage into soil, and they keep the soil loose and aerated by burrowing through it. They make soil by taking in the compost (food and yard clippings) and dirt, then pushing it out their tail. The dirt that comes out of the worms, called castings, is soft and very fine — perfect for gardening!

To help you study these fascinating, hard-working worms indoors, make a pretty home for them from an old, used, large glass jar. Borrow a few earthworms from your garden soil, but, when you are finished studying them, be sure to return them to your garden, yard, or a park, where they can continue their good work for the earth.

Put the soda pop can, open end down, inside the jar. Carefully spoon moist soil around the can, so the can stays in the center and the soil fills the area around it. (The can keeps the worms from always staying in the center of the jar where you can't see them.)

Once the jar is full of soil, the worms can be added. If you have a good spot to dig them in your yard, borrow a handful and put them in the jar. They will burrow down into the soil within a few minutes. If you need to buy worms, they can be purchased wherever fishing supplies are sold. You can get different types and sizes of worms; Red Wigglers are small and lively and won't crowd the jar. Don't put too many in — about a dozen is plenty for a gallon jar. Punch a few holes in the jar lid with the hammer and nail, so the worms get a good supply of oxygen.

Keep the soil lightly moist, but not wet. Don't let it dry out or the worms will dry out, too. To feed them, sprinkle on crushed, dry dog food or bits of shredded carrot peels. Worms also like coffee grounds and cornmeal.

Worms like darkness, just like under the ground. Cut the black paper to fit around the jar. Use colored chalks to decorate it with interesting designs. Draw on only one side of the paper.

Tape the ends of the paper together to make a ring that fits around the jar. Slide it up when you want to watch the worms, slide it back down over the glass when you are finished. They will burrow next to the glass so you will see them better. Notice how quickly they burrow away from the light when you are watching them.

When you are through studying them, turn them loose in your yard or at a park, putting them under a bit of sod or in some loose soil in a shady spot. They will burrow down below the surface and make a new home there.

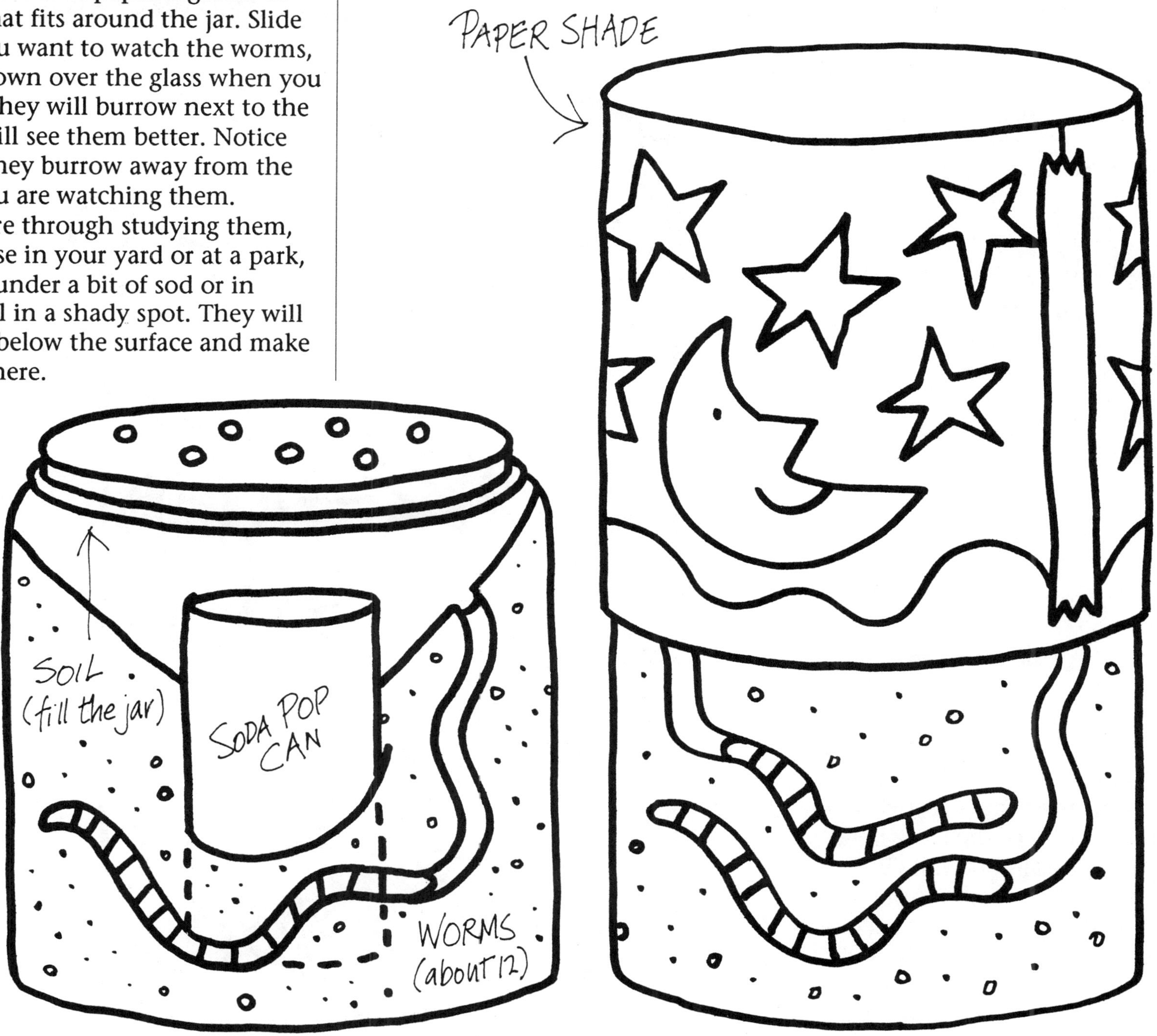

ANT RANCH

Ants are fascinating little creatures. They are fun to watch. The next time you find a trail of the little creatures entering your house, make an ant ranch and invite them in.

Materials

Large glass jar with a screw-on lid
Smaller jar with a lid or crushed aluminum foil ball
Pantyhose
Rubber band
Sandy soil
Hammer and nail

Punch some holes in the jar lid with the nail and hammer, so the ants will have air to breathe. Set aside.

Put the smaller jar or a clump of wadded, used aluminum foil into the larger jar. This will keep the ants from making their home in the center of the jar (where you can't watch them). Fill the area around the aluminum foil ball with soft sand or soil. Put a few drops of water on the soil. Ants need some water to drink, so be sure the soil doesn't dry out

The foil ball is covered with sand. Put a piece of panty-hose over the top and screw the lid on tight.

too much. Add a few drops of water each week.

When the soil is ready, add the ants. Ants are easy to find. Look for them along a sidewalk. You can use a pencil to make catching them easier. Point the pencil down to the ground, in front of an ant. It will climb up the pencil point. Hold the pencil over your ant ranch and gently push the ant off the pencil. It helps to have someone with you who can put the lid on the jar so the ants don't get away. Try to get at least 20 ants, so you have plenty to watch.

Warning! Be sure to get all your ants from the same place. If you get ants from different groups, they will kill each other.

Screw the lid on, and then, to keep the ants from escaping, fasten a piece of old pantyhose over the lid with a rubber band.

Finding food for ants is easy. They don't eat very much. One crumb of cornflake or a couple of grains of sugar is all they need. They get sick and die if they eat too much. Watch them, and when they are out of food, drop in another crumb or two. When you are done studying your ant guests, return them to where you found them.

After you have noticed the delicate shape and movements of your ants, you may want to make some ant prints to decorate notepaper or make cartoons with.

Use a black inked stamp pad and press your fingertips into the ink, then print with them to create ant bodies. Draw on the legs and antennae with a black pen. If you want to print with black paint, use the eraser end of a pencil to print the bodies of the ants, and draw on the detail with a fine-tip black pen. They look cute running across a notecard or decorating a book cover.

GOLDFISH BOWL

Materials

Gallon plastic jug

Heavy scissors

Permanent markers or stickers

To make a simple bowl for a single goldfish or guppy to live in, just cut a clean plastic jug in half. Wash away the label and decorate with bright colored permanent markers or stickers. Add a few interesting rocks and shells for your fish to explore.

Fill with lukewarm tap water. Let the tap water sit for a few hours or overnight so any chlorine will evaporate away, before you put your goldfish in. Your fish will need a tiny bit of food each day. Use breadcrumbs or purchase fish food.

It's fun to watch your fish move gracefully through the water. Perhaps you'd like to sketch it or use watercolors to create a painting of it as you watch.

Change the water every few days, when it begins to look cloudy, or if your fish tries to gulp air from the water's surface. Be sure to let the fresh water sit a bit to evaporate chlorine each time you refill the fish bowl.

ANIMAL TRACK PAPERWEIGHT

Materials

Plaster of Paris

Jug of water

Large can or cut-down jug to mix plaster in and stick to stir

First you have to locate some animal tracks to use. It's best right after a rain or after the ground has been irrigated. Look for firm, but soft mud with clear tracks that show up well.

If you are in the forest, look for tracks of wild animals near a pond, trail, or road. If you are visiting a beach or a park, look for bird tracks or dog paw prints.

As you study the prints, notice how they were made. If they were spaced closely, the animal was moving slowly. If the tracks are far apart, the animal was moving more quickly, taking longer strides. You can tell how large or heavy an animal is by the size of its track. It's easy to tell a fawn's tracks from those of an adult deer. The fawn's are smaller, closer together, and aren't pressed as far down into the mud. Isn't that the same with people?

If you can't find animal tracks, look for interesting tire tracks, or footprints. You can even do this project in your kitchen, with a dishpan full of mud, and a cooperative dog or cat to make the prints. If you don't have a pet, try your own footprints or handprints!

Now, follow the instructions on the package of plaster of Paris. Once it thickens, pour the plaster onto the print, letting some plaster surround the print. (If it is too runny, wait a few more minutes, until the plaster becomes thicker.)

The plaster will become solid enough to pick up in a few minutes. When it is hard, gently lift it up from the mud and put it in a sunny spot or indoors to dry. Brush any dirt away that sticks to the plaster. Let the cast sit overnight to dry harder.

It's fun to make a collection of casts from various animals. The casts can be used as book ends, paperweights, door stops, or as sculpture. Glue a piece of soft felt or flannel to the bottom of the plaster to protect furniture. If you want to paint the cast, use natural dyes (see page 16), tempera, latex paint, or watercolors. Seal with a waterproof finish if desired.

SHELL BUTTERFLY MAGNETS

Materials

Pairs of shells: mussel, clam, or oyster can be used
Antennae can be: twigs, broom straws, or pipe cleaner
Length of thread and scissors
Paint or markers
Tacky-type glue

If you have a chance, study a real butterfly closely, as it sits on a flower, but please don't touch it. Notice the wings are identical and how the designs create abstract sections of color and pattern. Moths have fascinating color patterns on their wings, too.

The coloration on butterflies and moths actually protects them in their environment. Butterflies have bright coloring that hides them as they feed at flower blossoms. Moths tend to have coloring that matches the bark of trees, where they can blend in and hide from birds, who think they are a tasty snack!

Now create an interesting butterfly or moth to attach to a magnet and mounted on the refrigerator. If you like, glue the finished butterflies to barrettes, or jewelry brooch backings. You can also tie a thread around the middle of your butterfly and hang from the ceiling to create a mobile.

Paint or decorate the shells with butterfly designs, decorating both sides alike. Let the swirls and texture of the shells inspire you. Cut the twig or pipe cleaner to make two antennae. Glue into position.

BUG GUEST HOUSE

Materials

- 1 quart milk carton
- Old pantyhose and rubber band
- Heavy scissors or craft knife
- Old magazines and glue

A bug guest house is the perfect way to get a close-up view, without harming the insect. Keep the insect or caterpillar just long enough to observe behavior and then return it to the wild, where you found it.

Be sure to put in whatever plant material your bug needs for food. Sprinkle a few drops of water on the leaves or bottom of the house.

To make the house, cut two window openings on the sides of the carton. Look through the magazines for colorful pictures. Trim and glue them to cover the milk carton, making a collage of interesting and beautiful pictures of nature.

When the glue is dry, cut off a leg from the pantyhose and pull it up over the box, having the toe at the base of the carton. Add your bug, some plant material, and a few drops of water. Then, pull the pantyhose up tightly, and trim, leaving about 3" to tie in a knot or fasten snugly with a rubber band. Watch your bug for a few hours or overnight, and then set it free. Save your bug house for another guest!

NATURE NOTE

BIRD CAFÉ

Bird Cupcakes

Materials ✱

1/2 cup peanut butter
1 cup birdseed
2 1/2 cups cornmeal
1/2 cup melted shortening
Muffin tin (greased)
Sticks: the size of a pencil
Yarn

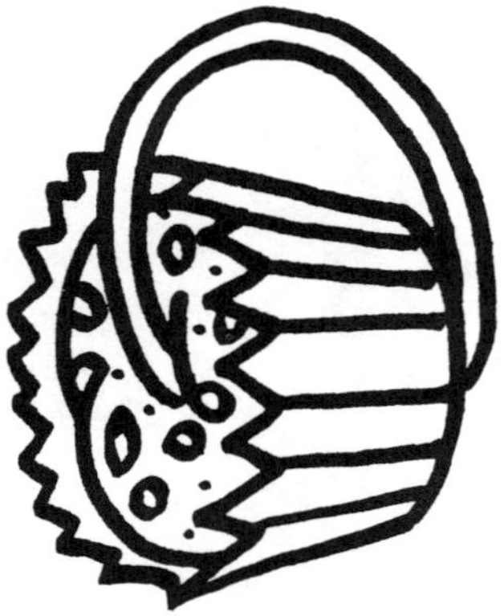

Combine the ingredients in a large bowl. Stir together. Drop the mixture into the muffin cups, pressing it down with your fingers. To create a hole for hanging, push a stick down in the middle. Let dry. Remove from the pan and take out the sticks. Thread yarn through the hole. Tie a loop and hang from a tree for the birds to enjoy.

Bird Bell

Materials ✱✱

Small yogurt container or paper cup
Ingredients as listed in Bird Cupcakes
Yarn
Cardboard circle, about 2" in diameter (a cereal box would be good for this)
Nail or sharp pencil

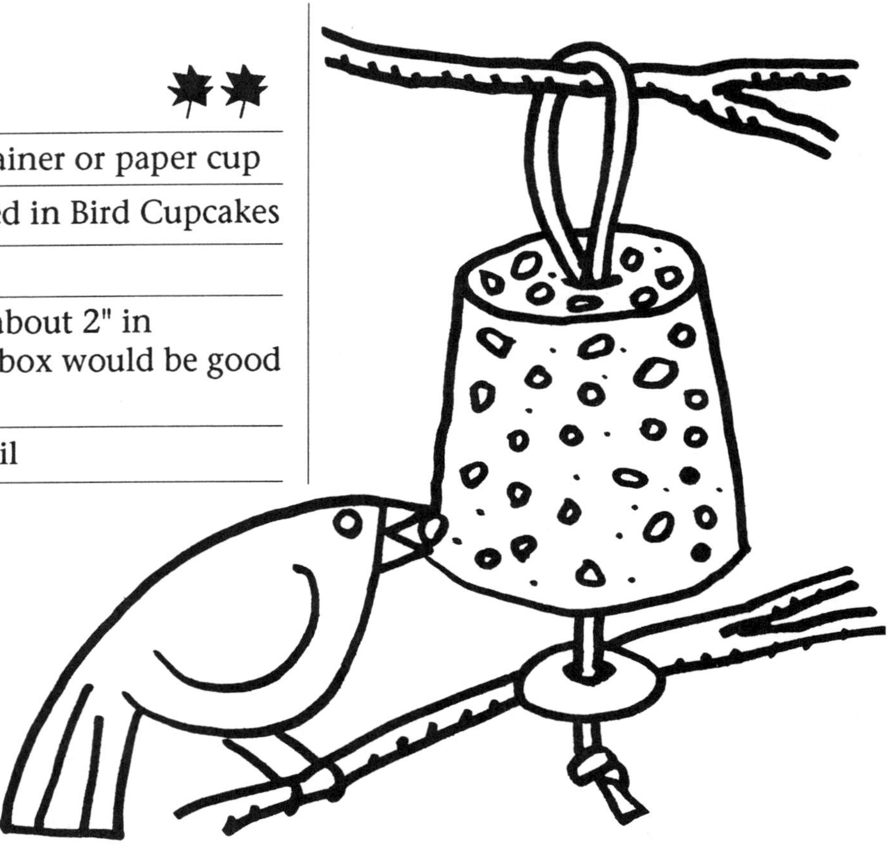

Prepare the ingredients as described in Bird Cupcake directions.

Punch a hole in the bottom of the yogurt container. Punch a hole in the center of the cardboard circle. Thread the yarn through the circle and knot the end. You may want to tie on a piece of twig to keep the yarn from pulling out through the hole. Thread the other end of the yarn through the hole in the bottom of the cup. Press the birdseed mixture into the cup, around the yarn, so the yarn will go right through the center of the birdseed. Pull the yarn up tight so the cardboard circle fits against the birdseed mixture. Let it harden. Tie a loop at the end of the yarn for hanging.

Peel the cup away, and the birdseed will be shaped like a bell, ready to hang from a tree so the flock can feast!

Winter Treat Garlands

Materials

- Oranges
- Bread: day-old is best
- Heavy-duty thread and yarn needle
- Knife

Tear the bread into fourths. Ask a grown-up to help you slice the oranges in rounds and then cut each round in fourths.

Thread the needle with about a yard of thread and string the food in a pattern, leaving a few inches between foods.

When you have several lengths strung, put on warm clothes and head outside to decorate a tree or bush with natural goodies for the winter birds.

This can be a fun holiday alternative to plastic and electric holiday decorations outdoors, plus the birds will love this treat.

WREATHS

Wreaths have long been used to show honor or joy. In ancient Egypt, flowers were sewn to cloth bands tied around the head. Wreaths were given as prizes to athletes in ancient Greece (at the first Olympic Games). Warriors, poets, and great speakers (orators) also won them. In Victorian England, a guest of honor at a party might have a wreath of flowers surrounding his or her chair. Wreaths are symbols of welcome and are popular decorating items year round, now.

Making wreaths gives you a chance to use fun and unusual natural materials, like cattails, grasses, and conifers, while creating something that makes a super gift or decoration. Consider using throwaways, too. Experiment with all those collectibles you've been saving, and use them to make a one-of-a-kind wreath with a message that's totally environment-friendly.

You need a base to glue or tie things onto. Cardboard or wire can be saved to make a base. Not all wreaths are round; yours can be oval, heart-shaped, square — or even football-shaped! Let your imagination and the materials guide you.

And, wreaths don't have to just hang on a wall. Use yours to honor someone with a thank-you, as a birthday surprise, or just to say, "you are special to me."

GRAPEVINE WREATH

Materials

Grapevines, several 3' sections
Decorations you've saved: ribbons, bells, dried flowers
Scraps of wire or twine for tying
Glue

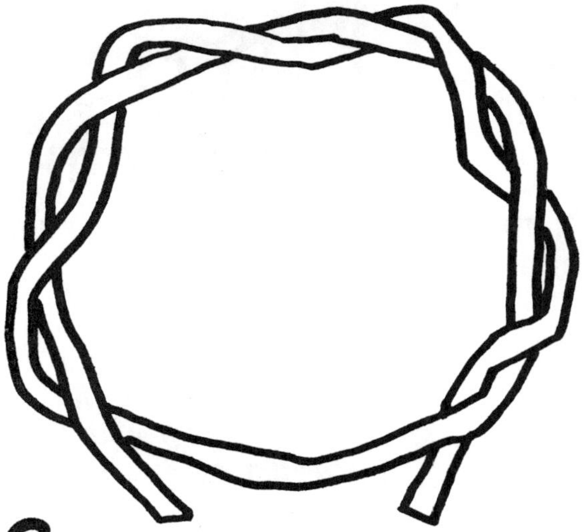

Grapevine cuttings can be obtained from gardeners doing fall pruning. Trim or pull the leaves away, leaving lengths of thin flexible vine. Take a single piece, and shape it into a circle, extending the ends so they can be wrapped over and under the rest of the circle. You may need to use thin wire or twine scraps to hold the vines in shape. Smaller wreaths are easier to form than large ones. Keep wrapping and adding new vines, until it is the thickness you want. Tuck the ends inside the wreath, and trim away any pieces that extend unevenly.

Grapevine wreaths are wonderful as they are, but you will be tempted to decorate them with dried flowers, leaves, ribbons, or almost anything you have around. You can stick little things in between the twisted vines. Until they are secure, use thin wire to hold items in place, or use a hot glue gun (grown-up use only).

You might turn yours into a "Get Well" wreath, with little surprises tucked in, or make a special personalized one for someone's graduation or birthday, by sticking in mementos and tiny surprises.

PINE CONE WREATH

Materials

- Pine cones in various shapes and sizes
- Wreath base
- Glue or thin wire scraps

Pine cone wreaths are a good family project. You need a wreath base to attach the cones to. It can be any size you'd like. If you choose a wire base, you can push the cones between the wire to secure them, or attach them with short scraps of thin wire.

If you use a base made by cutting a large donut shape from sturdy cardboard (such as a pizza base), you can attach the cones with a hot glue gun (grown-up use only). Tub and tile caulk, sold in tubes, works well, too.

Splatter paint your cones a shimmering silver if you'd like or leave them natural. Arrange them in a pattern or attach haphazardly. Add other natural materials such as dried flowers and autumn leaves, or use cones only, perhaps with a festive bow. Attach a sturdy wire loop to the back of the wreath and hang.

Glue each cone to the base with a squirt of caulk.

Cut cardboard bases in a variety of wreath shapes.

Pine cones are excellent art and craft materials. They are lightweight, unbreakable, come in lots of shapes and sizes, and they're free for the gathering during a walk in the woods.

When you go searching for cones, leave behind those that haven't opened to release seeds. They may grow seedlings for the next forest, or provide seeds for squirrels and chipmunks to eat. Instead, find cones that have the tips spread open. They look much prettier in your craft projects, too.

SEED MOSAIC WREATH

Materials

- Assorted dry beans and seeds
- Paper plate or sturdy cardboard
- Glue
- Scissors

Seeds are all around you. If you walk outdoors in the fall, you will find many different kinds. Check for pods, nuts, and seeds from wild grasses and from your flower garden. Look for seeds while you are eating, too. Many fruits and vegetables can provide interesting seeds to rinse and dry for project use. Watermelon, cherries, pumpkins — all are good sources for seeds. You are really reusing what would be thrown away! And don't forget dried peas and different varieties of colorful beans.

Use the scissors to cut out the center of a paper plate to create your wreath base, or use cardboard cut into a donut-shape (or other shape) for your base. Pizza box cardboard is excellent for this project.

Spread glue on small sections of the wreath at a time and position seeds and beans to create an interesting effect or design. You can use all the same seed or different textures, sizes, shapes, and colors. You can mix them together or create very interesting patterns. Whichever you decide, the wreath will be your wonderful creation — perfect for hanging in your kitchen!

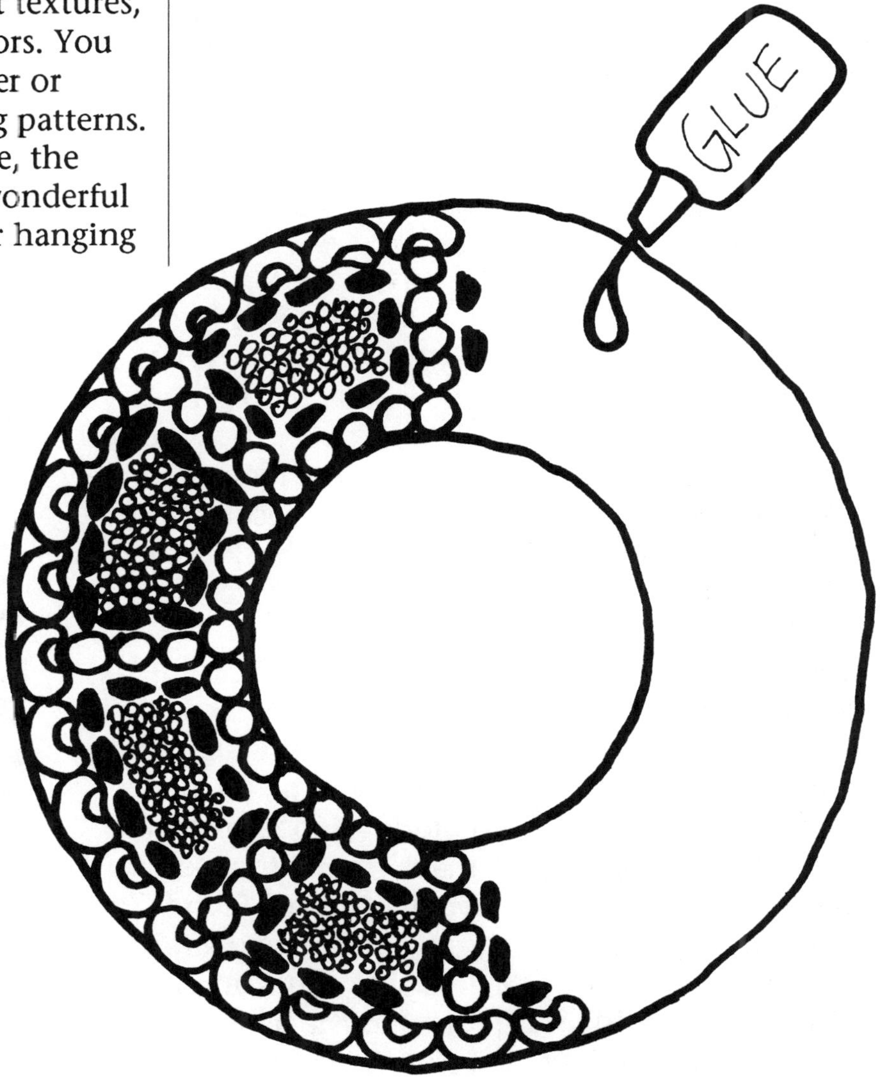

CORNHUSK WREATH

Materials

Cornhusks (save from corn on the cob or purchase)
Pan of water
Wire coat hanger and pliers
Masking tape

Husks are nature's protective jacket for the corn seeds, keeping out insects and birds that might eat the kernels before they can grow into new corn plants.

Cornhusks can be purchased in craft stores, in Mexican food sections of the grocery store, or saved when you prepare corn on the cob. If saving fresh husks, let them dry on newspaper, and then store uncovered in a box in a dry place. If you store them while they still contain moisture, they turn moldy.

Use pliers to shape the coat hanger into a round or other-shaped base for your wreath. (You may want a grown-up to help you.) Wrap the wire ends with masking tape to secure.

Wet the cornhusks as you use them, so they are easy to shape. Let them soak a bit in the pan of water, if they are very dry and brittle.

Fold the husk in half to make a loop. Lay it under the wire and pull the tail of the husk over the wire and through the loop, creating a knot. Pull securely. Knot on as many husks as will fit, completely covering the wire.

When the wire is filled with knotted husks, trim the ends of the husks to even them up. Tie on a colorful ribbon or bow made from a scrap of bright, printed fabric. You can slip thin wire around a few pine cones and fasten them to the base for accents, if you wish.

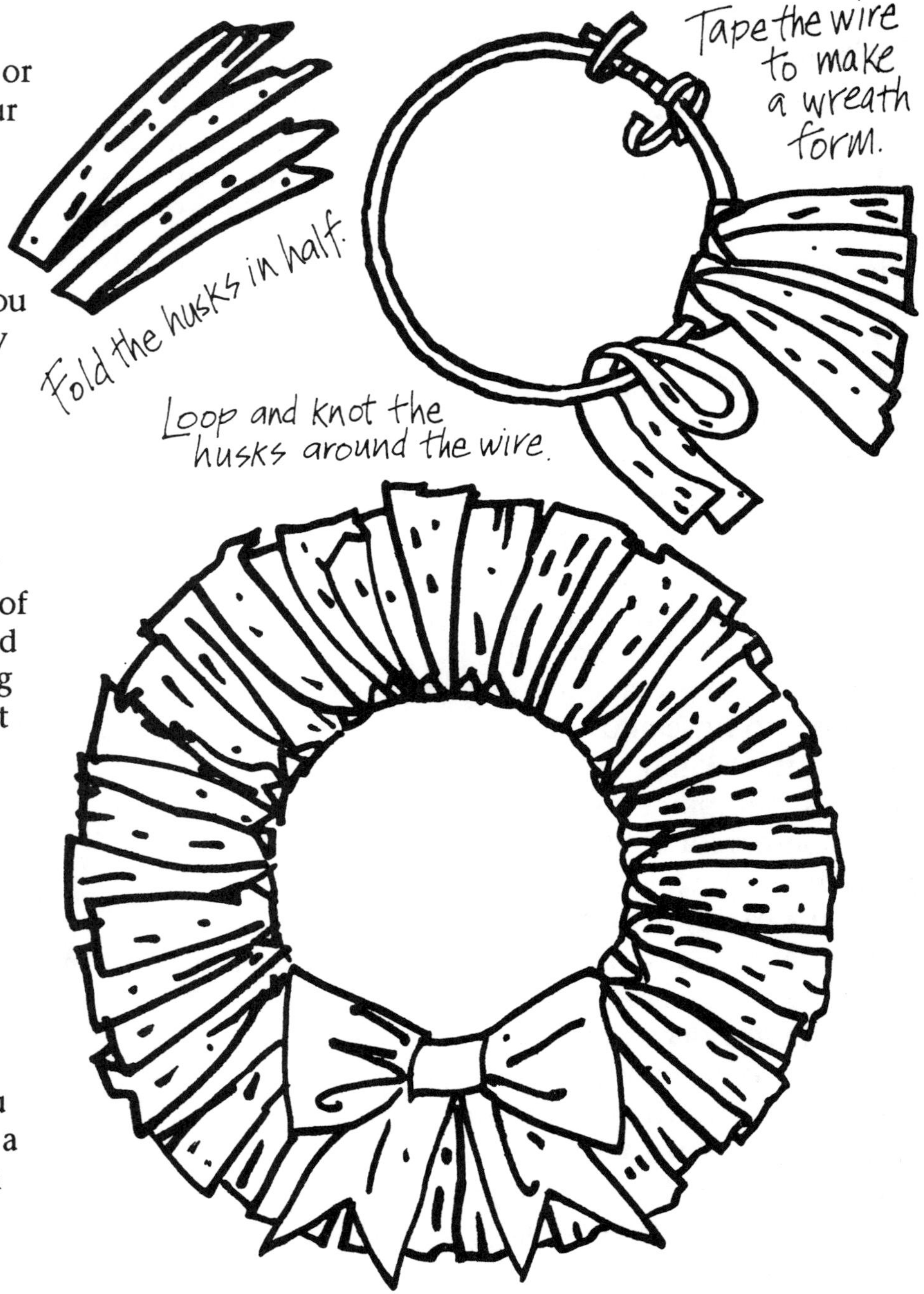

DRIED APPLE WREATH

Materials
1 dozen firm, fresh apples
1 cup lemon juice
2 teaspoons salt
12" cardboard wreath shape (use a pizza base)
Ribbon, if desired
6" wire or cord for hanging
Craft knife or scissors
Wire cake racks and cookie sheet
Towel
Adhesive: use thick, tacky-type glue, or latex caulking

Mix the lemon juice and salt in a bowl. Slice the apples about 1/8" thick, putting the slices in the lemon juice mixture to prevent browning.

Drain on a towel and pat dry. Spread the apple slices on the wire racks and place on the cookie sheet. Dry in the hot sun for a few days, bringing them indoors at night. You can also dry them in the oven at 140° F for 5 – 6 hours.

Trace the wreath shape around a dinner plate; ask a grown-up to cut out the center from the cardboard circle.

To assemble the wreath, glue the apple slices to the cardboard wreath shape. Do the inner and outer edges first, then overlap with a row down the center.

Poke a hole in the cardboard and tie the wire or cord in a loop, for hanging. If you would like a ribbon bow, tie it first, plumping it into shape, and then fasten it to the wreath with a piece of wire.

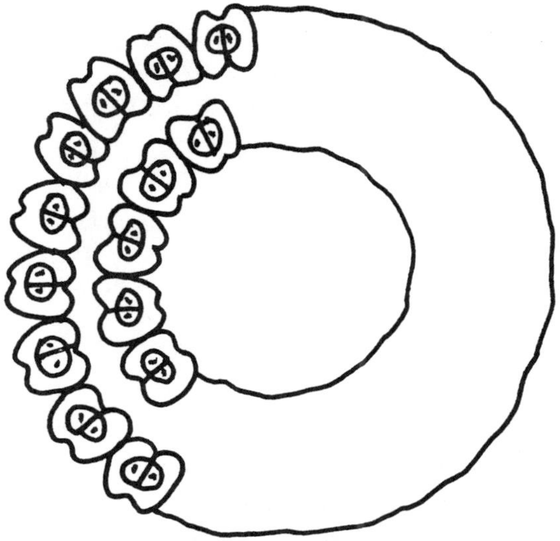

POPCORN WREATH

Materials

- Cardboard base (a pizza box is perfect)
- Lots of popped corn
- White glue
- Yarn, or ribbon, and scissors

Ask a grown-up to cut out the center of the cardboard to create the wreath base. Punch a hole near the edge and tie a loop of yarn through it to be used for hanging later.

Pour glue out on some newspaper or a recycled meat tray. Put the popped corn into two bowls — one to eat and one to dip in glue and stick onto the wreath base!

Cover the base by dipping popcorn in glue and pressing in place. Decorate with tiny yarn or ribbon bows, glued on here and there, if you wish.

GROWING THINGS

Nature is fun to observe, but you can take an active part in helping things along. You can grow a garden, plant a tree, provide habitat for wild animals — all while enjoying yourself, using all of your senses and sensibilities, and creating with your hands.

Look around you and decide what the possibilities are. Can you grow a garden? Fill a window box? Start seeds in a flower pot or cuttings in a jar and transplant them somewhere else later? Select flowers and plants with a variety of scents, colors, and shapes. Try planting some seeds that will surprise you, like gourds. Then, you can save them and create all kinds of things. If you have never done any planting, ask a neighbor who has a pretty garden or lots of plants in the window, or ask your teacher or librarian for some help. Once you get started, you'll see there are lots of opportunities to decide what you like to plant and grow. And remember, you can grow plants whether you live in a big city or in the country, or anywhere in between!

DISH GARDEN

Materials

- Used, large plastic jug
- Your choice of vegetable or fruit (see next page)
- Birdseed
- Charcoal briquettes
- Sponge
- Sand and water

Trim the jug so that you have a planting bowl about 1" high on the sides. (Decorate with permanent markers, if you wish.) If you have a piece of charcoal, such as a barbecue briquette, crush it and sprinkle at the bottom of the bowl to prevent the soil from turning moldy. Fill the bowl with moist sand.

Decide which plants you want to grow, selecting from the list on the next page. Follow the directions for each selection.

After you have planted your choices, tear a sponge into medium-sized pieces. Soak the pieces in water, and then sprinkle birdseed into the holes of the sponge pieces. Press the sponges down into the sand between your plantings. Keep the sponges moist until the birdseed sprouts. It'll be the first thing that starts to grow in your little garden. You can place some pretty shells or pebbles around the plantings. Keep the sand moist, but not too wet, and place in a sunny spot.

The Plants:

Carrots: Carrots must be started in water, so begin them a few days before you put your garden together. Cut the carrot tops off, leaving about 1" of carrot below the top. Set the tops in a bowl of water until they begin to sprout new leaves on top.

The other plants will sprout directly in the moist sand, if you prepare them as follows:

Pineapple: Cut off the top 2" of the fruit (the part with the spiky leaves). Let it dry for 2 – 3 days, and then plant it in the moist sand.

Beets: Cut the tops off, as you did for carrots. Trim the leaves off and plant the top in the sand.

Grapefruit: Soak the seeds overnight, before planting in the moist sand. (Grapefruit shells, filled with potting soil, make interesting pots for the plants themselves.)

Potato: Cut into sections, each with an eye or two, and plant.

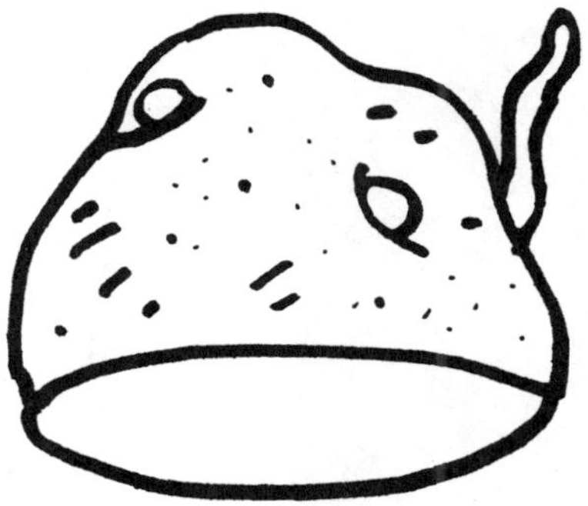

FOREST TERRARIUM

Materials

Two 2-liter soda pop bottles
Pebbles
Sand
Soil
Charcoal briquettes
Mosses, ferns, or small green plants

If you live where it's possible and can obtain the owner's permission, take a hike in a wooded area and gather a few tiny plants, such as moss from the side of tree trunks or rocks, and tiny ferns. Of course, you'll take only what you will use. As you know, never take the whole plant, but just a bit from a large clump, and be sure to re-cover the roots of the plant you have disturbed with soil.

When gathering, use a teaspoon to dig lightly and carefully around the roots. Lift them gently, leaving soil surrounding the roots. Take along some old newspapers to dampen and wrap around the plants to keep them moist and a small, cardboard box to lay your specimens in, as they are very delicate. Don't crowd them, and don't let the plants dry out. You will need to plant them immediately.

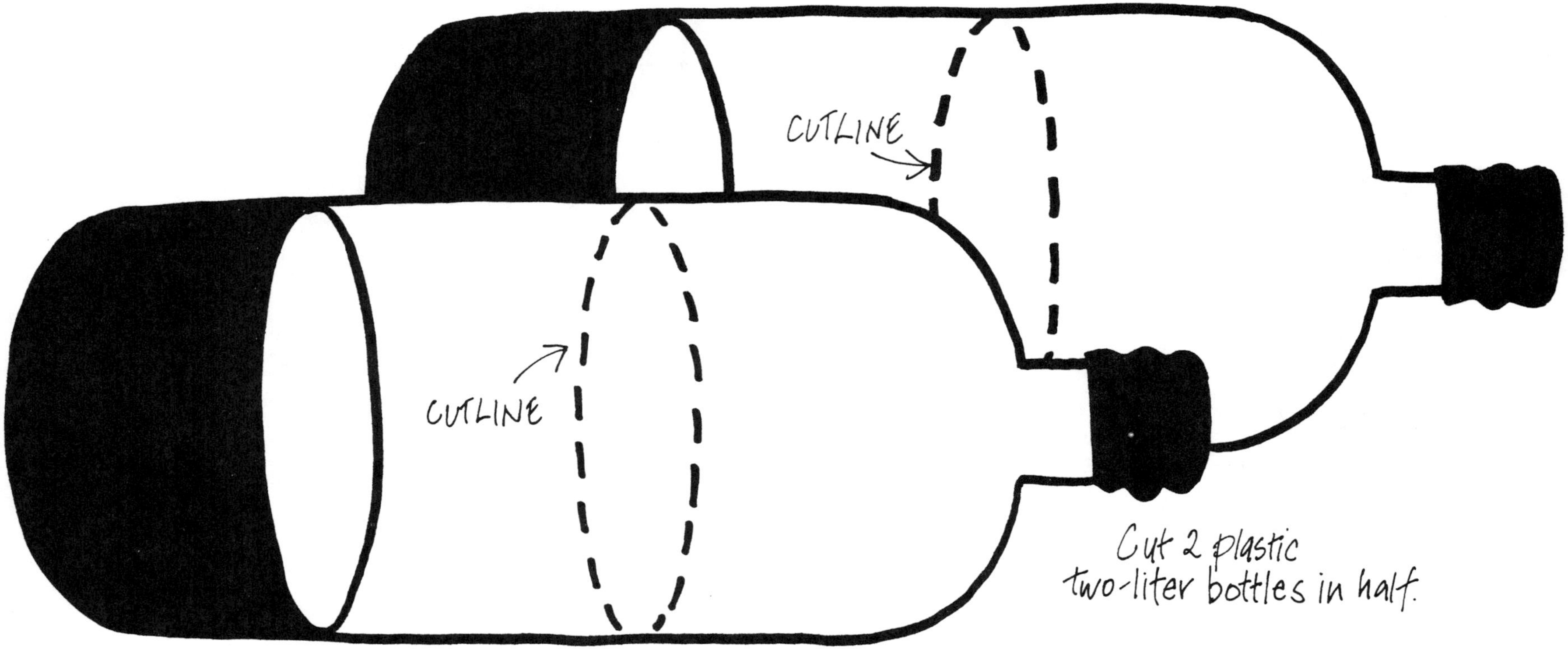

If you can't take a walk in the woods, look around for plant sources. You can take "cuttings" from established houseplants. Plants like philodendron and ivy are easy to grow from cuttings. Use a table knife or scissors to snip off a 6" piece at the end of a stem. Set it in a glass half-full of water until roots begin to appear. Then, it can be planted in a pot, or your terrarium. Share cuttings from your plants with friends, and create new plants from "old."

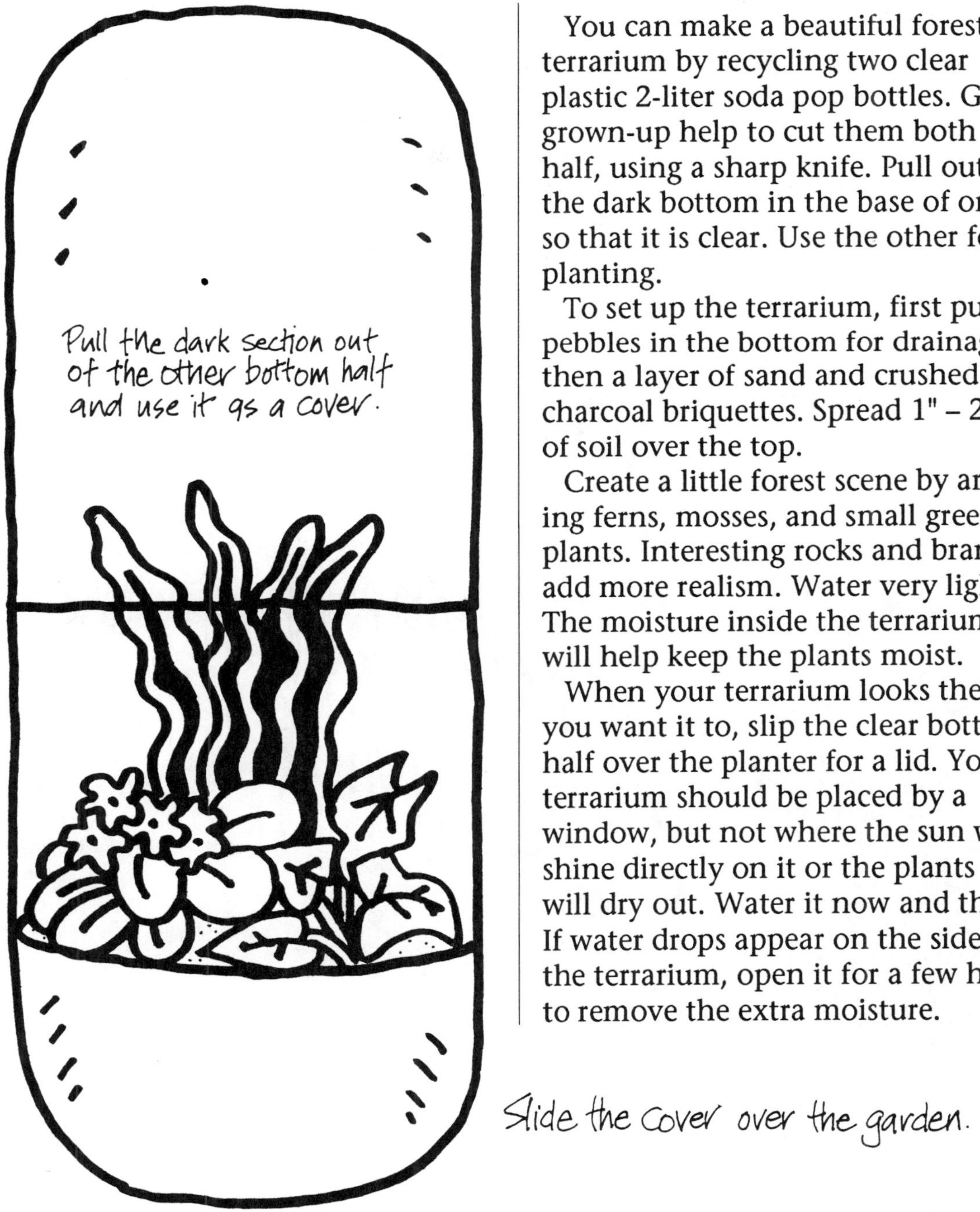

You can make a beautiful forest terrarium by recycling two clear plastic 2-liter soda pop bottles. Get grown-up help to cut them both in half, using a sharp knife. Pull out the dark bottom in the base of one, so that it is clear. Use the other for planting.

To set up the terrarium, first put pebbles in the bottom for drainage, then a layer of sand and crushed charcoal briquettes. Spread 1" – 2" of soil over the top.

Create a little forest scene by arranging ferns, mosses, and small green plants. Interesting rocks and branches add more realism. Water very lightly. The moisture inside the terrarium will help keep the plants moist.

When your terrarium looks the way you want it to, slip the clear bottle half over the planter for a lid. Your terrarium should be placed by a window, but not where the sun will shine directly on it or the plants will dry out. Water it now and then. If water drops appear on the sides of the terrarium, open it for a few hours to remove the extra moisture.

POTATO PORCUPINE

Materials

- Large potato
- Twigs or toothpicks
- Eyes: two whole cloves
- Grass seed
- Soil
- Spoon

Use the spoon to dig and hollow out one side of the potato. Fill the hollow with a little soil and sprinkle grass seed in it. Stick twigs or toothpicks in for legs. Position the cloves for eyes.

Keep moist and in a few days you will see the porcupine sprout its quills! In about two weeks, it will look really fluffy.

Try creating some other kinds of "furry" creatures, perhaps using more than one potato, twigs, and unusual plantings.

EGGHEADS

Materials

Eggshells and egg carton
Soil
Grass seed
Permanent marking pens or paint

Rinse and save eggshells in an egg carton for awhile, so you have several to work with. The best eggshells for this project are those broken straight across, slightly larger than half a shell.

To make an egghead, first select a large half shell. Draw on comical facial features with permanent marking pen or paint (or use both).

Fill the shell with some soil, sprinkle grass seed in it, and moisten with water. Set several eggheads in the egg carton near a sunny window, and in about a week, they will have a funny head of hair. You can trim the "hair" with scissors and watch it grow back again! When you are finished enjoying your smiling creations, plant the entire egghead in your garden; the shell will provide minerals for the soil as it decays.

Save eggshells. Fill with soil and grass seed, then decorate with pens or paint. Wait for your Egghead to sprout hair.

GLORIOUS GOURDS

Gourds appear in an amazing variety of shapes, colors, and textures. Fresh gourds look nice in centerpieces. Dried gourds can be cut, sanded, drilled, and wood-burned into clever and interesting objects.

Growing your own gourds is fun. They need a warm, sunny spot, with room to stretch out (or up). If you don't have garden space, you can purchase them fresh in grocery stores and garden markets, usually during the fall and winter.

If you are going to leave the gourds as they are for decoration , give them a shiny finish with a coat of acrylic floor wax or rub on some car wax. If you are going to make craft items from the gourds, don't a wax them.

There are rain forests in Alaska, California, and Washington. They are called wet conifer rain forests.

Gourd Bird House

Materials

- Dried gourd
- 1 wire coat hanger
- 3" stick
- Spoon and paring knife
- Nail and pliers

Choose a gourd that has a tear-drop shape. Use the nail to poke a hole through the top. Straighten the coat hanger and push it through the gourd. Use the pliers to twist the wire into a loop for hanging.

Using the paring knife and spoon, carefully hollow out a rounded hole about 2" across, for the bird to enter. You may want to ask for some grown-up help to puncture the gourd's tough outer skin. Shake out the seeds that have dried inside the gourd.

To make a perch for the birds, work a hole into the gourd below the opening and push the stick in through it.

Hang from a tree branch and wait for your new feathered neighbor to move in!

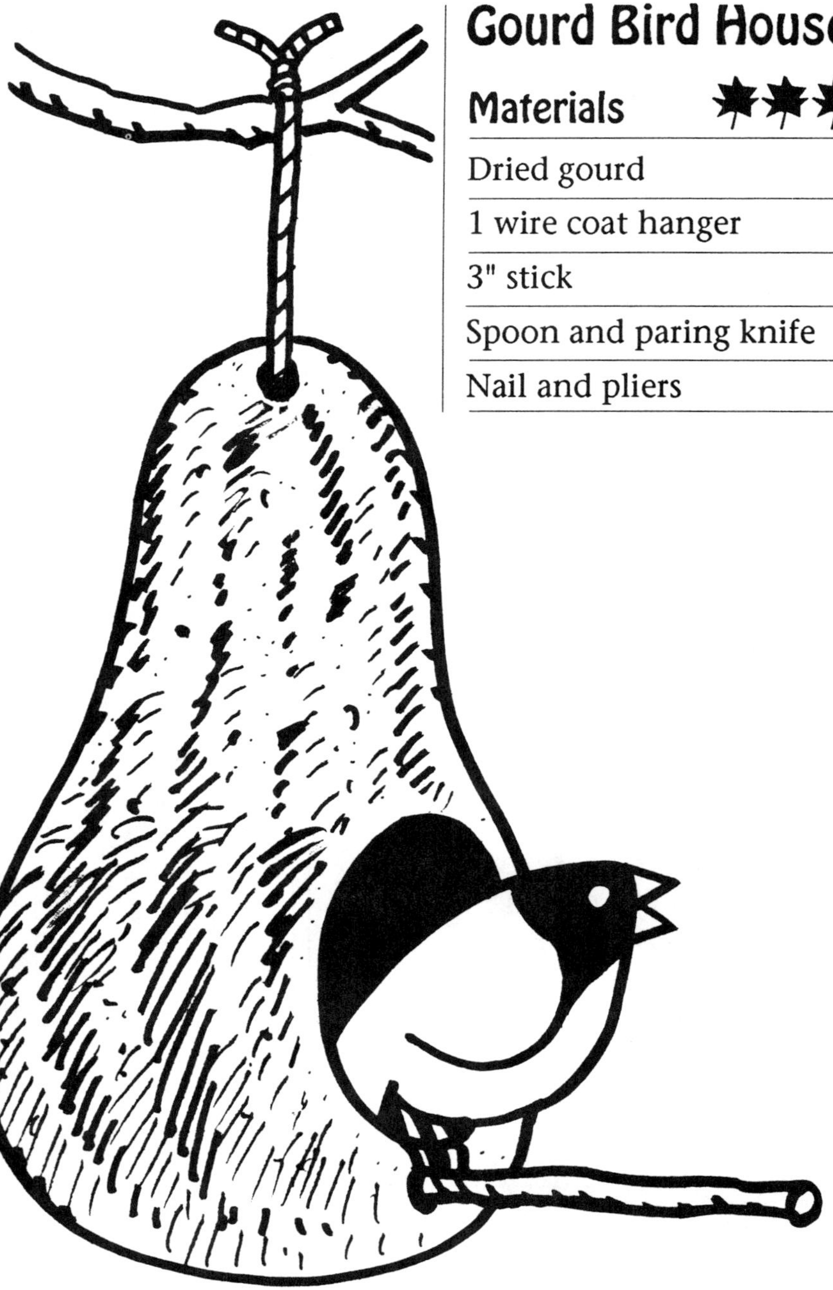

Gourd Bowl

Materials ★★★

- Dried gourd
- Sandpaper
- Small hand saw
- Spoon

Choose a gourd that's round in shape or has a rounded end that will make a good bowl shape. Ask a grown-up to help you saw an opening across the gourd. (You can cut it either vertically or horizontally, depending on how your gourd is shaped and what will give it the best balanced base.)

Scrape out the contents with a spoon, saving the seeds for another project such as the seed mosaic (see page 69). Scrape it clean and smooth the cut edges with sandpaper.

The outside can be decorated with paint, marking pens, or designs made with a wood-burning pen. Coat with acrylic finish, if you want a shiny look.

Useful items that Native American Indians made from dried gourds many, many years ago are on display in museums; your gourd bowl will last a long time if stored in a dry place. Fill it with dried flowers or leaves, for a truly natural piece of art!

CRYSTAL ROCK CANDY

Minerals form crystals when the atoms have room to grow freely, while the mineral is being formed. Some crystals are so rare and hard that they are used in jewelry. We call them gemstones. Diamonds, emeralds, sapphire, and rubies are good examples. Some common crystals are salt, sugar, ice, and quartz rock.

Not all crystals are edible, nor are most works of art, but these crystal works of art are old-time favorite candies that kids used to buy for a treat at the general store!

Materials

- 4 cups sugar
- 1 cup water
- String and pencil
- Drinking glass
- Saucepan and spoon
- Food coloring (optional)
- Magnifying glass (optional)

Ask a grown-up to help you heat 2 cups of sugar and the water in a saucepan. Stir until the sugar dissolves. Add 2 more cups sugar and continue heating and stirring until clear.

Carefully pour the solution into a drinking glass. Tie a length of string from the pencil so the string hangs in the solution. Crystals will form on the string within a few hours. Examine the crystals with a magnifying lens and touch them with your fingertips and tongue. What do you discover?

Try several different strings in one glass of sugar solution. Add food coloring to create colorful crystals. Create crystal sculptures you can taste!

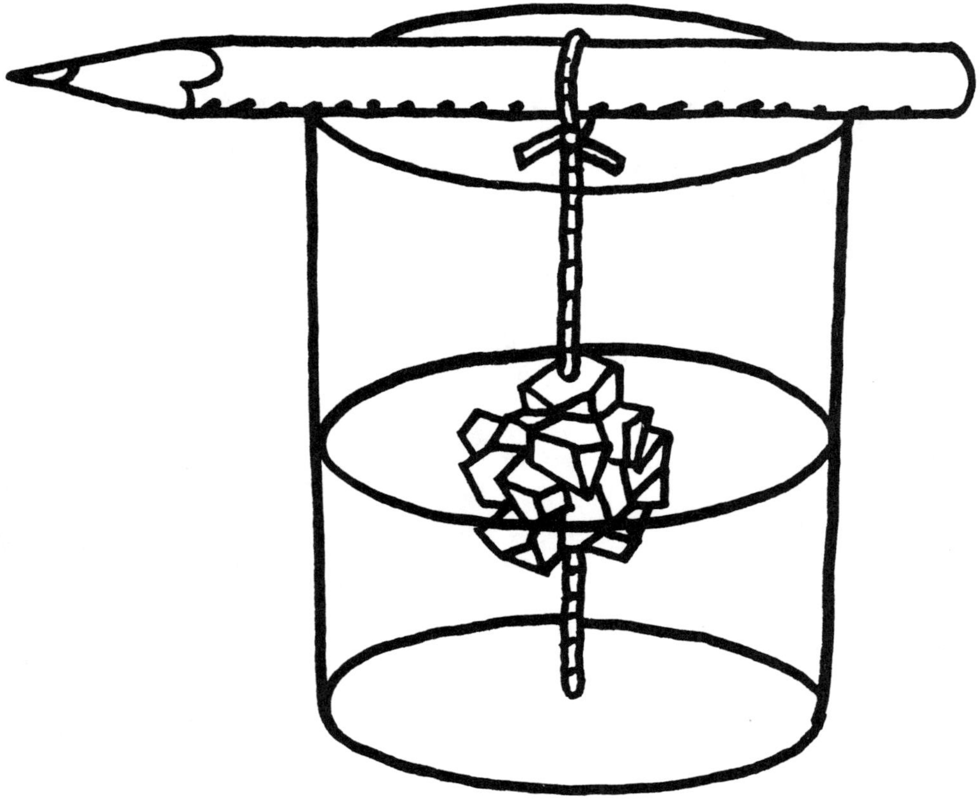

PRINTING

Making prints is a fun way to give life to discarded or reusable materials. Two things determine the nature of your print: your choice of brayer or tool to apply the ink with and your choice of material to print on. For printing, select from old sponges, stale bread, half a potato or orange, fallen leaves, empty thread spools, discarded nuts, bolts, or paper clips — whatever you can find!

Next, select a material to print on: paper grocery bags, tissue paper you have saved (ask a grown-up for help with pressing it smooth with a warm steam iron), cardboard and packaging materials, scrap paper, homemade paper (see page 18) — all provide good surfaces to print designs on.

You can also use old T-shirts, handkerchiefs, fabric scraps, pillow cases, and cut-up sheets (for making great personal flags to hang in your room and bandannas). Use acrylic or fabric paints for fabric printing.

You can use your printed materials to make gift bags, book covers, note cards, gift wrap, place mats, or artwork to frame. Your imagination plus the materials you gather will give new life to discarded items.

Spider Web Prints

Spiders eat insects that they catch in the sticky webs they build. Webs differ, depending upon the type of spider that makes them. A house spider creates a few strands that go in any direction, while some spiders make webs in sheets, and others create web funnels to trap insects. Some orb spiders create delicate works of art attached to stalks of grass.

It takes about an hour for a spider to build a web, usually at night. Look for one in the morning when the slant of the sun makes them easier to find. Look under fences, in grassy areas, or next to the base of buildings.

Don't disturb a web where a spider is working or where a fly has been caught. That might be a spider's breakfast! Instead, look for webs that have been deserted, and recycle that web into art!

Find an old, deserted spider web.

Spray with hairspray, so it will stick to a piece of cardboard. Braid some grass for a frame.

Materials

Spray paint or non-aerosol hairspray

Lightweight cardboard or stiff tag board — a piece about 6" x 6"

If you are using black spray paint, choose white cardboard. If using hairspray, choose black cardboard, or paint your cardboard a bright color. The contrast helps the web show up better.

Gently spray the deserted web from both sides, and then hold the cardboard behind the web. Pinch off the web's guide lines (where it is fastened to the grass or fence), so that now the web is resting on the cardboard. The wet hairspray will act like a glue, fastening it to the cardboard as it dries. Isn't it a beautiful, intricate design? Aren't you amazed that a tiny spider can quickly create such a beautiful work of art? This is nature at its artistic best! Why not weave or braid some grass to make a frame for your spider web art.

Incredible Food Printing

Almost any type of natural foodstuff can be used to make great prints. Potatoes are commonly used, but have you tried using nutshells, orange slices, uncooked macaroni shapes, or rolling corn on the cob in paint and printing with it? Search the pantry, then pull out the paints and newspapers and try food printing — buffet-style!

This type of printing is fun to do, and turns paper bags you have saved into gift wrap, book covers, or decorative shopping bags.

Lay out newspapers to protect your work surface. Prepare the foods by cutting or slicing, vertically or horizontally, or cutting the foods into shapes. (Cut apples horizontally to get a star shape in the center, and slice oranges horizontally to see the natural design of sections.)

Pour paint onto trays. Dip the foods and then press them in place on the printing paper. Experiment by using different patterns and colors, as well as different textures and colors of paper to print on.

You can give new life to old T-shirts, caps, pillowcases, sheets, or aprons, by printing fun designs on them. To print on fabric, use acrylic or fabric paints.

Materials
Fresh vegetables and fruits
Newspapers
Paint: tempera dries brightest
Paper to print on
Trays, plates, or recycled materials to hold paint

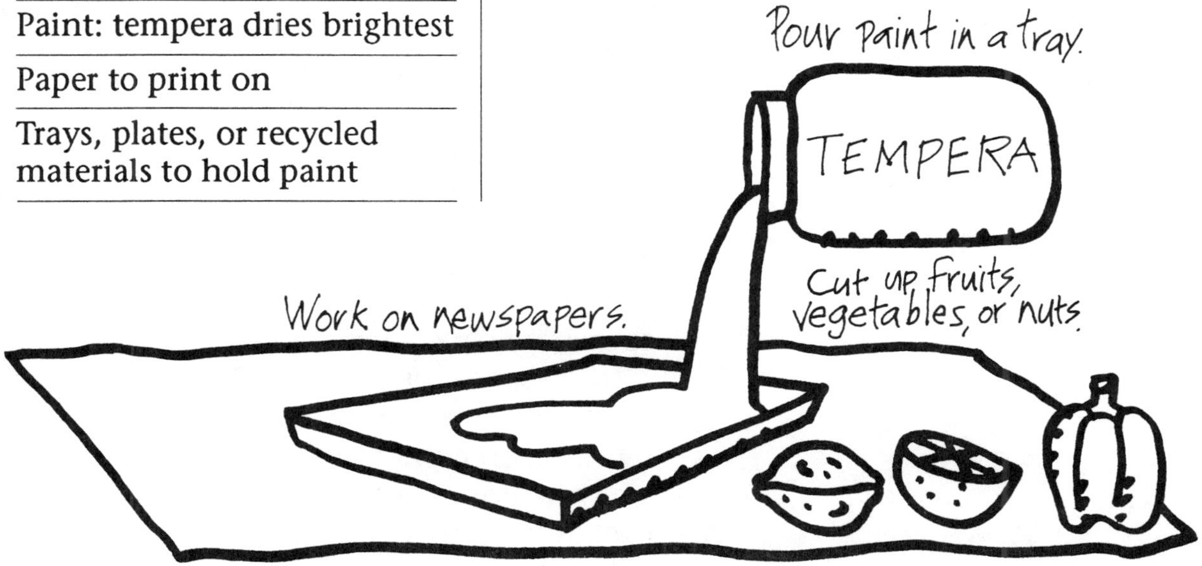

Mushroom Spore Prints

Materials

- Fresh mushroom: use one with a flat cap that hasn't opened yet
- Colored paper
- Glass jar

A mushroom isn't really a plant. It's a fungi, which means it grows from spores, not seeds.

Gently pull the stem away from the mushroom cap. Place the cap on a piece of colored paper, and cover with a glass jar. Leave it alone for about four hours. The mushroom cap will open, and the spores will drop onto the paper.

Try spore prints on different colors of paper, looking for interesting contrasts. Some spores are dark, some light.

To preserve your print and keep it from smearing, spray lightly with extra-hold hair spray in a non-aerosol pump can. Spore prints done on colorful pieces of paper make very attractive stationery.

Tin Can Printing

Materials

- Tin can
- Yarn or heavy string and scissors
- White glue in a small bowl
- Tempera paints
- Paper to print on
- Newspapers
- Packaging tray you have saved

Use the newspapers to protect your table top.

Remove both ends from the can. Pour some glue in the bowl. Cut a length of yarn about 12" long. Dip it in the glue and then wrap the yarn around the can, creating a pattern or design with the yarn. Add more lengths of yarn as needed. Let the glue dry completely.

Pour some paint on the tray. Roll the can in it, and then roll the can over the paper, pressing firmly to print. If you want to use several colors of paint at once, brush the paint onto the can in sections, then roll on the paper to print.

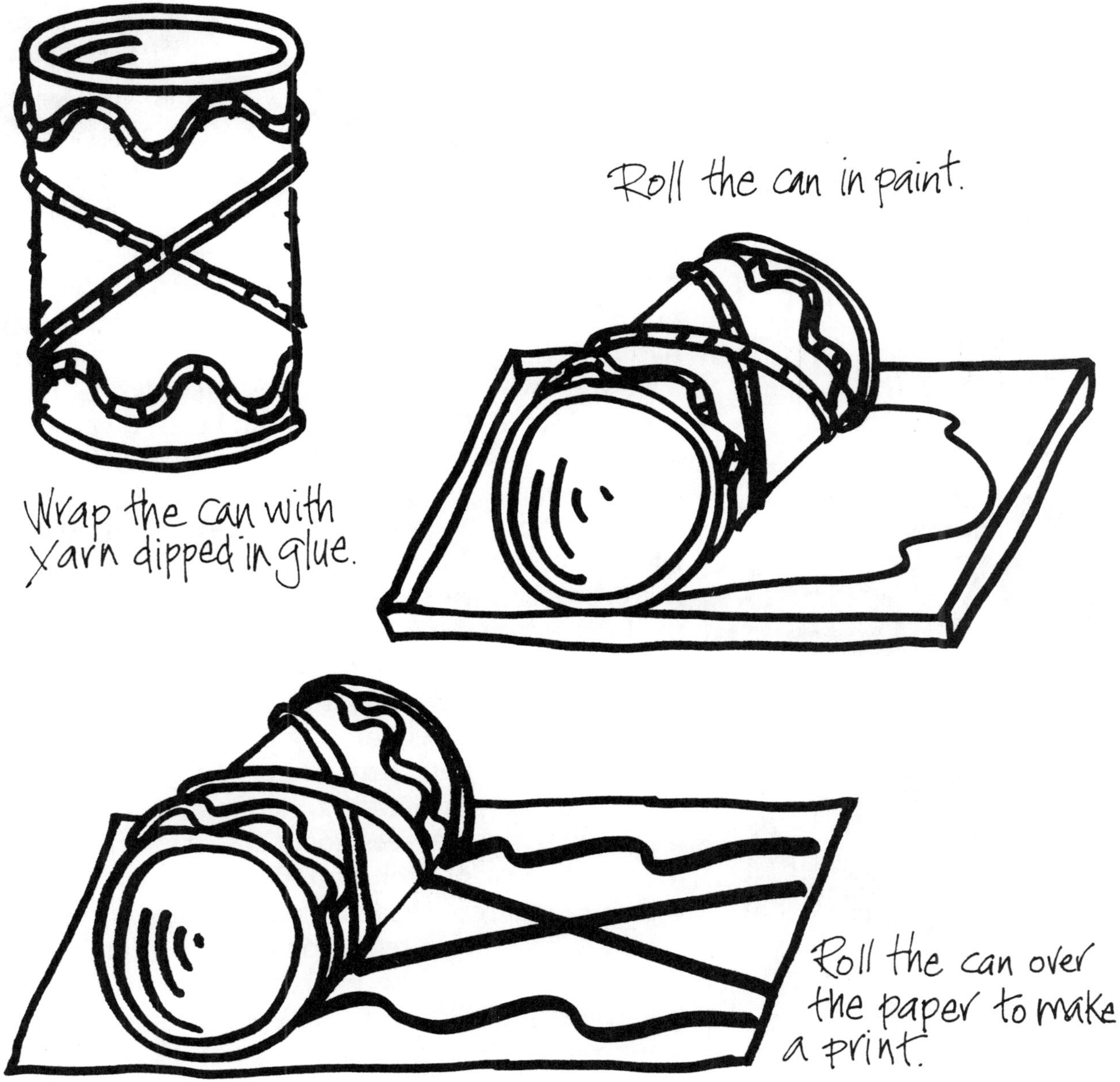

WEEDS, HERBS, & OTHER GREAT STUFF

No matter where you live, you can take a "walk on the wild side"! You can find plants, animals, and nature in its wildest form all around you. Can you find a weed growing in a crack in the sidewalk? Close your eyes and smell it's fragrance, then brush it gently against your cheek. Enjoy even the tiniest bit of nature around you. Whether in the city or in the country, nature is there if you open your eyes and mind to it. Did you notice the wasp's nest under the eave, the spider's web at the mailbox, the moss stuck between the bricks? You don't have to wander far to find wild things, because they are living right next to you.

Notice how many different kinds of plants are growing in just a small section of ground. Look at them from the ground up. Tiny plants may be hugging the ground, others surrounding them above. Look along walls and up in the trees, too. Close your eyes and sniff the different plants you find. Can you identify them without looking? Depending upon the time of year, you may find plants ready to send out seeds from pods. Blow or shake them, and watch the tiny seeds disperse into the air, to start next year's plants. And so nature's wondrous cycle continues.

TREAT NATURE WITH CARE

There are a few important things to consider, before helping yourself to any plants. Of course, you'll be polite and ask for permission, if you are on private property. You won't pick flowers in public gardens in parks — they are for everyone to enjoy. If the flowers you want to use are wildflowers, leave plenty of blossoms to turn to seed so the plants can reseed themselves. Never pull plants up by the root; instead, cut them with scissors, so plants that grow from the root mass can regenerate themselves.

There is plenty available free for the taking — autumn leaves, sprigs of different kinds of grasses, a tiny clump of moss, cattails, pine cones, pebbles, shells, and fallen bark.

Also, be careful that you aren't collecting in an area that has been recently sprayed with harmful chemicals that can contaminate your hands and your projects.

Take a paper sack and an empty box to carry your nature treasures in. You will also need a pair of blunt-ended scissors to clip stems, and some old string to tie small bundles of plants together. Plan your projects before going, so that you only collect the materials you will use, and you won't be wasting anything.

Flowers: Pressed & Dried

Pressed Flowers

Materials

Old newspapers
Flowers
Scissors

Is there a vacant lot near your home where purple violets or pink hepatica grow wild? Did you plant a box of pansies or violas this spring? If so, these are perfect for pressing.

Carefully collect a few flowers by snipping them on long stems, keeping all the leaves on them. Only pick as many as you need, and never too many from one plant.

Now, spread the flowers out on the newspapers, pressing with your fingers to flatten and shape them a bit. Cover the flowers with a few sheets of newspaper, stacking the flower-filled pages on top of each other. Press down with heavy books. Wait about a week before taking the pressed flowers out; store them in shoe boxes. You can make several projects with pressed flowers, so make up an ample supply to use another time. You can also dry leaves of different shapes and sizes.

Dried Flowers

Materials

1 cup borax (purchase in a supermarket)
2 cups cornmeal
Shoe box

Another way to preserve flowers is by drying them. Pressed flowers are flattened, while dried flowers are three-dimensional and can be arranged in a vase or basket, as if they were still alive. Roses, strawflowers, and purple statice all dry very well. Maybe you can plant some or ask a neighbor if you can pick a few flowers. Sometimes, a florist will let you have some old flowers to use for pressing and drying.

Mix the borax and cornmeal to make a drying agent. Spread some in the shoe box. Gently lay the flowers on the mixture. Carefully cover the flowers completely with the mixture. Put the lid on the box, and put it away in a closet for about a month. (Mark on your calendar when the flowers will be ready.)

Cover the flowers completely; then put on the lid.

Mini-Vase & Flowers

Materials

Thread spool (remove the labels; paint if you wish)
Tiny dried flowers or weeds
6" of narrow ribbon or yarn

This makes a simple, country-style gift for Mother's Day, May Day, or as party favors. A grouping of three of these looks very pretty on a bureau or mantel.

Break the flower stems off if they are too long, so they set nicely in the hole in the spool. Dip the stem ends in a little glue, and arrange them inside the hole of the spool.

Wrap the ribbon around the spool, and tie in a bow. Secure the bow with a dot of glue. Trim the ends evenly.

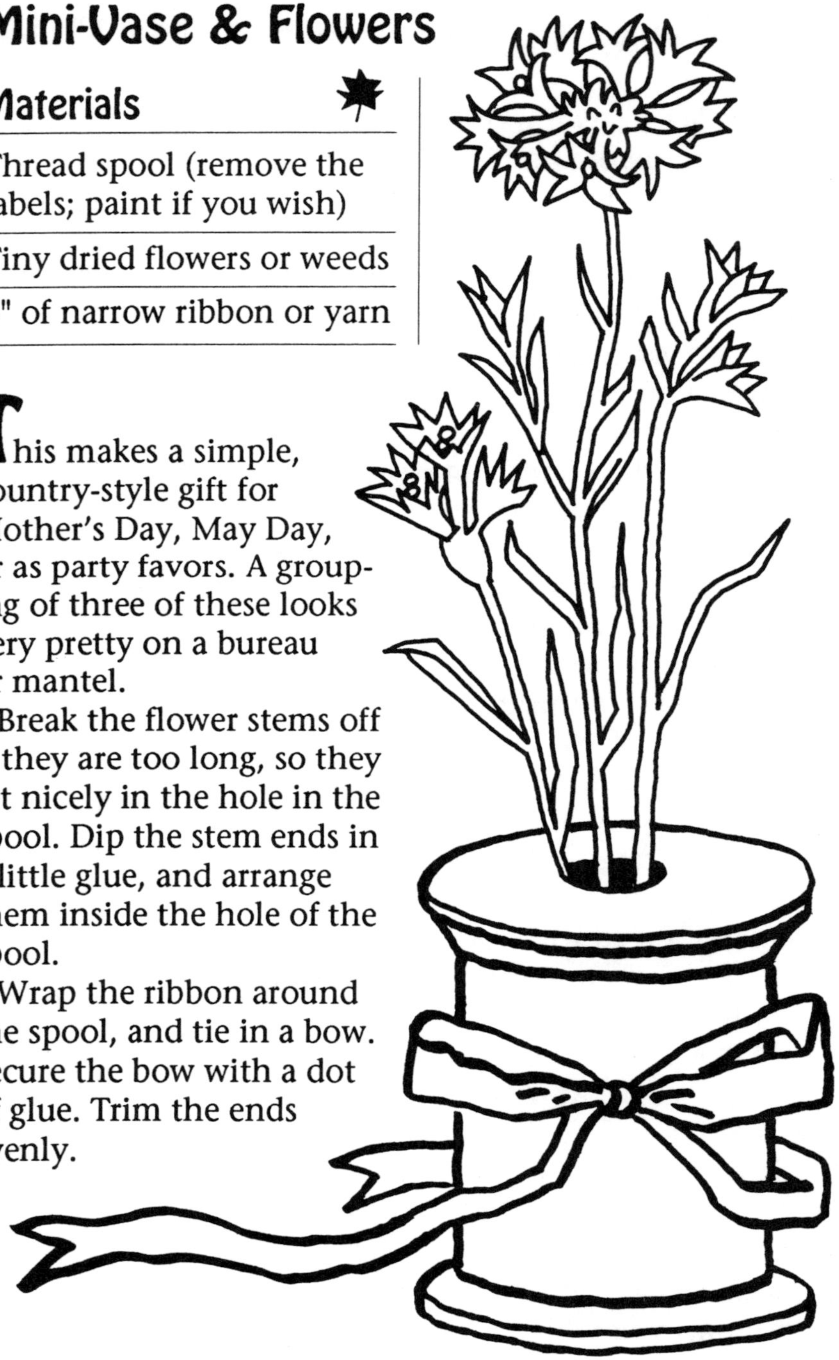

Pressed Flower Bookmarks

Materials

Homemade paper (see page 18) or tagboard the size you want your bookmark to be.
Pressed flowers or leaves
Small scrap of nylon net, tulle, or organdy fabric
Narrow ribbon or flat lace trim
Glue that dries clear

Here's a nice gift project using dried, pressed flowers. While you work on this, think of how pretty the flowers looked in the field or garden. That will help you arrange them in a very natural way.

Cut the paper and net the size you want to make your bookmark. Gently position the dried flowers on top of the paper. Use a few dots of glue to hold them in position. Using a tiny amount of glue around the edges, glue the net on top of the flowers. Position the ribbon or lace around the edges and glue in place.

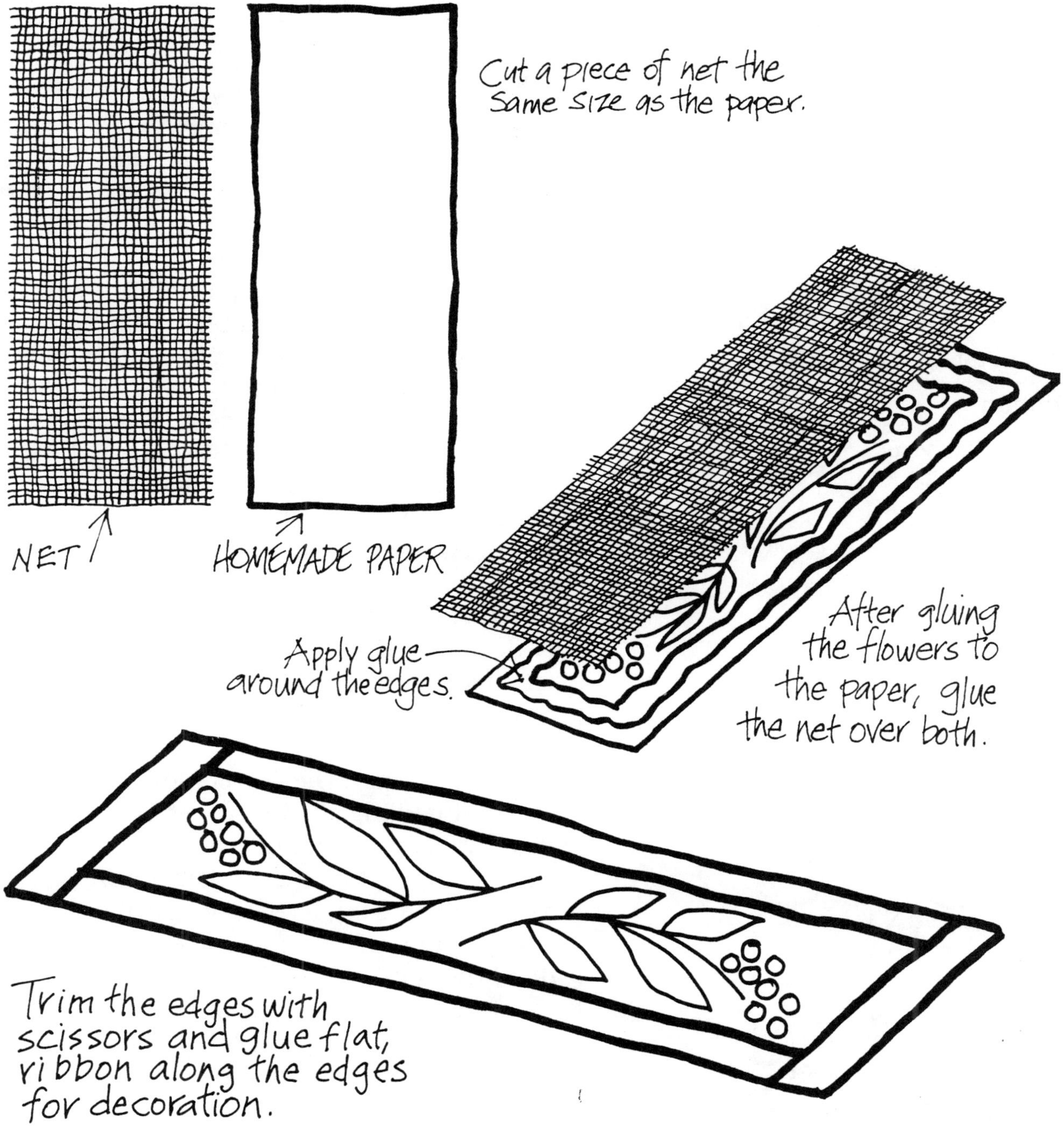

Potpourri

Materials

- Lots of flower blossoms, including roses
- 1 tablespoon mixed spices (cloves, cinnamon, nutmeg, mace, or allspice) and/or 1 tablespoon dry, mixed herbs
- Few drops potpourri oil (optional)
- Small, airtight containers
- Ribbon
- Pans for drying

What's one of the most wonderful things about outdoors? It smells so fresh and sweet — that is, if we take care of the air around us. Well, you can capture some of that outdoor goodness and bring it inside. You can make potpourri (poe-pour-REE) from just about any dried plant material that has a pleasant scent.

One way to obtain fresh flowers to use, if you don't have them in a garden, is to contact a florist shop, and ask for the flowers that have to be discarded. You may end up with lots of sweet-smelling roses, gardenias, and carnations for free.

To make the potpourri, gather lots of flower blossoms. Try to find different colors and scents. Roses are the most popular and should make up most of your mixture.

Now, pull apart the flower blossoms, discarding all but the petals. Place the petals in pans to dry, away from sunlight. Mix them a few times a day. When completely dry, sprinkle with a spoonful of mixed spices or dried herbs (rosemary, marjoram, cedar needles, mint, sage, or thyme). A few drops of potpourri oil (available at craft stores) can also be sprinkled on to intensify the scent.

Mix the dry petals with your hands and scoop them into clean, airtight containers. Baby food jars are perfect. Paint the lids and tie a ribbon around the jar to make a special gift.

To use potpourri, keep the lid closed until you want to scent a room; then, open the lid for a while. To maintain the nice scent, add drops of potpourri oil.

Potpourri Sachet

Materials

Dried potpourri mixture (see page 92)
6" square of nylon netting, or lightweight, cotton, print fabric
Rubber band
6" length of satin ribbon

Want to make a special gift for your sister or aunt, grandmother or neighbor? Here's a simple way to make a sachet to scent a bureau or desk drawer. These are also pretty hung from the tree as Christmas ornaments when made with red and green fabric squares.

Lay the fabric square on a table top and spoon about two tablespoons of the dried potpourri into the center. Bring the edges of the fabric to the center and secure with a rubber band. Then tie a pretty bow at the center with the satin ribbon.

Solar Art

Materials

Weeds, leaves, berries, flowers — whatever you have gathered
Studio proof paper and fixer (buy at a photography supply store)
Water
2 dishpans or square cake pans

Here's a way to use your environment to "capture" nature's beauty! This is a special kind of photography that uses the light from the sun to create shadow pictures. Select weeds and leaves with different shapes and feathery edges.

On a sunny day, arrange an assortment of your interesting weeds, thistles, and berries on a piece of studio proof paper and put it in bright sunlight. The plants will block the sun's rays, causing the paper under them to remain light colored, while the exposed paper turns a dark purple. It will only take a few minutes. (Lift the edge of a leaf carefully to see if it is "done.")

Ask a grown-up to prepare the fixer (it's poisonous) in one of the pans. Fill the other pan with water. Remove the plants and set the paper in the pan of fixer for five minutes. This will prevent the paper from turning completely dark in daylight. Take it out of the fixer bath, and set the paper in the pan of water for ten minutes.

You can soak more than one paper in the pans at once.

When the prints are done, lay them on newspapers to dry. If the print paper curls, stack a heavy book on it to flatten it. Your nature prints will look nice when matted or framed, and hung on the wall. You can also trim and glue the prints to folded construction paper to make greeting cards.

Rubbings

Materials

- Leaves of different shapes and sizes
- Paper
- Crayons (see page 30 to make your own), colored chalks, or soft lead pencils
- Newspapers

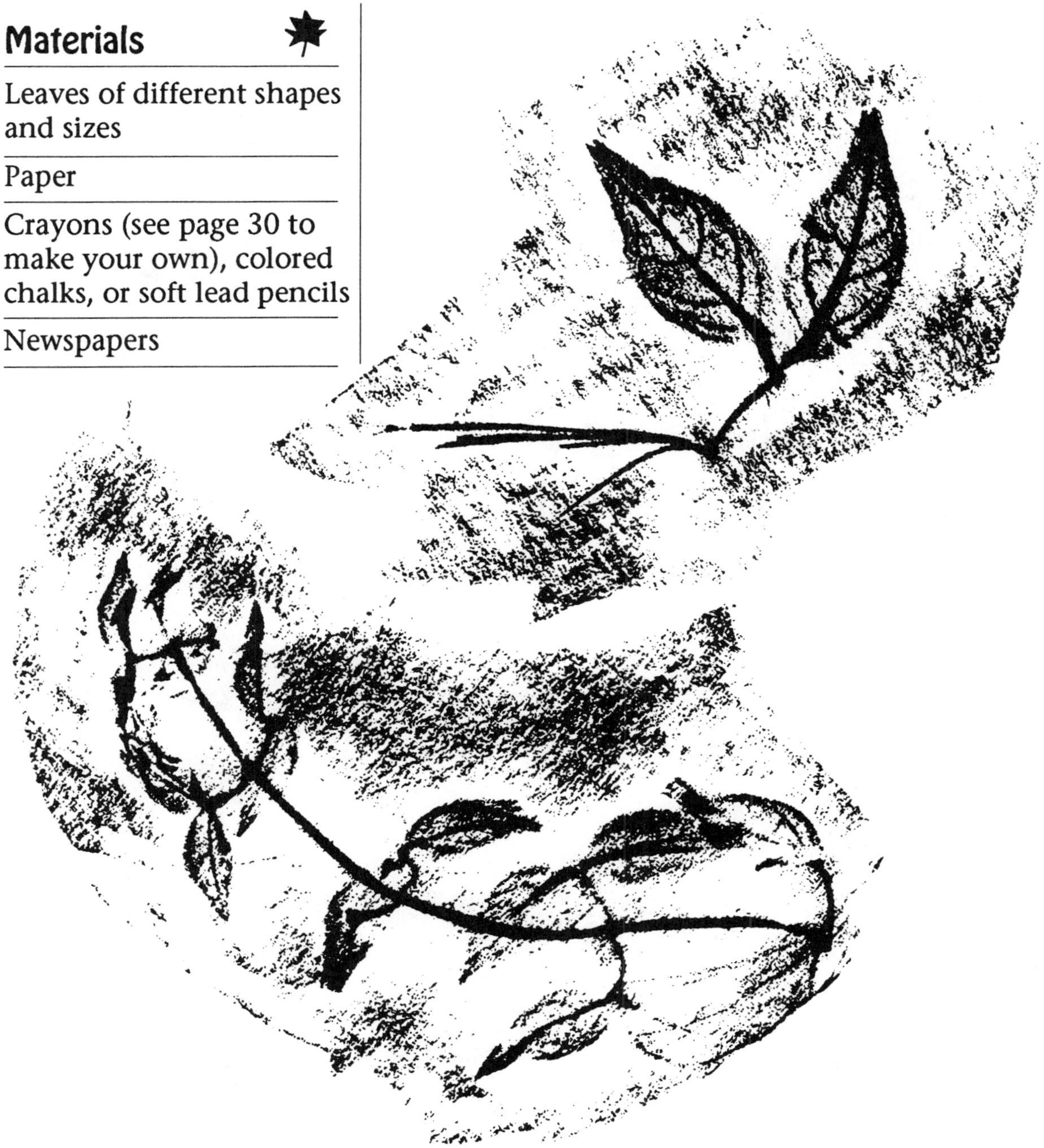

Isn't it fun to walk in the leaves, picking up different shapes and sizes that have fallen to the ground? Find a safe place to lie down on the ground and look up through the trees to the sky. Wow! Those trees are so very tall, and yet, the leaves float so slowly to the ground.

Collect several different types and sizes of leaves. Place some leaves on several layers of newspaper and position your rubbing paper over the leaves. Use the sides of the crayons to rub over the paper with steady, firm strokes, and the leaf shapes will be outlined on the paper. Try crayons, chalks, or pencil, or combinations of the three, for different effects.

Add other interesting textural items: coins, pieces of fabric and lace, paper doilies, cutouts from thin tag board, small washers, and pieces of sewing trims.

Take your crayons and paper outdoors to collect more textures. Hold the paper against different types of trees and make rubbings of the bark. Make rubbings of stucco walls, concrete sidewalks, asphalt streets, bricks. Manhole covers, tombstones, and old signs are also interesting.

Rose Petal Beads

In the past, rose petal beads were cherished remembrances of the blossoms in a grandmother's garden or a bride's bouquet. Here is a quick and easy way to make beads from the petals in your own garden or from discarded roses at the florist shop.

Materials

2/3 cup flour
2 tablespoons salt
1/3 cup water
6 cups of rose petals (pick them in the morning for best fragrance)
Large bowl and spoon
Toothpicks
Needle and thread

Mix the flour, salt, and water. Knead until smooth.

Tear the rose petals into tiny pieces. Crumble and crush them as you work to soften them and release their fragrance.

Mix the shredded petals into the dough, keeping it soft and pliable. Roll bits of dough into beads. Push toothpicks into the beads to make holes for stringing later. Set aside a few days for drying. Then, string the beads with a needle and double-knotted thread. Tie the ends of the thread together and wear as a fragrant, special necklace.

Add torn rose petals to the dough.

String with a needle and thread when dry.

Pomander

The first pomanders were made from gold or silver. They were shaped like balls and hung by a cord from the waist. They were filled with sweet-smelling herbs and spices, and used as perfumes. They were also thought to keep one from getting sick. Today, pomanders are made from fresh fruits and are hung in a closet to scent clothes and keep moths away.

Materials

- Firm, fresh oranges or lemons
- Whole dried cloves
- Toothpick or thumbtack with large plastic head
- Nylon net
- Ribbon or pretty yarn

Use a thumbtack with a large plastic head or a toothpick to poke holes in the orange skin, inserting a whole clove into each hole. You can randomly place the cloves in the orange, as close together as you can, or you can make a very neat vertical or horizontal pattern. If you want to add a richer, spicier scent, roll the finished pomander in a mixture of cinnamon, allspice, and nutmeg.

Now, set the pomander aside to dry for several weeks. It will shrink and get hard (as the orange gets dehydrated). Wrap it in a square of nylon net and tie the ends with the ribbon. It's ready to hang in a closet or kitchen, or give as a gift.

Poke holes with a thumbtack. Push the cloves into the holes.

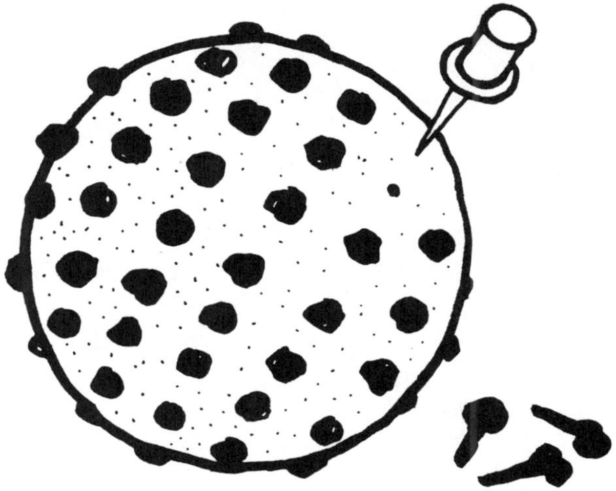

Wrap the dry pomander in nylon and tie with a ribbon.

Hooray for Herbs!

Herbs are aromatic plants used for cooking, medicine, household uses, and pest control. Some common herbs are the leaves of fragrant plants like mint, rosemary, and thyme.

Spices are similar to herbs except that they are usually made from tropical plants such as cinnamon, cloves, ginger, and pepper.

You can collect wild herbs, or you can easily grow your own — in a small garden, in flower pots, or window boxes. Just be sure to give them plenty of light and water them as needed. Herb seeds can be purchased anywhere garden supplies are sold.

When picking herbs from the wilds or your garden, use scissors to snip off only the leaves you will need, leaving the roots and some leaves for continued plant growth. Most herbs grow back after several cuttings.

When gathering fresh herbs, collect more than you think you need, as they will shrink while drying. Collect on a dry morning, and then dry the herbs further on newspapers, away from light. Once completely dry, separate the leaves from the stems. Crush the leaves and store in an airtight container until you're ready to use them.

If you are working on a project and run short of your dried herbs, mix in some uncooked rice to add bulk and to stretch your herb mixture.

Herb Vinegar

Materials

- Fresh or dried herbs: fennel, sage, rosemary, garlic, tarragon, or chives
- Vinegar (cider, white, or balsamic)
- Glass bottle with cork or nonmetal cap

Use several sprigs of fresh herbs or about 1/2 to 1 cup of loose herbs to make 1 quart of herb vinegar. You can use more or less, depending upon how strongly flavored you want the vinegar to be.

Fill the clean bottlewith herbs, gently arranging the sprigs. Then, fill the bottle with vinegar. Cap or cork, and let it sit for two weeks. Tie a pretty bow around the bottle for a perfect gift.

Here's a wonderful way to reuse old bottles and savor the flavor of fresh herbs in your salads all winter long. If the labels don't peel off easily, soak the bottles in warm water for a few minutes, then scrub off. Wash them thoroughly in hot, soapy water and air dry completely.

Sweet Dreams Pillow

Materials ✱✱✱

1 cup dried flower petals
1/2 cup dried mint
1 tablespoon crushed cloves
2 pieces of closely woven fabric, about 6" x 6" (Use broadcloth or gingham — cloth handkerchiefs are pretty, too.)
Needle, thread, and scissors
Ribbon or lace for trim (optional)
Large bowl

This pillow is for those nights when you just can't get to sleep. Place it inside your pillowcase. The scent of the herbs is said to have a relaxing effect.

Gently mix the herbs and petals in the bowl. With right sides of the fabric facing each other (so it looks inside out), sew the pillow together around the edges, leaving one side open for turning and filling. Clip the corners of the seam allowances. Turn right side out and fill gently with the dried herbs. Sew the opening closed.

You can decorate the pillow by gluing or sewing on lace or ribbon trims.

Mix herbs and dry petals.

Weed Casting

Materials

- Weeds, flowers, leaves
- Modeling clay
- Plaster of Paris and utensils
- Empty box, like a shoe box

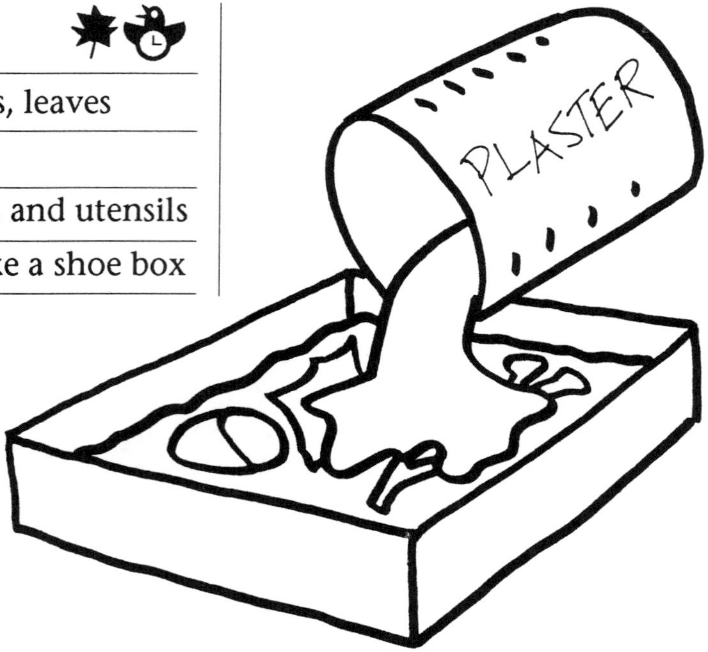

Press modeling clay into a box. Press the weeds into the clay, then remove them. Pour plaster into the box to cover the clay.

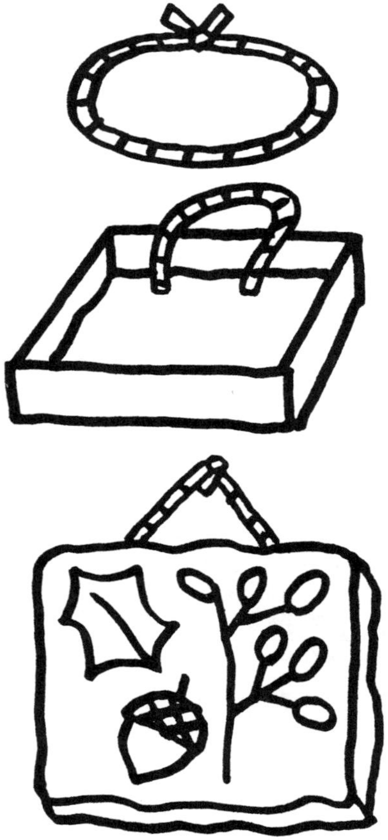

To make a cast that can be hung on the wall, tie a loop of old yarn or cord. Lay it on the wet plaster and push it down so it is covered by some wet plaster. 2 or 3" of yarn must be stuck within the plaster. When hard, hang by the yarn loop.

If working indoors, it's a good idea to spread old newspapers to cover your work area. Be sure that you don't wash any plaster down the sink drain. To discard leftover plaster, let it harden in the container, break it up, and add it to the compost heap.

To create an interesting sculpture, first press the modeling clay in the shoe box bottom, up to about half an inch thick. Arrange your weeds in a pleasing pattern on top of the clay. With your fingers, gently press the weeds down into the clay and then pull them out. Their imprints will remain. If you want to change your design, smooth the clay surface and press the weeds again. Once you have your final imprint, mix the plaster in the container, following the directions on the plaster box. Pour it over the clay until the plaster is about 2" thick.

Let the plaster harden and dry; overnight is best. Then, gently tear away the sides of the box, separating the clay from the plaster casting.

Paint or stain the plaster casting, if you wish. Dark shoe polish can also be gently rubbed onto the plaster surface with a soft rag. If you want a shiny finish, brush on a coat of acrylic finish or acrylic floor wax.

Peanut People

Materials

- Peanuts in the shell
- Fine-tip felt markers
- Glue and scissors
- Bits of stuffing, feathers, sequins, scraps of fabric or leather

Peanuts make nutty characters! Select the size and shape of nut you want for your person — some make wonderful babies, some tall and spindly characters, and others chubby and round folk.

Draw on a face and clothing details with the markers. Add scraps of cloth for hats, robes, scarves, or capes. Glue on pieces of embroidery thread or feathers for hair. Use bits of pillow stuffing or cotton balls for beards.

You can make clever family groupings by gluing several nuts of different sizes to a piece of bark or driftwood. This looks great on a desk or bookcase. Send a peanut family to work with your mom or dad!

Use a nail to poke holes in the nut shell's body for arms and legs made of twigs or pipe cleaners. Use tacky-type glue to hold them.

Finger puppets can be made from peanut shells, too, and . . . you get to eat the nut! All you need are peanuts and a fine-tip marking pen. Break the shell across, try to get one that is long. Draw on facial features, gluing details from scraps. Put it on your finger, and bring your puppet to life!

Pine Cone Owl Sculpture

Materials

- Small pine cones
- Felt scraps
- Glue and scissors
- Small branch
- Tin can with pebbles or soil

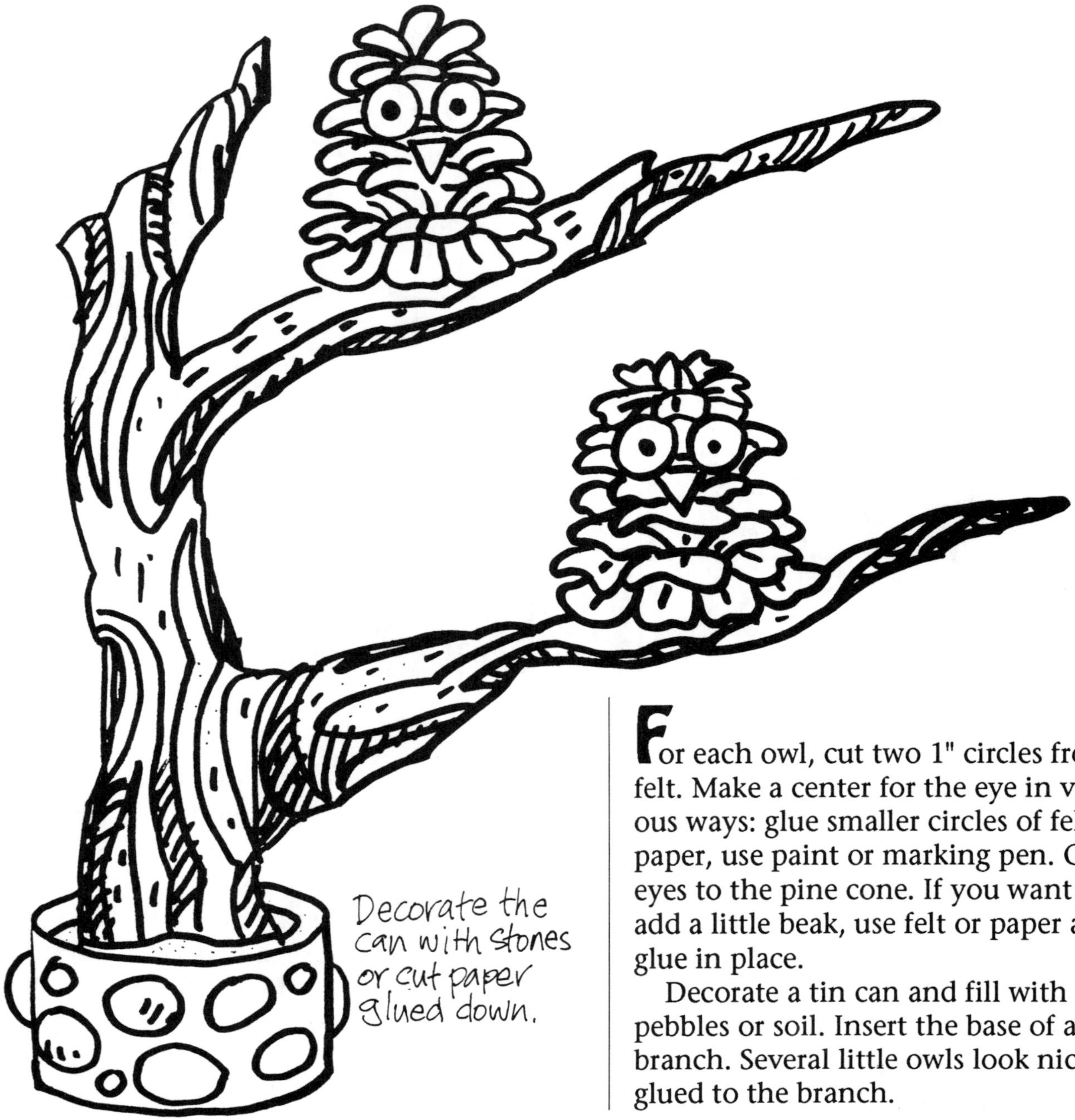

Decorate the can with stones or cut paper glued down.

For each owl, cut two 1" circles from felt. Make a center for the eye in various ways: glue smaller circles of felt or paper, use paint or marking pen. Glue eyes to the pine cone. If you want to add a little beak, use felt or paper and glue in place.

Decorate a tin can and fill with pebbles or soil. Insert the base of a branch. Several little owls look nice glued to the branch.

Weather Wonders

Have you noticed how much the weather affects you? It can change your plans for the day and your mood as well. It affects the kind of homes we live in, the type of clothing we wear, and the food we eat. It affects the plant and animal world, too. Many animals grow thick fur or go into hibernation when it's cold. Plants also have a period of inactivity during cold weather. Even fish live differently when the weather changes. Plants and animals are continually ***adapting*** *themselves to the weather around them.*

Rainy Day Drip Paintings

Materials

Butcher paper

Powdered tempera, several colors

Shaker dispensers for the paint (Old salt shakers or spice containers work very well. You will need one for each color of powdered paint.)

When the weather forecast is "light rain on the way," prepare for a rain painting. Work outside before the rain begins. Spread out a large sheet of paper, using stones or something heavy to weight down the paper's edges.

Fill the shaker dispensers with powdered paint. Sprinkle the powdered tempera randomly over the paper. As it rains, the raindrops will mix and blend the paint colors. After a few minutes, go out and discover what designs the rain has made for you. Bring in the wet painting and let dry on layers of old newspapers. You have a real "watercolor," created by a very famous artist — nature, herself!

Another way to do a rain painting, is to leave the paper outside to become wet. Once the drizzling stops, go outside with the shakers and sprinkle a design on the wet paper. Carefully, carry it inside to dry on newspaper. Which kind of rain painting do you like best?

Snow Painting

Materials

- Paint: tempera, food coloring, or natural dyes
- Colored chalk
- Large brushes or old spray bottles
- Cans or jugs to hold paint

Your painting technique will vary depending upon the type of snow: light, fluffy snow may be more difficult to work on than frozen, crusted snow. Snow banks with a frozen surface are easiest to paint on, while wet snow makes chalking easier. That's right — all snow is not alike! Try different activities with a variety of snow conditions and materials.

Mix diluted tempera paint, food coloring, or natural food dyes in cans or jugs. Use large brushes or fill old spray bottles with the paints. Experiment using the paints on snow banks. Paint large swirls or bands of color. Rather than painting an object or something you've seen, experiment with color, design, and the shape of the snowbank. What colors look interesting together? How wild can your design get?

Try to work quickly, rather than fussing over the job you are doing. If you don't like it, move on to another snowbank, or pat fresh snow in place over the paint, and try something else.

Colored chalk can be used on snow, too. Break up several pieces of chalk and rub their colors into the wet snow.

4.

CREATING TREASURES FROM TRASH

Have you ever looked at garbage with ideas for its potential? Try watching for useful items that would be thrown away around your home — everything from milk containers and yogurt containers to plastic bubble wrap found on many items to microwaveable trays to birthday cards and holiday gift wrap. Use your wonderful imagination and you'll see potential everywhere! How about unraveling the yarn from a sweater that the moths got to or cutting up the fabric from some old curtains? Whatever you save, rinse it out, or fold it up, or wind it around an old tissue tube for safe storage. Keep a "craft box" of reusables in the kitchen or your closet. When you need craft supplies, check out your stashed items.

By being imaginative you can find lots of uses for stuff that would sit for years and years in a landfill. But you also need to think about items before you purchase them. Try to buy only what you need and can use; look for things that aren't packaged in lots of throwaway materials.

Do the earth a favor, and yourself, too, by creating some glorious treasures from trash!

EGG CARTON CUT-UPS

Pulp egg cartons are made from recycled paper products and can also be recycled again when you are through using them. Using recycled materials creates jobs, saves natural resources, and lessens the load on our landfills. Best of all, you can have a lot of fun making some wild and crazy cut-ups.

All the egg carton projects are made with the same materials and are at the same degree of difficulty.

Materials

- Pulp egg cartons
- White glue
- Paint
- Paper clips, toothpicks, straight pins — depending upon project
- Scissors

FISH

Cut 2 individual egg sections apart; trim the rough edges evenly. These will be the fish's body. Use the carton lid to cut a fin and tail section as shown. Glue the body sections to each side of the fin and tail sections. Hold the pieces together a few minutes until the glue sticks. To make a mouth, cut around one of the pop-up lid fasteners molded into the lower portion of the carton. Glue it on the body.

Paint with tempera. While wet you can sprinkle glitter onto the paint, so it will sparkle like wet fish scales. Decorate the details with markers when the paint is dry. Hang several fish from lengths of old fishing line or string to create a mobile.

Trace and cut 1 fin and tail section from carton lid.

Glue fin and tail piece between 2 egg cup sections.

Paint. Hang from a string tied to a paper clip inserted into the egg cups.

CAT

Cut 2 individual egg cup sections apart, leaving little tabs to become feet on one, and leaving 2 tabs for ears on the other. Glue the head section on top of the body section. Break twigs or dry grass and glue on for whiskers.

To create a cat nose, glue a small black pompon, triangle of felt, or cut out the pop-up lid fastener from the carton and glue it in place on top of the whiskers. Paint the cat unusual colors, and glue on a bit of yarn or string for a tail. Can you find some scraps to create a tiny mouse, too?

At the rate Americans are producing garbage, we need 500 new garbage dumps a year.

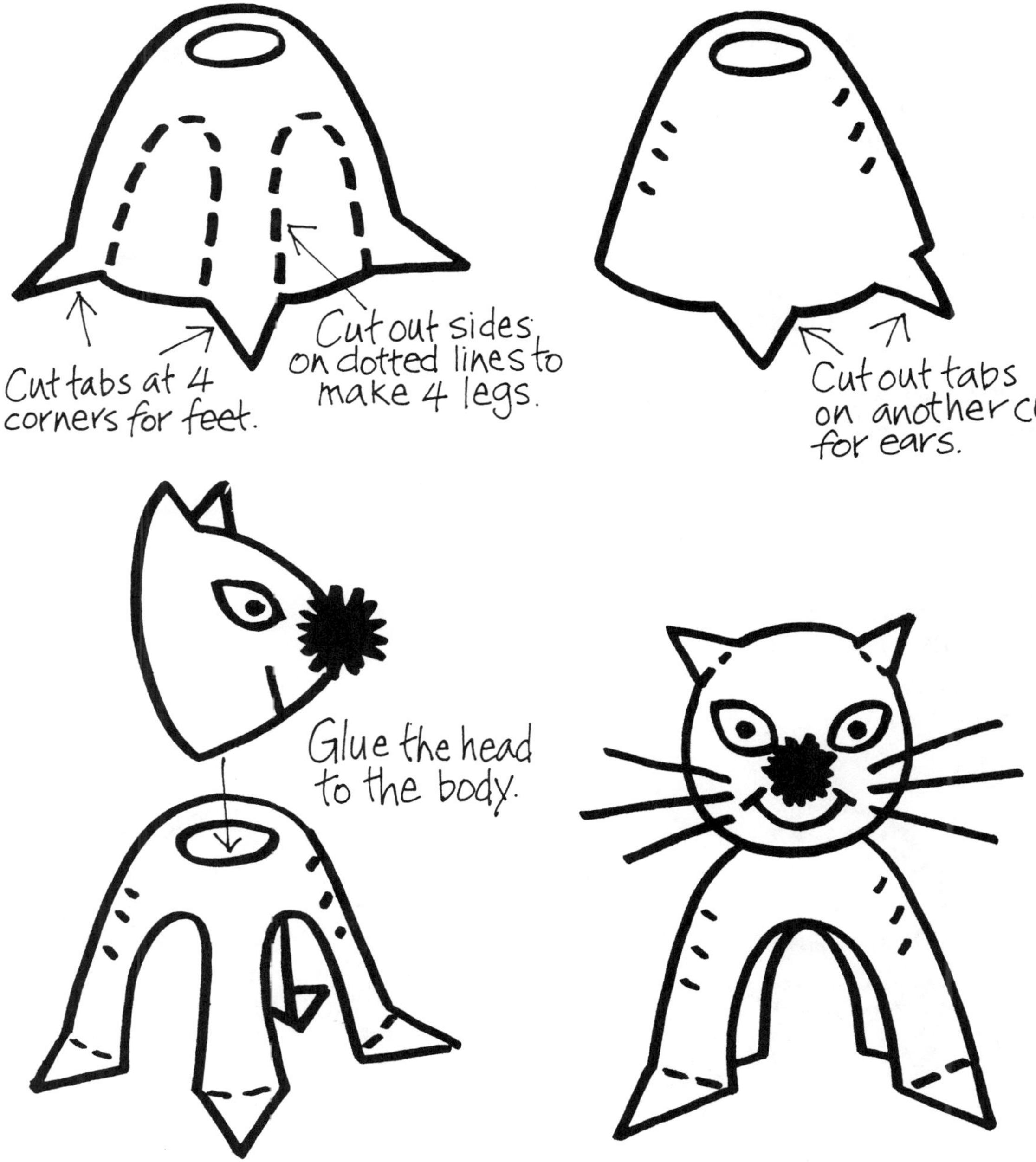

AIRPLANE

Cut 2 individual egg cup sections apart, and trim the rough edges away. Punch 2 holes in the top of one with a nail or sharp pencil. Thread a string through them for suspending the finished plane.

Cut wing and tail sections, and a propeller from the flat carton lid, as shown. Slide the 2 tail sections together at the slit. Now, cut a slit down the side of 1 egg cup section and insert the tail into the slit in the egg cup. Glue the wing section between the 2 cups.

Push a straight pin through the propeller and stick it onto the airplane. Paint as desired with tempera or poster paints. Hang several airplanes from different lengths of string to make a mobile.

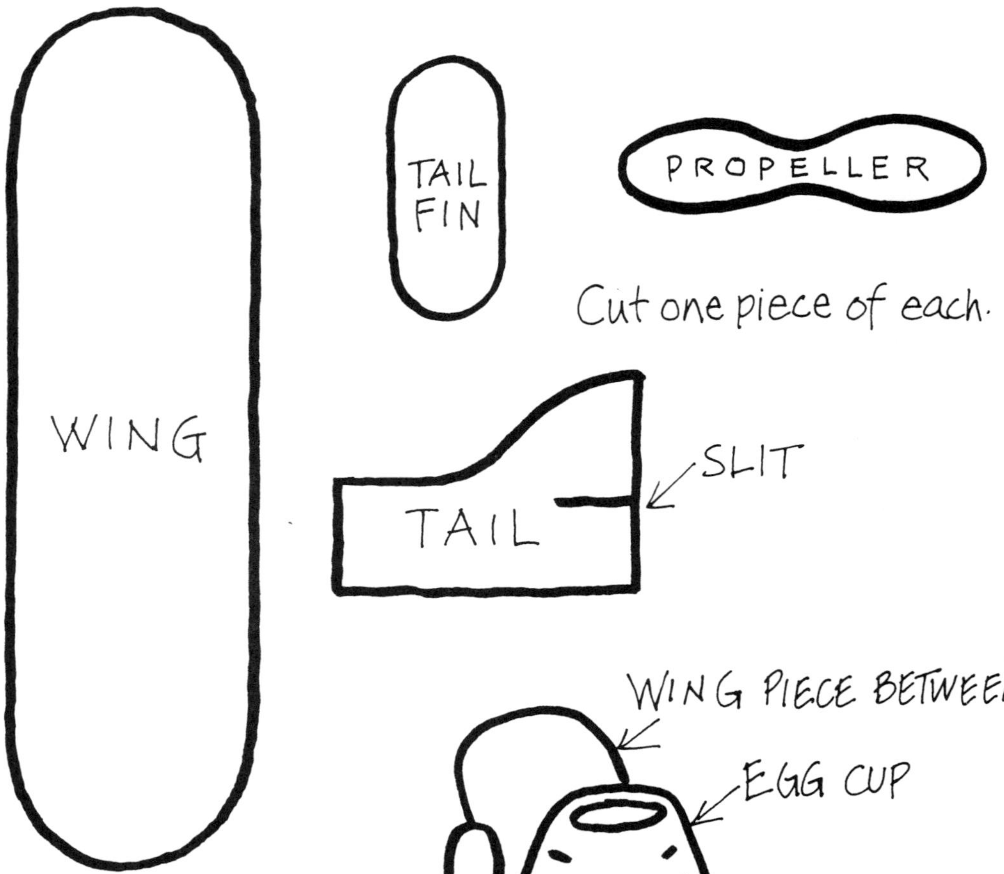

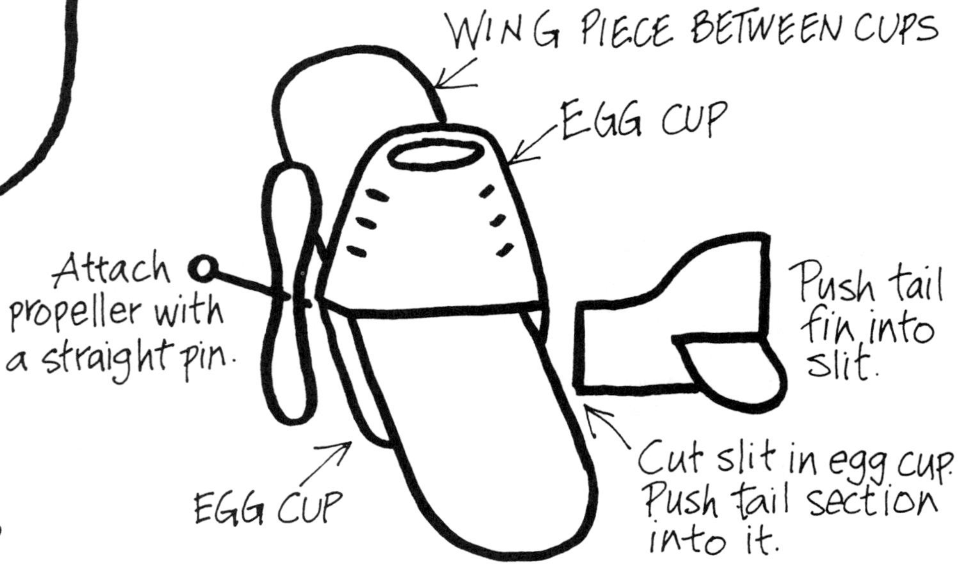

SANTA AND SLEIGH

Cut 4 individual egg cups; paint 3 red. Stack and glue them together to create a Santa as shown. Glue on bits of cotton to make the cap, beard, and jacket trim. Paint eyes and buttons, or glue paper cutouts in place.

To make a tiny sleigh, trim another egg cup into a sleigh shape. Paint it red, adding a bit of glitter along the edges for trim. Cut and shape 2 pipe cleaners (or cut out from lid) to make the runners. Glue them in place. Place tiny pine cones or special treats inside the sleigh, and use as a party favor or decoration.

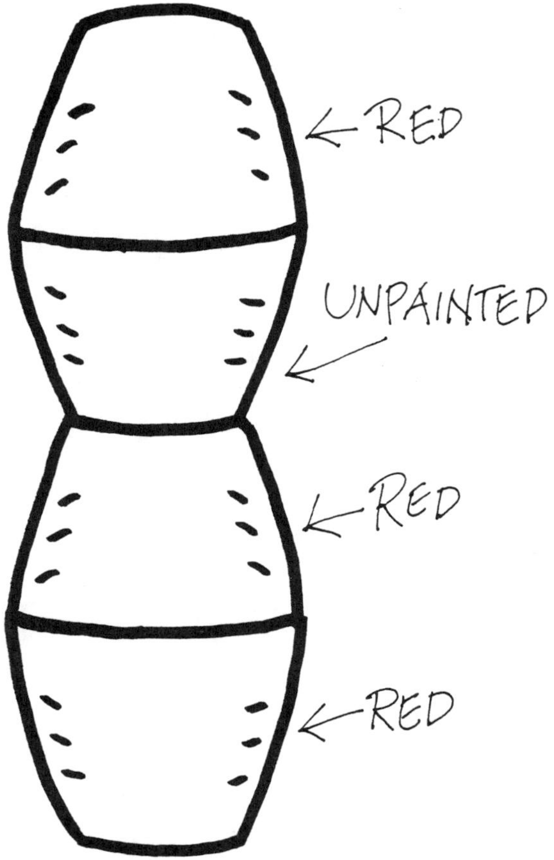

Glue cotton balls or stuffing as shown. Decorate with paint or cutouts.

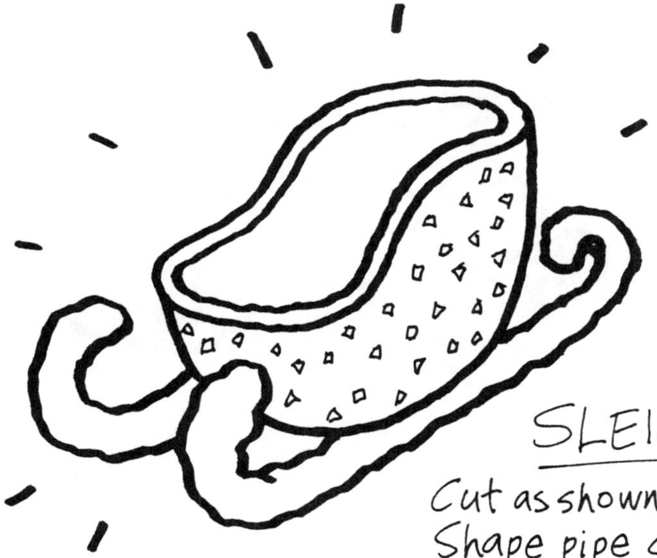

SLEIGH

Cut as shown. Paint and glue on glitter. Shape pipe cleaner runners and glue in place.

Use the egg cartons with high dividers between cups (rather than rounded ones). Cut a divider section away for the body, leaving turned-up edges for feet.

Cut 2 egg sections and trim away the uneven edges. Glue a cut-out beak between the two head sections. Glue head together, and then the head to the neck of the body. Paint or color with markers, if you wish; then glue on feathers. If you don't have real feathers, make some from cut tissue paper or curl lengths of paper around a pencil and glue in place.

You can make all sorts of egg carton creatures by "building" the basic shape and then adding the trims and details. Try a turtle, or dinosaur, or puppy. Use bits of paper, felt, yarn, and pipe cleaners to give each creative individual details. For eyes, use tiny buttons, beads, seeds, straight pins with black heads, or draw them on with a black pen. Use bits of shag carpet, stuffing, grass, yarn, or string for fur.

Glue together. Paint and glue on paper bag "feathers."

GENEROUS GIFTS & CLEVER CRAFTS

When you reuse discards to make something for someone else, you give two gifts. One is the item you give to the special person, the other gift is to the Earth and all its peoples, by reusing and recycling something that would have become trash.

Not only can you save money by making gifts, you save raw materials that would have gone into making, shipping, and packaging the purchased item. Besides, you get the fun of using your imagination and creativity, while making something you can be proud of. And there is no gift more special to receive than the one made especially by you!

COASTERS

Materials *

Yarn

Plastic snap-on lids saved from cans (like coffee and shortening)

Glue

Scissors

Spread glue generously over the inside of the lid. Lay yarn in the glue, working around and around from the outside to the middle. Change colors of yarn, if desired. When the entire lid is yarn-filled, and you are at the center, trim the yarn and tuck the end under to hide it. Let dry.

Great gift for Mom's desk!

DESK ORGANIZER

Materials **

Soup or juice cans, both ends cut out

Glue: latex epoxy

Spray paint, if desired

Clothespins

Paint the cans in a decorative pattern or solid color, or wrap old gift wrap around each can and glue. When dry, glue the cans together to create a pyramid. Use the clothespins to hold the cans securely in place while the glue dries.

Decorate another can to use as a matching pencil holder.

SPECTACULAR FLOWER VASES

Materials ✱✱

Glass bottles or jars with an interesting vase shape

Other materials by choice

Wash out the bottles and let dry. You can then decorate in several ways.

Decoupage: Colorful pictures cut from magazines, scraps from wallpaper, gift wrap, or fabric scraps can be decoupaged by gluing the pictures to the bottle and brushing several coats of white glue over it. Choose a white glue that dries clear and is waterproof. If your glue is too thick to brush on, dilute it with a bit of water.

Waxed: With grown-up help, a lighted candle can be held at an angle, and dripped down the sides of the bottle to make a stunning vase. Try using a variety of colors.

Yarn and grasses: Dip yarn in glue and wrap around the bottle, continuing from the base to the top until the whole bottle is covered. You'll love the results! Grasses can also be dipped in glue and wrapped around the vase, or around a can, for a wonderfully natural look. Dry grass is difficult to use, so gather tall fresh grass. It will shrink tightly around the vase after drying.

EGG CARTON FLOWERS

Materials

Pulp egg carton
Wire, 6" to 8" long, and button for each flower
Small can or plastic bottle cap (from laundry detergent bottle)
Clay, soil, or plaster of Paris
Gravel, small pebbles, or fluffy moss
Green tissue paper, floral tape, or green construction paper
Scrap of green paper or fabric
Glue and scissors

Cut apart the egg carton, trimming one egg cup into a flower shape. Cut the petals rounded or pointed, depending upon the type of flower you want. Poke 2 small holes in the flower base.

Push the wire up through one hole, through the button, and down through the second hole, threading the button to become the flower's center. Carefully twist the wire ends together, straightening them to make a nice sturdy stem. Cut out paper or fabric leaves, and tape to the wire. Wrap a strip of green tissue paper or floral tape around the wire, gluing the ends in place.

Set some clay or soil in the can or lid to anchor the stem, or mix a small amount of plaster of Paris and pour into the can or plastic lid. Position the flower stem as the plaster sets up. Sprinkle gravel or press moss into the surface of the clay or plaster before it hardens, to make it look more decorative. You can also make a bunch of these flowers to put in one of the vases you've made (see page 115) or to "plant" in the patchwork flower pot on the next page.

Cut one egg cup into a flower shape.

Thread a button to the center on a wire.

Cut a leaf from green paper. Glue to stem.

Wrap the wire with green paper. Position in a can or plastic cup with clay, soil, or plaster.

PATCH FLOWER POT

Materials

- Flower pot: terracotta or reuse a plastic one
- White glue and bowl
- Fabric scraps: cotton prints with pretty colors and designs
- Scissors
- Paint brush

Using fabric, you can decoupage an old pot and turn it into something very special with just old fabric scraps and glue.

Cut the fabric into 2" squares. Pour some glue into the bowl and then brush glue on an area of the pot. (If the glue is too thick, add a bit of water to thin it.) Press a fabric piece into the glue. Continue covering the pot with fabric patches, overlapping them so the entire surface of the pot is covered. Now, brush the entire surface with another coat of glue. Let dry. Give the entire pot one more coat of glue to make it nice and shiny.

Now it's ready to fill with rich soil and cuttings or seeds, or some of your egg carton flowers (see page 116)!

NAPKIN RINGS

Materials

- Paper tubes
- Cloth or gift wrap scraps
- Glue
- Scissors or pinking shears, if desired

Ask a grown-up to help cut the paper tubes into sections about an inch wide.

If you are using pinking shears, cut the fabric and paper into small pieces, about 1" x 1". Glue on the pieces and press them in place to cover the tubes, inside and out. Glue on bits of yarn, lace, braid, or feathers for decoration. Nuts and evergreen sprigs make nice autumn touches.

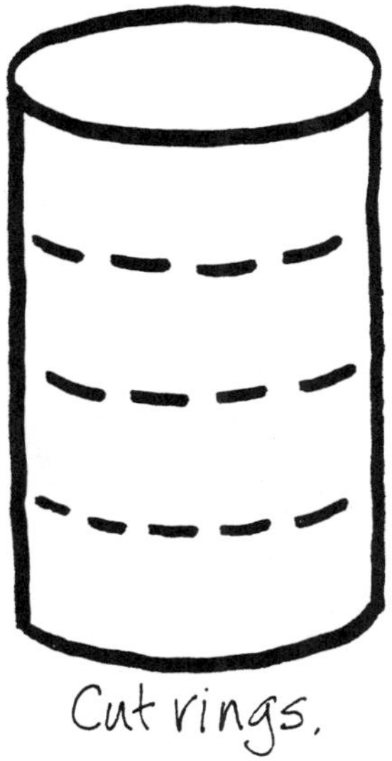

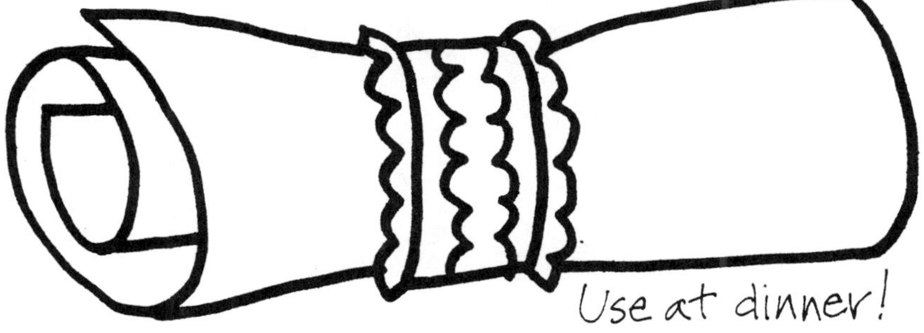

MAGAZINE HOLDER

Materials

- Large cereal box or detergent box
- Something to cover the box with: gift wrap, adhesive paper, leftover latex paint, or fabric
- Glue, if needed
- Ruler

Cut the box at an angle, as shown in the illustration, leaving about 4" at the shorter side. Use the ruler to be sure both sides are even. Paint, or cut fabric or paper and glue on to cover.

NIFTY NOTE PAD

Materials

- Papers
- Yarn or ribbon
- Hole punch or stapler

This is an easy way to use up small-size papers. Fold a larger piece of colored paper (wallpaper, gift wrap, or colored construction paper) over a stack of smaller papers to form a header.

Punch holes and tie with yarn or ribbon. Or, staple it and glue on a ribbon to cover the staples.

Decorate the top sheet with crayon designs, prints (see page 85), or rubber stamps. Use as an assignment pad, address book, or for telephone messages.

LITTLE WORLDS

Our planet Earth is really very small when compared to the rest of the universe. It's our home, and we need to be as careful with it as we can. We're all living in one community, and how each one of us lives affects all of the other living things. The amount of fresh water and the number of growing trees are really very small when compared to living things depending on these resources. We need to use what we have left wisely.

One way to do this is to look at objects around your house with imagination and a creative eye. Boxes, tubes, cans, containers can all be used to make something out of nothing. All it takes is the simple step of looking at a common object and asking yourself, "How many different ways can I use this?"

CASTLES

Materials

- Reused cardboard boxes
- Tissue tubes in assorted sizes
- Tempera paint, or leftover latex house paint
- Scissors
- White glue

Cut a large cardboard base to glue your castle to from a large carton. You may want to look in a few books for some details from real castles, or simply use your imagination.

Assemble the boxes and cans, arranging and re-arranging, until you have an idea of how your castle might look. Once everything is arranged to your liking, begin the construction by gluing the bottom boxes to the base. Use white glue, or, with a grown-up's help, use a hot glue gun.

SHOE BOX CASTLE

You can make towers by using scissors to cut paper tubes, or use frozen juice cans. A paper half-circle can be taped into a cone to roof the towers. Cardboard can be cut for a drawbridge that pulls up and down on lengths of yarn. You can create colorful flags from fabric scraps glued to twigs and stuck in the roof. And this is just the beginning . . . the possibilities are endless.

Once all the glue is dry, paint the finished castle with leftover latex paint or tempera.

To make a shoe box castle, use shoe boxes and tissue tubes. Cover the outside of the box and the tissue tubes with paint or colored paper. Glue a tube in each corner of the box. Cut colored paper in half circles and glue on top of the tubes for tower roofs. Cut paper triangles and tape to twigs for flags.

DOLL HOUSE

Materials

Boxes, large ones for the house, small for furniture
Glue
Fabric and wallpaper scraps, used gift-wrap
Small caps, spools, lids
Leftover latex paint, brush
Hot glue gun (for grown-up use) or heavy adhesive

Dolls of any size can be comfortable in houses created from cardboard cartons. Create a house with different floor levels to suit your needs, by gluing two or three boxes together. A hot glue gun used by a grown-up works best, but heavy-duty adhesive will work, too.

Give the cartons a coat or two of leftover latex paint. It helps make the house look great and strengthens the cardboard. A roof can

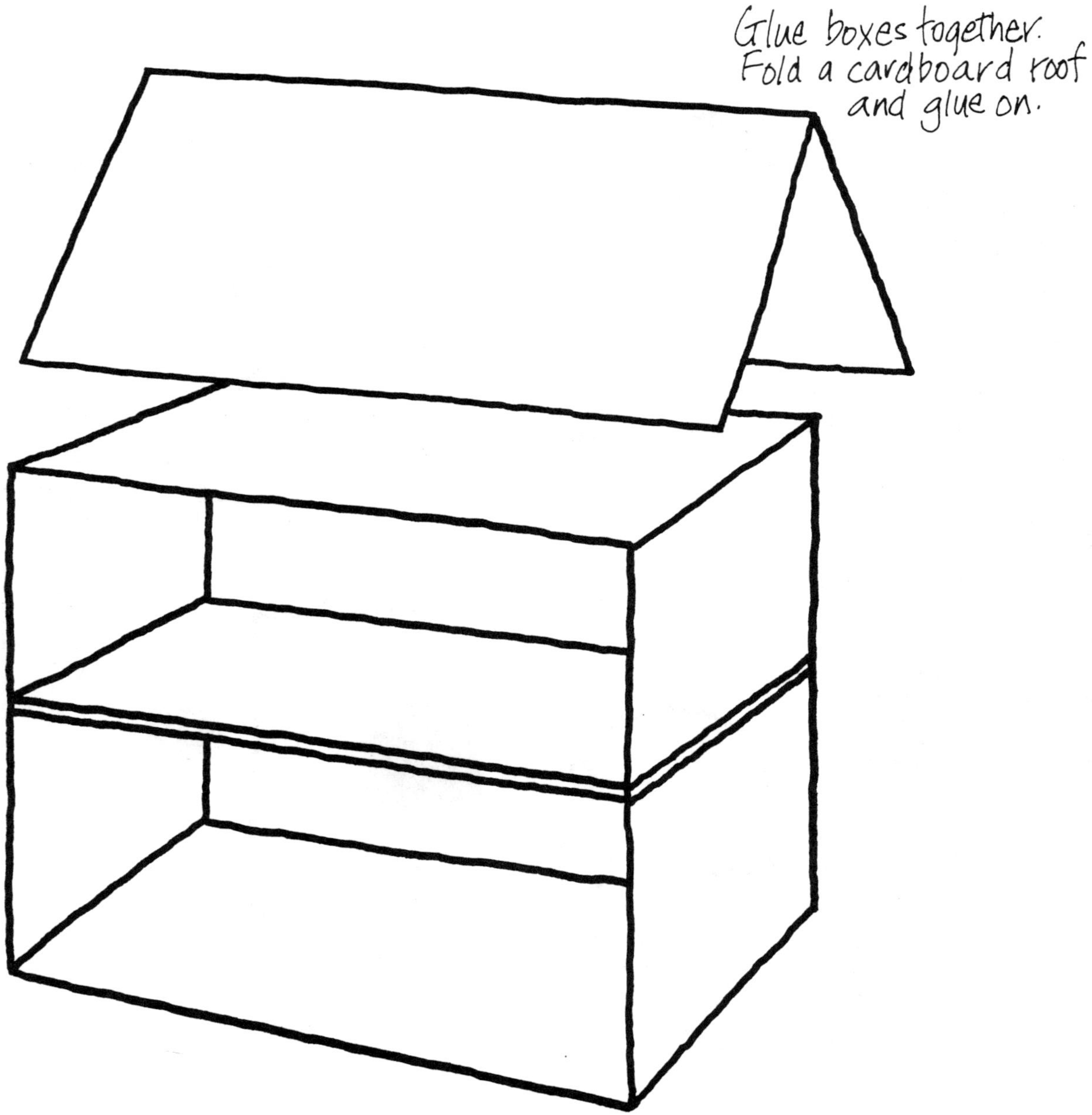

be made by scoring a large flat piece of cardboard down the center, and then folding to create a roof. Ask a grown-up to glue the top onto the house with a hot glue gun.

Begin searching and scrounging for decorating materials to give the house its personality. Select heavy fabric scraps like felt and toweling for carpeting. Used gift wrap or pieces of extra wall paper (sometimes you can get an old sample book from a store) can be glued in place to cover the walls.

You can cut out rectangles and glue on windows made from pieces of clear acetate saved from packaging materials. Cut out tiny pictures from magazines to hang as paintings on the walls. Make mirrors by gluing pieces of old aluminum foil to cardboard.

Make the furniture from small boxes and spools. Glue them together to create dressers, tables, chairs, and sofas. Use lids from jars, plastic tubs, and screw-on caps as platters, bowls, lamps, basins, or flower pots.

Fabric scraps become tablecloths, bedding, and curtains. A twig stuck in a bottle cap filled with modeling clay becomes a houseplant. Food can be shaped from homemade play dough.

The more materials you gather, the more ideas you will generate for additional furniture and decorations. The secret is to build and furnish your house with materials that would end up in the trash.

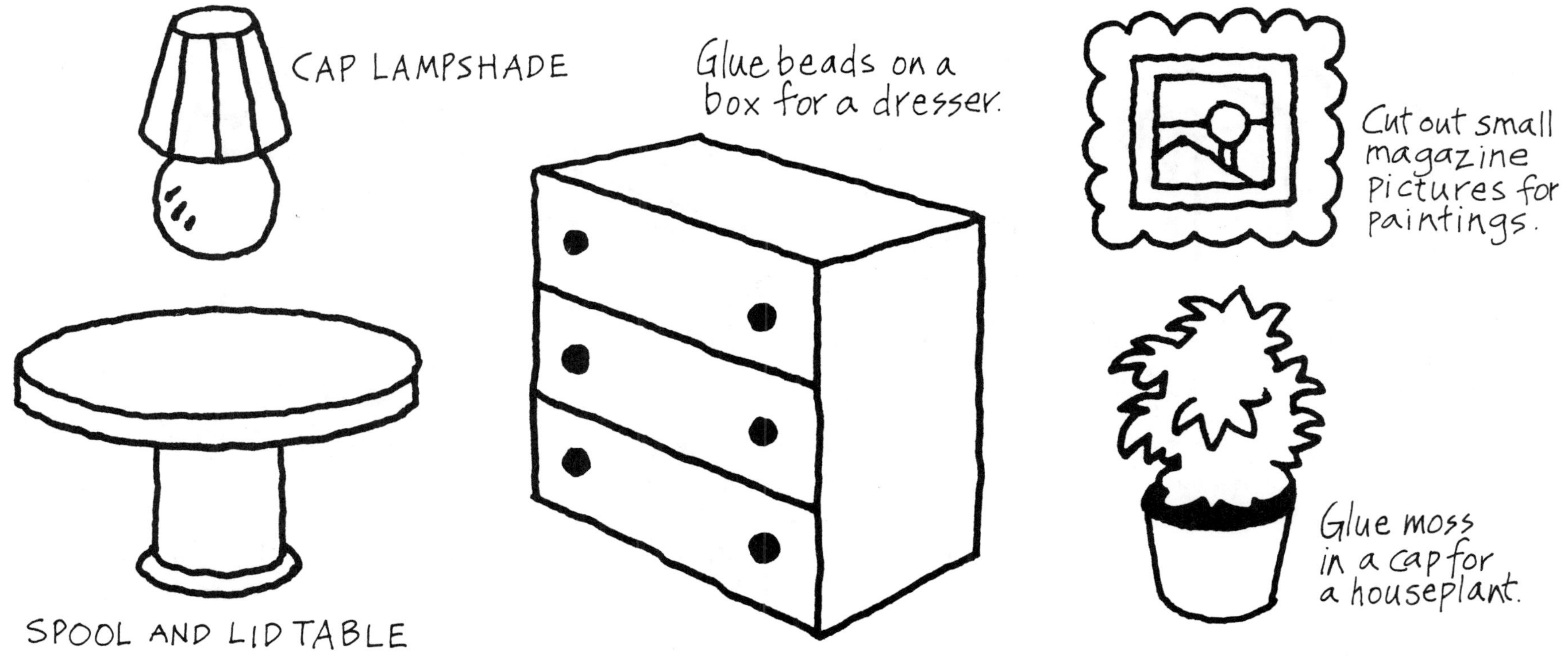

TERRIFIC LITTLE TOWN

Materials

Several small boxes, different sizes and shapes
Colored paper
Paint and brushes; marking pens
Assorted items you have saved to reuse
Tape, glue, and scissors

Save small boxes, such as different-sized milk cartons, until you have enough to create several buildings. Think about shapes for houses, stores, post office, a school, fire station, church, synagogue, or whatever else you would like in your town. Your town can look like a typical town, or you may want to develop a town from the Wild West, or imagine a town on Mars!

You may want some construction paper, paints, marking pens, straws, tissue tubes, buttons, twigs, clay, and assorted reusable odds and ends for the details.

The boxes can be painted with tempera or leftover latex paint. Add

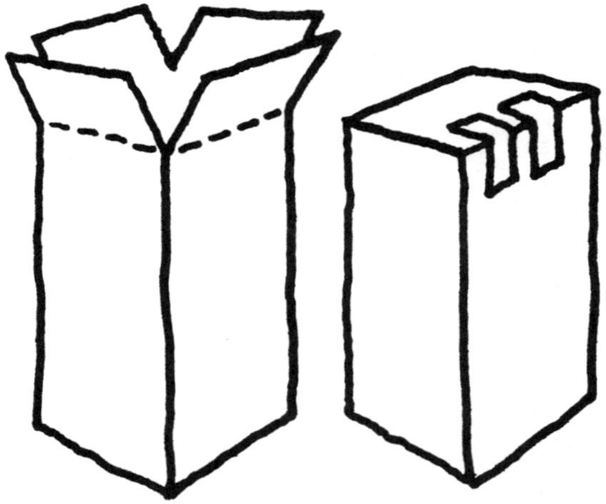

Cut slits in carton top. Fold down and tape.

Cut 1 milk carton to make the roof. Cut out the side of another milk carton for the base. Tape. Cut and fold doors and windows.

CARTON COTTAGE

Tape top closed. Glue on a folded rectangle of colored paper for a roof. Glue on colored paper siding, windows, and doors.

a little liquid detergent to help the paint adhere to the boxes better. Or, you can tape or glue paper to cover the boxes, or just leave the boxes as they are.

It's fun to arrange the houses on a table top or floor, or outdoors in a sandpile. If you want to create a mat to set your town on, use an old plastic shower curtain or a sheet. Draw the streets and parks with a permanent marking pen. The mat can be rolled up when you are not playing with it.

To create a simple house from a milk carton, tape it at the top. Glue on a folded rectangle of construction paper for the roof. Cut a door and windows, or just paint them on.

A larger house can be made from two milk cartons. Cut one to make the roof, and the side of another for the base. Tape them together. Cut and fold doors and windows.

Larger boxes can become apartment buildings. Draw many windows with a heavy marking pen, or paste on several small paper rectangles.

Use short pieces of shrubbery for trees. Stick the ends in balls of modeling clay. Street lights can be made by squeezing used scraps of aluminum foil to one end of a drinking straw and pressing the other end into modeling clay. You can even make a cobblestone sidewalk by gluing pebbles or shells to cardboard.

Make people by drawing faces on Popsicle sticks, gluing on clothing cut from fabric scraps or paper, and pushing the sticks into balls of modeling clay for support.

Make tall buildings by gluing on lots of cut paper windows.

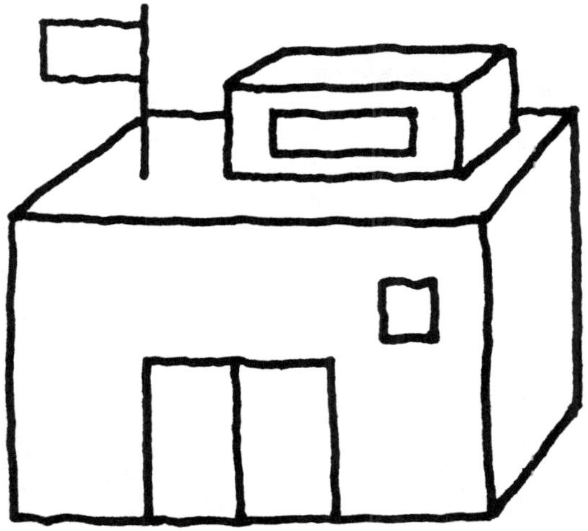

Use boxes to make a fire station.

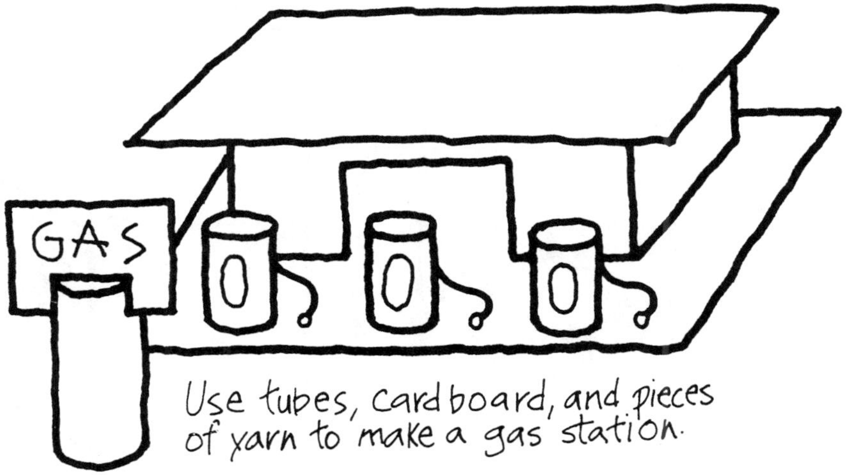

Use tubes, cardboard, and pieces of yarn to make a gas station.

PLAY HOUSE

Materials

Large cardboard carton, from furniture or appliances

Serrated knife, for grown-up use

Leftover latex paint, optional

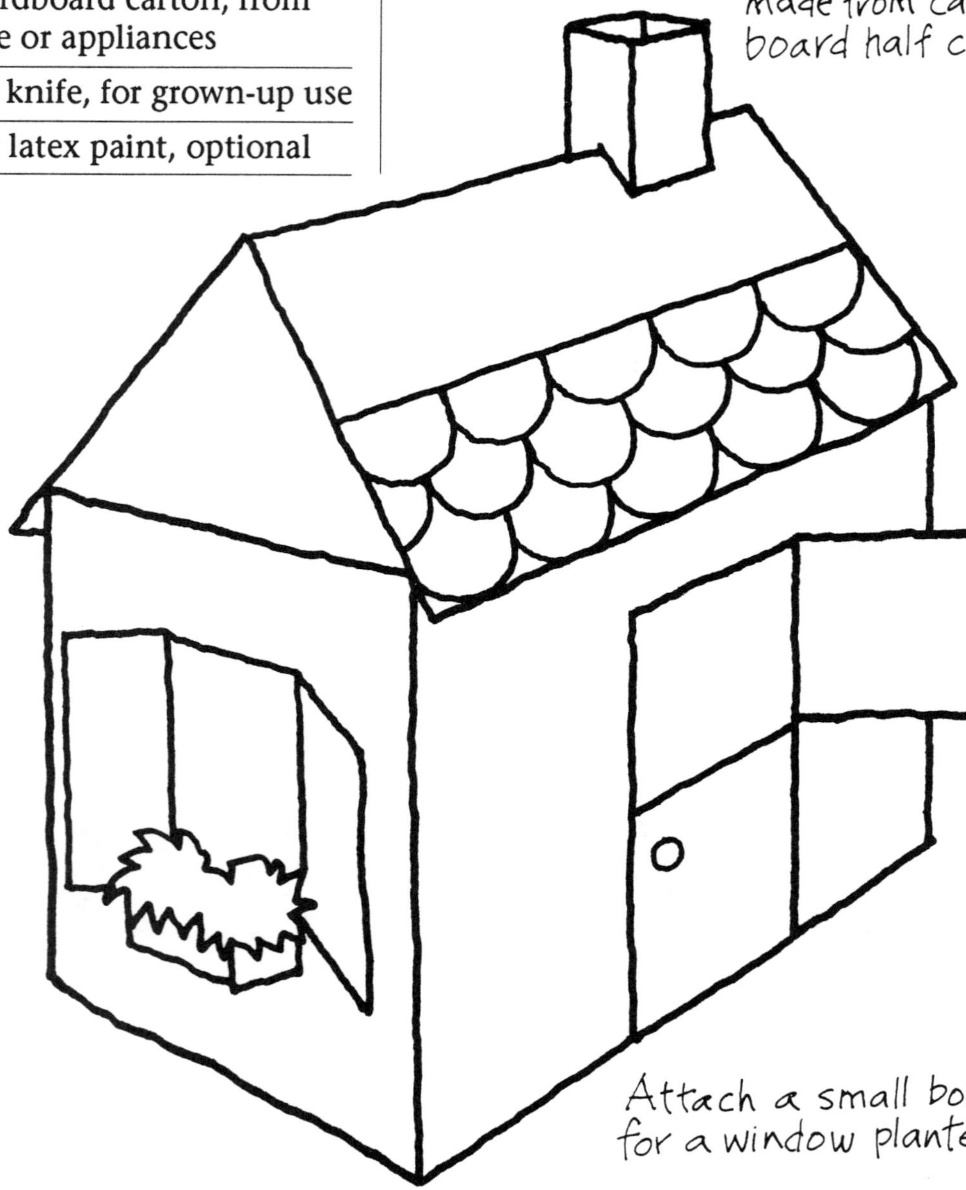

Large-sized play houses that you and your friends can play in can be made from large, corrugated cartons, obtained from appliance stores. Ask a grown-up to help you cut out any door or window areas you want with a serrated knife.

The house can be painted with leftover latex paint, or left as is. Cut a large piece of cardboard, fold in half, and attach for a roof. Trace large circles (about the size of a dinner plate) onto thin cardboard or copier paper you have saved. Cut out, cut them in half, and staple in overlapping rows to create roof shingles.

A window box can be attached beneath the window; just staple or glue a shoe box in place and fill it with greenery — real or your creation. Narrow boxes can be stacked on top of each other, end to end, and glued in place for a chimney.

Your play house can be anything you think of — a fort, cabin, castle, igloo, or space shuttle. Decorate with whatever you have on hand. When you are through with the house, take it to a cardboard bundler for recycling.

PLASTIC JUG CRAFTS

Plastic jugs are everywhere, it seems. Look around your home, and you will find them holding water, milk, soda pop, syrup, juice, and more. If you rinse them out and squash them flat (use your foot to stomp them), you can save them for the recycling center. Some plastics are now being recycled into heavier plastic items, such as fencing materials, park benches, even home insulation. If your recycling center doesn't take plastic, ask your parents to find one that does.

Before you send all the jugs to the recycling center, here are a few ways you can create (instead of buying) some fun and useful things — in the true spirit of environmental awareness.

Plastic bottles can be cut with scissors or a craft knife (you may want to ask for grown-up help). Sand the rough edges with sandpaper, if needed. Decorate with markers, glued on fabrics, or paints.

Note: Projects vary from one to three leaves in skill levels, once the jugs have been cut by a grown-up.

SCOOPS

Cut different-sized bottles to make useful scoops for the sandbox or beach.

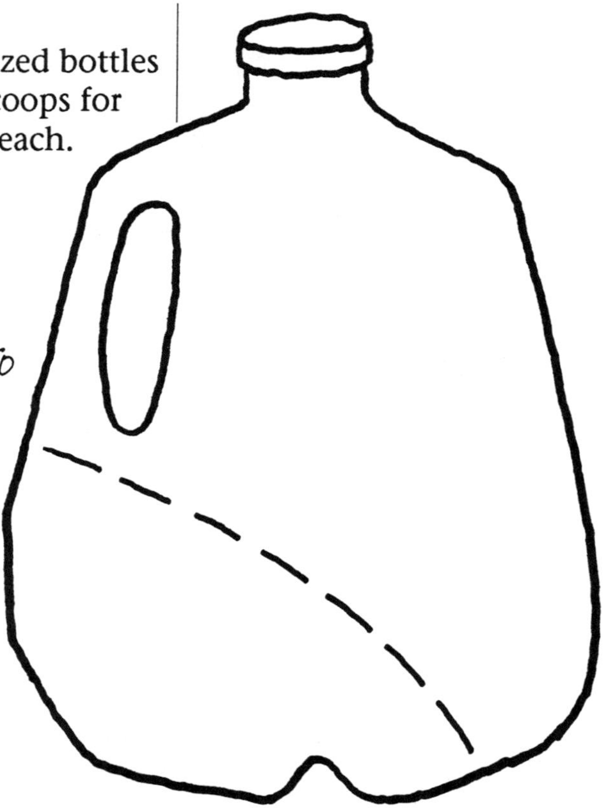

Cut a milk jug to make a scoop.

Tape a "ball" from old newspapers to make a toss and catch game.

FUNNEL

Cut a bottle in half, and use the top half for a funnel in the sand box, wading pool, or bathtub.

Cut from any size bottle.

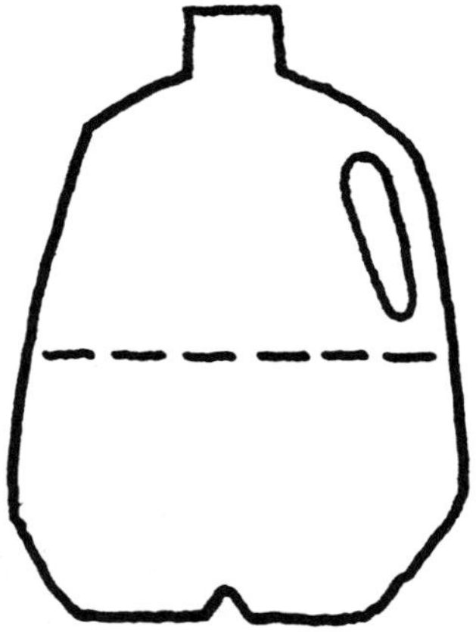

Use to fill containers.

FLOWER POT

The bottom half of a jug or large bottle makes a good flower pot. Decorate it with marking pens, stickers, or leftover paint. Cut a scallop edge along the top, and use a hole punch to create a decorative design. Use a hole punch to place four holes equal distances around the top edge. Tie on yarn or heavy cord to make a hanging planter.

Punch 2 holes; tie on a cord. Decorate and fill with hanging plants.

Cut the edge in scallops. Punch holes for decoration.

DOOR STOP

Fill a bottle with sand, fasten the lid on with strong glue, and color with markers to make a door stop.

DOLL HOUSE OR GAS STATION

Make a portable doll house or a gas station for small toy cars. Cut a large window in the side of the bottle, leaving about 1/2" along the top and bottom of the bottle and going about half-way across the bottle. Decorate the outside with permanent markers. Glue scraps of cloth or colored papers inside. For dolls, make furniture from small boxes and spools. Make a fuel pump for the cars by punching a hole with a nail and tying on a length of shoelace for a fuel hose.

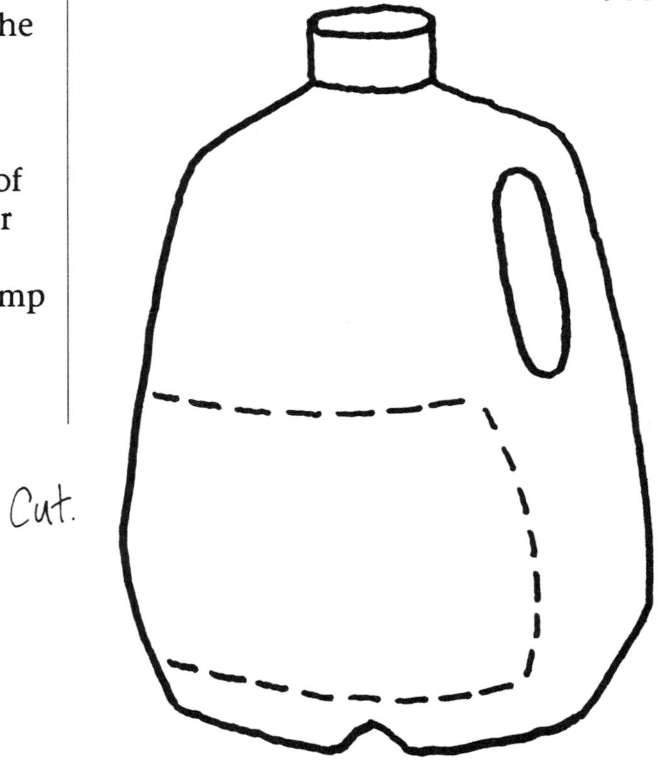

PIGGY BANK

Of course, the piggy bank is traditional. Collect four wine corks and a half-gallon bottle. You'll need fabric or leather scraps for ears, and a pipe cleaner or fabric scrap for the tail.

To make the legs, cut four circles the size of the wine corks in the side of the bottle. Push the corks in firmly, adding glue if necessary. Cut a slit in the top of the pig for the coins. Cut a slash for inserting the triangle-shaped ears into the pig; add glue if needed. Punch a hole in the rear with a nail and insert the tail. Give it a curl. Paint the entire pig pink or cover with papier-mache made from newspaper strips dipped in flour and water glue. Finish by gluing or painting on eyes.

What else could your bank become? How about an armadillo bank or a porcupine bank? Decorate with paint or pieces of colored papers.

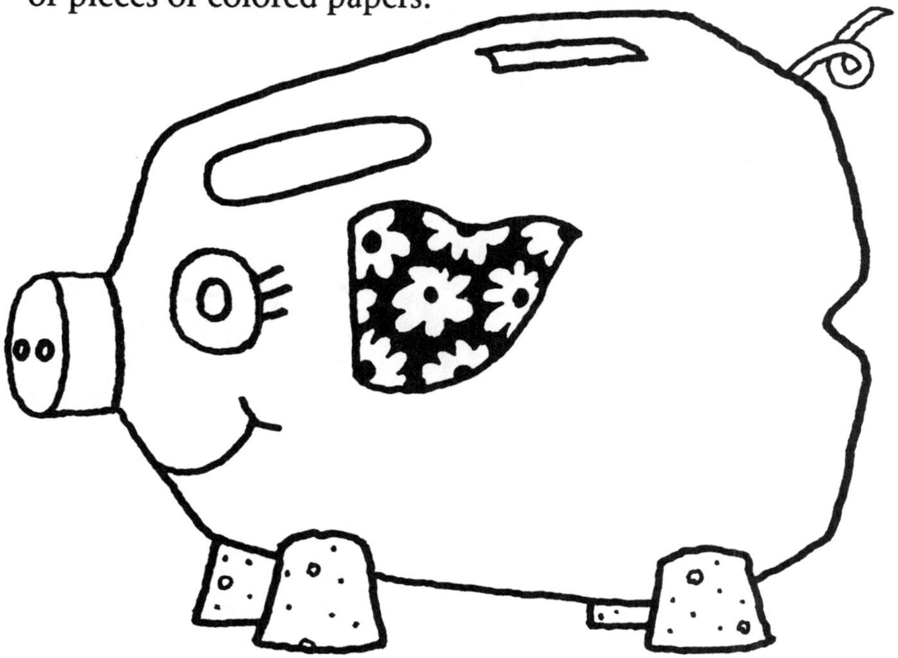

WATERING CAN

Make a watering can for the garden by punching holes near the top of the bottle with a sharp nail. Decorate with markers or stickers.

BASKET

You can make a lovely basket by cutting away the lower part of a jug, and then cutting vertical slits in the side. Make an even number of slits. Cut them about 3/4" apart. Use fabric strips to weave in and out between the slits, continuing around the bottle until the slits are filled in. Use the top of the bottle to cut a handle. Punch holes in the handle ends and the sides of the basket and use brass paper fasteners or pieces of yarn to tie the handle in place. Omit the slits and weaving, and you'll have a beach bucket.

MASKS

Large milk bottles are perfect masks. The handle can become a nose; cut out large circles for eyes (always make sure you can see in your mask). Decorate with leftover paints, dimensional fabric paints, or permanent marking pens. Glue on cut-out shapes from colored papers, gift wrap, or paper bags. To create hair around the edges of the mask, use a hole punch to punch holes about 3/8" apart along the top edge. Knot loops of yarn through the holes, pulling to secure (see Homemade Yarn, page 27). To keep the mask in place, punch two holes at the sides and tie a piece of elastic braid through the holes, or staple it in place at the sides.

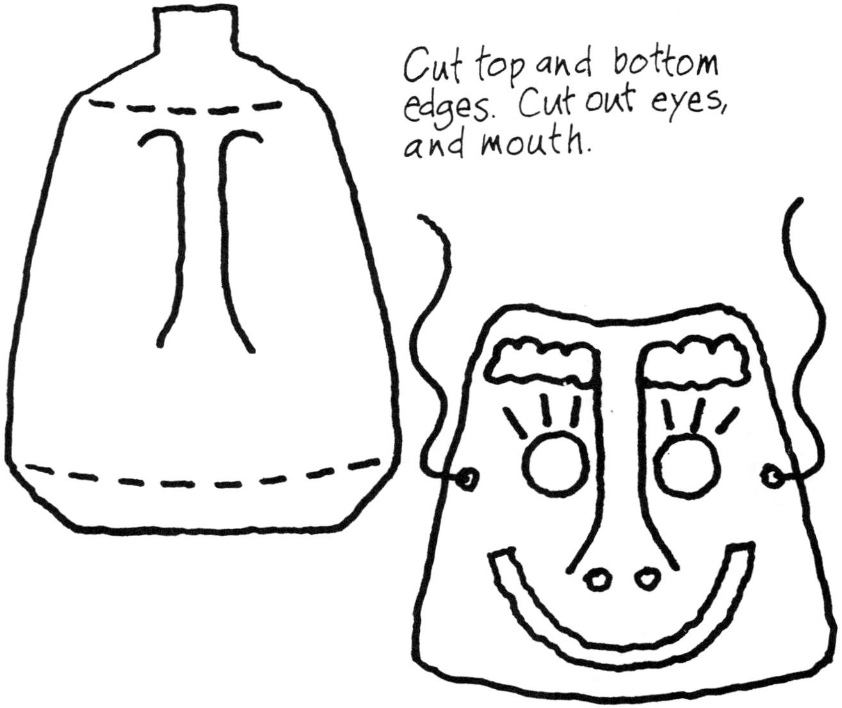

BOTTLE DOLL

Turn a bottle into a doll, ghost, or fairy tale character. Use a two-liter bottle for a slender figure, a gallon jug for a chubbier one.

Weight the bottle with some sand or gravel, and glue the lid on securely. Make the head by wadding stuffing in the end of a sock and tying securely. Slip this down over the neck of the bottle and tie in place with heavy string. Make the face with paint, embroidery, or by gluing on cut pieces of felt. Dust the cheeks with powder blusher. Hair can be made from wool, stuffing, yarn, or narrow strips of torn fabric. Sew or glue in place. Create clothing from scraps.

FUN & GAMES

There are lots of reasons why "new" toys aren't always best: their manufacture, packaging, and shipping place an additional burden on the earth; they cost money that we can use for other things; and they eventually break or bore us and find their way into the landfill.

Sometimes homemade toys — made out of reusable and recycled materials — have a special something that the shiniest new toy doesn't have. Making these toys is half of the fun, and playing with them is the other half! Giving them as gifts provides added satisfaction. As if that is not enough, you are doing something good for the earth.

BEAN BAG TOSS

Materials

- Strong cloth (a good way to use old denim jeans)
- Dry beans: soybeans, pinto, or navy beans
- Plastic soda bottles (various sizes)
- Cardboard box
- Sewing machine (optional)
- Needle, thread, and scissors

Here's a great game you can make yourself — all with recycled materials. To make each bean bag, cut 2 identical pieces of fabric, with the right sides facing each other. The easiest shape is a 5" square. An adult can sew the pieces together or show you how to do it. Leave a 2" opening for filling with the beans.

Trim the corners away, close to the stitching. Turn the bag right side out through the opening. Put about a cup of beans into each bag; it should be loosely filled and sort of limp. Turn the edges of the fabric in and handstitch the opening closed with small stitches.

Simple, sturdy bean bags are just plain fun to toss around. Create games of skill by cutting different-sized plastic jugs in half and tossing the bags into them. Cut holes in the side of a large cardboard box, and toss bean bags through the holes. Label the holes or jugs with numbers, and tally up everyone's scores.

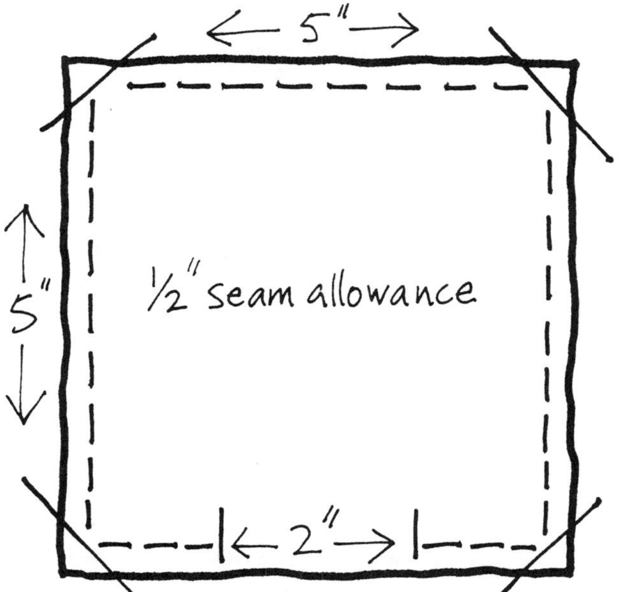

Trim away corners after stitching. Turn. Stitch opening closed.

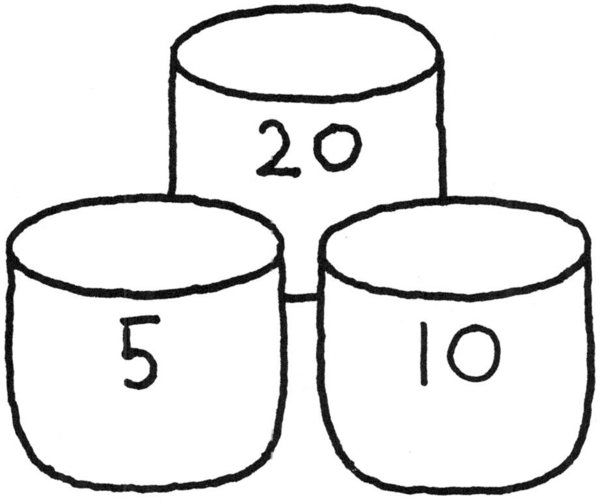

Cut plastic bottles and label for a toss game.

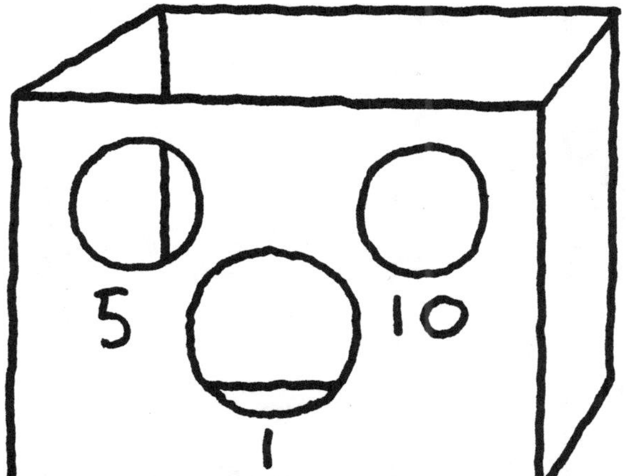

Cut holes in the sides of a box. Label with points.

PAPER BAG KITE

Materials ✱✱

Large, paper, grocery bag

Tape, string, scissors

Pencil

Hole punch (optional)

Cut away bottom of the bag.

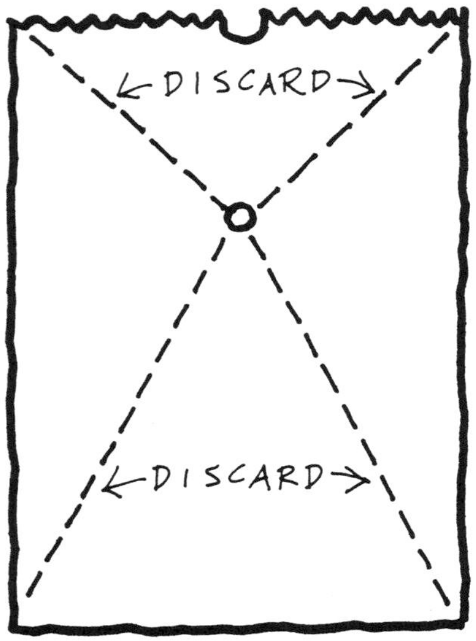

Cut one side of the bag on dotted lines to create 2 "wings." Cut through the dot to separate the sides.

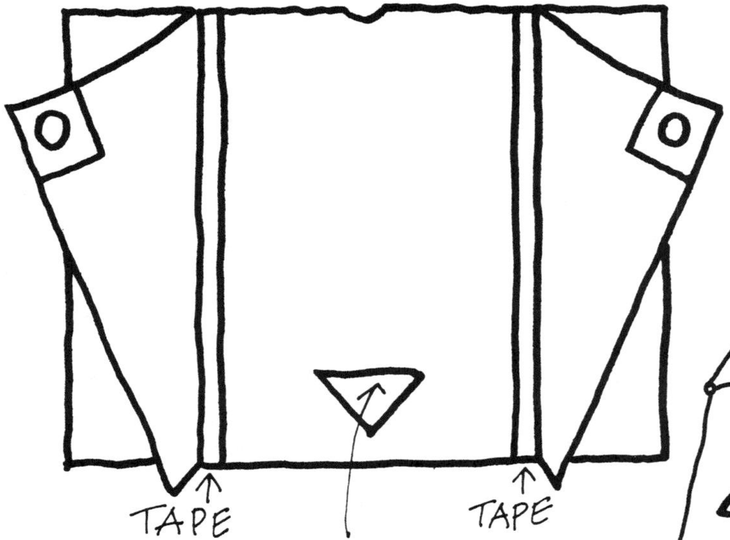

Cut out a vent.

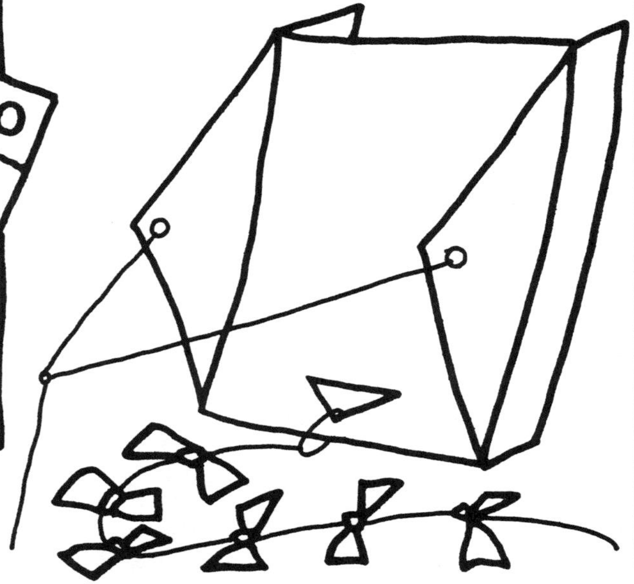

The best thing about this kite is that you probably have all of the materials you need in your house right now. You also don't need to obtain any sticks.

Cut the bottom out of the bag. Lay the bag flat on the table top. Pencil a dot about 1/3 down from the top center of the bag. Draw wings from the corners to that dot. Cut away the top and bottom triangle areas, cutting along the dotted lines, as shown.

Turn the bag over, and fold the wings to the front. Tape them to the bag. Put a piece of tape at the tip of each wing to strengthen it; then, punch a hole through it.

Cut out a triangle-shaped vent near the bottom of the bag. A tail made from pieces of tissue tied on a string can be tied below the vent.

Be sure to decorate your kite before flying. Short streamers can be cut from tissue paper and glued or stapled in place.

CAN WALKERS

Materials ✱✱

12 cans the same size: 48-ounce juice cans are good

6' – 8' of rope, cut in 2 equal lengths

Punch-type can opener

These are simple to make and great fun to use. They're not too difficult to walk on and are perfect for a backyard Olympics or circus.

Remove the tops of the cans. Punch 2 holes in the sides of each can, just below the rim, directly across from each other. Thread the rope through the holes and knot securely.

To use, stand on the end near the holes and hold the ropes in each hand. Try walking. Practice makes perfect!

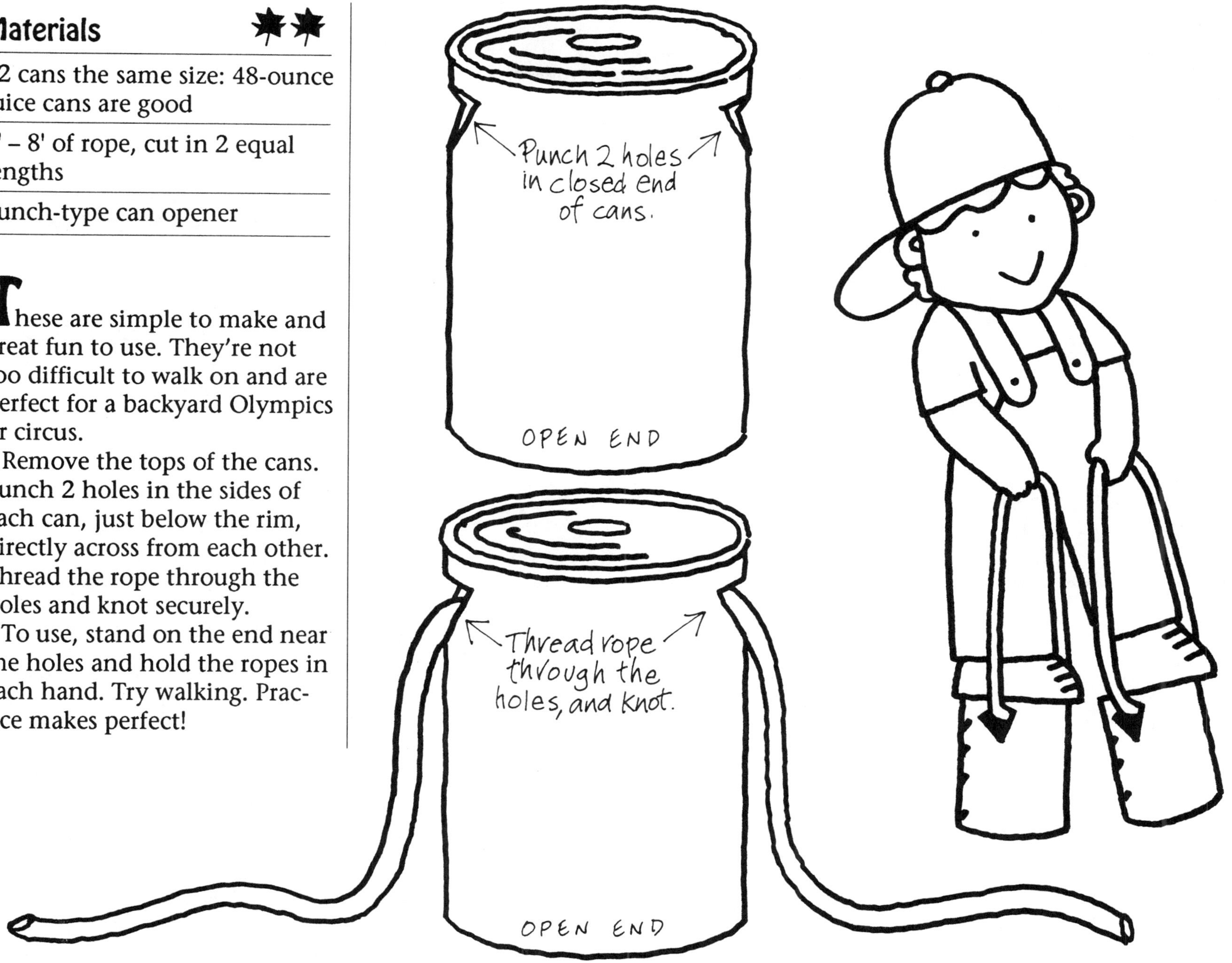

CHECKERS GAME

Materials

24 small, flat, plastic lids: 12 of each color (save the plastic lids from milk, water, and juice bottles)

Large cardboard pizza box, at least 16" x 16" inside

Paint or markers in two colors

Ruler and pencil

Rule the cardboard inside the box into 64 two-inch squares (see illustration). There should be 8 squares down each side. Color or paint alternating squares so you have a checkerboard pattern.

Line up the opposing game pieces on each side of the board (12 lids for each player) and let the game begin! When you are finished, store the game pieces inside the box.

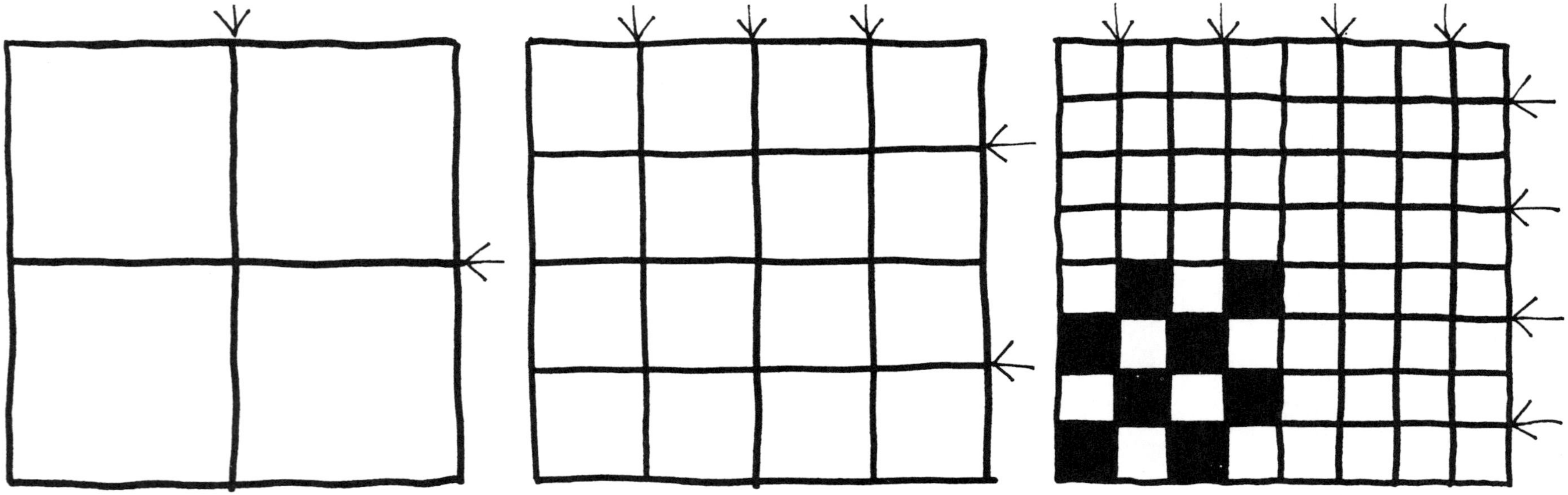

BOX PUZZLES

Materials

9 or more small, identical boxes: raisin, pudding, or gelatin boxes are ideal

Old magazine

Paste (see Pastes & Glues, page 24)

Tape

Pencil and ruler

Scissors

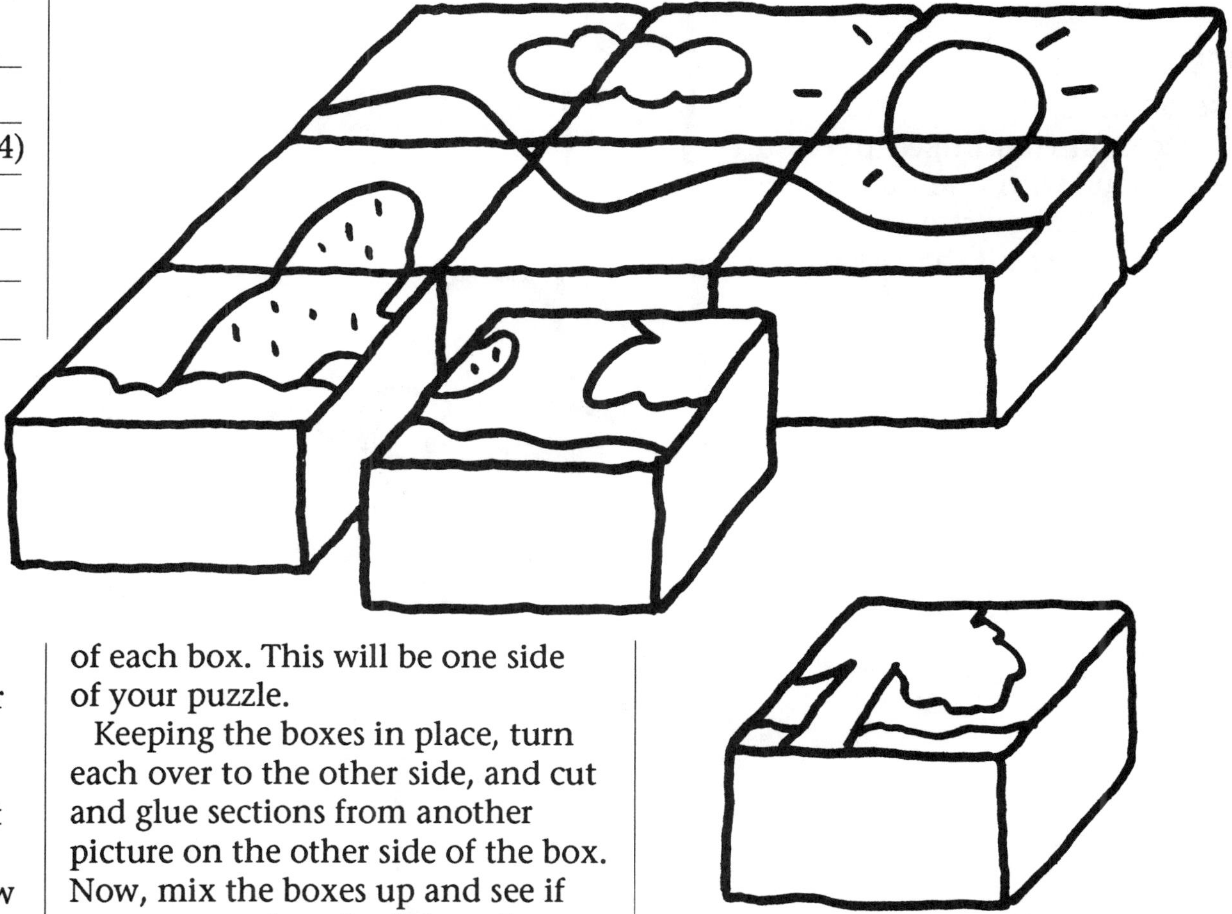

Tape the boxes closed. Lay the boxes out to create a rectangle or square.

Find a picture in a magazine that is colorful and fun, and that is the size of all of the boxes together. If you want, you can draw a picture yourself, using plenty of interesting design and color.

Use the ruler to measure and divide the picture into sections the size of each box. Cut the picture and glue each section to one side of each box. This will be one side of your puzzle.

Keeping the boxes in place, turn each over to the other side, and cut and glue sections from another picture on the other side of the box. Now, mix the boxes up and see if you can put them back in order to solve the puzzle.

To make the pieces last longer, you can cover the finished boxes with a coat of white glue diluted with water, or with clear adhesive paper.

PLENTY OF PUPPETS

Puppets are such a great, fun-filled way to enjoy art and drama. A puppet can be made from just about anything. Search through your box of odds and ends, your button box, and you're sure to find just what you need to make a one-of-a-kind puppet creation.

Finger puppets

These are the simplest to create. Draw faces on your fingertips or on your hand with fine-tip marking pens. You can also draw on peanut shells or paper strips that are taped and worn on your fingertips.

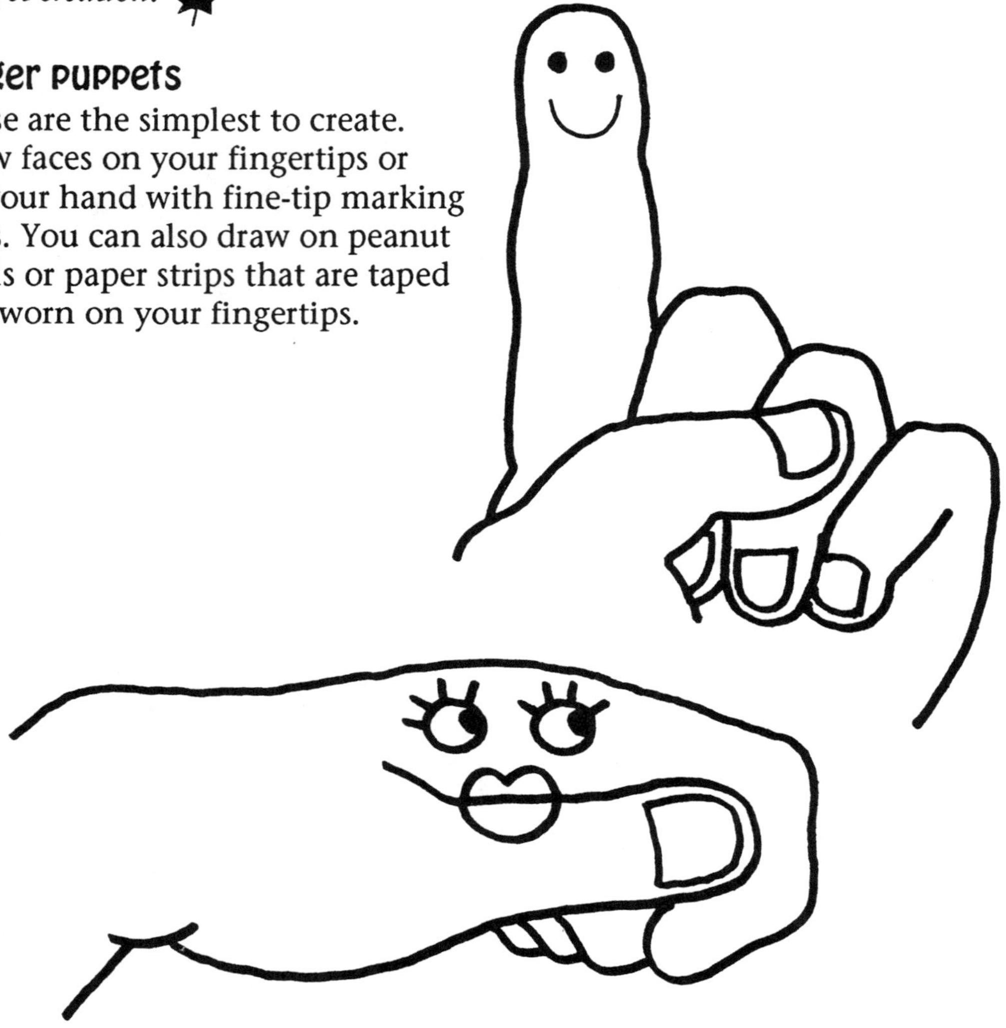

Decorate your hands for the easiest hand puppets.

Stick puppets

Sticks can be Popsicle sticks, paint stirring sticks, or long twigs. You can also roll a newspaper page tightly into a tube and tape. Draw your puppets on paper or cardboard; decorate with markers or paint. Hair can be cut from yarn, moss, fabric, or curled paper strips. Glue or staple in place. Tape or glue the puppet to the stick.

Glue drawings to sticks for puppets.

Box puppets

These puppets have mouths that move. Use a small box, like a gelatin box. Cut one side down the center and sides. Fold the ends of the boxes back, and you have a mouth. Cover with colored paper or paint. You can glue feathers, cut paper, yarn, or whatever you have for decoration.

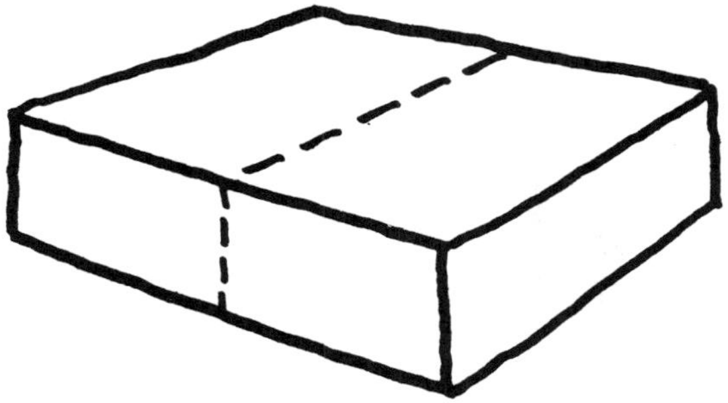

Cut a box in half on 3 sides. Decorate, fold, and put your fingers inside to make it move.

Cut and fold cardboard oval in half.

Glue inside sock. Decorate and slip over your hand.

Sock puppets

Here is a fun way to use old socks. They just naturally lend themselves to becoming arm puppets. To create a working mouth, cut an oval from cardboard, score it down the center, and fold. Insert the cardboard into the sock's toe, and glue it in place for a mouth. Sew on buttons for eyes, or cut shapes from felt and glue in place. Use your imagination and create all sorts of wild and crazy characters. Then put on a great puppet show.

Envelope puppets

Old envelopes make instant puppets, too. Tape an envelope closed. Fold it in half, and cut one side open along the fold. Insert your fingers in one section and your thumb in the other. Decorate with crayons, markers, or pieces of colored paper.

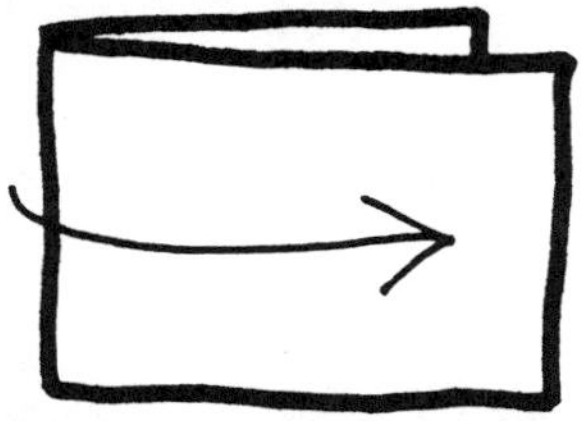

Fold to crease the middle.

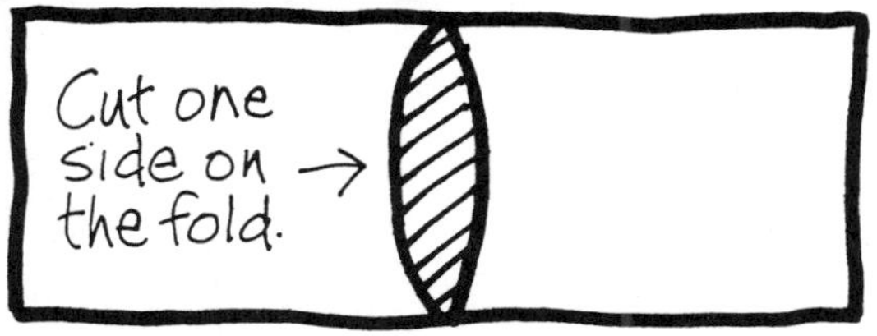

Decorate.

Slip fingers and thumb into the envelope to make the mouth open and close.

Puppet Stage

If you have a large cardboard carton, you can cut out a window, hang a cloth for a curtain, and give a real show. You can also stretch a sheet across a table or chair, or stretch a clothesline between trees and hang a tablecloth.

Cut a box for a stage.

BOOMERANG

Australians invented the boomerang, which is a flat, curved shape that can be thrown so that it returns to the thrower.

Materials ✱✱

- Cardboard
- Scissors
- Pencil

Draw and cut a boomerang shape from the cardboard. Decorate with markers or paint. You may want to change the design a bit, making several in different sizes and shapes. Toss and compare how they soar.

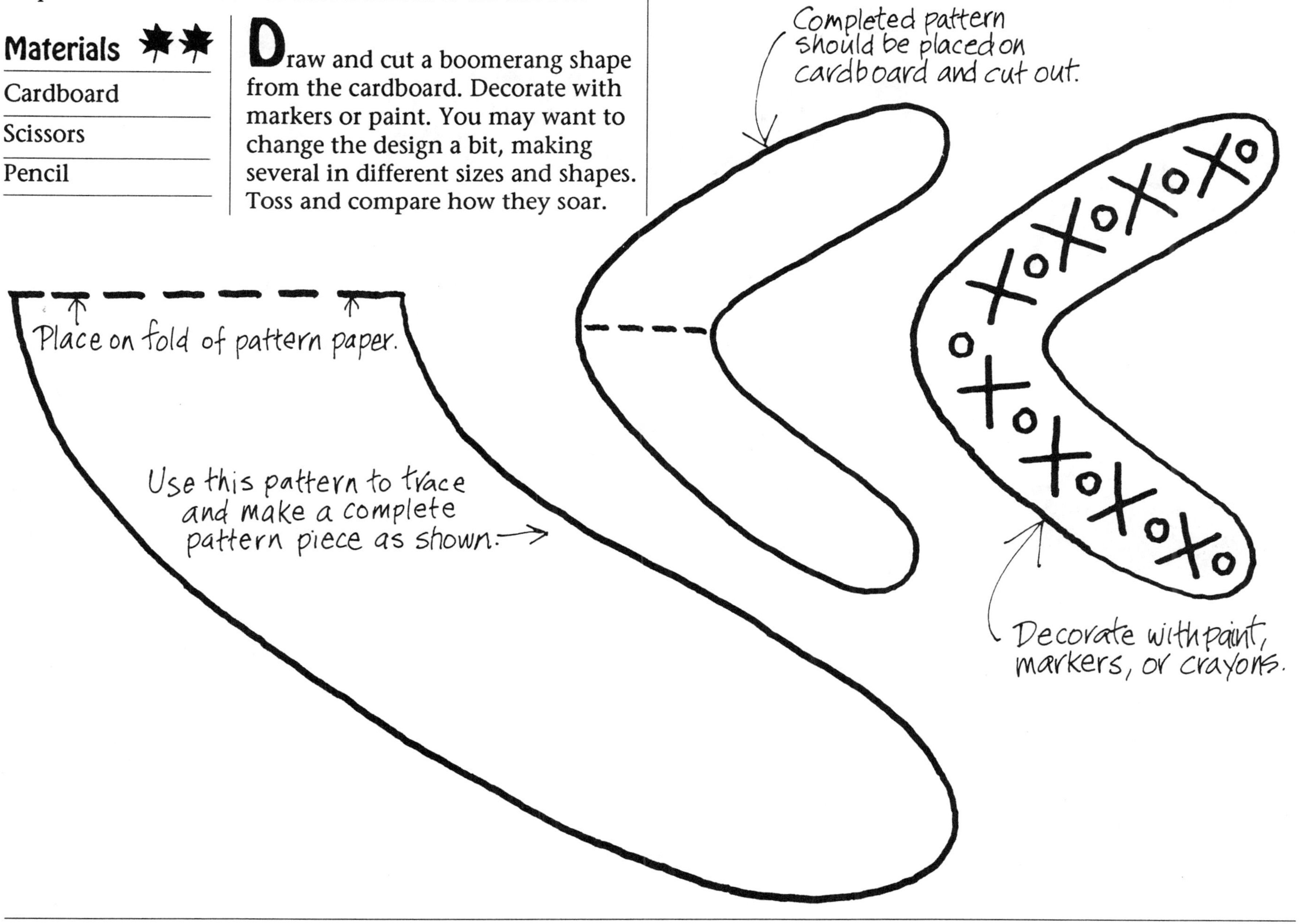

GIFTS FOR THE EARTH

Although every project in this book has helped the earth by reusing and recycling, here are some creations that are fun to make, but that also save our natural resources.

The following projects will begin to change your family's habits. Once you make your family a set of cloth napkins, you won't need to purchase disposable paper ones, made from our majestic forests. Saving recyclables in your own bin saves natural resources, prevents overfilling the landfills, and creates jobs in the recycling industry. By creating compost, you are recycling nutrients and developing good "earth" that will nourish plants and living things.

These projects are certainly fun to make with your family, but using them together is where the real satisfaction comes. By choosing these alternate lifestyle activities, you are doing something positive and lasting. It won't be the efforts of business or industry that change our quality of life. It will be our individual efforts, small but consistent, that change the tide. Little things do mean a lot.

INSPIRATION BOX

Materials

Assorted boxes including 2 large ones

Paints and permanent markers

Make a box just for those unusual things you find now and then that might be useful in art and craft projects. Find a sturdy carton and decorate it to suit your personality: perhaps graffiti with markers, or a collage cut from magazines. Add a few smaller boxes to keep tiny findings inside — like small shells you have gathered, unusual pebbles, or buttons you've collected. Ask your family to help you watch for useful items. A broken necklace, pretty stamps or stickers from the mail, corks, magnets, fake flowers, fabric remnants, yarn, gift wrap, and ribbons — whatever you come across that might be useful some day — can be saved until you are ready for it.

You'll also want to keep a separate, larger box to store clean jars, margarine tubs, and yogurt containers, tissue rolls, egg cartons, styrofoam meat trays (rinse in hot water first), and pieces of foil you have sponged off and folded flat. Paint or decorate it and write "Crafts" on it.

CLOTH NAPKINS

Materials

- Fabric: woven cotton is best
- Scissors
- Sewing machine, or needle and thread

What a great way to add sophistication to your meals, while saving trees that would be cut down for paper pulp! As a logger once said, "We are the only people that grind up our forests to wipe our mouths."

Years ago, everyone had cloth napkins. In the Pilgrim's time they used large napkins that were draped over their shoulders while eating.

You can make a whole set of cloth napkins for your family. Buy some woven cotton broadcloth fabric remnants at a fabric store (each napkin can be from different fabric), or better yet, recycle an old sheet, curtain, or dress.

To make napkins, cut the fabric into 17" x 17" squares, one for each napkin. If you have a sewing machine, ask a grown-up to help you turn the edges under and stitch

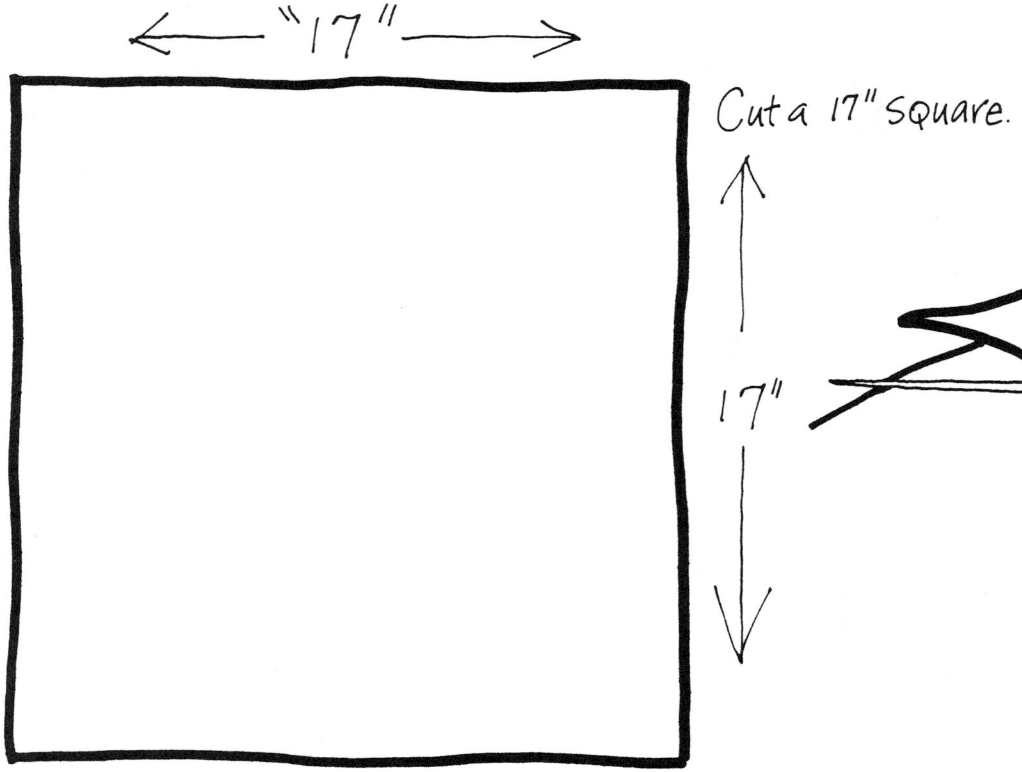

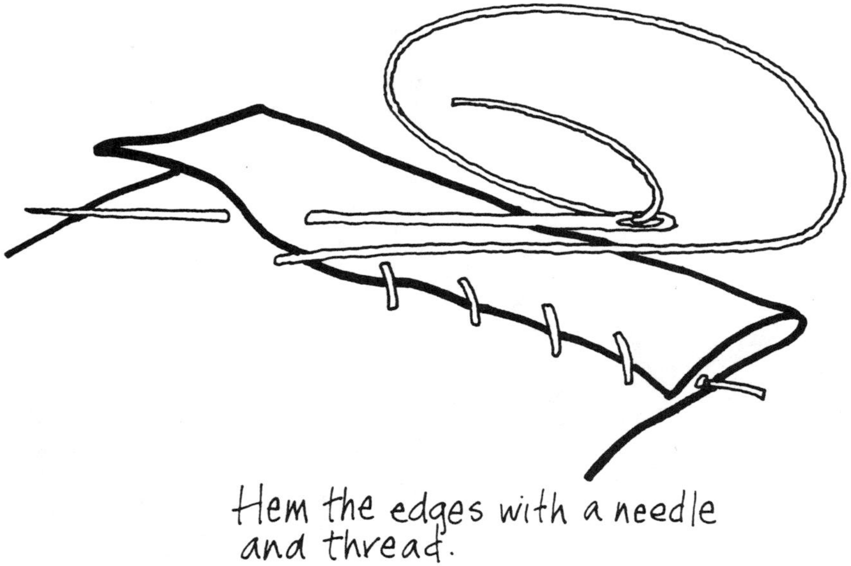

them down, making a hem. If not, you can roll the cut fabric edges under, and stitch them in place with a needle and thread. (If you don't know how to sew yet, this is an easy project for you to learn the basic hemming stitch.)

When your squares are all hemmed, you can use old pieces of sponge, or cut shapes from potatoes to print designs on the napkins with acrylic or fabric paints, or your own homemade natural dyes (see page16).

Put the napkins into napkin rings you have made for everyone in your family (see page 117), or put names on the napkins. Then, there will be a personal napkin for everyone, and you won't have to wash the napkins after every meal.

After you have completed making the napkins, fold them up neatly and place them in an old basket, or decorate the outside of an empty coffee can or shoe box. Your family can store them there — each with its own napkin ring — keeping them ready for the next meal.

RECYCLING BINS

Set a good example for your family by creating recycling bins and then using them! If you do this, chances are your whole family will join in the effort, and you will have moved everyone in your family one step closer to being good earth citizens.

Try to place your bins where they are accessible, but not in the way. Talk over the place to keep them with your parents. Offer to go on the weekly visit to the nearest recycling center, too. Your interest in making recycling work in your home will be a real gift to the earth.

Materials ✱✱

- Large cardboard boxes
- Leftover latex paint, or used gift wrap
- Permanent markers
- Cord and scissors

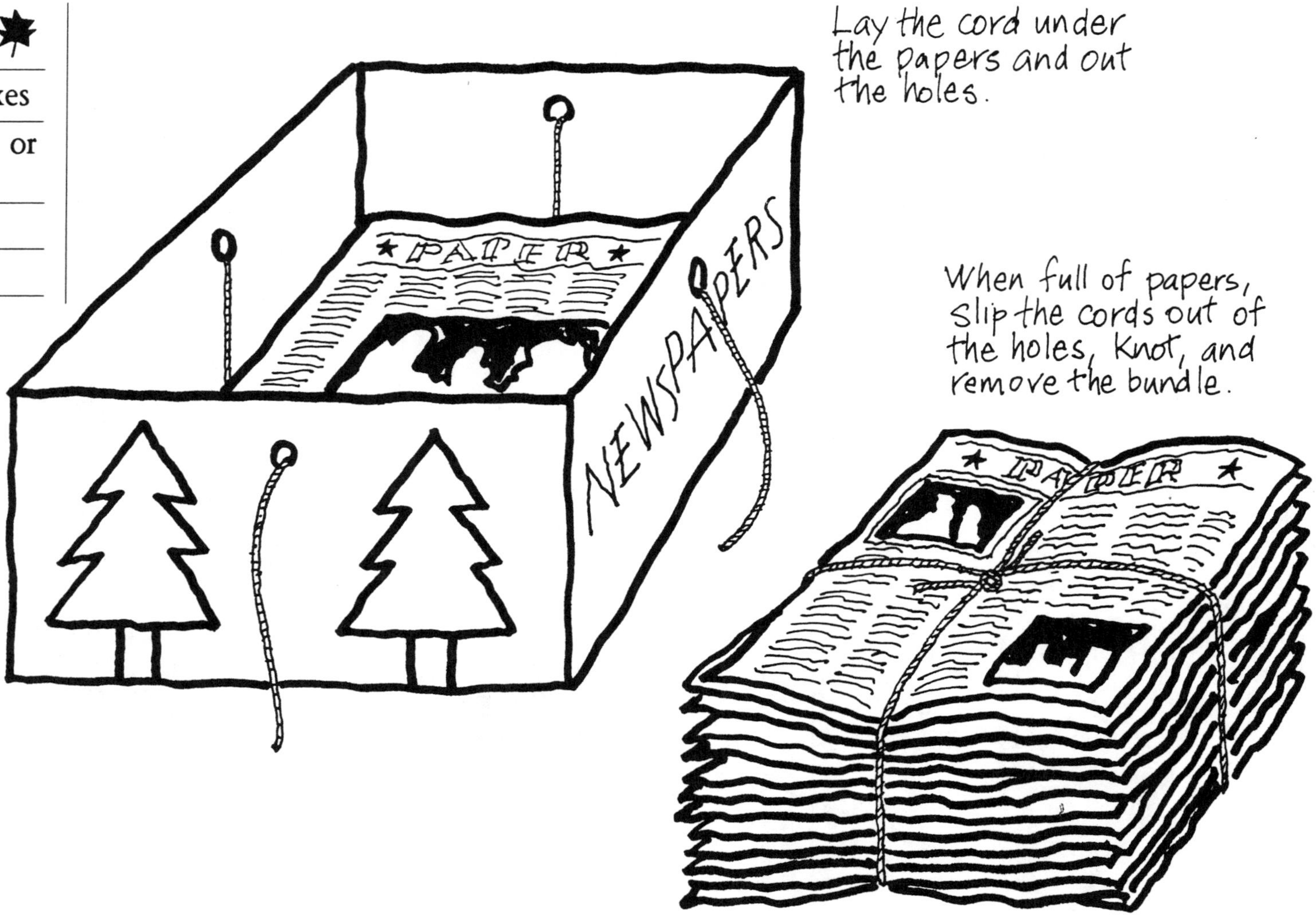

Create separate storage areas for the variety of items you recycle. Save sturdy cardboard boxes and paint them with leftover latex house paint, which gives the cardboard more strength and makes them look special, too. Or, decorate them with used gift wrap. Make separate boxes for aluminum, for plastics, and for glass, clearly labelling each one with a permanent marker. Make a small box to put near the computer or typewriter for saving white bond paper.

Now, make a special box for newspapers by punching holes in the four sides near the top of the box, and then placing the cord across the inside of the box and up through the holes. Pile in the newspapers each day, until it's full, and then just pull the loose ends of cord from the holes and tie securely to bundle. Slide the bundle out of the box to take to the recycling center, and restring the box for the next pile of newspapers.

COMPOST HOLDER

Materials

Large plastic jug from milk or water

Permanent markers or paints

Scissors or serrated knife

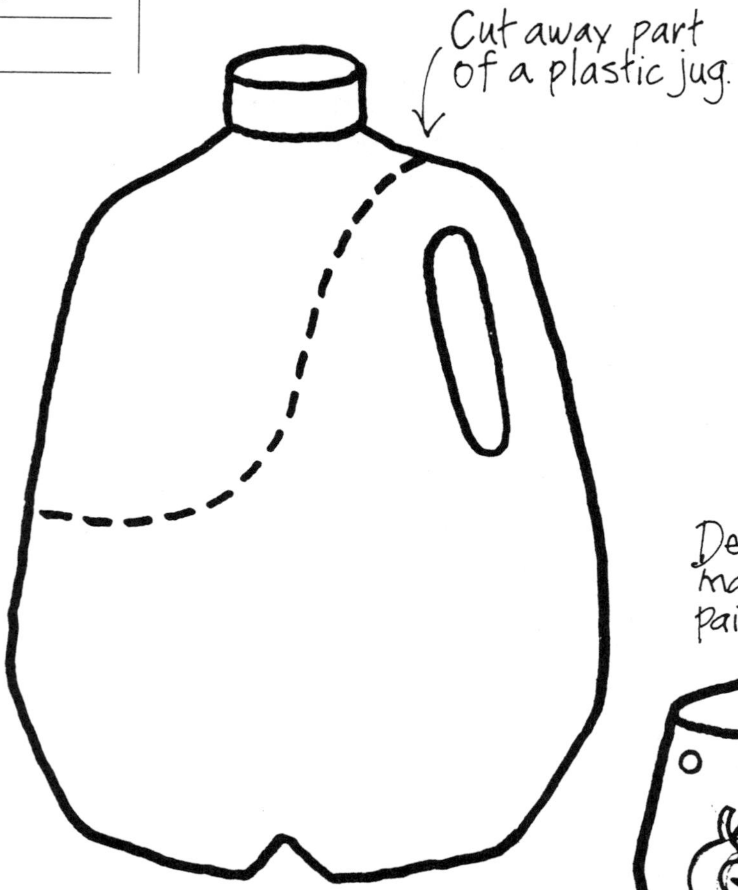

Make a compost holder by cutting a large opening in a plastic bottle, as shown. Draw on fruits and veggies with permanent markers. Keep the holder by the sink for food scraps (no bones or meat), and carry it out to dump on your compost heap in the yard after dinner. Your holder can be washed with hot, soapy water and reused each day.

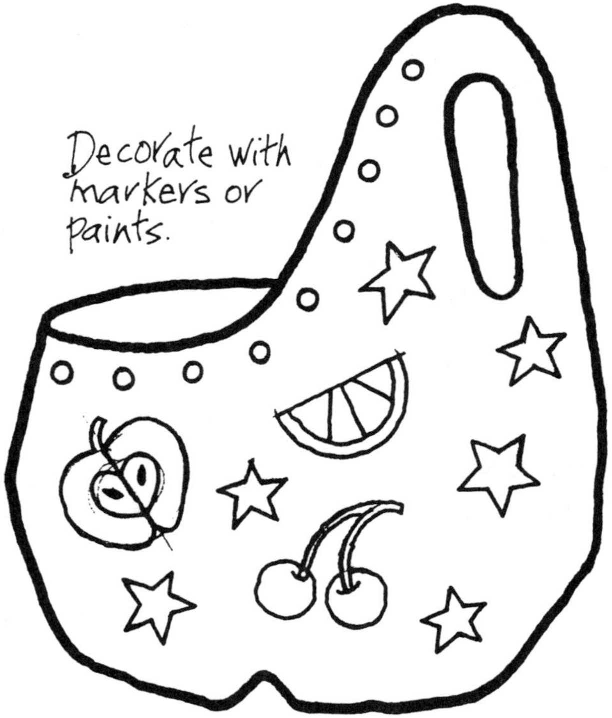

DRAFT DODGER

Make a crazy-looking snake that will help you stay warm and save energy, too. Place it across the bottom of doors and windows to prevent warm air from escaping in winter, or cool air escaping in the summer.

Materials ✱✱

- Old tights
- Rags or old clothing
- Needle and thread
- Scraps of felt and glue

Cut a leg off the old tights. Stuff with cut-up pieces of old clothing or rags. Stitch the end closed. Glue on some felt pieces for eyes and mouth. Decorate with pieces of felt to make an attractive, playful critter.

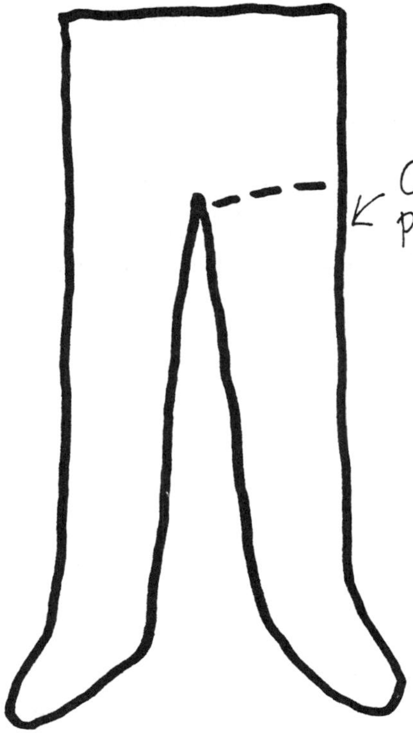

Cut the leg from a pair of tights.

Place under a door to keep cold air out.

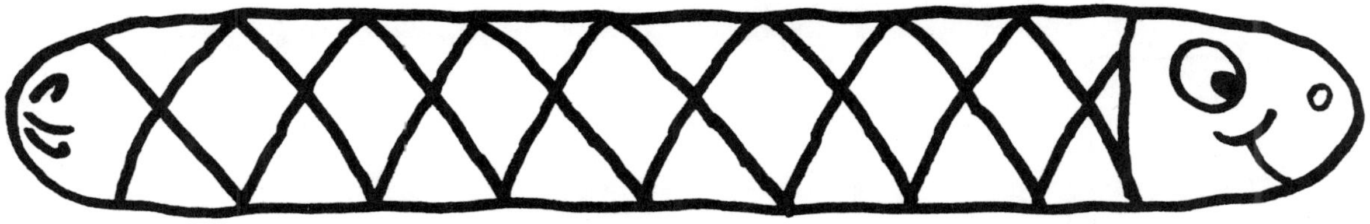

Stuff, stitch, and glue on a face.

SHOPPING BAG

Cloth shopping bags are useful as well as ecologically sound. You won't have to decide between "paper or plastic," and your bag can be folded up and carried in a purse or pocket. Make up several for gifts or to sell in a money-making venture for your club or group.

Materials

Heavy canvas or denim fabric

Sewing machine or needle and thread

Scissors

You can do this "by hand," but it really is easier with a sewing machine. Ask a grown-up to help you. Cut the fabric to the following dimensions: 38" x 18" rectangle for the bag, and two 4" x 12" pieces for handles.

Fold the rectangle in half, right side of fabric facing inside, and stitch the side together. Now, refold the bag so the seam is in the center, and stitch the bottom. Use a double row of stitching to make it sturdy.

1. Fold and stitch side seam of the bag.

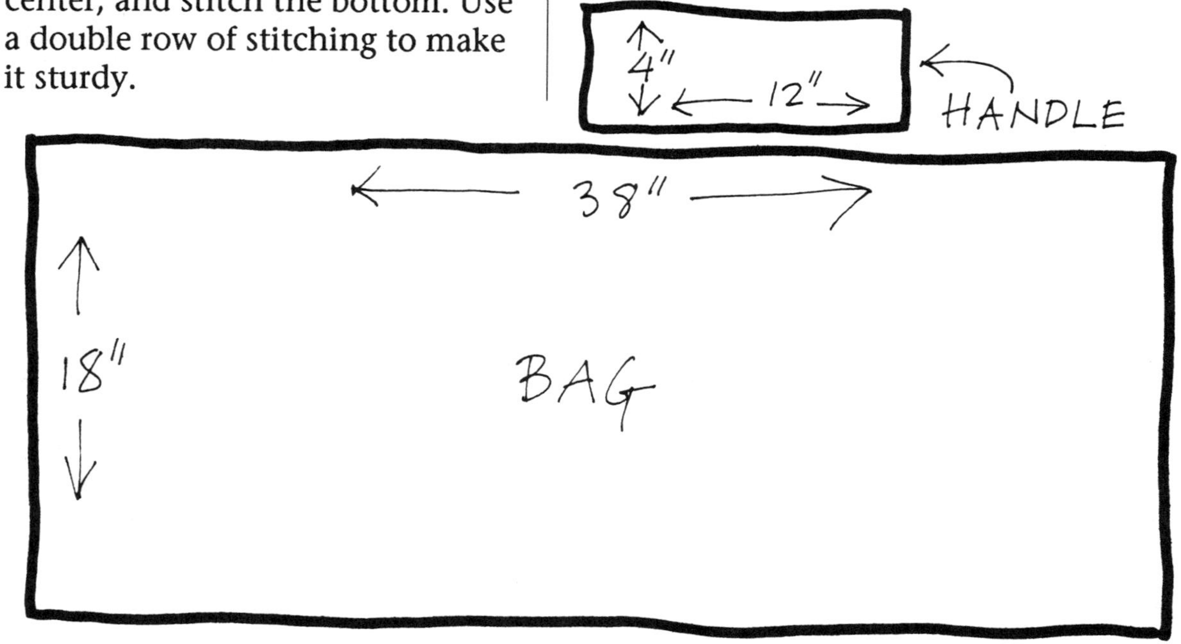

Pull the bag up at the ends to create two triangular corner areas. Stitch across these ends with a double seam.

Turn the bag right side out and hem the top edge.

Make the handles by sewing a seam down the center of each smaller rectangle. Turn right side out and stitch securely to each side of the bag.

Decorate the finished bag with fabric or acrylic paints. Use a cut-up sponge or potato to print with acrylic paints. Tie dye or paint with your homemade dyes (see page 16).

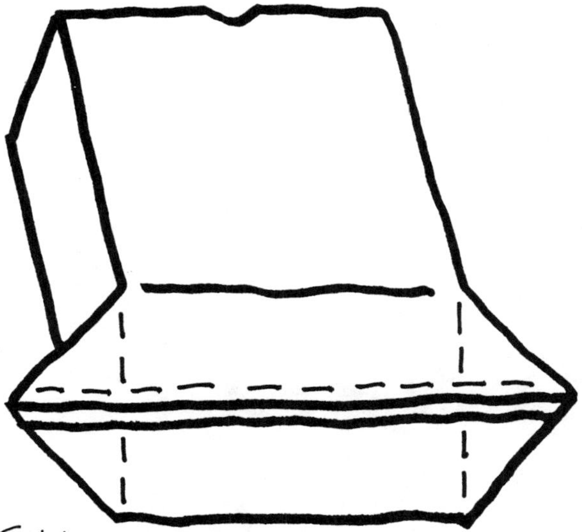

Fold corners out and stitch across them.

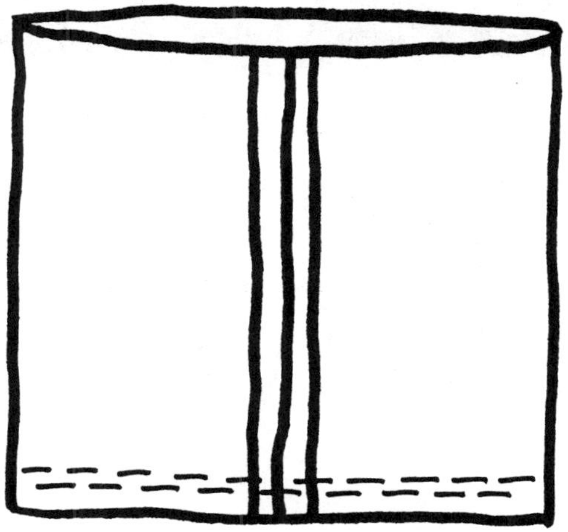

Fold and stitch bottom of bag.

Turn. Hem top. Sew on handles. Decorate with markers or paint.

Simple shopping bags can be made from the mesh bags that onions and potatoes are sold in. Remove the paper labels and decorate by weaving or stitching with colorful yarn and a yarn needle. Run a piece of heavy cord or leather boot lace through the top to make a drawstring.

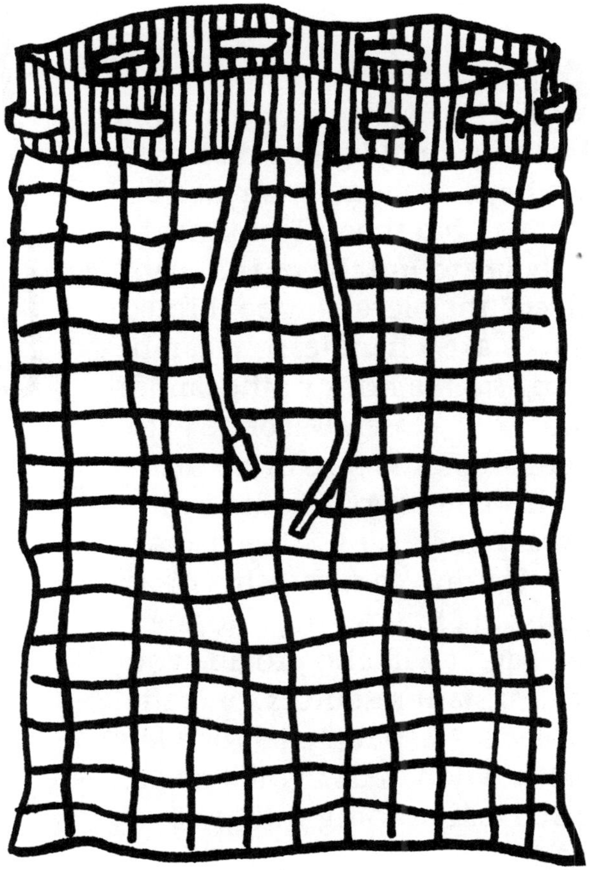

RAG BAG

Materials ✱✱

- Old pillowcase
- Piece of rope
- Needle and thread
- Permanent markers or homemade dyes (see page 16)

Make a rag bag for your family by using an old pillowcase or sewing a rectangular-shaped bag from an old sheet. Turn under a 2" hem around the opening and "feed" the piece of rope through it to make a handle, so it can be hung from a hook in the laundry room or a closet. Decorate with permanent markers or tie-dye with some of your homemade dyes. Whenever you need a rag for cleaning paint brushes or polishing the car, dig into the rag bag. It will also provide you with instant resources for craft projects. Need material for a kite tail or a doll dress? You'll be prepared and nothing will go to waste!

INDEX 5.

More Good Books from Williamson

See last page for ordering information, or visit your favorite bookseller. Thank you.

Williamson *Kids Can!*® Books

The following award-winning *Kids Can!*® books are for children ages 6 to 12. Each book is 144-176 pages, fully illustrated, trade paper, 11 x 8½, $12.95 US.

Parent's Guide Children's Media Award
Parents' Choice Approved
BOREDOM BUSTERS!
The Curious Kids' Activity Book
by Avery Hart & Paul Mantell

Parents' Choice Gold Award
Dr. Toy Best Vacation Product
THE KIDS' NATURE BOOK
365 Indoor/Outdoor Activities and Experiences
by Susan Milord

Parents' Choice Approved
Dr. Toy Best Vacation Product
KIDS GARDEN!
The Anytime, Anyplace Guide to Sowing & Growing Fun
by Avery Hart and Paul Mantell

Parents' Choice Recommended
American Bookseller Pick of the Lists
ADVENTURES IN ART
Art & Craft Experiences for 8- to 13-Year-Olds
by Susan Milord

Dr. Toy Best Vacation Product
American Bookseller Pick of the Lists
KIDS' CRAZY ART CONCOCTIONS
50 Mysterious Mixtures for Art & Craft Fun
by Jill Frankel Hauser

Parent's Guide Children's Media Award
Parents' Choice Approved
MAKING COOL CRAFTS & AWESOME ART!
A Kids' Treasure Trove of Fabulous Fun
by Roberta Gould

Selection of Book-of-the-Month;
Scholastic Book Clubs
KIDS COOK!
Fabulous Food for the Whole Family
by Sarah Williamson and Zachary Williamson

Parents' Choice Gold Award
American Bookseller Pick of the Lists
Oppenheim Toy Portfolio Best Book Award
THE KIDS' MULTICULTURAL ART BOOK
Art & Craft Experiences from Around the World
by Alexandra M. Terzian

Benjamin Franklin Best Multicultural Book Award
Skipping Stones Multicultural Honor Award
THE KIDS' MULTICULTURAL COOKBOOK
Food & Fun Around the World
by Deanna F. Cook

Children's Book-of-the-Month Club Selection
KIDS' COMPUTER CREATIONS
Using Your Computer for Art & Craft Fun
by Carol Sabbeth

Parent's Guide Children's Media Award
Benjamin Franklin Best Education/Teaching Book Award
HAND-PRINT ANIMAL ART
by Carolyn Carreiro
full color, $12.95

Parents' Choice Gold Award
Benjamin Franklin Best Juvenile Nonfiction Award
KIDS MAKE MUSIC!
Clapping and Tapping from Bach to Rock
by Avery Hart and Paul Mantell

American Bookseller Pick of the Lists
Oppenheim Toy Portfolio Best Book Award
EcoArt!
Earth-Friendly Art & Craft Experiences for 3- to 9-Year-Olds
by Laurie Carlson

THE KIDS' WILDLIFE BOOK
Exploring Animal Worlds through Indoor/Outdoor Crafts & Experiences
by Warner Shedd

HANDS AROUND THE WORLD
365 Creative Ways to Build Cultural Awareness & Global Respect
by Susan Milord

Parents' Choice Approved
KIDS CREATE!
Art & Craft Experiences for 3- to 9-Year-Olds
by Laurie Carlson

American Bookseller Pick of the Lists
Oppenheim Toy Portfolio Best Book Award
Benjamin Franklin Best Juvenile Nonfiction
Teachers' Choice Award
SUPER SCIENCE CONCOCTIONS
50 Mysterious Mixtures for Fabulous Fun
by Jill Frankel Hauser

Oppenheim Toy Portfolio Best Book Award
American Bookseller Pick of the Lists
THE KIDS' SCIENCE BOOK
Creative Experiences for Hands-On Fun
by Robert Hirschfeld and Nancy White

Parent's Guide Children's Media Award
Teachers' Choice Award
CUT-PAPER PLAY!
Dazzling Creations from Construction Paper
by Sandi Henry

Early Childhood News Directors' Choice Award
VROOM! VROOM!
Making 'dozers, 'copters, trucks & more
by Judy Press

Parents Magazine Parents' Pick
KIDS LEARN AMERICA!
Bringing Geography to Life with People, Places, & History
by Patricia Gordon and Reed C. Snow

THE KIDS' NATURAL HISTORY BOOK
Making Dinos, Fossils, Mummies & Zulu Huts
by Judy Press

GIZMOS & GADGETS
Creating Science Contraptions that Work (& Knowing Why)
by Jill Frankel Hauser

Williamson's *Kaleidoscope Kids*™ Books

Kaleidoscope Kids™ books encourage kids, ages 7-12, to explore places, subjects, peoples, and history from many different perspectives, using many different skills. Each book is 96-104 pages; two-color, fully illustrated, 10 x 10, $10.95.

Children's Book Council Notable Book
American Bookseller Pick of the Lists
Dr. Toy 10 Best Educational Products
PYRAMIDS!
50 Hands-On Activities to Experience Ancient Egypt
by Avery Hart & Paul Mantell

Parent's Guide Children's Media Award
American Bookseller Pick of the Lists
KNIGHTS & CASTLES
50 Hands-On Activities to Experience the Middle Ages
by Avery Hart & Paul Mantell

ANCIENT GREECE!
40 Hands-On Activities to Experience This Wondrous Age
by Avery Hart and Paul Mantell

MEXICO!
40 Activities to Experience Mexico Past and Present
by Susan Milord

BRIDGES!
Amazing Structures to Design, Build & Test
by Elizabeth Rieth and Carol Johmann

GEOLOGY ROCKS!
50 Hands-On Activities to Explore the Earth
by Cindy Blobaum

THE BEAST IN YOU!
Activities & Questions to Explore Evolution
by Marc McCutcheon

Williamson's *Tales Alive!®* Books . . .

A feast of folklore fun for ages 4 and up! These beautiful, full-color books focus on retellings of multicultural folktales accompanied by original paintings and activities to round out a child's understanding of a tale and its subject. Books are 96-128 pages, full color with original art, 8½ x 11.

Benjamin Franklin Best Juvenile Fiction
Parents' Choice Honor Award
Skipping Stones Multicultural Honor Award

TALES ALIVE!
Ten Multicultural Folktales with Activities
by Susan Milord
Trade paper, $12.95

Benjamin Franklin Best Juvenile Fiction
Benjamin Franklin Best Multicultural Book Award
Teachers' Choice Award

TALES OF THE SHIMMERING SKY
Ten Global Folktales with Activities
by Susan Milord
Trade paper, $12.95

TALES ALIVE!
BIRD TALES
from Near and Far
by Susan Milord
Trade paper, $12.95

Visit our Website:
http://www.williamsonbooks.com
or, call 800-234-8791 **for catalog.**

To order Books

Williamson books are available from your favorite bookseller, or directly from Williamson Publishing.

Toll-free phone orders: **800-234-8791**
Visa or Mastercard accepted.
E-mail orders with charge card: **orders@williamsonbooks.com**
Or, send check or money order to:

WILLIAMSON PUBLISHING

P.O. Box 185, Charlotte, Vermont 05445

Postage is $4.00 for first book plus $1.00 for each additional book. Satisfaction is guaranteed or full refund without questions or quibbles. Books shipped within 48 hours.

Prices may be slightly higher when purchased in Canada.